Computer graphics

Computer graphics

Mathematical first steps

P. A. Egerton
and
W. S. Hall
University of Teesside

PRENTICE HALL
EUROPE

LONDON   NEW YORK   TORONTO   SYDNEY   TOKYO   SINGAPORE
MADRID   MEXICO CITY   MUNICH   PARIS

First published 1998 by
Prentice Hall Europe
An Imprint of
Pearson Education Limited
Edinburgh Gate
Harlow
Essex CM20 2JE, England

Typeset in 10/12pt Galliard

Printed and bound in Great Britain by
Biddles Ltd, Guildford and King's Lynn

Library of Congress Cataloging-in-Publication Data

Available from the publisher

A catalogue record for this book is available from the British Library

ISBN: 0–13–599572–8

This book is dedicated to
Terry, Christine and James
(PAE)
Pauline, Charlotte, Andrew and Clare
(WSH)

Contents

Preface

Our intention in writing this book is to provide an accessible introduction to the many varied areas of mathematics that have relevance and application in the modern study of computer graphics. The materials have been developed for a one semester module for students studying on the MSc CAGTA ('Computer Aided Graphical Technology and Applications') at the University of Teesside in Middlesbrough. At Teesside there is a tradition of high-quality research and development in computer graphics, and in this Masters programme, run successfully for over nine years, graduates from a wide variety of backgrounds develop and enhance their computer graphics skills. On the course there are students who hold degrees in fine art, architecture or design, as well as those with computing, engineering or mathematics degrees. While all are graduates, many of them have little recent exposure to mathematics, and so we assume a minimum of prerequisite knowledge. However we provide the tools for a wide breadth of applications, so students can feel confident in their mathematical skills in the context of computer graphics.

We chart a careful path, focusing only on techniques that are essential. Our approach is now being used for degree and diploma students, and we feel it is relevant also for those undergoing technician training, or even pre-college students seeking enrichment topics. For those who have basic high-school mathematics up to age 16 (GCSE level or equivalent) this book will support a secure development in the subject; those who have studied mathematics at higher levels (even at degree level) will probably find that, while much material is familiar, we include many new aspects that can profitably be considered. We aim to impart a sound working knowledge of the techniques needed, and rigorous proofs are omitted.

Computer graphics, or visualization, is a rapidly expanding area of activity that has practitioners involved in a vast spectrum of enterprises, from creative animation through virtual reality environments to scientific imaging. The key to the theory of all of this is the mathematical language by which objects can be represented and manipulated. Thus we deal with the geometry of points, lines, angles, curves and surfaces using the numerical techniques consistent with computers. We wish to help those who read this book to understand the ideas behind computer graphics, and to become confident in their abilities to perform appropriate mathematical manipulations. Then they will appreciate the manoeuvres and activities that graphics packages make possible, and also be capable of building on their skills by studying more advanced texts. Above all, we hope to provide readers with a firm foundation for developing practical and professional skills in graphical technology.

This book has been brought forward for publication as the result of much collaboration with many colleagues. We are pleased to be able to acknowledge the considerable amount of help given us by Mr Simon Alexander, Dr John Dormand, Mr Matthew Holton, Mr Hamish Lawson and Mr Alex Parkinson in producing the computer graphics images included, and to acknowledge also the help given us by Mr Simon Alexander, Mr David Briggs, Dr Michael Cummings, Mr Eudes Diemoz, Mr Matthew Holton and Mr Alex Parkinson for ongoing discussions, sharing notes and proof reading. Thanks must also be given to Mrs Lynn Wildmore for the typing she did and to the publisher's team.

A note about working with this book: in order to help the reader there is a Glossary of the meanings of common terms included at the end, and there are 'worked examples', clearly identified, in the text. In addition we have included a set of exercises (with their answers) on the material of each chapter. Wherever an electronic calculator has been used we have, in general, worked with three or more decimal places, then normally given each answer correct to two decimal places, in places using the symbol '$\simeq$' to indicate the approximation. Despite the fact that most questions have been tested by at least two cohorts of our students (our thanks to them!) it is still possible that some errors remain: our apologies if this is the case. Any inaccuracies in the calculations or in the text are our responsibility; we shall be pleased to acknowledge any that are brought to our attention.

If this book leads people to appreciate the way that mathematical ideas underpin the exciting modern developments in computer graphics, and if it helps people to master mathematical techniques that can lead to further involvement in graphics production or study or research then we have achieved our objective.

Patricia A. Egerton

William S. Hall

University of Teesside

Part 1
Points, lines and planar curves:
Vector algebra

Shapes inside a computer:
Review of geometry and trigonometry

1.1 Computer graphics

Let us start with a consensus about what **computer graphics** and **visualization** are. The word graphics is associated with charts, graphs, images, pictures and patterns, often in the context of art, design or animation; visualization is the process of making graphical images, of putting things into picture form. Computer graphics or computer visualization involves the computer with the visual forms: it is the interface of graphical communications with computer technology. The term computer graphics was first used by the Boeing Corporation in 1960; it involves using a computer to create and hold pictorial information and also to adapt and manipulate the display in different ways.

The types of display available when computer graphics are used vary enormously. We are familiar with simple, static two-dimensional displays of rectangular objects, including bar graphs and histograms. Then there are curved plots of surfaces, used in displaying realistic objects, and even more complex representations that include moving and developing images of perspective views of three-dimensional objects. The number of uses for computer graphics continues to grow rapidly. Apart from the field of computer games and animation, there are vast areas where the skilled use of computer graphics is in the vanguard of modern technological development. Among such uses you may have heard of simulation models, for practising techniques and for stability testing; there are established applications such as the computerization of surgeons' instruments and pilots' controls; and as well as these there are developments in vehicle design, architectural design, analysis of crystal structures and many, many more, where computer graphics now provide a vital, integral tool.

Even though there is such a wide variety of applications, we shall be dealing only with systems where the display is two dimensional, on a screen, even when it is a three-dimensional reality that is being represented. Until the time when computer technology permits genuinely three-dimensional representations of our three-dimensional world, we are restricted to two-dimensional representations. However,

re-presentations

most of us today are fully conversant with the conventions by which three-dimensional reality is conveyed via two dimensions. For us, two-dimensional images are the norm, in paintings, photographs, films etc. and we have grown up readily able to interpret graphical devices such as foreshortening, perspective views and shading. These skills that we have developed through experience and training are by no means trivial. Techniques in graphical mathematics will allow us to build into the two-dimensional screen display appropriate conventions which allow a realistic interpretation of three-dimensional reality.

In Figure 1.1(a), (b) and (c) we show some images that illustrate the scope of computer graphics display. In Figure 1.1(a) computer graphical techniques have been used to display a realistic model of human hair, Figure 1.1(b) shows a simulated model of a human organ being held and cut, for the purposes of surgeons' training, and Figure 1.1(c) illustrates some computer-generated forms of trees.

On a computer screen an image is produced using minute subdivisions of the screen called **pixels**. Each pixel is assigned a shade of grey, or of a colour, and the

Figure 1.1 (a) Computer modelling of human hair *(source: Alex Parkinson, University of Teesside).*

Figure 1.1 (b) Model of human organ for surgeon training *(source: Simon Alexander, University of Teesside).*

Figure 1.1 (c) Computer-generated tree *(source: Matthew Holton, University of Teesside).*

groups of pixels are interpreted as points or lines or surfaces. In Figure 1.2 we show a computer-generated image to demonstrate this: the border between the light and dark areas is magnified to illustrate the pixel composition. In fact, a computer assigns an appropriate position, shade or colour by dealing with numbers only, so we shall consider the mathematical (numerical) ways of representing points and lines, and hence surfaces too. We shall also consider mathematical techniques for manipulating these points and lines.

The ways in which points and lines are dealt with using mathematics can vary, and we shall look at methods that use coordinates, and also vectors and parameters. The manipulations to be investigated will include scaling, rotation, shifting, projection and perspective views; these will be carried out using matrices. We shall start by looking at simple cases: at points and lines in two dimensions, and their transformations. These ideas are then extended to three dimensions, to three-dimensional objects represented in two dimensions (pictures on a screen), and different methods for dealing with surfaces are introduced.

no shear-ing or twisting?

moire, moire, moire!

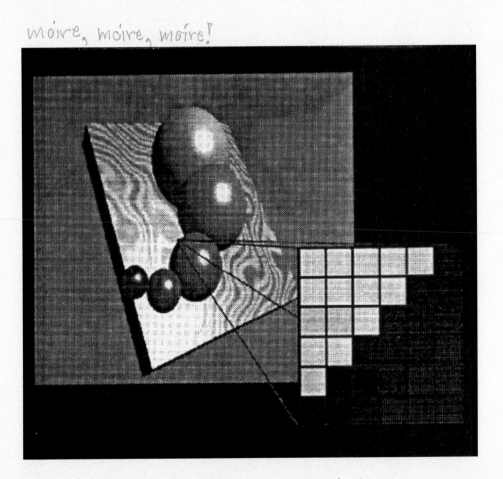

Figure 1.2 A magnification to illustrate the pixel composition of an image
(source: Matthew Holton, University of Teesside).

1.2 Objects inside a computer

We know that a computer monitor (or a television) does not actually contain the object depicted, as suggested in Figure 1.3. What a computer does is to hold, in numerical form, representations of points of an object; these are then transformed by mathematical techniques so that the image on the screen matches the reality we wish to display. In Figure 1.4 we have a diagram of the different ways of considering the activities involved. In the first column we have the geometric and visualization activities; in the second column we have the mathematical terms for the activities; in the third column we have the computer activity. The essential starting point is a knowledge of the mathematical tools needed to deal with an appropriate computer model of our three-dimensional world; then our screen display will correspond to reality.

1.3 Geometry

all of which are fuzzy

Basic elements of our study are points, lines, planes and angles. We must be able to use mathematical language to describe these, and also to quantify relationships between them. Thus a review of some basic geometrical ideas is necessary here, and you are warmly advised to brush up on your own 'school-level' work on geometry before proceeding past this chapter!

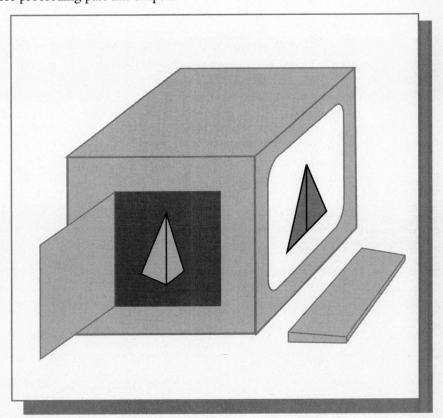

Figure 1.3 Object inside a computer.

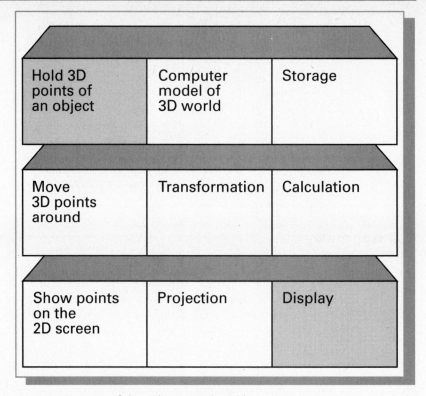

Figure 1.4 Computer capture of three-dimensional world.

One of the first things we expect from geometry is that it will help us to describe precisely any **point,** that is a specific position in space, or on a plane. In Figures 1.5 to 1.8 we have some very straightforward ways of specifying positions. In each example you will be able to identify the starting point or **reference point**, the measuring system and information about direction, by which the point P is precisely described. In Figures 1.5 and 1.6 we notice that the point P is specified by a single distance and a single direction from the starting point, whereas in Figures 1.7 and 1.8 the measurements are consecutive. Both of these methods will be used as we proceed; at every stage we shall use the most appropriate technique.

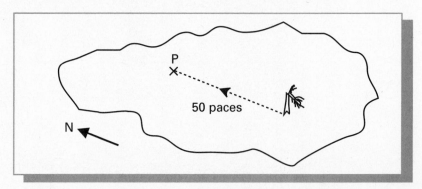

Figure 1.5 'The treasure is buried 50 paces due north from the broken pine.'

And the broken pine is a distinctive marker.

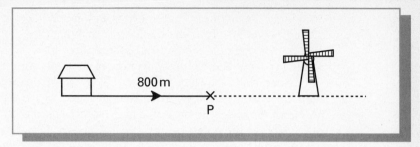

Figure 1.6   'He walked to a position 800 metres from his house in the direction of the windmill.'

in the direction of
towards

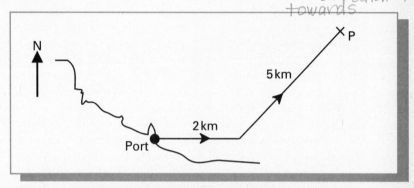

Figure 1.7   'The boat sailed 2 km due east, then 5 km due north-east, to reach the rendevous with the submarine.'

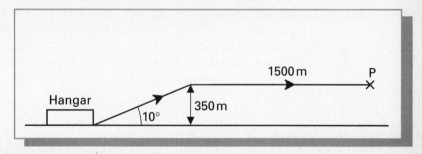

Figure 1.8   'The glider was towed up from its hangar at 10° to the ground until it reached 350 m, then it flew horizontally for 1500 m.'

1.4 Geometrical language

In order to communicate with a computer to fix the position of a point in space, we must deal with a frame of reference, and measurements of distance and direction, in purely numerical form.

We start in a simple way by considering how we might determine numerically the position of a person in a room. As shown in Figure 1.9(a), the position of the person's feet, F, could be identified as being 1 metre from the wall in front, and 2 metres from the wall on his or her left. In addition, the eye position, E, could be described as being 1.8 metres above the floor. Thus the person's position is fully described using the distances from three fixed **plane** (that is, flat) surfaces which are at right angles (i.e. 90°) to each other, as the walls and floor of a room usually are.

When we are thinking geometrically, these three plane surfaces at right angles (that is the two walls and the floor, meeting in a corner) would usually be replaced by the simpler picture shown in Figure 1.9(b). Here we retain only the lines where the planes meet, and we call the lines **axes**; this gives us a **frame of reference**. The distances from the planes are measured in the directions of these axes, and are called the **coordinates** of the points considered. The corner, O, where the three axes join is called the **origin**; this is the starting point, from which distances along the axes are measured.

A coordinate frame like this one based on the walls and floor of a room gives us a **rectangular coordinate system**. Each axis is at right angles to both the other axes, and along each axis we have a **scale**, by which distances can be measured and the position of any point identified. According to the scale shown in Figure 1.9(b), measured in metres, the coordinates of the feet, F, are $(1, 2, 0)$ and the coordinates of E, the eye position, are $(1, 2, 1.8)$.

Although the scales on different axes can be different, for most of our graphical work the scales will be kept the same, to preserve true proportions. As seen in Figure 1.9(b), a standard way of labelling the axes is as the **x-axis**, the **y-axis** and the **z-axis** in the arrangement indicated. In future work we shall use shorthand symbols, so that a distance along the x-axis may be denoted by 'x' or 'X', etc., and the coordinates of a point may be generalized as (x, y, z) or (X, Y, Z), where the letters stand for numbers that may be known or unknown.

In two dimensions (see Figure 1.10) we have a simpler diagram since only the x-axis and the y-axis need to be shown, and the z-axis is not required. As before, the scales on the axes will nearly always be the same, and the origin is the zero on both. Any point in two dimensions in this **x–y plane** can be specified by a pair of numbers, which are its coordinates. (We must always take care over the order of these coordinates: the first number always refers to a distance measured along the

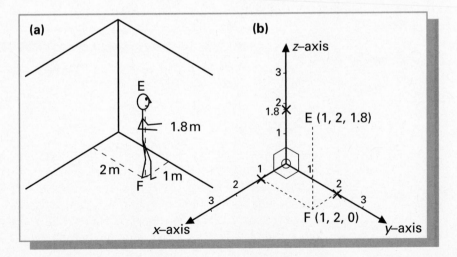

Figure 1.9 A coordinate system based on measurements taken in a room.

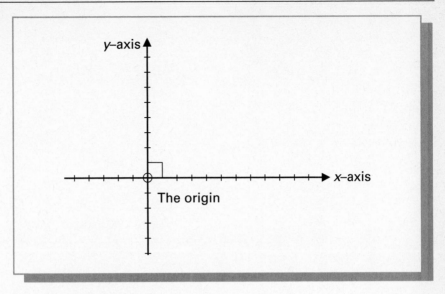

Figure 1.10 Two-dimensional rectangular axes.

direction of the *x*-axis, and the second to a distance in the direction of the *y*-axis; the order follows alphabetical order.) In Figure 1.11, we see that the point A has coordinates (6, 2), B is (3, −2) and C is (−4, −1). Using this coordinate system, we need to be able to calculate the length and gradient or slope of a line which joins two points. We must be able to determine the coordinates of the midpoint of a line, and to identify when pairs of lines are parallel or perpendicular. The following examples illustrate these calculations in two dimensions; the points and lines are shown in Figure 1.12.

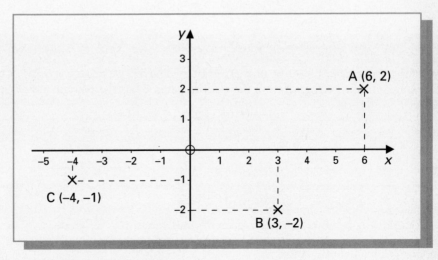

Figure 1.11 Two-dimensional coordinates.

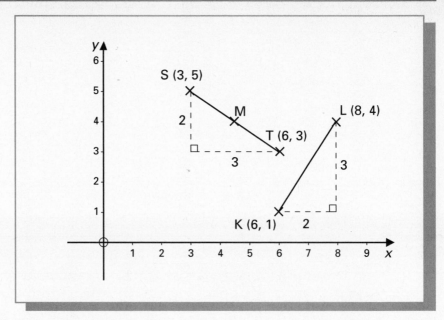

Figure 1.12 Line segments.

Example 1.1 The length of a line segment

The **length** of the line between the points S and T is the distance between them; it is denoted by |ST|, and it is calculated as follows:

$$|ST|^2 = 3^2 + 2^2$$
$$= 9 + 4$$
$$= 13$$

Thus the length of ST = |ST| = $\sqrt{13}$ ≈ 3.61. (This is an application of **Pythagoras' Theorem**, described in Appendix A.)

Example 1.2 The mid-point of a line   *The average*

For the coordinates of M, the **mid-point** of the line ST, we use <u>the average</u> of both the x-coordinates, and the average of both the y-coordinates. Thus the coordinates of M are

$\left(\frac{1}{2}(x_1 + x_2), \frac{1}{2}(\bar{y}_1 + y_3)\right)$ $\longrightarrow$ $\left(\frac{1}{2}(3+6), \frac{1}{2}(5+3)\right)$

What is the corresponding formula   *How about*

that is

for the midpoint or centroid of a △? $\left(4\frac{1}{2}, 4\right)$ *($\frac{1}{3}(x_1+x_2+x_3), \frac{1}{3}(y_1+y_2+y_3)$)*

for centroid of △? It works.

Example 1.3 The gradient of a line

The **gradient** or **slope** of a line is given by 'difference in y/difference in x' or, more informally, by 'distance up/distance along'. Thus the gradient of the line KL is $\frac{3}{2}$ and the gradient of the line ST is $-\frac{2}{3}$.

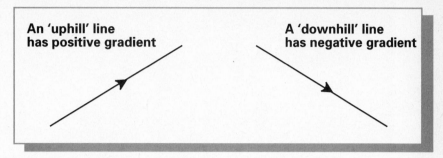

An 'uphill' line
has positive gradient

A 'downhill' line
has negative gradient

Figure 1.13 Slopes of lines.

We note that an 'uphill' line, whose direction is 'bottom left to top right' always has **positive gradient**. Similarly, a 'downhill' line, with direction 'top left to bottom right', always has **negative gradient** (see Figure 1.13).

Example 1.4   Parallel lines

Lines are said to be **parallel** when they have the same direction; thus in two dimensions lines are parallel when they have the same gradient. Thus every line with gradient $= \frac{3}{2}$ is parallel to the line KL in Figure 1.12.

Example 1.5   Perpendicular lines

Lines are said to be **perpendicular** or **normal** to each other when they are at right angles, and in two dimensions this is the case whenever the result of multiplying their gradients is -1. Since we have the gradient of

$$KL = \frac{3}{2}$$

$$\frac{a}{b} \times \frac{b}{a} = -1$$

and the gradient of

$$ST = -\frac{2}{3} \quad \text{or} \quad \left(\frac{y_2 - y_1}{x_2 - x_1}\right) \times \left(\frac{y_4 - y_3}{x_4 - x_3}\right) = -1$$

from Example 1.3, and since when we multiply these together we obtain

$$\frac{3}{2} \times \frac{-2}{3} = -1$$

we deduce that the lines KL and ST are perpendicular.

This is the neatest & cleanest way to think about it.

1.5 Angles and trigonometry

The usual understanding of an **angle** is that it is used to quantify turning or rotation (see Figure 1.14(a)), but from the outset we must realize that there are two different systems by which angles can be measured. We most commonly measure angles in **degrees**: there are 360°(degrees) in one complete revolution, so there are 180° in half a revolution and 90° in a quarter of a revolution, called a **right angle**; these are shown in Figure 1.14(b).

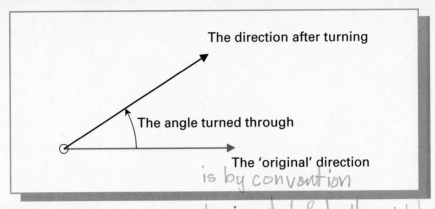

Figure 1.14 (a) An angle.

is by convention horizontal & to the right in reference to this page.

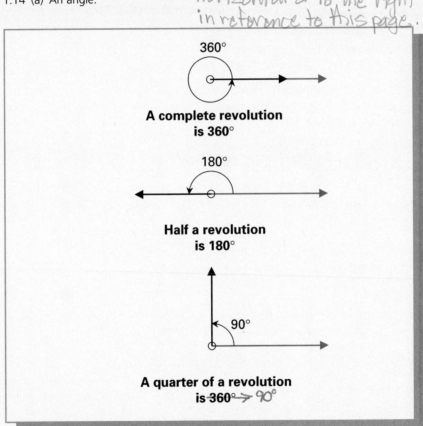

Figure 1.14 (b) Angles in degrees.

— I've never seen this notation before.

An alternative form of measurement, which we need in later chapters, uses **radians**. 1^c (that is, 1 radian) is the angle at the centre of a circle when <u>the length of the arc</u> is the same as the radius (see Figure 1.15(a)). The circumference of a circle is $2\pi \times$ its radius, as indicated in Figure 1.15(b), where π is a real number just bigger than 3, approximately 3.1416 correct to four decimal places. Thus one

times

3.14159

The curved length of the arc.

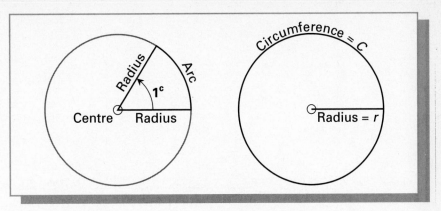

Figure 1.15 (a) One radian. Figure 1.15 (b) $C = 2\pi r$.

The ^{c} sign is defined by visual analogy to the ^{o} sign.

Thus $2\pi^c = 360°$

Maybe think of ^{c} for circumference. Most mathematicians never write the ^{c}. ↑

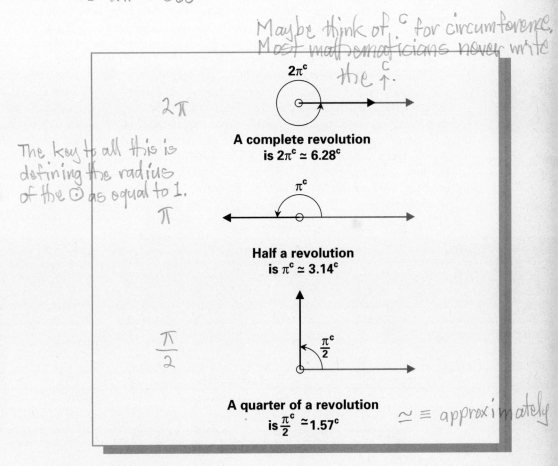

2π

The key to all this is defining the radius of the ⊙ as equal to 1.

π

$\dfrac{\pi}{2}$

$2\pi^c$

A complete revolution is $2\pi^c \simeq 6.28^c$

π^c

Half a revolution is $\pi^c \simeq 3.14^c$

$\dfrac{\pi^c}{2}$

A quarter of a revolution is $\dfrac{\pi^c}{2} \simeq 1.57^c$

$\simeq \equiv$ approximately

Figure 1.15 (c) Angles in radians.

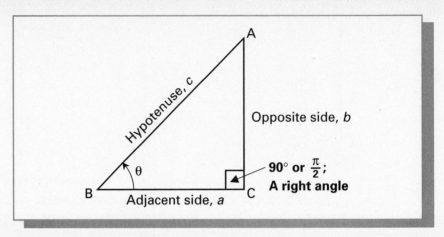

Figure 1.16 A right-angled triangle.

complete revolution is $2\pi^c$, half a revolution is π^c, and a right angle is $(\frac{\pi}{2})^c$. These angles are shown in Figure 1.15(c). When no units are quoted it is generally taken to mean that radians are being used, or that units are optional. Calculators operate either in 'degree mode' or in 'radian mode', so care must be taken to set the calculator correctly when performing calculations.

Take note {

The word **trigonometry** comes from 'triangle-measuring', and the essence of trigonometry is that certain numbers are assigned to particular angles, which aids us in calculating the lengths of sides of triangles, and other angles. The most useful of these numbers are named as the **sine**, **cosine** and **tangent** of the angle in question.

As already mentioned, an angle of 90° is a right angle. Angles less than 90° are termed **acute angles** (where acute means sharp or pointed), and any acute angle can be shown in a **right-angled triangle**, from the measurements of which its sine or cosine or tangent can be calculated. Referring to Figure 1.16, we state the essential definitions:

$$\text{sine of angle } \theta = \sin\theta = \frac{\text{opposite}}{\text{hypotenuse}} = \frac{b}{c} \quad = \frac{y}{x}$$

$\theta = theta$

$\phi = phi$

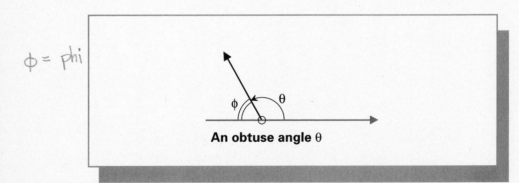

Figure 1.17 An obtuse angle θ.

$$\text{cosine of angle } \theta = \cos\theta = \frac{\text{adjacent}}{\text{hypotenuse}} = \frac{a}{c} = \frac{x}{r} \quad \textit{where } r =$$
$$\textit{radius of}$$
$$\text{tangent of angle } \theta = \tan\theta = \frac{\text{opposite}}{\text{adjacent}} = \frac{b}{a} = \frac{y}{x} \quad \textit{unit } \odot.$$

They are ratios pure and simple.

These are called **trigonometric ratios** and they have the same value whatever the size of triangle drawn, so they have a fixed value for any given angle. We usually obtain the numerical value of any trigonometric ratio from a calculator, using the SIN or COS or TAN button. Thus, for example, we can verify that $\tan 40° \simeq 0.84$, $\sin 72° \simeq 0.95$ and $\cos\left(\frac{\pi}{5}\right)^c \simeq 0.81$.

An angle that lies between one and two right angles, i.e. between 90° and 180°, is called an **obtuse angle** (since obtuse means blunt). For an obtuse angle, as in Figure 1.17, the trigonometric ratios are defined by:

→ but not necessarily in other places in this book

By definition here
$$\sin\theta° = \sin(180° - \phi°) = \sin\phi°$$
∠φ + ∠θ = 180°
$$\cos\theta° = -\cos(180° - \phi°) = -\cos\phi° \quad \text{] since x direction}$$
or π^c
$$\tan\theta° = -\tan(180° - \phi°) = -\tan\phi° \quad \text{) is now minus.}$$

An angle is deemed to be a **positive angle** if it is measured in an anticlockwise sense. Angles measured in a clockwise sense are **negative angles**, and for these, as shown in Figure 1.18, we have the following definitions:

−,+ *+,+*
$$\sin(-\theta) = -\sin\theta$$
$$\cos(-\theta) = \cos\theta \quad \textit{adjacent over hypotenuse is still +}$$
−,− *+,−*
$$\tan(-\theta) = -\tan\theta$$

Calculators give the trigonometric ratio for any size of angle; in particular we can obtain $\tan 162° \simeq -0.32$, $\sin 3.5^c \simeq -0.35$ and $\cos(-20°) \simeq 0.94$.

Whenever we are given any two sides of a right angled triangle we can calculate both its acute angles. Suppose we are given the lengths of the sides opposite to and adjacent to an angle: this allows us to calculate the tangent ratio. By using the INVERSE TAN (sometimes shown as TAN⁻¹ or SHIFT TAN or 2nd FUNCTION TAN) on the calculator we can work backwards from this number to get the angle we need. Thus if the tangent of an angle is 3/4 say, that is 0.75, the calculator will tell

I do not know if Inverse Tan is same as ArcTan.

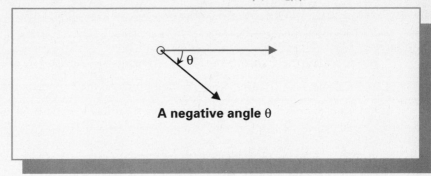

A negative angle θ

Figure 1.18 A negative angle θ.

us that the angle is approximately $36.87°$; in other words, if $\tan\theta = 0.75$ then $\tan^{-1}(0.75) \simeq 36.87°$. Then since the angles of any triangle add up to $180°$, the other acute angle is $(180 - 90 - 36.87)° \simeq 53.13°$.

We conclude this chapter with an important result. Whatever the size of an angle θ, the following is true:

A variant of the Pythagorean theorem (handwritten)

$$\sin^2\theta + \cos^2\theta = 1 \qquad (\sin\theta)^2 + (\cos\theta)^2 = 1$$

We verify this result for an acute angle by referring to Figure 1.16. Since we have

$$\sin\theta = \frac{b}{c} \text{ and } \cos\theta = \frac{a}{c} \quad \text{by definition}$$

we can write

better (handwritten)   *better* (handwritten)

$$\sin^2\theta = (\sin\theta)^2 = \frac{b^2}{c^2} \text{ and } \cos^2\theta = (\cos\theta)^2 = \frac{a^2}{c^2}$$

Adding these together gives

$$\sin^2\theta + \cos^2\theta = \frac{b^2}{c^2} + \frac{a^2}{c^2}$$

$$= \frac{b^2 + a^2}{c^2} \quad \text{very roundabout (handwritten)}$$

But triangle ABC is right angled, and so by Pythagoras' Theorem we have

$$b^2 + a^2 = c^2 \text{ and hence } \sin^2\theta + \cos^2\theta = \frac{c^2}{c^2} = 1$$

This is a key result, frequently needed whenever trigonometry is being used.

Nota bene (handwritten)

A certain facility in dealing with sines, cosines and tangents will be expected as we proceed. Thus, if it is necessary, time spent in mastering these ideas, and also getting to know your calculator, will be very worth while.

Exercises

In the exercises that follow evaluate each answer exactly, where possible, or else correct to two decimal places. A sketch graph will enhance each answer.

1.1 Calculate the lengths of the line segments joining the following pairs of points:

a) $P(1, 2)$, $Q(4, 6)$ b) $R(2, 7)$, $S(7, -5)$ c) $M(-12, 3)$, $N(12, 10)$

d) $F(7, 6)$, $G(6, 7)$ e) $T(12, 5)$, $U(17, 8)$ f) $J(3.6, 8)$, $K(19, 8)$

1.2 Calculate the gradients of the line segments in Exercise 1.1.

1.3 Calculate the coordinates of the mid-points of the line segments in Exercise 1.1.

1.4 Determine whether the following pairs of line segments are parallel, perpendicular or neither:

a) $P(1, 3)$, $Q(4, 10)$; $R(-1, 6)$, $S(6, 3)$

b) $P(2, 8)$, $Q(4, 12)$; $R(-3, -5)$, $S(0, 1)$

c) P(5, 2), Q(5, 11.2); R(9.6, 5), S(9.6, 17)

d) P(–6, 8), Q(2, –4); R(2, 5), S(5, –1)

1.5 Refer to the triangle shown in Figure 1.16, and give the angles in degrees:

a) If $a = 6$, $b = 7$, what is angle θ?

b) If $b = 1.42$, $c = 2.1$, what is angle θ?

c) If $a = 0.72$, $c = 3.5$, what is angle θ?

d) If $c = 1$, $b = 0.68$, what is angle θ?

e) If $b = 1$, $c = 1.68$, what is angle θ?

1.6 If the triangle whose vertices have coordinates A(1, 3), B(2, 5), C(7, 3) is enlarged and becomes the triangle whose vertices have coordinates P(2, 6), Q(4, 10), R(14, 6), by what factor does its area increase? (Hint: the area of a triangle can be calculated using the formula 'Area $= \frac{1}{2}$ base $\times$ height'.)

In Exercises 1.7 and 1.8, use your knowledge of Pythagoras' Theorem and the basic trigonometry of right-angled triangles to determine the answers. Solutions using an alternative method will be provided in Section 3.4.

1.7 One night, a spider began spinning a web inside a shoebox, whose dimensions are: length 33 cm, width 18 cm, depth 12 cm; see Figure 1.19. It started at a top corner and climbed down to the base, inside; it crawled along the length to the next corner and then crawled along the width, ending up at the corner furthest from where it started. It tightened a filament of web fixed between its starting and finishing positions. How long was this filament of web?

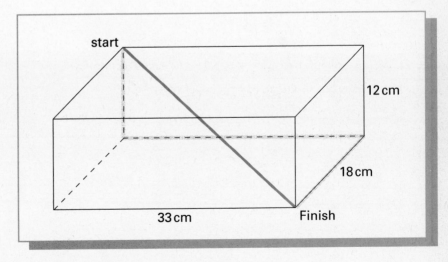

Figure 1.19 The first web of the nocturnal spider.

1.8. The shoebox was cleaned out next day, so the following night the spider began to spin a new web, as shown in Figure 1.20. It started at a top corner, as before, and managed to stretch a filament from there to the mid-point of the opposite base edge and then back to the adjacent top corner. What was the angle between these two strands of filament?

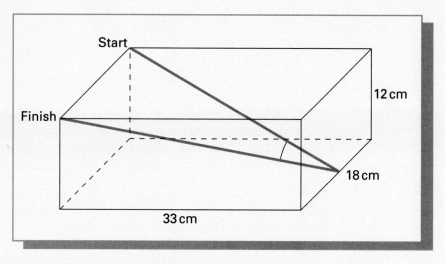

Figure 1.20 The second web of the nocturnal spider.

Answers

1.1 a) 5; b) 13; c) 25; d) 1.41; e) 5.83; f) 15.4.

1.2 a) 4/3; b) –12/5; c) 7/24; d) –1 e) 3/5; f) 0.

1.3 a) $(2\frac{1}{2}, 4)$; b) $(4\frac{1}{2}, 1)$; c) $(0, 6\frac{1}{2})$; d) $(6\frac{1}{2}, 6\frac{1}{2})$; e) $(14\frac{1}{2}, 6\frac{1}{2})$; f) (11.3, 8).

1.4 a) perpendicular; b) parallel; c) parallel; d) neither.

1.5 a) 49.40°; b) 42.55°; c) 78.13°; d) 42.84°; e) 36.53°.

1.6 The area is increased by a factor of 4.

1.7 39.46 cm.

1.8 28.75°.

2

Points in a plane: *Position vectors*

2.1 Vectors and vector notation

So that a computer can deal with points, lines and planes we need to be able to specify these in purely numerical terms. The chief tool that enables us to do this is the **vector**. The word vector is used for a type of quantity that has magnitude or size as well as direction. Vectors come in many guises: there are physical quantities such as displacement or velocity or force, where a complete description involves both direction and size, and there are more abstract quantities. Wherever a quantity can be depicted by an 'arrow', with the length of the shaft representing its size and the arrowhead its direction, then we have a vector. In this book we adopt a standard notation and show **vector** quantities in **bold type** but **scalar** quantities (like real numbers) in standard type. Thus the arrow from A to B will be written **AB** and the arrow from B to A will be written **BA**; in both cases the length of the line (the size of the vector) is the same. (In handwriting, we usually underline vector quantities.)

Heaviside's convention

They underline. Oh? I usually overline.

We start by looking at vectors in two dimensions, that is, those that can be represented by arrows drawn on a plane. A **free vector** is shown by a directed line segment whose length is a measure of its magnitude. In Figure 2.1 the lines **AB**, **CD** and **EF** are all of equal length and, being parallel, they have the same direction. Thus, since these three lines all have the same length and direction they represent the same vector quantity.

It is sometimes important to 'anchor' a vector, to know its starting point as in Section 1.3. When our arrow diagram shows a line of a particular length, going in a particular direction and starting at the origin, then we have a **position vector**. The position vector $\mathbf{p} = \mathbf{OP}$ shown in Figure 2.2 specifies the position of the point P with respect to the origin, O.

We identify vectors using notation based on the coordinates described in Section 1.4. In the same plane as a vector **OP** under consideration we superimpose a rectangular coordinate system, with its origin at O. Then, obviously, everything about **OP** is determined by the coordinates of the point P (see Figure 2.3). We have **OP** =

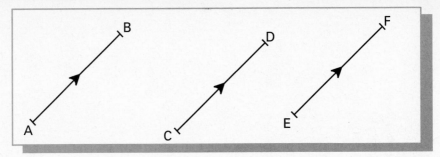

Figure 2.1 These line segments have the same length and the same direction; they all represent the same vector quantity.

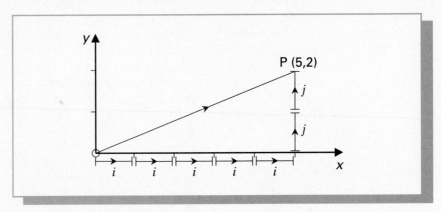

Figure 2.2 A position vector 'anchored' at the origin O.

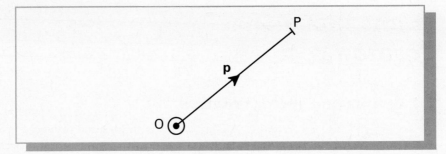

Figure 2.3 Combining the unit vectors **i** and **j**.

(5 2) using **row vector** notation; row vectors are commonly used among computer graphics professionals, and there is an obvious correspondence between the row vector for **OP** and the coordinates (5, 2) of the point P. Sometimes **column vector** notation is used; our choice of row vectors is discussed in the Postscript to the book.

A **unit vector** is a vector whose size is '1', so it can be represented by an arrow of length 1. A unit vector in the direction of the x-axis is called **i**, and a unit vector in the direction of the y-axis is called **j**. Thus for the vector **OP** in Figure 2.3 we can also write **OP** = 5**i** + 2**j**, which is the **component form** of the vector.

We note that **i** = (1 0) and **j** = (0 1). In most situations it is a matter of personal preference as to which notation, row vectors or component form, is used. Each notation has advantages in different circumstances. We shall continue to use each of them, sometimes in alternate examples, to encourage equal familiarity with both.

2.2 Measurements associated with vectors

The following examples refer to the vectors **OP** and **OQ** in Figure 2.4(a) and (b). We have shown above that there are different ways to write **OP**; so also we can write **OQ** in different ways, as **q**, or as the row vector (2 − 4), or in component form as **2i − 4j**.

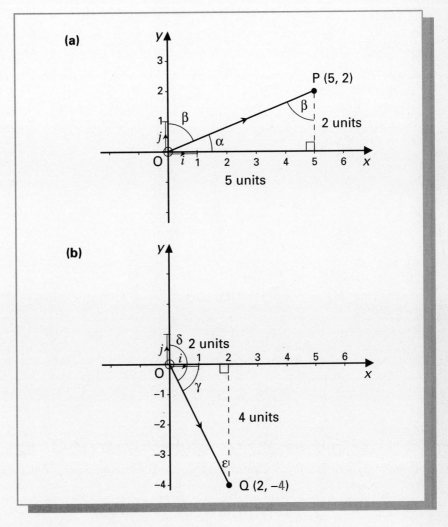

Figure 2.4 Vectors in two dimensions.

Example 2.1 The modulus of a vector

The **modulus** of a vector is given by the length of the arrow, using a method similar to that of Example 1.1. Thus the modulus of **OP** is

$$|OP| = \sqrt{5^2 + 2^2}$$
$$= \sqrt{25 + 4}$$
$$= \sqrt{29}$$
$$\approx 5.39$$

We can also calculate the modulus of **OQ**:

$$|OQ| = \sqrt{2^2 + (-4)^2}$$
$$= \sqrt{4 + 16}$$
$$= \sqrt{20}$$
$$\approx 4.47$$

Example 2.2 A unit vector

The unit vector in the direction of **OP** is written $\hat{OP}$, which is calculated as follows:

$$\hat{OP} = \frac{\text{vector } OP}{\text{modulus of } OP}$$
$$= \frac{OP}{|OP|}$$
$$= \frac{5i + 2j}{5.39}$$
$$= \frac{5i}{5.39} + \frac{2j}{5.39}$$
$$\approx 0.93i + 0.37j$$

Similarly we have

$$\hat{OQ} = OQ/|OQ|$$
$$= \frac{2i - 4j}{4.47}$$
$$= \frac{2i}{4.47} - \frac{4j}{4.47}$$
$$\approx 0.45i - 0.89j$$

Example 2.3 Angles between vectors and axes

The size of the angles that a vector makes with the positive directions of the axes can be determined as follows:

1. The angle between **OP** and **i** is α, where $\tan \alpha = \frac{2}{5} = 0.4$, so $\alpha = 21.80°$.

2. The angle between **OP** and **j** is β, where $\beta = 90° - 21.80° = 68.20°$.

3. The angle between **OQ** and **i** is γ, where $\tan \gamma = \frac{4}{2} = 2$, so $\gamma = 63.43°$.

4. The angle between **OQ** and **j** is δ, where $\delta = 90° + 63.43° = 153.43°$

Example 2.4 Direction cosines

The cosines of the angles which a vector makes with the positive axes are called its **direction cosines**; these numbers are most useful for fixing the direction of a vector. We have for **OP**

$$\cos \alpha = \frac{5}{|OP|} = \frac{5}{5.39} \approx 0.93$$

$$\cos \beta = \frac{2}{|OP|} = \frac{2}{5.39} \approx 0.37$$

Similarly for **OQ**:

$$\cos \gamma = \frac{2}{|OQ|} = \frac{2}{4.47} \approx 0.45$$

and since angle δ is obtuse, with $\delta = (180° - \varepsilon)$, we use a result from Section 1.5 and so

$$\cos \delta = \frac{-4}{|OQ|} = \frac{-4}{4.47} \approx -0.89$$

We see that when two vectors are parallel (as in Example 1.4) they have the same gradient and thus they will have the same direction cosines. It is by comparing the direction cosines of vectors that we can extend the idea of parallel vectors from two to three dimensions when required.

2.3 Manipulating vectors

The system of vectors, which we have introduced above, will be seen to give us the terminology and techniques for dealing with points, lines, angles and surfaces too, as will be seen later. Moreover, as this system deals with geometrical quantities in numerical terms, it is extremely valuable for computer technology. To exploit their potential we must be able to manipulate vectors, so next we look at aspects of adding and subtracting vectors and 'scaling' them by a number.

2.3.1 Adding vectors

As shown in Figure 2.5, to see what is meant by $(\mathbf{p} + \mathbf{q})$ we move $\mathbf{q}$ parallel to itself,

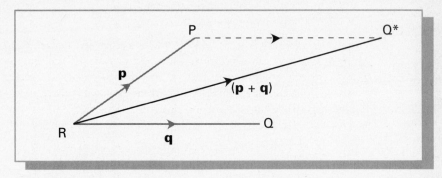

Figure 2.5 Vectors added graphically.

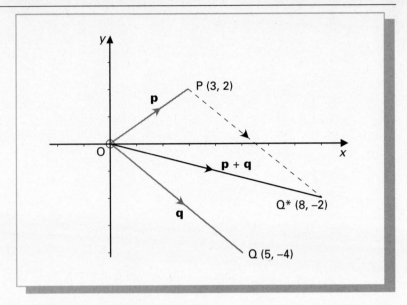

Figure 2.6 Vectors added using coordinates.

so that it starts where **p** finishes (this is a different arrow, but it represents the same vector as we saw in Section 2.1). The **sum** or **resultant** (**p** + **q**) is obtained by completing the triangle, as shown; this is called **triangle addition**. If you let your fingers 'walk' along in the direction of the vectors, then the overall displacement is the same if you 'walk' from R to P and then to Q*, or if you 'walk' from R to Q* direct.

The calculations are quite straightforward when we add vectors that are specified using a coordinate system. Referring to Figure 2.6, in component form we have **p** = 3**i** + 2**j** and **q** = 5**i** − 4**j**. Adding these gives

$$\mathbf{p} + \mathbf{q} = (3\mathbf{i} + 2\mathbf{j}) + (5\mathbf{i} - 4\mathbf{j})$$
$$= 3\mathbf{i} + 2\mathbf{j} + 5\mathbf{i} - 4\mathbf{j}, \text{ removing the brackets,}$$
$$= 8\mathbf{i} - 2\mathbf{j}, \text{ collecting together the } \mathbf{i} \text{ and } \mathbf{j} \text{ components}$$

Alternatively, referring still to Figure 2.6 but now using row vectors, we have **p** = (3 2) and **q** = (5 − 4) so that

$$\mathbf{p} + \mathbf{q} = (3 \quad 2) + (5 \quad -4)$$
$$= ((3 + 5) \quad (2 - 4))$$
$$= (8 \quad -2).$$

Whichever method is used, the resultant vector **p** + **q** is the same, as expected. Moreover, the resultant vector **q** + **p** is identical to **p** + **q**, which illustrates the fact that vector addition is **commutative**, that is 'order does not matter'.

Another feature of vector addition is that logically there must exist a **zero vector**, one with zero magnitude and no direction. This zero vector 'stays at the origin', and is written **0**. We have

$$\mathbf{0} = 0\mathbf{i} + 0\mathbf{j}$$
$$= (0 \quad 0)$$

and for any vector **p** the zero vector satisfies

$$p = 0 + p = p + 0$$

so that, in other words, adding nothing makes no difference.

2.3.2 Negative vectors and subtracting vectors

$-\mathbf{q}$ is a **negative vector**, by which we mean a vector with the same magnitude as $\mathbf{q}$ but in the opposite direction, as shown in Figure 2.7. We are able to calculate $\mathbf{p} - \mathbf{q}$ by finding $\mathbf{p} + (-\mathbf{q})$: we reverse the direction of $\mathbf{q}$ and, starting from $\mathbf{Q}$, we then use triangle addition as in Section 2.3.1.

When we subtract vectors given in a coordinate system then we follow one of the following methods. Referring to Figure 2.8, in component form we have

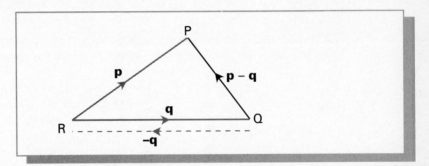

Figure 2.7 Vectors subtracted graphically.

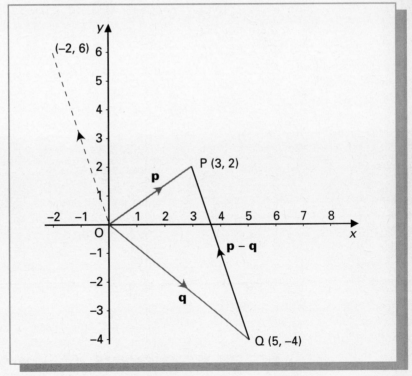

Figure 2.8 Vectors subtracted using coordinates.

$\mathbf{p} = 3\mathbf{i} + 2\mathbf{j}$ and $\mathbf{q} = 5\mathbf{i} - 4\mathbf{j}$. We subtract these vectors to get

$$\mathbf{p} - \mathbf{q} = (3\mathbf{i} + 2\mathbf{j}) - (5\mathbf{i} - 4\mathbf{j})$$
$$= 3\mathbf{i} + 2\mathbf{j} - 5\mathbf{i} + 4\mathbf{j}, \text{ removing the brackets,}$$
$$= -2\mathbf{i} + 6\mathbf{j}, \text{ collecting together the } \mathbf{i} \text{ and } \mathbf{j} \text{ components.}$$

Alternatively, referring still to Figure 2.8 but now using row vectors, we have

$$\mathbf{p} = (3 \quad 2) \text{ and } \mathbf{q} = (5 \quad -4), \text{ and subtraction gives}$$
$$\mathbf{p} - \mathbf{q} = (3 \quad 2) - (5 \quad -4)$$
$$= ((3 - 5) \quad (2 + 4))$$
$$= (-2 \quad 6)$$

We see that the vector we obtain for $\mathbf{p} - \mathbf{q}$ is the same whichever method is used: row vectors and vectors in component form are completely equivalent.

If we wish to determine the vector between any two points whose coordinates are known, then we use vector subtraction. Suppose we require the vector from P(2, 7) to Q(4, 10) as shown in Figure 2.9: we note that the direction matters, it is **PQ** that we want. First we identify the position vectors **OP** = **p** and **OQ** = **q**, and then we use these to calculate the vector **PQ** using triangle addition in triangle OPQ:

$$\mathbf{PQ} = \mathbf{PO} + \mathbf{OQ}$$
$$= -\mathbf{p} + \mathbf{q}$$
$$= -(2 \quad 7) + (4 \quad 10)$$
$$= (2 \quad 3)$$

Similarly we can show that $\mathbf{QP} = (-2 \quad -3)$, which is as expected since this is the negative of the vector **PQ**.

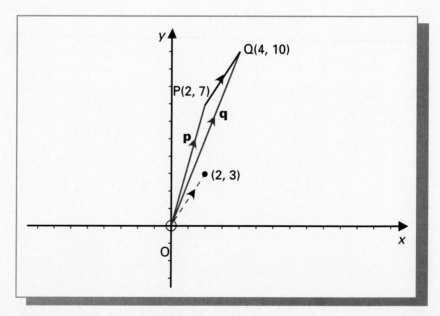

Figure 2.9 The vector between given points.

2.3.3 Scaling vectors

We can **scale** any vector by multiplying it by a scalar number (just a number). To 'scale it by 3' we make it three times bigger in the same direction, that is we multiply the vector by 3. Then where **p** is $(4 \quad 3)$, as in Figure 2.10, we have

$$3\mathbf{p} = 3(4 \quad 3)$$
$$= (12 \quad 9)$$

Similarly a scale factor of $\frac{1}{2}$, say, will yield a vector just half the size, in the same direction; thus for the same vector **p**

$$\tfrac{1}{2}\mathbf{p} = \tfrac{1}{2}(4 \quad 3)$$
$$= (2 \quad 1\tfrac{1}{2})$$

A negative scale factor reverses the direction of a vector. When the scale factor is -1, then the effect is just to reverse the vector, so that it has the same modulus but the opposite direction. If a negative scale factor is other than -1, then it alters the modulus of the vector as well. Thus referring to the same vector **p** in Figure 2.10:

$$(-2)\mathbf{p} = -2(4 \quad 3)$$
$$= (-8 \quad -6)$$

The effects of these scalings are indicated in Figure 2.10.

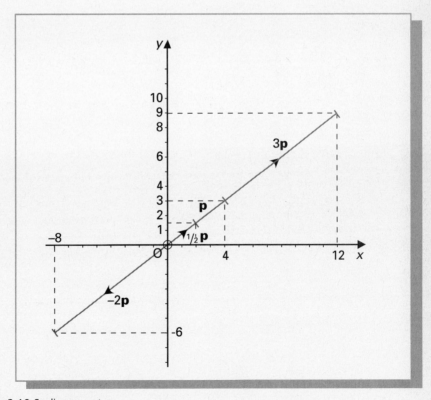

Figure 2.10 Scaling a vector.

Exercises

In the exercises that follow evaluate each answer exactly, where possible, or else correct to two decimal places. A sketch graph will enhance each answer.

2.1 Sketch the following vectors with initial points located at the origin:

a) $\mathbf{p} = 2\mathbf{i} + 3\mathbf{j}$ b) $\mathbf{q} = -3\mathbf{i} + 4\mathbf{j}$ c) $\mathbf{r} = -2\mathbf{i} - 4\mathbf{j}$ d) $\mathbf{s} = 3\mathbf{i} - 2\mathbf{j}$

2.2 Calculate the modulus of each vector in Exercise 2.1, and also the angle that it makes with the positive x-axis.

2.3 Determine the unit vector in the direction of each of these:

a) $\mathbf{h} = (3 \quad 6)$ b) $\mathbf{k} = (-4 \quad -8)$ c) $\mathbf{m} = (5 \quad -4)$ d) $\mathbf{n} = (3 \quad 0)$

2.4 Calculate the direction cosines for the vectors in Exercise 2.3.

2.5 If $\mathbf{u} = -3\mathbf{i} + \mathbf{j}$, $\mathbf{v} = 4\mathbf{i} - 8\mathbf{j}$, and $\mathbf{w} = \mathbf{i} + 2\mathbf{j}$, calculate the following:

a) $\mathbf{u} + \mathbf{v}$ b) $\mathbf{u} - \mathbf{w}$ c) $6\mathbf{v} + 2\mathbf{w}$ d) $\mathbf{u} + \mathbf{w} - \mathbf{v}$ e) $5(\mathbf{v} - 4\mathbf{u})$ f) $-3(\mathbf{u} + 2\mathbf{w})$
g) $2\mathbf{u} - 3\mathbf{v} + \frac{1}{2}\mathbf{w}$

2.6. Find the components of the vectors with initial points P and final points Q, where

a) P(4, 8), Q(3, 7) b) P(3, −5), (−4, −7)

c) P(−5, 0), (−3, 1) d) P(3, 3), Q(4, 4)

Answers

2.2 a) $\sqrt{13} \approx 3.61, 56.31°$; b) 5, 126.87° c) $\sqrt{20} \approx 4.47, -116.57°$,
d) $\sqrt{13} \approx 3.61, -33.69°$

2.3 a) $\hat{\mathbf{h}} = (0.45 \quad 0.89)$; b) $\hat{\mathbf{k}} = (-0.45 \quad -0.89)$; c) $\hat{\mathbf{m}} = (0.78 \quad -0.63)$;
d) $\hat{\mathbf{n}} = (1 \quad 0)$.

2.4 a) 0.45, 0.89; b) −0.45, −0.89; c) 0.78, −0.63; d) 1, 0.

2.5 a) $\mathbf{i} - 7\mathbf{j}$; b) $-4\mathbf{i} - \mathbf{j}$; c) $26\mathbf{i} - 44\mathbf{j}$; d) $-6\mathbf{i} + 11\mathbf{j}$; e) $80\mathbf{i} - 60\mathbf{j}$;
f) $3\mathbf{i} - 15\mathbf{j}$; g) $-17\frac{1}{2}\mathbf{i} + 27\mathbf{j}$.

2.6 a) $-\mathbf{i} - \mathbf{j}$; b) $-7\mathbf{i} - 2\mathbf{j}$; c) $2\mathbf{i} + \mathbf{j}$ d) $\mathbf{i} + \mathbf{j}$.

Angles between lines – introducing the third dimension: *Scalar products*

3.1 Multiplying vectors

To obtain all the results we want from vectors we must extend our ideas beyond the addition, subtraction and multiplying by a scalar that we met in the last chapter. The combination of quantities in this fashion is called an **algebra**, and we shall soon find that the 'algebra of vectors' is more intricate than the corresponding 'algebra of numbers'. While there is only one way in which two numbers can be multiplied together, there are two – essentially different – ways in which vectors can be multiplied together. We now look at the first of these ways; it is termed the **scalar product** of vectors, because the result is a scalar number, or alternatively the **dot product** of vectors because of the dot notation that is used. In computer graphics we shall use this product as a way of finding the angle between two vectors, and also of showing when two vectors are perpendicular.

3.2 The dot product

The general definition of the dot product of two vectors involves the modulus of each (see Example 2.1) and the angle between the directions of the vectors. If the angle between the two vectors **a** and **b** shown in Figure 3.1 is θ, where $0 \leq \theta < 180°$, then we define their dot product by

$$\mathbf{a} \cdot \mathbf{b} = |\mathbf{a}|\,|\mathbf{b}| \cos\theta$$

It is important to notice that when $\mathbf{a} \cdot \mathbf{b}$ is calculated the result is a pure (scalar) number, and not a vector. This is because the quantities involved, $|\mathbf{a}|$, $|\mathbf{b}|$ and $\cos\theta$, are each scalar numbers. From the definition we can obtain the formula that is used to calculate the angle between two vectors; it is

$$\cos\theta = \frac{\mathbf{a} \cdot \mathbf{b}}{|\mathbf{a}|\,|\mathbf{b}|}$$

In order to develop a feel for this way of multiplying, we shall apply it to the

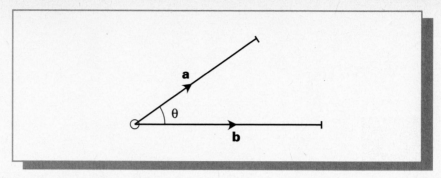

Figure 3.1 The angle between vectors.

vectors **i** and **j**, which are unit vectors in the directions of the axes we met in Section 2.1. First, we multiply **i** by **i** using the dot product. Because the vectors are coincident, the angle between them is $0°$ (see Figure 3.2a)), and so we have

$$\mathbf{i} \cdot \mathbf{i} = |\mathbf{i}|\,|\mathbf{i}|\cos 0°$$

$$= 1 \times 1 \times 1$$

since **i** is a unit vector and $\cos 0° = 1$ (which may be checked on your calculator). Thus

$$\mathbf{i} \cdot \mathbf{i} = 1$$

and similarly we can show that

$$\mathbf{j} \cdot \mathbf{j} = 1$$

We see that the dot product of any unit vector with itself will always yield the number '1'.

Next we multiply **i** by **j** using the dot product. Because the vectors are perpendicular, as shown in Figure 3.2(b), the angle betwen them is $90°$, and so

$$\mathbf{i} \cdot \mathbf{j} = |\mathbf{i}|\,|\mathbf{j}|\cos 90°$$

$$= 1 \times 1 \times 0$$

$$= 0$$

since here again **i** and **j** are unit vectors, and also $\cos 90° = 0$. Exactly similarly,

$$\mathbf{j} \cdot \mathbf{i} = 0$$

and we can deduce that 'The dot product = zero' implies *either* that at least one vector is the zero vector *or* that the vectors are perpendicular. This provides us with an easy check to determine whether non-zero vectors are perpendicular.

We now use the above results to find a method of calculating the dot product **a** · **b** when we know the components of the two-dimensional vectors **a** and **b**, but do not necessarily know the angle between them. We take $\mathbf{a} = a_1\mathbf{i} + a_2\mathbf{j}$, and $\mathbf{b} = b_1\mathbf{i} + b_2\mathbf{j}$, then

$$\mathbf{a} \cdot \mathbf{b} = (a_1\mathbf{i} + a_2\mathbf{j}) \cdot (b_1\mathbf{i} + b_2\mathbf{j})$$

which we multiply together in the standard way to get

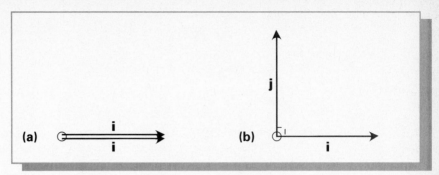

Figure 3.2 (a) $\mathbf{i} \cdot \mathbf{i}$, coincident unit vectors. (b) $\mathbf{i} \cdot \mathbf{j}$, perpendicular vectors.

$$\mathbf{a} \cdot \mathbf{b} = (a_1 \times b_1)\, \mathbf{i} \cdot \mathbf{i} + (a_2 \times b_2)\, \mathbf{j} \cdot \mathbf{j} + (a_1 \times b_2)\, \mathbf{i} \cdot \mathbf{j} + (a_2 \times b_1)\, \mathbf{j} \cdot \mathbf{i}$$

and we apply the above results, $\mathbf{i} \cdot \mathbf{i} = \mathbf{j} \cdot \mathbf{j} = 1$ and $\mathbf{i} \cdot \mathbf{j} = \mathbf{j} \cdot \mathbf{i} = 0$ to get

$$\mathbf{a} \cdot \mathbf{b} = (a_1 \times b_1) + (a_2 \times b_2)$$

(The '$\times$' here signifies the ordinary multiplication of scalar numbers.) We now have two equally useful formulae:

$$\mathbf{a} \cdot \mathbf{b} = |\mathbf{a}|\,|\mathbf{b}|\cos\theta \ \text{ and } \ \mathbf{a} \cdot \mathbf{b} = (a_1 \times b_1) + (a_2 \times b_2)$$

Like vector addition, we see that this form of vector multiplication is commutative, that is the order in which the vectors are multiplied does not affect the result. The value of this definition of vector multiplication is now evident: use of these alternative formulae gives us a direct way to calculate θ, the angle between any two vectors. We now illustrate this.

Example 3.1 Calculating the angle between vectors

We calculate the angle between the vectors $\mathbf{a} = 3\mathbf{i} + 5\mathbf{j}$ and $\mathbf{b} = 2\mathbf{i} + \mathbf{j}$, shown in Figure 3.3.

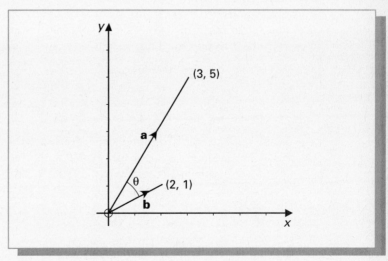

Figure 3.3 Calculating the angle between vectors in the coordinate plane.

Using the method of Example 2.1 we first calculate:

$$|\mathbf{a}| = \sqrt{34} \text{ and } |\mathbf{b}| = \sqrt{5}$$

From above we know that

$$\mathbf{a} \cdot \mathbf{b} = 3 \times 2 + 5 \times 1 = 6 + 5 = 11$$

then since

$$\mathbf{a} \cdot \mathbf{b} = |\mathbf{a}| \, |\mathbf{b}| \cos\theta$$

we have

$$11 = \sqrt{34} \times \sqrt{5} \times \cos\theta$$

Hence

$$\cos\theta = \frac{11}{\sqrt{34} \times \sqrt{5}}$$

$$= \frac{11}{\sqrt{170}}$$

$$\simeq 0.8437$$

Thus

$$\theta \simeq 32.47°.$$

3.3 The third dimension

Although a computer graphics display is two dimensional and shown on a screen, the images that are stored and manipulated are usually those of three-dimensional 'solid' objects. All the techniques we developed earlier for dealing with two-dimensional vectors can easily be extended to the three-dimensional case.

The idea behind the rectangular Cartesian system we use for three dimensions has already been introduced, based on the lines where the walls and floor of a room meet (see Section 1.4). Before proceeding, however, we must note that the standard coordinate system is based on a **right-handed set**, that is, when the thumb of a right hand twists from the direction of the x-axis to the direction of the y-axis, then the motion is similar to that needed to screw in an ordinary (right-handed) screw along the positive z-axis. The notation and results for vectors in three dimensions are summarized in the examples below and also in Figure 3.4.

A unit vector in the direction of the z-axis is **k**, and in three dimensions the unit vectors in the directions of the axes are written as the following row vectors:

$$\mathbf{i} = (1 \quad 0 \quad 0)$$

$$\mathbf{j} = (0 \quad 1 \quad 0)$$

$$\mathbf{k} = (0 \quad 0 \quad 1)$$

The position of any point P in three dimensions can be shown by three coordinates (X, Y, Z). The position vector of the point P is the vector **OP** which is written as $(X \quad Y \quad Z)$, or in component form as $X\mathbf{i} + Y\mathbf{j} + Z\mathbf{k}$. The modulus of **OP** is given by

$$|\mathbf{OP}| = \sqrt{X^2 + Y^2 + Z^2}$$

so a unit vector in the direction of **OP** is given by

$$\widehat{\mathbf{OP}} = \frac{\mathbf{OP}}{|\mathbf{OP}|} = \frac{X\mathbf{i} + Y\mathbf{j} + Z\mathbf{k}}{\sqrt{X^2 + Y^2 + Z^2}}$$

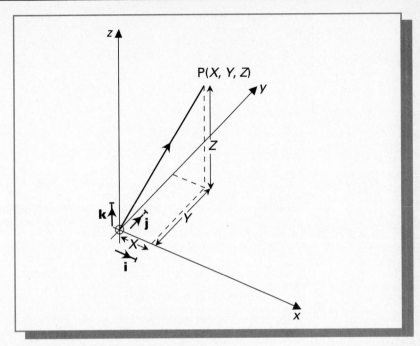

Figure 3.4 A three-dimensional coordinate system.

Example 3.2 Direction cosines in three dimensions

As in the two-dimensional case, the direction cosines of a three-dimensional vector enable us to calculate the angles made between the vector and the axes. Two vectors that have identical direction cosines have the same direction, and thus are parallel (see also Examples 1.4 and 2.4). Using the notation of Figure 3.5, the direction cosines of the vector shown are defined by

$$\cos \alpha = \frac{X}{|OP|}$$

$$\cos \beta = \frac{Y}{|OP|}$$

$$\cos \gamma = \frac{Z}{|OP|}$$

These are a most useful way of specifying the direction of a vector.

Example 3.3 Adding and subtracting vectors in three dimensions

Three-dimensional vectors are added and subtracted just as those in two dimensions. Thus we can calculate using the component form:

$$(3\mathbf{i} + 2\mathbf{j} - \mathbf{k}) + (4\mathbf{i} - \mathbf{j} - 2\mathbf{k}) = (7\mathbf{i} + \mathbf{j} - 3\mathbf{k})$$

Similarly, using row vector notation we can calculate

$$(6 \quad 3 \quad -1) - (2 \quad 4 \quad -3) = (4 \quad -1 \quad 2)$$

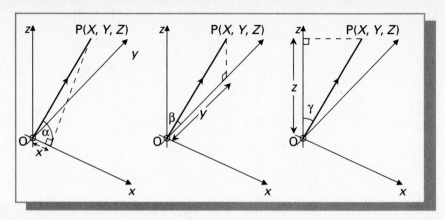

Figure 3.5 Direction cosines.

The zero vector is

$$\mathbf{0} = 0\mathbf{i} + 0\mathbf{j} + 0\mathbf{k} = (0 \quad 0 \quad 0)$$

Example 3.4 The vector between two points in three dimensions

As shown in Figure 3.6, there is a vector from the point P(3, 4, 7) to the point Q(2, 1, 9). Following the method of Section 2.3.2, this vector, **PQ**, is given by

$$\mathbf{PQ} = \mathbf{PO} + \mathbf{OQ}$$
$$= -\mathbf{p} + \mathbf{q}$$
$$= \mathbf{q} - \mathbf{p}$$
$$= (2 \quad 1 \quad 9) - (3 \quad 4 \quad 7)$$
$$= (-1 \quad -3 \quad 2)$$

Example 3.5 The angle between two vectors in three dimensions

The angle θ between **OP** and **OQ** in Figure 3.6 may be calculated using the dot product, thus

$$|\mathbf{p}|\,|\mathbf{q}|\cos\theta = (3 \times 2) + (4 \times 1) + (7 \times 9)$$
$$= 73$$

Since we have

$$|\mathbf{p}| = \sqrt{3^2 + 4^2 + 7^2} = \sqrt{74}$$

and

$$|\mathbf{q}| = \sqrt{2^2 + 1^2 + 9^2} = \sqrt{86}$$

we can write

$$\cos\theta = \frac{73}{\sqrt{74} \times \sqrt{86}} \approx 0.9151$$

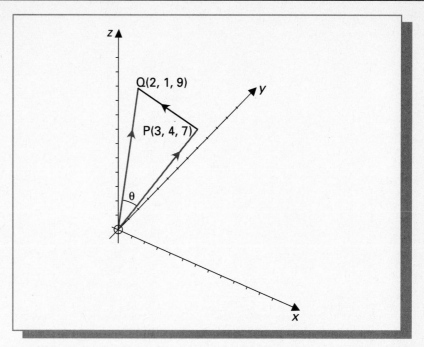

Figure 3.6 The vector between points and the angle between position vectors in three dimensions.

which gives

$$\theta = 23.78°$$

In this example we have extended the definition of the dot product of two vectors to allow for three components in each. Thus for $\mathbf{a} = a_1\mathbf{i} + a_2\mathbf{j} + a_3\mathbf{k}$ and $\mathbf{b} = b_1\mathbf{i} + b_2\mathbf{j} + b_3\mathbf{k}$ we now have the dot product defined as follows:

$$\mathbf{a} \cdot \mathbf{b} = (a_1 \times b_1) + (a_2 \times b_2) + (a_3 \times b_3).$$

3.4 Model solutions

We complete this chapter by including some examples which are model solutions to exercises. The first two refer back to Exercises 1.7 and 1.8, but here we offer solutions that rely on vector methods – the advantages to be gained are obvious. The third example is more formally worded, and it will readily be appreciated that its solution using traditional geometry would be very awkward indeed.

Example 3.6 The first web of the nocturnal spider

'One night, a spider began spinning a web inside a shoe box, whose dimensions are: length 33 cm, width 18 cm, and depth 12 cm. It started at a top corner and climbed down to the base, inside; it crawled along the length to the next corner and then crawled along the width, ending up at the corner furthest from where it started. It tightened a filament of web fixed between its starting and finishing positions. How long was this filament of web?'

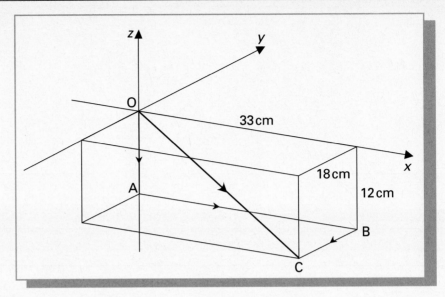

Figure 3.7 The first web of the nocturnal spider: use of vectors.

As shown in Figure 3.7, we construct three-dimensional rectangular axes aligned with the edges of the shoebox. As usual, **i**, **j** and **k** are the unit vectors along the *x*-, *y*- and *z*-axes. Then, with the notation indicated, the filament made by the spider is given by the vector **OC**. Using vector addition

$$\mathbf{OC} = \mathbf{OA} + \mathbf{AB} + \mathbf{BC}$$

$$= -12\mathbf{k} + 33\mathbf{i} - 18\mathbf{j}$$

Hence, taking the components in their standard order,

$$\mathbf{OC} = 33\mathbf{i} - 18\mathbf{j} - 12\mathbf{k}$$

For the length of **OC**, we calculate its modulus:

$$|\mathbf{OC}| = \sqrt{33^2 + 18^2 + 12^2}$$

$$\approx 39.46$$

Thus the length of the filament is approximately 39.46 cm.

Example 3.7 The second web of the nocturnal spider

'The shoe box was cleaned out next day, so the following night the spider began to spin a new web. It started at a top corner, as before, and managed to stretch a filament from there to the mid-point of the opposite base edge and then back to the nearest adjacent top corner. What was the angle between these two strands of filament?'

As shown in Figure 3.8, we use rectangular axes and notation similar to that in Example 3.6. The two strands of filament are given by the vectors **PO** and **PQ**, with θ the angle between them. Note that in calculating this angle, we must arrange that the direction of each vector is away from the point of their intersection. Then, as before, by vector addition we have

$$OP = OA + AB + BP$$
$$= -12k + 33i - 9j$$
$$= 33i - 9j - 12k$$

Hence, reversing the direction of this we get

$$PO = -33i + 9j + 12k$$

Similarly,

$$QP = QD + DC + CP$$
$$= -12k + 33i + 9j$$
$$= 33i + 9j - 12k$$

Hence

$$PQ = -33i - 9j + 12k$$

The angle θ is found by using the value of the dot product of these vectors:

$$\cos \theta = \frac{PO \cdot PQ}{|PO| \, |PQ|}$$

Thus

$$\cos \theta = \frac{(-33 \times -33) + (9 \times -9) + (12 \times 12)}{\sqrt{(33^2 + 9^2 + 12^2)} \times \sqrt{(33^2 + 9^2 + 12^2)}}$$

$$= \frac{1152}{\sqrt{1314} \times \sqrt{1314}}$$

$$\approx 0.8767$$

Hence the angle between the filaments is approximately 28.75°.

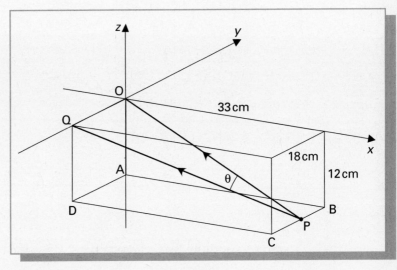

Figure 3.8 The second web of the nocturnal spider: use of vectors.

Example 3.8 The angle between two lines in space

Where A(−1, 0, 2), B(3, 2, 5) and C(−2, 2, 4) are three points in space, we use vector methods to find the angle between the lines AB and AC.

We can see from Figure 3.9 that

$$\mathbf{OB} = \mathbf{OA} + \mathbf{AB} \text{ and hence}$$

$$\mathbf{AB} = \mathbf{OB} - \mathbf{OA}$$

Using the component form of the vectors we have

$$\mathbf{AB} = (3\mathbf{i} + 2\mathbf{j} + 5\mathbf{k}) - (-\mathbf{i} + 2\mathbf{k})$$

$$= (4\mathbf{i} + 2\mathbf{j} + 3\mathbf{k})$$

Similarly

$$\mathbf{AC} = \mathbf{OC} - \mathbf{OA}$$

$$= (-2\mathbf{i} + 2\mathbf{j} + 4\mathbf{k}) - (-\mathbf{i} + 2\mathbf{k})$$

$$= (-\mathbf{i} + 2\mathbf{j} + 2\mathbf{k})$$

To calculate the angle θ, we use the formula

$$\mathbf{AB} \cdot \mathbf{AC} = |\mathbf{AB}| \, |\mathbf{AC}| \cos \theta$$

We first evaluate $\mathbf{AB} \cdot \mathbf{AC}$:

$$\mathbf{AB} \cdot \mathbf{AC} = (4 \times -1) + (2 \times 2) + (3 \times 2)$$

$$= -4 + 4 + 6$$

$$= 6$$

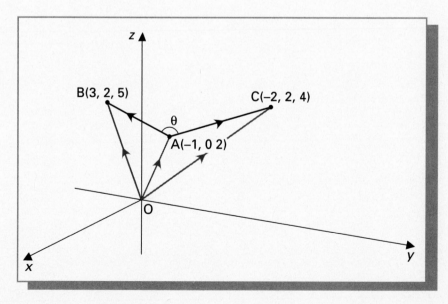

Figure 3.9 The angle between two lines in space.

Then we evaluate $|\mathbf{AB}|$ and $|\mathbf{AC}|$:

$$|\mathbf{AB}| = \sqrt{4^2 + 2^2 + 3^2}$$
$$= \sqrt{29}$$

and

$$|\mathbf{AC}| = \sqrt{(-1)^2 + 2^2 + 2^2}$$
$$= \sqrt{9}$$
$$= 3$$

Thus from the formula

$$6 = \sqrt{29} \times 3 \times \cos\theta$$

so that

$$\cos\theta = \frac{6}{\sqrt{29} \times 3}$$
$$\approx 0.3714$$

Hence the angle between the lines $\mathbf{AB}$ and $\mathbf{AC}$ is approximately $68.20°$.

Exercises

3.1   Given the vectors $\mathbf{a} = 3\mathbf{i} - 4\mathbf{j} + 2\mathbf{k}$, $\mathbf{b} = \mathbf{i} + \mathbf{j} + \mathbf{k}$ and $\mathbf{c} = -2\mathbf{i} + 5\mathbf{j} + \mathbf{k}$, calculate each of the following:

a) $\mathbf{b} - \mathbf{a}$ b) $\mathbf{a} + \mathbf{c}$ c) $\mathbf{a} + \mathbf{b} + \mathbf{c}$ d) $2\mathbf{a} - 3\mathbf{b} + \frac{1}{2}\mathbf{c}$ e) $|\mathbf{b}|$ f) $|\mathbf{c}|$

3.2   Determine the vector $\mathbf{PQ}$ whose initial point is at $P(2, -1, 3)$ and whose final point is at $Q(3, 2, -4)$.

3.3   Four points are defined by their position vectors as follows: $\mathbf{OP} = 3\mathbf{i} + 0.5\mathbf{j} - \mathbf{k}$; $\mathbf{OQ} = 2\mathbf{OP}$; $\mathbf{OR} = -\mathbf{OP}$; $\mathbf{OS} = \frac{1}{2}\mathbf{OP}$. What are the coordinates of the points P, Q, R and S?

3.4   Calculate the dot products of the following pairs of vectors:

a) $3\mathbf{i} + 2\mathbf{j}$, $4\mathbf{i} - 3\mathbf{j}$ b) $(-1 \quad 1)$, $(4 \quad -2)$ c) $\mathbf{i} - 2\mathbf{j} + 3\mathbf{k}$, $2\mathbf{i} - \mathbf{j} + \mathbf{k}$
d) $(4 \quad -6 \quad 1)$, $(2 \quad 0 \quad -1)$

3.5   Are the following vectors at right angles to each other?

a) $\mathbf{a} = 7\mathbf{i} + \mathbf{j} - 2\mathbf{k}$ and $\mathbf{b} = \mathbf{i} + 7\mathbf{j} - \mathbf{k}$ b) $\mathbf{c} = (2 \quad 3 \quad -1)$ and $\mathbf{d} = (-2 \quad 1 \quad -1)$

3.6   Determine the value of the scalar number h that will make the vectors

$\mathbf{p} = 2\mathbf{i} + h\mathbf{j} + \mathbf{k}$ and $\mathbf{q} = 4\mathbf{i} - 2\mathbf{j} - 2\mathbf{k}$ perpendicular to each other.

3.7   If $\mathbf{a} = \mathbf{i} + 3\mathbf{j} + 2\mathbf{k}$, $\mathbf{b} = -\mathbf{j} + 4\mathbf{k}$ and $\mathbf{c} = 3\mathbf{i} - 4\mathbf{j} - \mathbf{k}$, find the values of
a) $(\mathbf{a} + \mathbf{b}) \cdot \mathbf{c}$ and b) $\mathbf{a} \cdot \mathbf{c} + \mathbf{b} \cdot \mathbf{c}$ and compare the results.

3.8   Find the angles between the following pairs of vectors:

a) $\mathbf{p} = 3\mathbf{i} + 2\mathbf{j} - 6\mathbf{k}$ and $\mathbf{q} = 4\mathbf{i} - 3\mathbf{j} + \mathbf{k}$ b) $\mathbf{r} = (4 \quad -2 \quad 4)$ and $\mathbf{s} = (3 \quad -6 \quad -2)$

3.9   Calculate the angle at B between the lines joining the points whose coordinates are
A$(-1, -1, -1)$, B$(2, 3, 1)$ and C$(-2, 5, 2)$.

3.10 With respect to rectangular coordinate axes, three points have the following coordinates: P(1, 4, 2), A(4, −1, 4), B(5, 3, 6). Determine whether or not **OP** and **AB** are parallel.

3.11 Four points are represented by the following coordinates: P(3, 1, 1), Q(4, 4, 2), A(1, 2, 1) and B(3, 8, 3). Calculate the vectors **PQ** and **AB** and show that they are parallel.

3.12 Calculate the lengths and the direction cosines of the vectors **AB**, where the coordinates of the points A and B are as follows:
a) A(1, 1, 1) and B(2, 0, 1)
b) A(2, −1, 1) and B(−2, 2, 2)
c) A(−1, 3, 1) and B(−2, −1, 0)

Determine the angles α, β, γ between each of these vectors and the positive directions of the coordinate axes.
Show that in each case $\cos^2\alpha + \cos^2\beta + \cos^2\gamma = 1$.

3.13 The direction cosines for three different vectors are $\left\{ \dfrac{\sqrt{3}}{2}, 0, \dfrac{1}{2} \right\}$, $\left\{ \dfrac{1}{\sqrt{3}}, \dfrac{1}{\sqrt{3}}, \dfrac{1}{\sqrt{3}} \right\}$ and $\left\{ \dfrac{1}{3}, \dfrac{-1}{3}, \dfrac{\sqrt{7}}{3} \right\}$.

Calculate the angles each of these vectors makes with the positive directions of the coordinate axes.

Answers

3.1 a) $-2\mathbf{i} + 5\mathbf{j} - \mathbf{k}$; b) $\mathbf{i} + \mathbf{j} + 3\mathbf{k}$; c) $2\mathbf{i} + 2\mathbf{j} + 4\mathbf{k}$; d) $2\mathbf{i} - 8\frac{1}{2}\mathbf{j} + 1\frac{1}{2}\mathbf{k}$; e) 1.73; f) 5.48.

3.2 $\mathbf{PQ} = \mathbf{OQ} - \mathbf{OP} = \mathbf{i} + 3\mathbf{j} - 7\mathbf{k}$.

3.3 P(3, 0.5, −1); Q(6, 1, −2); R(−3, −0.5, 1); S(1.5, 0.25, −0.5).

3.4 a) 6; b) −6; c) 7; d) 7.

3.5 a) No ; b) Yes.

3.6 $h = 3$.

3.7 a) −11; b) −11.

3.8 a) 90°; b) 67.61°.

3.9 85.35°.

3.10 Yes, parallel, both given by $(\mathbf{i} + 4\mathbf{j} + 2\mathbf{k})$.

3.11 $\mathbf{PQ} = \mathbf{i} + 3\mathbf{j} + \mathbf{k}$; $\mathbf{AB} = 2\mathbf{i} + 6\mathbf{j} + 2\mathbf{k} = 2\mathbf{PQ}$; hence parallel.

3.12 a) $|\mathbf{AB}| \simeq 1.41$; $\{1/\sqrt{2}, -1/\sqrt{2}, 0\}$; 45°, 135°, 90°.
b) $|\mathbf{AB}| \simeq 5.10$; $\{-0.78, 0.59, 0.20\}$; 141.67°, 53.96°, 78.69°.
c) $|\mathbf{AB}| \simeq 4.24$; $\{-0.24, -0.94, -0.24\}$; 103.63°, 160.53°, 103.63°.

3.13 30°, 90°, 60°; 54.74°, 54.74°, 54.74°; 70.53°, 109.47°, 28.13°.

4

Finding normals to planes:
Vector products

4.1 The 'other' form of multiplication

In the last chapter we had practice with manipulating vectors in three dimensions; we now extend the usefulness of vectors by presenting a technique that will enable us to determine the normal to any set of vectors in a plane. A **normal** to a pair of vectors is a vector that is at right angles to both of them, so that a **normal to a plane** is a vector that is at right angles to all the vectors that are in that plane (see Figure 4.1(a) and (b)). Finding normals will enable us to communicate numerically about many real phenomena, including rectangular constructions and the reflections of rays of light from surfaces. The key to all these possibilities is the technique based on the second way in which vectors can be multiplied together, termed the **vector product** of vectors (since the result is itself a vector) or the **cross product** of vectors (named after the cross notation used, the ordinary symbol used also for the multiplication of scalar numbers).

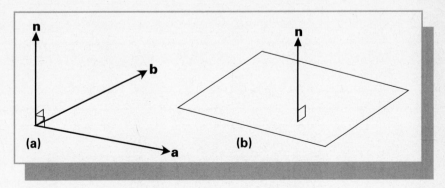

Figure 4.1 (a) **n** is normal to **a** and **b**. (b) **n** is normal to the plane.

4.2 The cross product

The definition of the cross product of two vectors demands the consideration of more than two dimensions. Like the dot product, the cross product depends on the modulus of each vector and the angle between them, but the result of the cross product is essentially different: it is another vector, at right angles to both the originals.

For an understanding of the cross product $\mathbf{a} \times \mathbf{b}$, we first imagine drawing a plane through the two vectors $\mathbf{a}$ and $\mathbf{b}$ as shown in Figure 4.2(a). This can always be done: either the given vectors intersect from the outset, or, if not, then we apply the technique of Section 2.3.1, and move $\mathbf{b}$ parallel to itself until it does intersect with $\mathbf{a}$. In this plane we show the angle θ between the directions of the vectors, where θ is chosen so that $0 \leq \theta < 180°$. Then by definition we have

$$\mathbf{a} \times \mathbf{b} = |\mathbf{a}|\,|\mathbf{b}|\,\sin\theta\,\hat{\mathbf{n}}$$

where $\hat{\mathbf{n}}$ is a unit vector at right angles to both $\mathbf{a}$ and $\mathbf{b}$, shown in Figure 4.2(b), with $\mathbf{a}$, $\mathbf{b}$ and $\hat{\mathbf{n}}$ forming a right–handed set (as described in Section 3.3).

Obviously the order of multiplication affects the result, since requiring that we have a right-handed set will cause directions to reverse if the order of $\mathbf{a}$ and $\mathbf{b}$ is reversed; this form of vector multiplication is not commutative. Thus in the Figure 4.3(a) and (b) we see that $\mathbf{a} \times \mathbf{b}$ yields a vector perpendicular and up out of the plane, whereas $\mathbf{b} \times \mathbf{a}$ yields a vector perpendicular down from the plane.

There are always two opposite directions possible for a normal, and we see that here $\mathbf{a} \times \mathbf{b} = -(\mathbf{b} \times \mathbf{a})$. In more advanced computer graphics applications, care has to be taken with the direction of normals, and it is not uncommon to need to 'reverse normals' in certain practical situations. We note, however, that these two normals are very closely related, and since

$$|\mathbf{a} \times \mathbf{b}| = |\mathbf{b} \times \mathbf{a}| = |\mathbf{a}|\,|\mathbf{b}|\,\sin\theta$$

their magnitude is the same.

We now develop our understanding of the cross product of vectors by applying the basic definition to the unit vectors $\mathbf{i}$, $\mathbf{j}$ and $\mathbf{k}$. First, we multiply $\mathbf{i}$ by $\mathbf{i}$ using the cross product. As shown in Figure 4.4(a) the vectors are coincident, so as in Section 3.2 the angle $\theta = 0°$ and hence

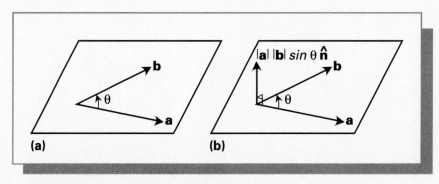

(a) (b)

Figure 4.2 (a) Looking down on vectors in a plane.
(b) Looking down on the result of a vector product.

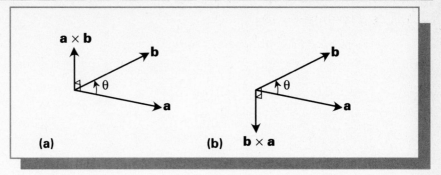

Figure 4.3 (a) $\mathbf{a} \times \mathbf{b}$ (b) $\mathbf{b} \times \mathbf{a}$.

$$\mathbf{i} \times \mathbf{i} = |\mathbf{i}|\,|\mathbf{i}|\, \sin 0° \,\hat{\mathbf{n}}$$

Since $\mathbf{i}$ is a unit vector and $\sin 0° = 0$ (which may be checked on your calculator), this gives

$$\mathbf{i} \times \mathbf{i} = (1 \times 1 \times 0)\,\hat{\mathbf{n}}$$

and hence

$$\mathbf{i} \times \mathbf{i} = \mathbf{0}, \text{ the zero vector}$$

Similarly,

$$\mathbf{j} \times \mathbf{j} = \mathbf{0} \text{ and } \mathbf{k} \times \mathbf{k} = \mathbf{0}$$

so we see that the cross product of any vector with itself is always the zero vector. Conversely, whenever the cross product of vectors is identically the zero vector, then we may deduce *either* that at least one vector is the zero vector, *or* that the vectors are parallel, having the same direction ($\theta = 0°$). If we can be sure that the vectors are not zero, then this provides us with a straightforward test to discover whether or not vectors are parallel.

Next we multiply $\mathbf{i}$ by $\mathbf{j}$ using the cross product. As we see in Figure 4.4(b) these vectors are perpendicular to each other, thus $\theta = 90°$ as in Section 3.2. Then

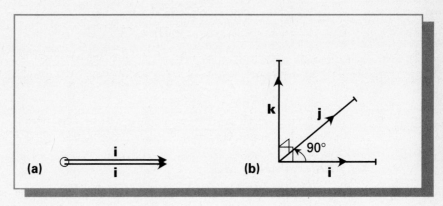

Figure 4.4 (a) $\mathbf{i} \times \mathbf{i} = \mathbf{0}$ (b) $\mathbf{i} \times \mathbf{j} = \mathbf{k}$.

$$i \times j = |i| \; |j| \sin 90° \; \hat{n}$$

Since i and j are unit vectors and $\sin 90° = 1$, this gives

$$i \times j = (1 \times 1 \times 1)k$$

because i, j and k form a right-handed set.

Thus

$$i \times j = k$$

Similarly, we can show that

$$j \times k = i \text{ and } k \times i = j$$

The order of the vectors in these results may appear strange, but it can easily be remembered if we notice that each result contains a 'cycle' within alphabetical ordering.

There remain three other possible cross products of these unit vectors to consider. Since the effect of multiplying the vectors in a different order is to reverse the direction of the cross product, we have immediately that

$$j \times i = -k \text{ and } k \times j = -i \text{ and } i \times k = -j$$

Using the above results, we now calculate the cross product $a \times b$ of any three-dimensional vectors a and b. We assume that the vectors are given in component form, but we need not know explicitly the angle between them. We take

$$a = a_1 i + a_2 j + a_3 k \text{ and } b = b_1 i + b_2 j + b_3 k$$

Then

$$
\begin{aligned}
a \times b &= (a_1 i + a_2 j + a_3 k) \times (b_1 i + b_2 j + b_3 k) \\
&= [a_1 i \times (b_1 i + b_2 j + b_3 k)] + [a_2 j \times (b_1 i + b_2 j + b_3 k)] \\
&\quad + [a_3 k \times (b_1 i + b_2 j + b_3 k)]
\end{aligned}
$$

by the usual rules of multiplying brackets. Thus

$$
\begin{aligned}
a \times b &= (a_1 b_1 i \times i + a_1 b_2 i \times j + a_1 b_3 i \times k) \\
&\quad + (a_2 b_1 j \times i + a_2 b_2 j \times j + a_2 b_3 j \times k) \\
&\quad + (a_3 b_1 k \times i + a_3 b_2 k \times j + a_3 b_3 k \times k)
\end{aligned}
$$

This looks far worse than it is. We use our first set of results to replace $i \times i$, $j \times j$ and $k \times k$ by 0. Then we apply the other results to tidy up the expression as follows:

$$a \times b = (a_2 b_3 - a_3 b_2)i + (a_3 b_1 - a_1 b_3)j + (a_1 b_2 - a_2 b_1)k$$

This still may appear hard to remember, and perhaps here it is worthwhile to learn a pattern of multiplying numbers based on what is called a determinant.

4.2.1 Determinants

A **determinant** consists of numbers arranged in a square, but the determinant itself has a single value. In the case of a '2×2' determinant its value is the product on one diagonal minus the product on the other diagonal. Thus for the determinant

$$D = \begin{vmatrix} 3 & 7 \\ 2 & 8 \end{vmatrix}$$

the value of D is obtained from

$$\begin{vmatrix} 3 & 7 \\ 2 & 8 \end{vmatrix} = (3 \times 8 - 2 \times 7) = 24 - 14 = 10$$

If we return to our expression for the cross product of **a** and **b**, and rewrite the middle bracket to obtain a change of sign, we get

$$\mathbf{a} \times \mathbf{b} = (a_2 b_3 - a_3 b_2)\mathbf{i} - (a_1 b_3 - a_3 b_1)\mathbf{j} + (a_1 b_2 - a_2 b_1)\mathbf{k}$$

The three brackets can be seen to be the values of three determinants, respectively

$$\begin{vmatrix} a_2 & a_3 \\ b_2 & b_3 \end{vmatrix}, \begin{vmatrix} a_1 & a_3 \\ b_1 & b_3 \end{vmatrix} \text{ and } \begin{vmatrix} a_1 & a_2 \\ b_1 & b_2 \end{vmatrix}$$

It is often easiest to remember the expression above by means of the following composite determinant pattern:

$$\begin{vmatrix} \mathbf{i} & \mathbf{j} & \mathbf{k} \\ a_1 & a_2 & a_3 \\ b_1 & b_2 & b_3 \end{vmatrix}$$

The numerical value of each component is the value of the 2×2 determinant found by deleting the row and column containing that vector. As long as we make sure to subtract the component of **j** calculated in this way, this method enables us to calculate the cross product of any pair of three-dimensional vectors.

Example 4.1 Calculating a cross product

We calculate the cross product of $\mathbf{a} = 3\mathbf{i} + 2\mathbf{j} + 5\mathbf{k}$ and $\mathbf{b} = 7\mathbf{i} + 11\mathbf{j} + 13\mathbf{k}$. We start by setting the components of the vectors into the determinant pattern as

$$\begin{vmatrix} \mathbf{i} & \mathbf{j} & \mathbf{k} \\ 3 & 2 & 5 \\ 7 & 11 & 13 \end{vmatrix}$$

Deleting the row and column containing **i**, we obtain the numerical value of the **i**-component of the product:

$$\begin{vmatrix} 2 & 5 \\ 11 & 13 \end{vmatrix} = (2 \times 13 - 11 \times 5) = (26 - 55) = -29$$

Deleting the row and column containing **j**, we obtain the numerical value of the **j**-component:

$$\text{MINUS} \begin{vmatrix} 3 & 5 \\ 7 & 13 \end{vmatrix} = -(3 \times 13 - 7 \times 5) = -(39 - 35) = -4$$

Deleting the row and column containing **k**, we obtain the numerical value of the **k**-component:

$$\begin{vmatrix} 3 & 2 \\ 7 & 11 \end{vmatrix} = (3 \times 11 - 7 \times 2) = (33 - 14) = 19$$

Thus in this case

$$\mathbf{a} \times \mathbf{b} = -29\mathbf{i} - 4\mathbf{j} + 19\mathbf{k}$$

4.3 Calculating a normal

In computer graphics applications we calculate a cross product in order to determine a vector that is normal to a given pair of vectors, and hence normal to the plane that contains them. Equivalently, such a vector may be described as perpendicular to, or orthogonal to, or at right angles to, a given pair of vectors. By calculating $\mathbf{a} \times \mathbf{b}$, we immediately get a vector perpendicular to both $\mathbf{a}$ and $\mathbf{b}$. If a unit vector, $\hat{\mathbf{n}}$, normal to both is required, then we must divide $\mathbf{a} \times \mathbf{b}$ by its own magnitude $|\mathbf{a} \times \mathbf{b}|$ to obtain

$$\hat{\mathbf{n}} = \frac{\mathbf{a} \times \mathbf{b}}{|\mathbf{a} \times \mathbf{b}|}$$

Example 4.2   Finding a unit normal to a plane

We find a unit normal to the plane containing the three points A(−1, 0, 1), B(2, 3, −1) and C(1, 4, 2) sketched in Figure 4.5.

The plane which contains the points A, B and C is defined by any two vectors along the lines AB, BC or CA. Without loss of generality, we choose to consider the pair of vectors **BA** and **BC**. (Other pairs of vectors could be chosen, but we must remember to direct them away from their point of intersection in each case.) We first find the component form for each of **BA** and **BC**:

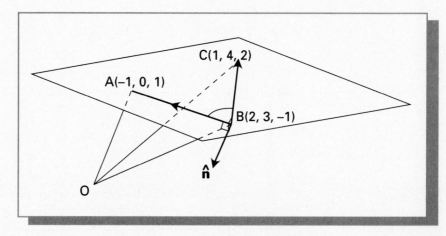

Figure 4.5 The unit normal to a plane containing three given points.

$$BA = OA - OB$$
$$= (-i + k) - (2i + 3j - k)$$
$$= -3i - 3j + 2k$$
$$BC = OC - OB$$
$$= (i + 4j + 2k) - (2i + 3j - k)$$
$$= -i + j + 3k$$

We next write down the determinant pattern for $\mathbf{BA} \times \mathbf{BC}$ which is

$$\begin{vmatrix} i & j & k \\ -3 & -3 & 2 \\ -1 & 1 & 3 \end{vmatrix}$$

Then

$$\mathbf{BA} \times \mathbf{BC} = ((-3) \times 3 - 1 \times 2)i - ((-3) \times 3 - (-1) \times 2)\,j + ((-3) \times 1 - (-1) \times (-3))k$$
$$= (-9 - 2)i - (-9 + 2)j + (-3 - 3)k$$
$$= -11i + 7j - 6k$$

The vector $\mathbf{BA} \times \mathbf{BC}$ is normal to the plane of A, B and C. To find a unit normal, we divide by the modulus of $\mathbf{BA} \times \mathbf{BC}$ calculated as

$$|\mathbf{BA} \times \mathbf{BC}| = \sqrt{(-11)^2 + (7)^2 + (-6)^2}$$
$$= \sqrt{121 + 49 + 36}$$
$$= \sqrt{206}$$

Thus a unit normal is

$$\hat{\mathbf{n}} = \frac{1}{\sqrt{206}} (-11i + 7j - 6k)$$
$$\simeq -0.77i + 0.49j - 0.42k$$

With a calculator we can easily verify that

$$|\hat{\mathbf{n}}| = \sqrt{(0.77)^2 + (0.49)^2 + (0.42)^2} \simeq 1$$

$\hat{\mathbf{n}}$ is indeed a unit vector. Moreover, we can verify that

$$\hat{\mathbf{n}} \cdot \mathbf{BA} = 0$$

and

$$\hat{\mathbf{n}} \cdot \mathbf{BC} = 0$$

and thus show that $\hat{\mathbf{n}}$ really is perpendicular to both $\mathbf{BA}$ and $\mathbf{BC}$, and hence to the whole plane containing A, B and C.

4.4 Model solutions

We conclude this chapter with worked examples based on graphical problems involving models of real artefacts. A coordinate system is superimposed on the structure in each case, and vector methods are used. The techniques involved include determining the moduli of vectors, and calculating dot products and cross products in order to find angles and normals.

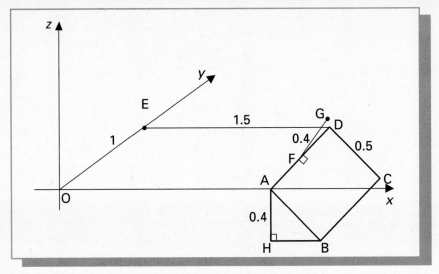

Figure 4.6 Model for the roof, rear window and aerial of a car.

Example 4.3 The car aerial

A familiar design feature of some modern cars is the radio aerial jutting out from the middle of the top of the rear window – just like a feather jauntily placed at the back of a cap. If we consider a simplified version of the roof of such a car, with very simplified dimensions based on metres, as shown in Figure 4.6, we can model the structure using a fairly obvious coordinate system. Assuming that the aerial is at right angles to the rear window, we set ourselves the task of using vector methods to calculate the coordinates of the tip of the aerial.

Using the notation on the diagram and the axes shown, we first determine the coordinates of the vertices; we have O(0, 0, 0), A(1.5, 0, 0), D(1.5, 1, 0), E(0, 1, 0), and F(1.5, 0.5, 0). To find the coordinates of B and C we need |HB|, the length of HB, which we calculate using Pythagoras' Theorem:

$$|HB|^2 + (0.4)^2 = (0.5)^2$$

so that

$$|HB| = \sqrt{(0.25 - 0.16)}$$

$$= \sqrt{0.09}$$

$$= 0.3$$

Thus we have coordinates for the remaining vertices: B(1.8, 0, −0.4) and C(1.8, 1, −0.4).

Since **FG** is assumed to be normal to the plane ABCD, its direction will be given by the cross product of any two vectors in that plane: we take these to be **AB** and **AD**. The product **AB** × **AD** will be in the direction of **FG**. We next calculate the components of the vectors **AB** and **AD**:

$$AB = OB - OA$$

$$= (1.8i - 0.4k) - (1.5i)$$

$$= 0.3i - 0.4k$$

$$AD = OD - OA$$

$$= (1.5i + 1j) - (1.5i)$$

$$= 1j$$

Now we need to calculate $AB \times AD$ so we consider the following determinant pattern:

$$\begin{vmatrix} i & j & k \\ 0.3 & 0 & -0.4 \\ 0 & 1 & 0 \end{vmatrix}$$

Thus

$$AB \times AD = (0 - 1 \times (-0.4))i - (0 - 0)j + (0.3 \times 1 - 0)k$$

$$= 0.4i + 0.3k$$

A unit vector in the direction of $AB \times AD$ is given by

$$\frac{AB \times AD}{|AB \times AD|}$$

where

$$|AB \times AD| = \sqrt{(0.4)^2 + (0.3)^2}$$

$$= \sqrt{0.25}$$

$$= 0.5$$

Since FG is of length 0.4 we have

$$FG = (0.4/0.5)\,(0.4i + 0.3k)$$

$$= 0.32i + 0.24k$$

In conclusion, the position vector of G is

$$OG = OF + FG$$

$$= (1.5i + 0.5j) + (0.32i + 0.24k)$$

$$= 1.82i + 0.5j + 0.24k$$

and so the coordinates of G, the tip of the aerial, are $(1.82, 0.5, 0.24)$.

Example 4.4   The garage

Now we consider the construction of a computer model of the garage for our car. The sketch of the garage, and its simplified dimensions in metres, are shown in Figure 4.7. The task we set ourselves is in three parts; we shall use vector methods to find the following

1. The distance between A and B, and between B and C.
2. The angle between AB and BC.
3. The outward unit normal vector to the sloping roof CDFE.

We first superimpose on the sketch of the garage a system of coordinate axes as shown in Figure 4.7, with the origin at O. To calculate the distances in part (1) we first identify the coordinates of vertices as A(0.5, 0, 2.5), B(4, 5, 2.5) and C(2, 6, 5). In order to calculate the required distances we determine the moduli of the appropriate vectors; thus:

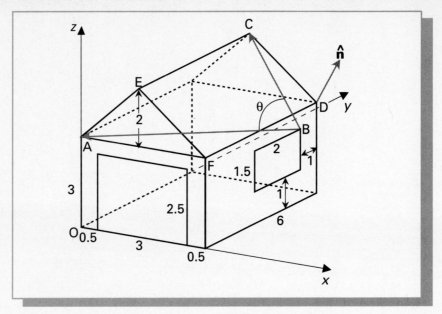

Figure 4.7 Model for the garage.

$$\mathbf{AB} = \mathbf{OB} - \mathbf{OA}$$
$$= (4\mathbf{i} + 5\mathbf{j} + 2.5\mathbf{k}) - (0.5\mathbf{i} + 2.5\mathbf{k})$$
$$= (3.5\mathbf{i} + 5\mathbf{j})$$

so that

$$|\mathbf{AB}| = \sqrt{3.5^2 + 5^2}$$
$$= \sqrt{12.25 + 25}$$
$$= \sqrt{37.25}$$
$$\simeq 6.103$$

Also

$$\mathbf{BC} = \mathbf{OC} - \mathbf{OB}$$
$$= (2\mathbf{i} + 6\mathbf{j} + 5\mathbf{k}) - (4\mathbf{i} + 5\mathbf{j} + 2.5\mathbf{k})$$
$$= (-2\mathbf{i} + \mathbf{j} + 2.5\mathbf{k})$$

so that

$$|\mathbf{BC}| = \sqrt{(-2)^2 + 1^2 + 2.5^2}$$
$$= \sqrt{4 + 1 + 6.25}$$
$$= \sqrt{11.25}$$
$$\simeq 3.354$$

Hence the approximate distances are: from A to B, 6.10 m, and from B to C, 3.35 m.

For part (2) we must find the size of angle θ shown in Figure 4.7. We need to calculate $\mathbf{BA} \cdot \mathbf{BC}$, which is given by

$$\mathbf{BA} \cdot \mathbf{BC} = (-\mathbf{AB}) \cdot \mathbf{BC}$$
$$= (-3.5\mathbf{i} - 5\mathbf{j} + 0\mathbf{k}) \cdot (-2\mathbf{i} + \mathbf{j} + 2.5\mathbf{k})$$
$$= (-3.5) \times (-2) + (-5) \times 1 + 0 \times 2.5$$
$$= 7 - 5$$
$$= 2.$$

Thus

$$|\mathbf{BA}| \, |\mathbf{BC}| \cos\theta = 2$$

and we can use the values of $|\mathbf{BA}|$ and $|\mathbf{BC}|$ calculated in part (1) above.

Thus

$$6.103 \times 3.354 \times \cos\theta = 2,$$

and hence

$$\cos\theta = \frac{2}{6.103 \times 3.354}$$

$$\simeq 0.0977$$

so that

$$\theta \simeq 84.39°$$

Thus the angle between AB and BC is approximately 84.39°.

To determine the normal $\hat{\mathbf{n}}$ required in part (3) we must calculate

$$\hat{\mathbf{n}} = \frac{\mathbf{DC} \times \mathbf{DF}}{|\mathbf{DC} \times \mathbf{DF}|}$$

where the coordinates of F are (4, 0, 3), and the coordinates of D are (4, 6, 3). The required vectors $\mathbf{DC}$ and $\mathbf{DF}$ are given by

$$\mathbf{DC} = \mathbf{OC} - \mathbf{OD}$$
$$= (2\mathbf{i} + 6\mathbf{j} + 5\mathbf{k}) - (4\mathbf{i} + 6\mathbf{j} + 3\mathbf{k})$$
$$= (-2\mathbf{i} + 0\mathbf{j} + 2\mathbf{k})$$

and

$$\mathbf{DF} = \mathbf{OF} - \mathbf{OD}$$
$$= (4\mathbf{i} + 0\mathbf{j} + 3\mathbf{k}) - (4\mathbf{i} + 6\mathbf{j} + 3\mathbf{k})$$
$$= (0\mathbf{i} - 6\mathbf{j} + 0\mathbf{k})$$

To find $\mathbf{DC} \times \mathbf{DF}$ we consider the determinant pattern

$$\begin{vmatrix} \mathbf{i} & \mathbf{j} & \mathbf{k} \\ -2 & 0 & 2 \\ 0 & -6 & 0 \end{vmatrix}$$

Then

$$DC \times DF = (0 \times 0 - 2 \times (-6))i - ((-2) \times 0 - 0 \times 2)j + ((-2) \times (-6) - 0 \times 0)k$$

$$= 12i - 0j + 12k$$

$$= 12i + 12k$$

Hence we have

$$|DC \times DF| = \sqrt{12^2 + 12^2}$$

$$= \sqrt{144 + 144}$$

$$= \sqrt{288}$$

$$\simeq 16.97$$

and so

$$\hat{n} = \frac{12}{16.97}i + \frac{12}{16.97}k$$

$$\simeq 0.707i + 0.707k$$

Thus the outward unit normal vector to the sloping roof CDFE has components $(0.71i + 0.71k)$, correct to two places of decimals, and we note in passing the absence of a component in the direction of j: this fits with our expectations.

Exercises

4.1 Calculate $a \times b$ and $|a \times b|$ where

a) $a = i + j - k$ and $b = 2i - j + 3k$
b) $a = 3i + 2j + k$ and $b = -i + 4k$

4.2 If $a = i + 2j + k$, $b = -i + k$ and $c = 3i + j - k$, evaluate

a) $a \times b$; b) $b \times a$; c) $b \times c$; d) $a \times (b \times c)$; e) $a \cdot (b \times c)$

4.3 Find a vector that is perpendicular to both $(i + j + k)$ and $(i + 3j - k)$.

4.4 What is wrong with the expression $a \cdot b \cdot c$?

4.5 By calculating their dot products and their cross products, determine whether the following pairs of vectors are parallel or perpendicular or neither:

a) $(-i + 2j)$, $(3k)$ b) $(-i + j - 3k)$, $(4i - 4j + 12k)$
c) $(4j + 3k)$, $(8j + 6k)$ d) $(3i + 2j + k)$, $(6i + 4j + 2k)$
e) $(i + j)$, $(j + 2k)$ f) $(i - 2j + 3k)$, $(3i + 5k)$

4.6 Find two unit vectors perpendicular to both of

a) $3i + 2j + 5k$ and $3j - k$ b) $i + j - k$ and $j + 2k$

4.7 Find a unit vector that is normal to the plane that passes through the points $O(0, 0, 0)$, $P(1, 2, 0)$ and $Q(3, -1, 0)$.

4.8 Find both the unit vectors that are normal to the plane that passes through the points $R(0, 4, 0)$, $S(1, 1, 1)$ and $T(-2, 1, -3)$.

Answers

4.1 a) $2\mathbf{i} - 5\mathbf{j} - 3\mathbf{k}$, 6.16; b) $8\mathbf{i} - 13\mathbf{j} + 2\mathbf{k}$, 15.39.

4.2 a) $2\mathbf{i} - 2\mathbf{j} + 2\mathbf{k}$; b) $-2\mathbf{i} + 2\mathbf{j} - 2\mathbf{k}$; c) $-\mathbf{i} + 2\mathbf{j} - \mathbf{k}$; d) $-4\mathbf{i} + 4\mathbf{k}$; e) 2.

4.3 $-4\mathbf{i} + 2\mathbf{j} + 2\mathbf{k}$.

4.4 Having calculated $\mathbf{a} \cdot \mathbf{b}$ first, we then have a dot product of a scalar number times a vector: this does not exist, since the dot product is defined for two vectors only.

4.5 a) Perpendicular; b), c), d) parallel; e), f) neither.

4.6 a) $\pm (0.87\mathbf{i} - 0.15\mathbf{j} - 0.46\mathbf{k})$; b) $\pm (0.80\mathbf{i} - 0.54\mathbf{j} + 0.27\mathbf{k})$.

4.7 $\mathbf{k}$.

4.8 $\pm (0.80\mathbf{i} + 0.07\mathbf{j} - 0.60\mathbf{k})$.

5

Following a line:
Parameters

5.1 Points, lines and parameters

O ur use of vectors up until now has been confined to describing directions, and distances, and the positions of points. We have not yet dealt in any way with the descriptions of lines, which of course are an intrinsic part of computer graphics displays.

Once a coordinate system has been agreed upon, any point in space can be precisely described, and 'anchored', by listing its coordinates, which are the components of its position vector (see Section 2.1). However, only one point is fixed by a position vector, as shown in Figure 5.1, and we wish now to go further than the specification of single points and move on to the specification of **lines**.

How then can we describe a particular line in space, and do so in an unambiguous way? Let us look for the answer to this question using our intuition. In a very general context, a straight line can be thought of as the path left behind a point moving in a 'straight' direction – think, for example, of watching a vapour trail left behind an aeroplane. Assuming that we all have the same understanding of the word 'straight' ('kept on a steady course', 'with no corners, bends or kinks', 'like a string held taut'), this notion of a line **generated** by a moving point is very useful.

Until now we have had a static idea of a vector; for example, using two dimensions, we may think of the position vector $\mathbf{r} = \mathbf{OP} = 2\mathbf{i} + 4\mathbf{j}$, where the components $x = 2$ and $y = 4$ are fixed (they are the coordinates of P). Now let us suppose that the $\mathbf{i}$- and $\mathbf{j}$-components of $\mathbf{r}$ vary in proportion with each other, so that the $\mathbf{j}$-component is always double the $\mathbf{i}$-component. As they change, for example we might have $x = 3$ with $y = 6$, or $x = -1$ with $y = -2$, or $x = 1$ with $y = 2$, so we see that the end of the vector $\mathbf{r}$ apparently moves along the line of $\mathbf{OP}$, as shown in Figure 5.2. The whole line along the direction of $\mathbf{OP}$, through O, is then said to be the **locus**, that is the **path**, of the end of the position vector $\mathbf{r}$.

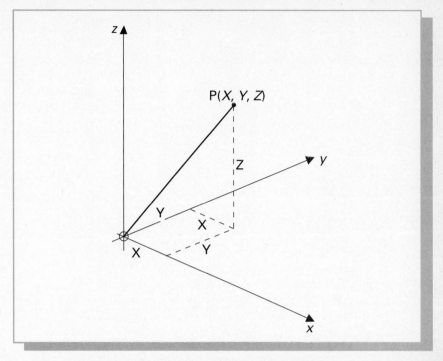

Figure 5.1 The coordinates of point P with unique position vector (X   Y   Z).

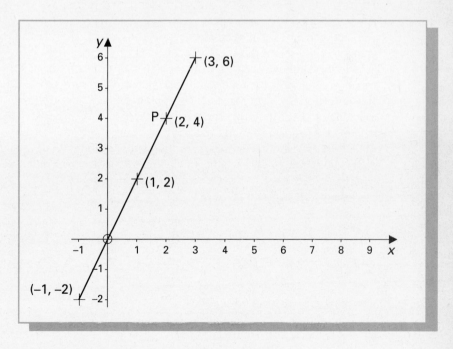

Figure 5.2 The locus of a point along the direction of **OP**.

Thus we see that if this vector **r** is varying so that its **j**-component is always twice its **i**-component, then the formula **r** = x**i** + y**j** does not give us a single position vector. Rather we can say that since x can be any number (call it 'u'), then y will always be double that number (and hence '$y = 2u$'), and we see that the points that have position vectors such as **r** = 1**i** + 2**j**, **r** = 2**i** + 4**j**, **r** = 3**i** + 6**j**, **r** = $\frac{1}{2}$**i** + 1**j**, **r** = (−4)**i** + (−8)**j**, etc., will all lie on the line in question. The **vector equation** of this line is then **r** = u**i** + 2u**j**, and the **variable** 'u' (which can take any value we choose) is called a **parameter**. As a matter of notation we shall often include the parameters and parameter values in square brackets, as [u] or [$u = 3$] for instance; by this means we emphasize the difference between parameters and coordinates.

5.2 Plotting straight lines

Where the **i**- and **j**-components of a vector vary according to a given rule, we are always able to plot the resulting line (or curve). Taking another example, suppose we have a vector formula **r** = x**i** + y**j**, and we know that 'whatever the value x takes, y is always 2 greater', then we can introduce a parameter u in this case too. If x takes any value call it 'u', then we have '$x = u$', and so 'y is 2 greater' will give us '$y = u + 2$'. Hence we have the vector equation **r** = u**i** + (u + 2)**j**, and we can choose any values at all for u, say in the range between −2 and +2, and so plot the line segment betwen these given end values.

As shown in Table 5.1, we place our choice of values of u as the first row in a table; in the subsequent rows we place the calculated values of x and y. Then the pairs of values of x and y are taken as the coordinates of points, namely (−2, 0), (−1, 1), (0, 2), (1, 3) and (2, 4), and we discover that these points all lie on a straight line (see Figure 5.3).

Using their position vectors, we plot the points with these coordinates on a graph and join them; this gives a segment of the straight line, shown in Figure 5.3. Strictly speaking, we need to provide very many points to display the full line, and, when a computer is used, enough pairs of coordinates must be calculated and suitably displayed so that the resulting points appear on the screen as if they are touching, and merging together to form the line. However, we get a good idea of this process by joining up the five points we have calculated, and we see that, as the value of the parameter u varies, it indicates the position along the line.

It is both interesting and important to note that the same line can arise from different parametric vector formulae. If we take **r** = (3v)**i** + (3v+2)**j**, then we see that the **parametric equations** are

$$x = 3v \text{ and } y = 3v + 2$$

where this time the parameter is called 'v'. We show in Table 5.2 a table of values with our choices for v (taken once more from the range between −2 and +2), where

Table 5.1 To determine some points on the line **r** = u**i** + (u + 2)**j**.

u	−2	−1	0	1	2
$x = u$	−2	−1	0	1	2
$y = u + 2$	0	1	2	3	4

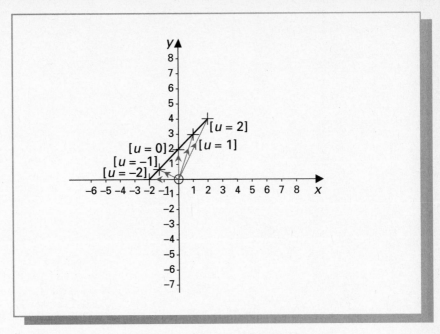

Figure 5.3 For $-2 \leq u \leq 2$, $\mathbf{r} = u\mathbf{i} + (u + 2)\mathbf{j}$ gives a straight line segment.

the corresponding values for x and y are calculated. In this case we see that the points to be plotted have coordinates $(-6, -4)$, $(-\frac{3}{2}, \frac{1}{2})$, $(0, 2)$, $(3, 5)$ and $(6, 8)$, and the line is shown in Figure 5.4.

Table 5.2 To determine points on the line $\mathbf{r} = 3v\mathbf{i} + (3v + 2)\mathbf{j}$.

v	-2	$-\frac{1}{2}$	0	1	2
$x = 3v$	-6	$-\frac{3}{2}$	0	3	6
$y = 3v + 2$	-4	$+\frac{1}{2}$	2	5	8

The two lines shown in Figures 5.3 and 5.4 are segments of the same straight line! Different ranges of the parameters may give different portions of this line, but the vector equations

$$\mathbf{r} = u\,\mathbf{i} + (u + 2)\mathbf{j}$$

and

$$\mathbf{r} = 3v\,\mathbf{i} + (3v + 2)\mathbf{j}$$

represent exactly the same straight line. This coincidence can be anticipated by examining both pairs of parametric equations. From the first vector equation we have

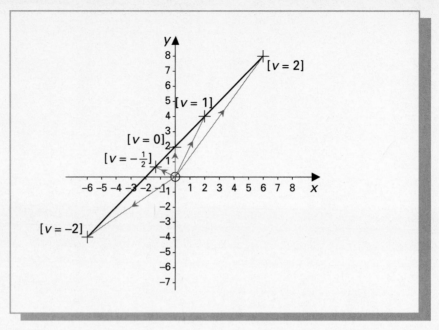

Figure 5.4 For $-2 \leq v \leq 2$, $\mathbf{r} = 3v\mathbf{i} + (3v + 2)\mathbf{j}$ gives a different segment of the same straight line.

$$\begin{cases} x = u \\ y = u + 2 \end{cases}$$

Substituting the top equation into the bottom (a standard technique when dealing with **simultaneous equations**), we get

$$y = x + 2$$

From the second vector equation we have

$$\begin{cases} x = 3v \\ y = 3v + 2 \end{cases}$$

and substitution gives

$$y = x + 2$$

Thus the parametric equations of both lines can be reduced to the same **Cartesian equation**, namely '$y = x + 2$'.

Example 5.1 Different vector equations can yield the same line

We shall plot the graphs of the two lines given by

(i) $\mathbf{r} = (u + 1)\mathbf{i} + (u - 3)\mathbf{j}$

(ii) $\mathbf{r} = (v + 5)\mathbf{i} + (v + 1)\mathbf{j}$

and show by algebraic methods that these lines are the same.

Table 5.3 Table of values for $\mathbf{r} = (u + 1)\mathbf{i} + (u - 3)\mathbf{j}$.

u	-4	-2	-1	0	$+\frac{1}{2}$	1	3	5
$x = u + 1$	-3	-1	0	1	$1\frac{1}{2}$	2	4	6
$y = u - 3$	-7	-5	-4	-3	$-2\frac{1}{2}$	-2	0	2

For the first vector equation, we choose values for u (taken in this case from the range between -4 and 5) and calculate the corresponding values for x and y (see Table 5.3). For the parameter value $[u = -2]$ we plot the point $(-1, -5)$. In similar fashion we plot the points that correspond to the other values of the parameter, and when we join these points we obtain the line shown in Figure 5.5.

For the second vector equation we set up a table of values based on our choices for v, and in Table 5.4 we see some results based on values of v being taken between -3 and 4. For the parameter value $[v = 1]$ we plot the point $(6, 2)$, and we continue for the other values of the parameter. On joining these points we obtain the line shown in Figure 5.6.

We now show that these lines are the same. From (i) we have the parametric equations

$$\begin{cases} x = u + 1 \\ y = u - 3 \end{cases}$$

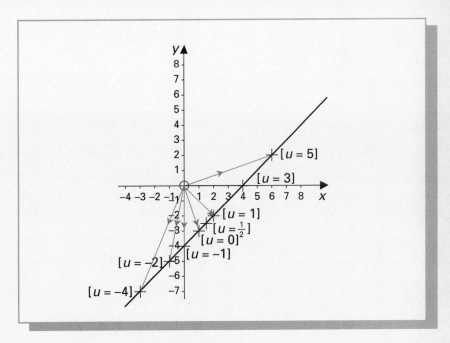

Figure 5.5 Graph of line $\mathbf{r} = (u + 1)\mathbf{i} + (u - 3)\mathbf{j}$.

Table 5.4 Table of values for $\mathbf{r} = (v + 5)\mathbf{i} + (v + 1)\mathbf{j}$.

v	−3	−1	0	1	2	4
$x = v + 5$	2	4	5	6	7	9
$y = v + 1$	−2	0	1	2	3	5

From the top equation we get $u = x - 1$, and substituting this into the bottom equation gives $y = (x - 1) - 3$, so that the Cartesian equation is

$$y = x - 4$$

From (ii) we have the parametric equations

$$\begin{cases} x = v + 5 \\ y = v + 1 \end{cases}$$

This top equation gives $v = x - 5$, which substituted into the bottom equation gives $y = (x - 5) + 1$, so that the Cartesian equation is again

$$y = x - 4.$$

Since they have the same Cartesian equations, these two lines are the same.

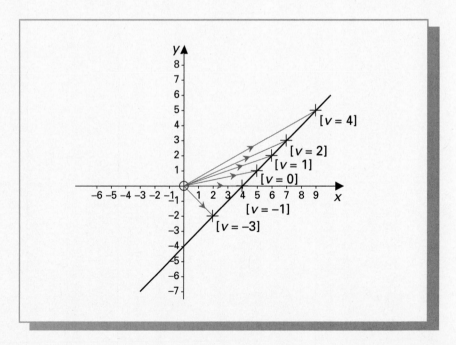

Figure 5.6 Graph of line $\mathbf{r} = (v + 5)\mathbf{i} + (v + 1)\mathbf{j}$.

5.2.1 Some important features

There are some points about straight lines that it is useful to make clear at the outset.

Firstly, if you were to construct your own table of values for any of the lines we have dealt with, with your own choice of different values for the parameter in question, then you might well plot points with different Cartesian coordinates: but be assured that they would all lie on the same line.

Secondly, the minimum number of points needed to fix a straight line is just two (think of stretching a piece of thread between two pins). It is, however, usually advisable to plot a third point as a check on accuracy. In the examples above a larger number of points are plotted to show how the varying of the value of the parameter alters the position of points on the line.

Finally, it is important to be clear in our minds about the difference between the free vectors of Section 2.1 and the lines that we are now able to describe using vector equations. A free vector is any line segment whose length and direction, but not position, are specified. For example, any of the vectors shown in Figure 5.7(a) can be represented by (3 2) or (3**i** + 2**j**): they are free vectors, starting at any point then going 3 units in the x-direction and 2 units in the y-direction, and each has length $\sqrt{3^2 + 2^2} = \sqrt{13}$ and gradient 2/3. A free vector is not anchored at the origin of the coordinate axes and, unless we have more information about it, we can think of it as 'floating'. On the other hand, the straight lines that we are now able to plot from the vector equations are definitely fixed in position; each of them marks the track of the end of a moving position vector. For example, the formula $\mathbf{r} = 3u\mathbf{i} + (2u + 4)\mathbf{j}$ yields a fixed line as shown in Figure 5.7(b): depending on the range of values chosen for the parameter it can stretch without limit in both directions; it has gradient 2/3, and it passes through the point (0, 4). In the same way, the formula $\mathbf{r} = 3u\mathbf{i} + 2u\mathbf{j}$ also yields a fixed line, as shown in Figure 5.7(b), and this line too is 'unlimited' with gradient 2/3. Despite the fact that this line passes through the origin (0, 0), we must be clear that it is not a position vector (nor a free vector); it is formed from a moving position vector but is itself a line fixed in the plane.

5.3 A 'natural' parameter for straight lines

As we have seen, a straight line has a unique Cartesian equation, but its vector equation can come in many guises, involving different parameters or different ranges for a parameter. Depending on the circumstances, different parametric forms may be chosen for particular purposes. However, it is interesting to consider whether there might be a parametric form that is more 'natural' than the others. The question is: can we design the parameter in the vector equation of a straight line so that its increase in value corresponds to length along the line? In other words, we seek to arrange that a unit increase in the value of the parameter measures unit distance along the line.

To illustrate what is involved here we consider the straight line whose Cartesian equation is

$$y = 2x + 1$$

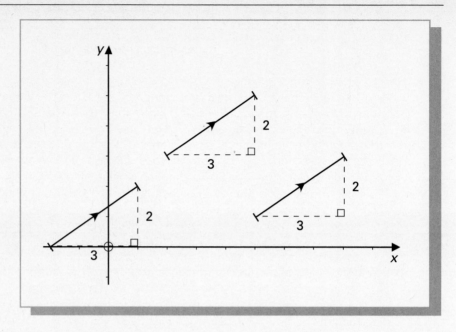

Figure 5.7 (a) Different free vectors given by (3 2).

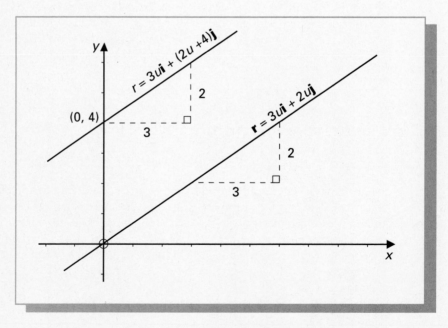

Figure 5.7 (b) The lines given by $\mathbf{r} = 3u\mathbf{i} + 2u\mathbf{j}$ and $\mathbf{r} = 3u\mathbf{i} + (2u + 4)\mathbf{j}$.

Table 5.5 Values for $\mathbf{r} = u\mathbf{i} + (2u + 1)\mathbf{j}$.

u	0	1	2
$x = u$	0	1	2
$y = 2u + 1$	1	3	5

We can produce a simple parametric form by assigning

$$x = u$$

so that

$$y = 2u + 1$$

and then we have a vector equation for this straight line given by

$$\mathbf{r} = u\,\mathbf{i} + (2u + 1)\mathbf{j}$$

Choosing three values of u allows us to complete a table (see Table 5.5), and then plot the line (see Figure 5.8).

Where $[u = 0]$ we have the point P(0, 1), and where $[u = 1]$ we have the point P*(1, 3). Thus referring to Figure 5.9, and using Pythagoras' Theorem (see Example 1.1), we see that for consecutive integer values of the parameter u the distance d between the points on the line is given by

$$d^2 = 2^2 + 1^2$$

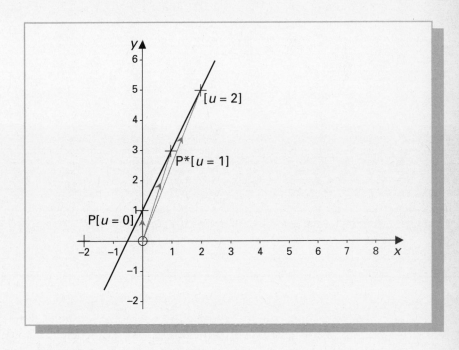

Figure 5.8 Graph of line $\mathbf{r} = u\mathbf{i} + (2u + 1)\mathbf{j}$.

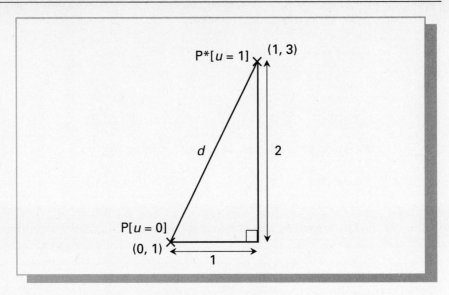

Figure 5.9 Finding the distance between P and P*.

Thus

$$d^2 = 5$$
$$d = \sqrt{5}$$

If we now replace the original parameter u by a new parameter v, with $u = v/d$, then we find that each difference of 1 unit in the new parameter corresponds to a distance of 1 unit measured along the line, as we require.

In the case we are considering,

$$d = \sqrt{5} \simeq 2.236$$

so we replace u by

$$\frac{v}{2.236} \simeq 0.447v$$

The new forms of the parametric equations are thus

$$\begin{cases} x = 0.447v \\ y = 2 \times 0.447v + 1 \end{cases}$$

and hence the new form of the vector equation is

$$\mathbf{r} = 0.447v\mathbf{i} + (0.894v + 1)\mathbf{j}$$

that is

$$\mathbf{r} \simeq 0.45v\mathbf{i} + (0.89v + 1)\mathbf{j}$$

It is straightforward to verify that this new vector equation has the same Cartesian form as the original. Moreover, if we check by taking any two consecutive integer values of v, and calculating the distance between the corresponding points on the line, we get '1' as the answer. For example, if we take the new parameter values [$v =$

2] and $[v = 3]$, then the corresponding points have coordinates

$$(0.447 \times 2, 0.894 \times 2 + 1) = (0.894, 2.788)$$

and

$$(0.447 \times 3, 0.894 \times 3 + 1) = (1.341, 3.682)$$

Using Pythagoras' Theorem again, the distance between these points is

$$\sqrt{(3.682 - 2.788)^2 + (1.341 - 0.894)^2}$$
$$= \sqrt{0.894^2 + 0.447^2}$$
$$= 1$$

This technique for finding a parameter whose unit increase corresponds to unit length always works for straight lines.

Exercises

5.1 The vector equation of a straight line is $\mathbf{r} = u\mathbf{i} + (2u + 5)\mathbf{j}$. Draw up a table of values for x and y, the $\mathbf{i}$- and $\mathbf{j}$-components of $\mathbf{r}$, when u is $-3, -2, -1, 0, 1, 2, 3$, and hence sketch the graph of the line. By eliminating u using algebraic methods, determine the Cartesian equation of the line (that is, an equation in terms of x and y only).

5.2 Four straight line segments are given by the following equations, involving the parameters u, v, w and e:

$$\mathbf{r}_1 = \mathbf{i} + u\mathbf{j}, \quad -1 \leq u \leq 1$$
$$\mathbf{r}_2 = v\mathbf{i} + \mathbf{j}, \quad -1 \leq v \leq 1$$
$$\mathbf{r}_3 = -\mathbf{i} + w\mathbf{j}, -1 \leq w \leq 1$$
$$\mathbf{r}_4 = e\mathbf{i} - \mathbf{j}, \quad -1 \leq e \leq 1$$

Sketch and name the shape they make. Give the coordinates of its vertices.

5.3 Two of the following are vector equations of the same line. Which two? What is its Cartesian equation?

a) $\mathbf{r} = (u + 2)\mathbf{i} + (1\frac{1}{2}u + 4)\mathbf{j}$

b) $\mathbf{r} = (2u + 1)\mathbf{i} + (u + 4)\mathbf{j}$

c) $\mathbf{r} = (2u)\mathbf{i} + (3u + 1)\mathbf{j}$.

5.4 A vector equation for a particular straight line is given by

$$\mathbf{r} = (3u - 1)\mathbf{i} + (2u + 1)\mathbf{j}$$

Calculate the coordinates of the points P and Q on the line whose position vectors correspond to the values of $\mathbf{r}$ given by $[u = 1]$ and $[u = 2]$. Use Pythagoras' Theorem to determine the distance between P and Q. Hence write down a form for a vector equation of this same line using a different parameter, v, such that unit increase in the new parameter corresponds to unit distance along the length of the line.

Answers

5.1 $y = 2x + 5$.

5.2   A square, with vertices at $(1, 1)$, $(-1, 1)$, $(-1, -1)$, $(1, -1)$.

5.3   a) and c) both represent the line given by $2y = 3x + 2$.

5.4 $P(2, 3)$, $Q(5, 5)$. Distance $= \sqrt{13} \approx 3.61$. $\mathbf{r} = (0.83v - 1)\mathbf{i} + (0.55v + 1)\mathbf{j}$.

Lines in space:
Vector equations

6.1 Lines in two-dimensional space

In Chapter 5 we extended the idea of the position vector of a single point so that we could deal with the vector representation of a straight line. We explored how a parameter works when it appears in the components of a position vector, and how we can plot the graph of a straight line by choosing particular values for the parameter (in an appropriate range) and then calculating the x- and y-coordinates for the ends of a succession of position vectors. The ordered sequence of these parameter values corresponds to an ordered sequence of points on the line.

We now approach this matter from a different viewpoint: how to write down a vector representation for a line ℓ which passes through two points shown as A and B in Figure 6.1(a). This line, like any other, is potentially infinitely long and can extend without limit in both directions, but we shall use the line segment AB as our starting point. With the notation shown in Figure 6.1(b), where the coordinates of the given points are A(1, 6) and B(4, 8), and the method of Section 2.3.2, we first calculate the vector **AB** which gives us the direction of the line ℓ:

$$\begin{aligned} \mathbf{AB} &= \mathbf{OB} - \mathbf{OA} \\ &= \mathbf{b} - \mathbf{a} \\ &= (4\mathbf{i} + 8\mathbf{j}) - (\mathbf{i} + 6\mathbf{j}) \\ &= 3\mathbf{i} + 2\mathbf{j} \end{aligned}$$

or, alternatively, as a row vector:

$$\mathbf{AB} = (3 \quad 2)$$

In order to describe the line ℓ, we imagine a point P on it which can move along it in either direction (see Figure 6.1(c)). (We might think of P as a small ring which is free to slide along the whole length of the taut wire that is ℓ.) As P moves along the line its coordinates vary, and we call them (x, y). Then we see that the position vector of P is **OP**, which can be written as **p**, or in components as $(x\mathbf{i} + y\mathbf{j})$, or as a row vector $(x \quad y)$.

For the point P on the line ℓ, we can use the triangle addition of Section 2.3.1 and write

$$\mathbf{p} = \mathbf{a} + \mathbf{AP}$$

We see that the vector $\mathbf{AP}$ has the same direction as the vector $\mathbf{AB}$, but only some (variable) proportion of its length. Thus we can write

$$\mathbf{AP} = u\,\mathbf{AB} = u\,(\mathbf{b} - \mathbf{a})$$

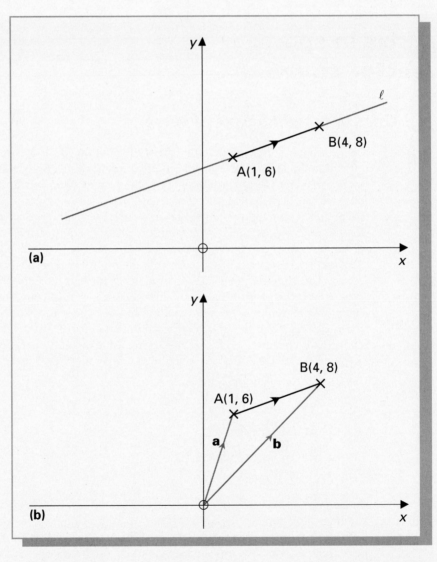

Figure 6.1 (a) A line ℓ passing through points A and B in the x–y plane. (b) The vector $\mathbf{AB}$ gives the direction of ℓ.

where u is some variable scale factor (compare this with Section 2.3.3). Combining these statements we have

$$p = a + u(b - a)$$

and as u varies this gives us all possible position vectors for P at any point on the line ℓ. In fact, this expression completely defines the whole line ℓ, and you will recognize that we are using the variable u as a parameter. As indicated in Figure 6.1(d), all the different values of u give us all the different positions for P on the

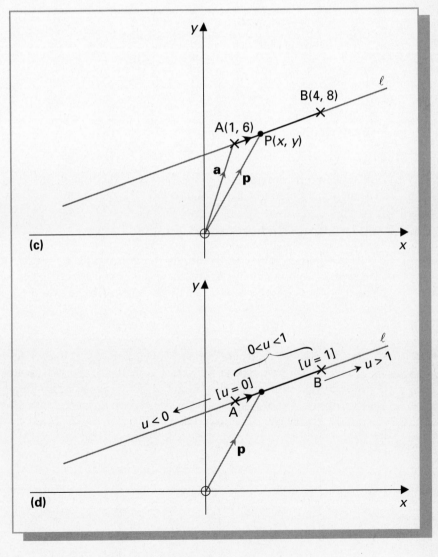

Figure 6.1 (c) A moving point P(x, y) on the line ℓ.
  (d) Different parameter values indicate different parts of the line ℓ.

line. If u is a positive number between 0 and 1 (that is, a positive fraction), then P lies between A and B; it is an **internal point** on the line segment. If u is greater than 1, then P lies to the right of B, and if u is negative, then P lies to the left of A; these positions are **external points** with respect to the line segment. If u is 0 then $\mathbf{p} = \mathbf{a}$, and so P is at A; if u is 1 then $\mathbf{p} = \mathbf{b}$, and so P is at B.

In the vector expression above for a straight line we replace $\mathbf{p}$ by '$\mathbf{r}(u)$', which means 'a variable vector where u is the parameter'. Then the **vector equation** of the straight line passing through points A and B is

$$\mathbf{r}(u) = \mathbf{a} + u(\mathbf{b} - \mathbf{a})$$

and in the particular case we started with (see Figure 6.1(b) and above) we have

$$\mathbf{r}(u) = (\mathbf{i} + 6\mathbf{j}) + u(3\mathbf{i} + 2\mathbf{j})$$
$$= (\mathbf{i} + 6\mathbf{j}) + (3u\mathbf{i} + 2u\mathbf{j})$$
$$= (1 + 3u)\mathbf{i} + (6 + 2u)\mathbf{j}$$

using techniques introduced in Sections 2.3.3 and 2.3.1. We can also write this as

$$x\mathbf{i} + y\mathbf{j} = (1 + 3u)\mathbf{i} + (6 + 2u)\mathbf{j}$$

or, using row vector notation:

$$\mathbf{r}(u) = ((1 + 3u) \quad (6 + 2u))$$

The formulae developed here correspond exactly with the vector equations of straight lines used in Chapter 5.

6.2 Lines in three-dimensional space

We now consider how to determine the vector equation of the straight line that passes through two points whose three-dimensional coordinates we are given. Our method for doing this will be exactly the same as in the two-dimensional case, since the formula

$$\mathbf{r}(u) = \mathbf{a} + u(\mathbf{b} - \mathbf{a})$$

from Section 6.1 is as valid in three dimensions as it is in two dimensions.

Suppose we wish to find the vector equation of the straight line L which passes through two different points A and B with coordinates (1, 6, 3) and (4, 8, 7) respectively, as shown in Figure 6.2.

First we calculate the vector **AB**:

$$\mathbf{AB} = \mathbf{b} - \mathbf{a}$$
$$= (4\mathbf{i} + 8\mathbf{j} + 7\mathbf{k}) - (\mathbf{i} + 6\mathbf{j} + 3\mathbf{k})$$
$$= 3\mathbf{i} + 2\mathbf{j} + 4\mathbf{k}$$

Then as above we have

$$\mathbf{r}(u) = \mathbf{a} + u(\mathbf{b} - \mathbf{a})$$
$$= (\mathbf{i} + 6\mathbf{j} + 3\mathbf{k}) + u(3\mathbf{i} + 2\mathbf{j} + 4\mathbf{k})$$

As we know, there are different ways of writing this, and some versions may be more

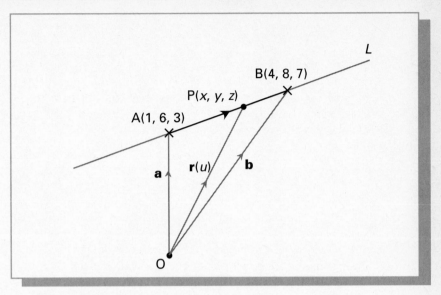

Figure 6.2 A line *L* passing through points A and B in space.

convenient in certain circumstances. For example, we can combine the vectors and write the result in component form:

$$\mathbf{r}(u) = (1 + 3u)\mathbf{i} + (6 + 2u)\mathbf{j} + (3 + 4u)\mathbf{k}$$

or like this:

$$x\mathbf{i} + y\mathbf{j} + z\mathbf{k} = (1 + 3u)\mathbf{i} + (6 + 2u)\mathbf{j} + (3 + 4u)\mathbf{k}$$

or we can use row vectors, as:

$$\mathbf{r}(u) = ((1 + 3u) \quad (6 + 2u) \quad (3 + 4u))$$

Any of these forms can be used as the vector equation of the straight line that passes through A and B.

6.3 Different parametric forms

It is interesting to consider, now, how it is that the vector equations arrived at in Sections 6.1 and 6.2 are not the only ones possible for the lines ℓ and L. Our way of working was quite straightforward, but we should recognize that we did assign the special parameter values of 0 and 1 to A and B respectively. It would be restricting if we had no choice in the allocation of parameter values, and moreover it is often advantageous to be able to assign the parameter values differently. Thus we now demonstrate how we can construct a vector equation for a straight line so that the two given points can take any parameter values we care to give them.

Let us return to the line L that passes through the points A(1, 6, 3) and B(4, 8, 7) as in the previous section. The vector equation we worked with was

$$\mathbf{r}(u) = \mathbf{a} + u(\mathbf{b} - \mathbf{a})$$

and this is based on the parameter u which takes value 0 at A and value 1 at B. Now it is certainly true that

$$u = \frac{u - 0}{1}$$

since for any value of u if we take away zero, and then divide by 1, we leave the original value unchanged. If we recognize the '0' here as the parameter value assigned to A, and the '1' as the **parametric distance** '1 – 0' between A and B, then the above vector equation can be written

$$\mathbf{r}(u) = \mathbf{a} + \frac{u - 0}{1 - 0}(\mathbf{b} - \mathbf{a})$$

(We can check that we still have the same line L. When $[u = 0]$ the term $(u - 0)/(1 - 0)$ has the value 0, and so P is at A; when $[u = 1]$ this term has value 1, and so P is at B.)

These ideas lead us towards the general form of the vector equation of a straight line passing through two points A and B. This general form is

$$\mathbf{r}(u) = \mathbf{a} + \frac{u - m}{n - m}(\mathbf{b} - \mathbf{a})$$

where 'm' is the value taken by the parameter at the first given point on the line, and 'n' is the parameter's value at the second given point. Thus '$n - m$' is the parametric distance between the points measured along the line. This is illustrated in Figure 6.3. For those who prefer remembering with words rather than relying on symbols, the fraction is 'u minus the first parameter value, divided by the parametric distance'.

We conclude this chapter with examples that show two different parametrizations for the vector equation of the line L.

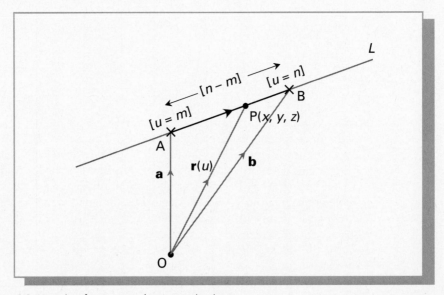

Figure 6.3 Notation for a general parametrization.

Example 6.1 A parametrization for a line in space

For the line L, which passes through the points A(1, 6, 3) and B(4, 8, 7), we construct a vector equation where the parameter takes the value 6 at the point A, and the value 10 at the point B.

As shown in Figure 6.4, the parametric distance between A and B is $10 - 6 = 4$. Thus the vector equation of L is

$$\mathbf{r}(u) = \mathbf{a} + \frac{u - 6}{4}(\mathbf{b} - \mathbf{a})$$

We can easily see that if $[u = 6]$, then $(u - 6)/4$ is zero, so that $\mathbf{r}(u) = \mathbf{a}$ and hence A is the point plotted. Similarly if $[u = 10]$, then $(u - 6)/4$ has the value 1, so that $\mathbf{r}(u) = \mathbf{b}$ and B is the point plotted.

We must be sure that we can rearrange this vector equation into its component form:

$$\mathbf{r}(u) = \mathbf{a} + \frac{u - 6}{4}(\mathbf{b} - \mathbf{a})$$
$$= (\mathbf{i} + 6\mathbf{j} + 3\mathbf{k}) + \frac{u - 6}{4}(3\mathbf{i} + 2\mathbf{j} + 4\mathbf{k})$$
$$= (1 + 3\frac{u - 6}{4})\mathbf{i} + (6 + 2\frac{u - 6}{4})\mathbf{j} + (3 + 4\frac{u - 6}{4})\mathbf{k}$$

In order to tidy this, we multiply every term by 4 and obtain

$$4\mathbf{r}(u) = (4 + 3(u - 6))\mathbf{i} + (24 + 2(u - 6))\mathbf{j} + (12 + 4(u - 6))\mathbf{k}$$
$$= (4 + 3u - 18)\mathbf{i} + (24 + 2u - 12)\mathbf{j} + (12 + 4u - 24)\mathbf{k}$$
$$= (3u - 14)\mathbf{i} + (2u + 12)\mathbf{j} + (4u - 12)\mathbf{k}$$

This gives us the following vector equation in component form:

$$\mathbf{r}(u) = \tfrac{1}{4}(3u - 14)\mathbf{i} + \tfrac{1}{4}(2u + 12)\mathbf{j} + \tfrac{1}{4}(4u - 12)\mathbf{k}$$

which of course can equally easily be written as a row vector:

$$\mathbf{r}(u) = (\tfrac{1}{4}(3u - 14) \quad \tfrac{1}{4}(2u + 12) \quad \tfrac{1}{4}(4u - 12))$$

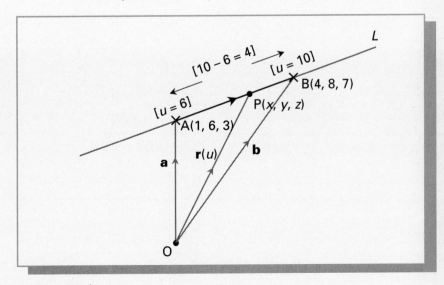

Figure 6.4 One parametrization for L.

As a check, it is possible to substitute in the values $[u = 6]$ and $[u = 10]$ in turn. This gives the components of the position vectors of the points A and B, from which we can take their coordinates.

Example 6.2 A different parametrization for the same line

For the same line L, passing through the points A(1, 6, 3) and B(4, 8, 7) we now construct a vector equation where the parameter takes the value $-\frac{1}{2}$ at A, and the value 2 at B. (We remember from work in Chapter 5 and Sections 6.1 and 6.2 above that it is quite possible to have negative values of parameters.)

As shown in Figure 6.5, the parametric distance between A and B here is $2\frac{1}{2}$. Thus the vector equation of L is

$$\mathbf{r}(u) = \mathbf{a} + \frac{u - [-\frac{1}{2}]}{2\frac{1}{2}}(\mathbf{b} - \mathbf{a})$$

$$= \mathbf{a} + \frac{u + \frac{1}{2}}{2\frac{1}{2}}(\mathbf{b} - \mathbf{a})$$

Multiplying all through by 5 (to eliminate the fractions) gives

$$5\mathbf{r}(u) = 5\mathbf{a} + (2u + 1)(\mathbf{b} - \mathbf{a})$$

and we can rearrange this into component form as

$$5\mathbf{r}(u) = 5(\mathbf{i} + 6\mathbf{j} + 3\mathbf{k}) + (2u + 1)(3\mathbf{i} + 2\mathbf{j} + 4\mathbf{k})$$
$$= (5 + 3(2u + 1))\mathbf{i} + (30 + 2(2u + 1))\mathbf{j} + (15 + 4(2u + 1))\mathbf{k}$$
$$= (5 + 6u + 3)\mathbf{i} + (30 + 4u + 2)\mathbf{j} + (15 + 8u + 4)\mathbf{k}$$
$$= (6u + 8)\mathbf{i} + (4u + 32)\mathbf{j} + (8u + 19)\mathbf{k}$$

So the vector equation in component form is

$$\mathbf{r}(u) = \tfrac{1}{5}(6u + 8)\mathbf{i} + \tfrac{1}{5}(4u + 32)\mathbf{j} + \tfrac{1}{5}(8u + 19)\mathbf{k}$$

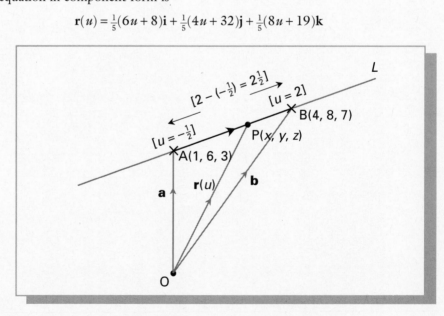

Figure 6.5 A different parametrization for L.

Using row vector notation this equation is

$$\mathbf{r}(u) = (\tfrac{1}{5}(6u+8) \quad \tfrac{1}{5}(4u+32) \quad \tfrac{1}{5}(8u+19)\,)$$

You can verify easily that substitution of the values $[u=-\tfrac{1}{2}]$ and $[u=2]$ in turn will yield the position vectors of the given points A and B.

Now that we have developed the theory of vectors, we can use them to specify not just directions, distances and the positions of points, but also straight lines in both two and three dimensions. The task for the next chapter is to extend the ideas about vector equations to curves as well. This is important, since realistic computer graphics images, like most real-world objects, involve curves even more than they involve straight lines.

Exercises

A sketch graph, showing the points and the lines involved, will enhance each answer.

6.1 Consider the line passing through the point A(1, 1, 0) to B(5, 2, 0) and find its vector equation in component form, in terms of the parameter u, which takes values 0 at A and 1 at B. Determine the coordinates of the points P, Q and R on this line, where u takes values $\tfrac{1}{2}$, $1\tfrac{1}{2}$ and $-\tfrac{1}{2}$ respectively.

6.2 Repeat Exercise 6.1 using the parameter v, which takes values 1 at A and 0 at B.

6.3 Repeat Exercise 6.1 using the parameter w, which takes values –1 at A and 1 at B. By eliminating w from the parametric equations, find the Cartesian equation of this straight line. By similarly eliminating the parameters u and v in Exercises 6.1 and 6.2 above, show that the same straight line is being considered in all three cases.

6.4 Find the vector equation of the line through the line segment MN, where M and N have coordinates (2, 2, 2) and (5, 1, 1), and the parameter is u, which takes values –1 at M and 1 at N. Find the coordinates of the internal points on this line that correspond to the parameter values $[u=-\tfrac{1}{2}]$, $[u=0]$ and $[u=\tfrac{1}{2}]$, and the coordinates of the external points that correspond to $[u=-2]$ and $[u=3]$.

6.5 Find the vector equation of the straight line that passes through P(–4, 1, 2) and R(2, 7, 6) in which the parameter u takes value 0 at Q, the midpoint of PR, and value 1 at R. Calculate the length of QR, and hence find the vector equation of this line using the parameter v where $v=0$ at Q and v measures length along the line.

Answers

6.1 $\mathbf{r}=(1+4u)\mathbf{i}+(1+u)\mathbf{j}$; P(3, $1\tfrac{1}{2}$, 0), Q(7, $2\tfrac{1}{2}$, 0), R(–1, $\tfrac{1}{2}$, 0).

6.2 $\mathbf{r}=(5-4v)\mathbf{i}+(2-v)\mathbf{j}$; P(3, $1\tfrac{1}{2}$, 0), Q(–1, $\tfrac{1}{2}$, 0), R(7, $2\tfrac{1}{2}$, 0).

6.3 $\mathbf{r}=(3+2w)\mathbf{i}+(1\tfrac{1}{2}+\tfrac{1}{2}w)\mathbf{j}$; P(4, $1\tfrac{3}{4}$, 0), Q(6, $2\tfrac{1}{4}$, 0), R(2, $1\tfrac{1}{4}$, 0); $4y=x+3$.

6.4 $\mathbf{r}=(3\tfrac{1}{2}+1\tfrac{1}{2}u)\mathbf{i}+(1\tfrac{1}{2}-\tfrac{1}{2}u)\mathbf{j}+(1\tfrac{1}{2}-\tfrac{1}{2}u)\mathbf{k}$; $(2\tfrac{3}{4}, 1\tfrac{3}{4}, 1\tfrac{3}{4})$, $(3\tfrac{1}{2}, 1\tfrac{1}{2}, 1\tfrac{1}{2})$, $(4\tfrac{1}{4}, 1\tfrac{1}{4}, 1\tfrac{1}{4})$; $(\tfrac{1}{2}, 2\tfrac{1}{2}, 2\tfrac{1}{2})$, (8, 0, 0).

6.5 $\mathbf{r}=(-1+3u)\mathbf{i}+(4+3u)\mathbf{j}+(4+2u)\mathbf{k}$;
$\mathbf{r}=(-1+0.64v)\mathbf{i}+(4+0.64v)\mathbf{j}+(4+0.43v)\mathbf{k}$.

7

Lines and common curves:
Parametric and Cartesian forms

7.1 Linearity and non-linearity

In the previous two chapters we have dealt with straight lines in considerable detail, but we know that points and straight lines alone can never provide us with graphical images that correspond realistically to the real world; we need **curves** of different types. In looking at the vector equations of straight lines we know that the **i**-, **j**- (and **k**-) components are written in terms of a parameter, and from the parametric equations we know we can determine the Cartesian equation of the line (see Section 5.2). We now proceed with a detailed look at the Cartesian equation of a straight line, and then consider what is meant by a function. We shall look at the Cartesian and vector equations of various common curves.

In considering the equations of straight lines you may have noticed that all the formulae used to represent them have recognizably simple structures. In both the parametric equations and the Cartesian equations of straight lines we deal only with linear expressions. **Linear expressions** contain a **variable** (such as u or v or x which can vary, taking different values), multiples of the variable, and numbers. Linear expressions never contain powers of a variable such as u^2 or v^2 or x^{-1}, or trigonometric functions such as $\sin \theta$ or $\cos \theta$ (see also Section 7.2 below). Thus in describing straight lines we need only linear expressions such as $(3u + 2)$, or $(\frac{1}{2}v - 10)$, or $(5 - 0.2x)$. This is illustrated in the standard form for the Cartesian equation of a straight line in two dimensions, which is

$$y = mx + c$$

The expression '$m\,x + c$' is linear, where 'x' is called the **independent variable** because its values are chosen first (and independently), and m and c are numbers fixed for each line. 'y' is called the **dependent variable** since its values depend on those of x.

Here we note two facts which may be familiar. As indicated in Figure 7.1(a),(b) and (c), and as you may verify for yourself, the number c always gives the **y-intercept**, that is, the position where the line cuts the (vertical) y-axis. The number m in the standard Cartesian equation of a straight line always gives the gradient of that

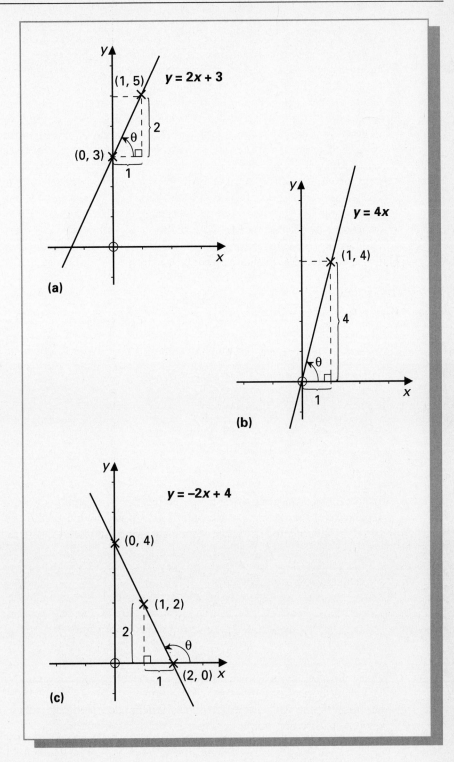

Figure 7.1 Graphs of (a) $y = 2x + 3$ (b) $y = 4x$ (c) $y = -2x + 4$.

line (compare with Example 1.3) and since the gradient is (distance up/distance along) we see that we can further identify $m = \tan \theta$, for each line.

We shall now extend our investigation to a selection of curves whose parametric equations and Cartesian equations are non-linear, and you will not be surprised to discover that these are not straight lines. In the following sections we describe some familiar curves whose equations involve powers of a variable, or trigonometric functions of a variable. We include each curve's Cartesian equation, since it is often useful to be able to recognize these standard equations of common curves. It is from each vector equation however, involving a parameter, that we obtain tables of values (the method is the same as that used in Section 5.2 for straight lines) and then plot the position vectors of points on the curve in order to indicate its shape. We recognize that, just as with straight lines, any curve can be represented by different vector equations: vector 'parametric' equations are not unique. It is important to be able to use these techniques confidently, in order to sketch the graph of a curve from a vector equation, and to appreciate the methods used in getting a computer to display a curve on a screen.

7.2 Functions

Before we proceed, we here clarify some words and ideas. In the section above we discussed how expressions are made up of variables and numbers. Expressions can be based on independent variables; some expressions are linear, such as these:

$$x$$
$$3u + 2$$
$$5 - 0.2x$$

and some are non-linear, such as these:

$$u^2$$
$$\sin \theta$$

Expressions are used in formulae to define the construction of other, dependent, variables and these formulae are called **functions**. Functions allow us to calculate a (single) value of y for any given value of x. For example, from the function

$$y = 2x + 7$$

we can calculate the following:

when $x = 1$, then $y = 2 \times 1 + 7 = 2 + 7 = 9$

when $x = 3$, then $y = 2 \times 3 + 7 = 6 + 7 = 13$

when $x = -2$, then $y = 2 \times (-2) + 7 = -4 + 7 = 3$

and so on: for any given value of x we can calculate the corresponding value of y.

Functions play an important role in our work. The idea is included at this point because it fits in with our discussion of independent and dependent variables. The essential nature of a simple function is that it can be written as

$$y = \text{(linear or non-linear expression in some independent variable)}$$

and whatever value we choose for our independent variable we can always calculate a single value for y. When we regard θ as a variable angle, then the expressions

$$y = \sin \theta$$
$$y = \cos \theta$$
$$y = \tan \theta$$

are called **trigonometric functions**, and a single value for y can be found for any specific angle θ using a calculator, as in Section 1.5.

7.3 The parabola

The **parabola** is a planar curve which is closely followed by the path of a ball thrown into the air (*bola* means ball), or indeed as the trajectory of any missile launched with a certain velocity but travelling under no force other than gravity. As shown in Figure 7.2, the lack of horizontal forces means that a parabola of flight has left–right symmetry and a smooth maximum point. A parabolic curve is used to construct mirrors, and aerials for receiving telecommunication signals (including satellite dishes for televisions, illustrated in Figure 7.3). This use depends on the property of parabolas indicated in Figure 7.4(a) and (b). All parallel rays (of light or of radio waves) reaching a parabolic reflector are reflected to a single **focus point** for onward transmission, and vice versa: rays emitted from a point at the focus are transmitted as parallel after reflection. Knowledge about the behaviour of reflected light, like this described here, is an important tool in making computer graphics models realistic.

It is possible that you have met the Cartesian equation $y = x^2$ whose graph is a parabola. The orientation of this curve shown in Figure 7.5(a) is often taken to be standard. However, for many purposes the 'sideways' orientation of Figure 7.5(b) is preferred, and this has the Cartesian equation $x = y^2$, or $y^2 = x$. When we take the

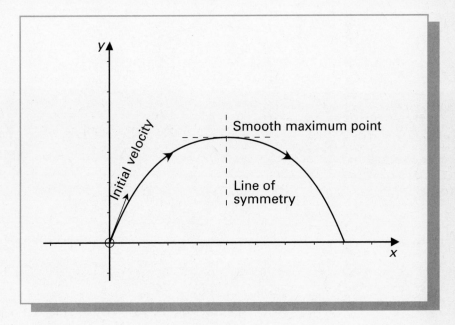

Figure 7.2 The path of a ball thrown into the air.

Figure 7.3 A computer-generated image of a satellite dish (*source: Matthew Holton, University of Teesside*).

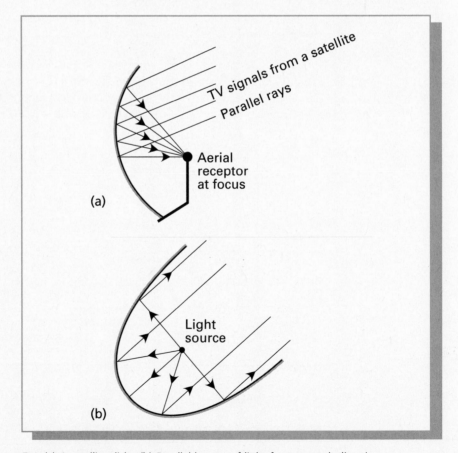

Figure 7.4 (a) A satellite dish. (b) Parallel beams of light from a parabolic mirror.

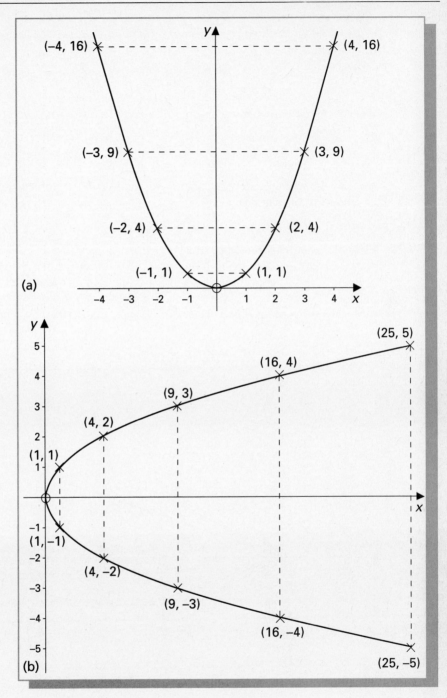

Figure 7.5 Graphs of (a) $y = x^2$. (b) $y = \pm x^{1/2}$

square root of any number we always get two possible answers, one positive and one negative, so we see that the equation for this curve can be written $y = \pm \sqrt{x}$, or, using index notation, $y = \pm x^{1/2}$.

We consider the vector equation

$$\mathbf{r}(u) = u^2\mathbf{i} + u\mathbf{j}$$

We have here the non–linear parametric equations

$$\begin{cases} x = u^2 \\ y = u \end{cases}$$

and by eliminating u between them, we verify that the corresponding Cartesian equation for this curve is precisely

$$y = \pm x^{1/2}$$

From the parametric equations, having chosen a sequence of values for the parameter u, we construct a table, as in Table 7.1, and then we plot the position vectors of points on the curve, shown in Figure 7.6. On joining these points with line segments as in Figure 7.7, we see an approximation to the expected parabola; obviously, the more position vectors that are plotted, then the more accurate, and

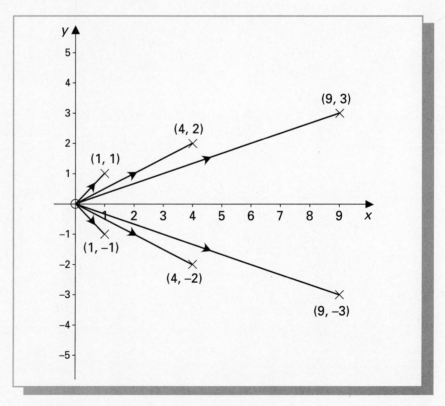

Figure 7.6 Some position vectors plotted from $\mathbf{r}(u) = u^2\mathbf{i} + u\mathbf{j}$.

Table 7.1 Values for components of $\mathbf{r}(u) = u^2\mathbf{i} + u\mathbf{j}$.

u	−3	−2	−1	0	1	2	3
$x = u^2$	9	4	1	0	1	4	9
$y = u$	−3	−2	−1	0	1	2	3

the smoother, is the curve. As the sequence of values taken for u increases, so the points follow around the sweep of the curve, from the bottom to the top, in order.

We now illustrate an important advantage that the use of parameters gives us. Suppose we take the Cartesian equation $y = \pm x^{1/2}$, and plot a sequence of points based on an increasing sequence of values for x (instead of the parameter u). If we take the same sequence of values we get the table shown in Table 7.2, which yields the graph shown in Figure 7.8. If we take a different sequence, where the square roots are more easily calculated, then we get the table of Table 7.3 and the graph of Figure 7.9. In both cases we do get the outline of the parabola, but only if the points are joined up out of sequence.

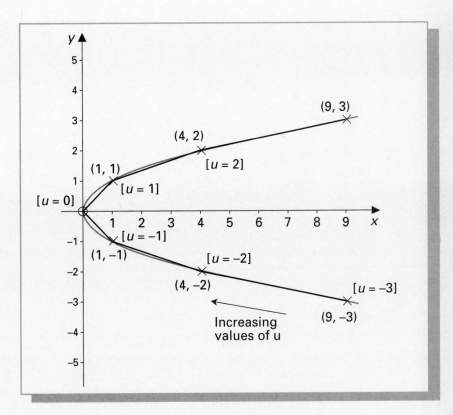

Figure 7.7 The points joined by line segments approximate to a parabola.

Table 7.2 Values for $y = \pm x^{1/2}$.

x	0	1	2	3	4
$y = \pm x^{1/2}$	0	−1 or +1	−1.41 or +1.41	−1.73 or +1.73	−2 or +2

Table 7.3 Values for $y = \pm x^{1/2}$ (all integer coordinates).

x	0	1	4	9	16	26
$y = \pm x^{1/2}$	0	−1 or +1	−2 or +2	−3 or +3	−4 or +4	−5 or +5

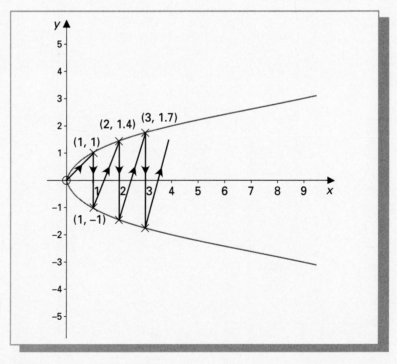

Figure 7.8 Points joined up in order of increasing x.

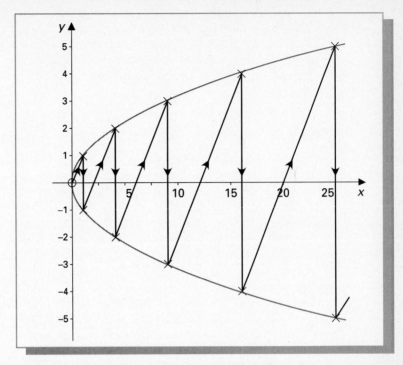

Figure 7.9 Points joined up in order of increasing x (integer coordinates).

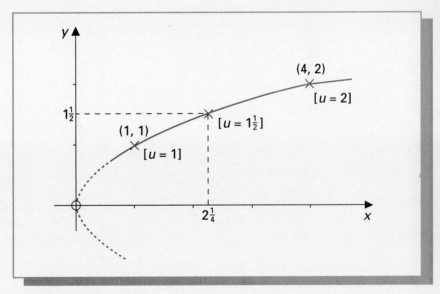

Figure 7.10 Interpolation on the curve $\mathbf{r}(u) = u^2\mathbf{i} + u\mathbf{j}$ (compare with Figure 7.7).
For $[u = 1\frac{1}{2}]$, the point will lie on the curve between the points shown:
$x = u^2 = 2\frac{1}{4}$; $y = u = 1\frac{1}{2}$.

By contrast with this, the use of parametric equations allows us to develop natural methods, which can be readily computerized, in which a curve is generated by taking points in order. In this case **interpolation** is always possible, so that whenever the parameter takes a value between two others, then the resulting point lies on the curve in between the corresponding pair of points (see Figure 7.10).

7.4 The circle

The **circle** is our best known planar curve. It is easily drawn using a loop of thread and a pin (see Figure 7.11(a)) and yet it is a key shape, providing the basic idea for wheels, cylinders, pipes, discs and disks. We are all aware of circular shapes in daily life, in the rim of a cup or plate, or the outline of a ball, and when we consider a small weight (shell or stone or nut) being whirled around on a string, we intuitively approach the dynamic description of a circle, which is 'the locus of a point which remains equidistant from a fixed centre'.

For the simplest graph of a circle we place its **centre** at the origin and give it a **radius** of unit length, as shown in Figure 7.12. With the circle so positioned, we apply Pythagoras' Theorem to a right-angled triangle such as OPN, where the point P(x, y) lies on the circumference of the circle, and deduce that

$$x^2 + y^2 = 1^2 = 1$$

which is the Cartesian equation of this circle. More generally, for a circle whose centre is at the origin, with radius R units, the Cartesian equation is

$$x^2 + y^2 = R^2$$

Different methods have been devised by which the graph of a circle may be plotted from an equation. We shall now consider how a circle can be plotted from its

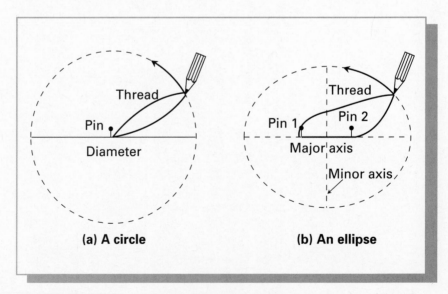

(a) A circle   (b) An ellipse

Figure 7.11 Constructing (a) a circle and (b) an ellipse using pins and a loop of thread.

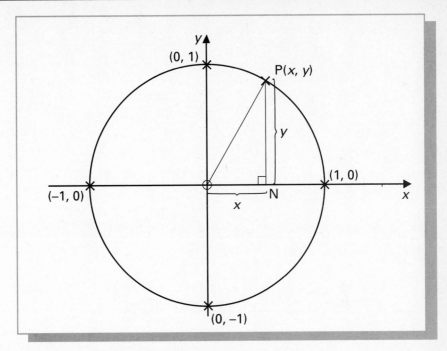

Figure 7.12 A unit circle centred at the origin.

Cartesian equation, and how it can be plotted from a standard form of vector equation. We note that these are not the only ways in which a circle can be plotted and, since the computation of both square roots and trigonometric functions can be relatively expensive, other methods are often used. The method that is most commonly used by computer graphics practitioners involves the technique known as **recursion**, which is beyond our present scope.

7.4.1 Graphing a circle from its Cartesian equation

If we take the Cartesian equation of even a simple unit circle and from it plot its graph, then we meet with several drawbacks. Starting with

$$x^2 + y^2 = 1$$

we get

$$y = \pm \sqrt{1 - x^2}$$

and then we set up a table of values (Table 7.4) based on our choice of values for x. We can see easily, as shown in Figure 7.13, that equal increments in x do not correspond to equal distances around the circumference or equal angles between position vectors; moreover the ambiguity of the + and − signs hinders ordered progression, and interpolation, around the curve. We have mentioned also that the calculation of square roots is a comparatively expensive computation; for all these reasons a computerized method to graph a circle is not normally based on the Cartesian equation.

Table 7.4 Values for $y = \pm\sqrt{1-x^2}$.

x	0	$\frac{1}{4}$	$\frac{1}{2}$	$\frac{3}{4}$	1
x^2	0	$\frac{1}{16}$	$\frac{1}{4}$	$\frac{9}{16}$	1
$1-x^2$	1	$\frac{15}{16}$	$\frac{3}{4}$	$\frac{7}{16}$	0
$y = \pm\sqrt{1-x^2}$	± 1	± 0.97	± 0.87	± 0.66	0

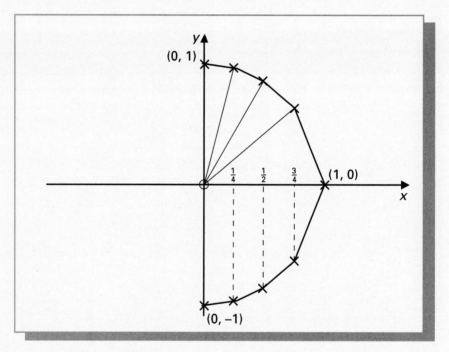

Figure 7.13 Graph based on Table 7.4.

7.4.2 Graphing a circle from a vector equation with a standard parameter

The standard vector equation of a circle with radius R involves the parameter θ, which is the angle between the position vector of a point $P(x, y)$ on the circle and the x-axis. Applying the results from Section 1.5 to triangle OPN in Figure 7.14 we have

$$\frac{x}{R} = \cos\theta \text{ and } \frac{y}{R} = \sin\theta$$

from which we obtain the parametric equations

$$\begin{cases} x = R\cos\theta \\ y = R\sin\theta \end{cases}$$

Using these parametric equations we write down a vector equation for the circle

$$\mathbf{r}(\theta) = (R \cos\theta)\mathbf{i} + (R \sin\theta)\mathbf{j}$$

and if we deal with a unit circle, for simplicity, the vector equation is

$$\mathbf{r}(\theta) = \cos\theta\, \mathbf{i} + \sin\theta\, \mathbf{j}$$

We now take a sequence of values of the parameter θ (between 0° and 360°), and we calculate the corresponding values of x and y from the parametric equations

$$\begin{cases} x = \cos\theta \\ y = \sin\theta \end{cases}$$

These are shown in Table 7.5, and from them we plot a sequence of points shown on the circle in Figure 7.15. The order in which these points are plotted matches the order in the values of the parameter; they are consecutive, with no ambiguity.

Table 7.5 To graph the circle $\mathbf{r}(\theta) = \cos\theta\,\mathbf{i} + \sin\theta\,\mathbf{j}$.

θ	0°	45°	90°	135°	180°	225°	270°	315°
$x = \cos\theta$	1	0.71	0	−0.71	−1	−0.71	0	0.71
$y = \sin\theta$	0	0.71	1	0.71	0	−0.71	−1	−0.71

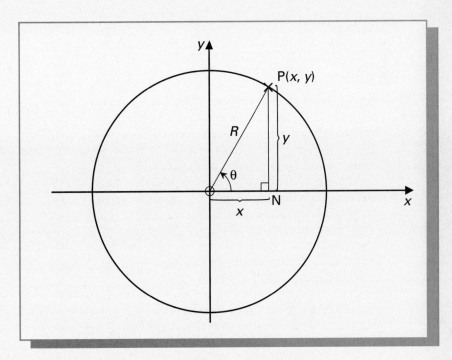

Figure 7.14 The parameter θ used in a vector equation of a circle.

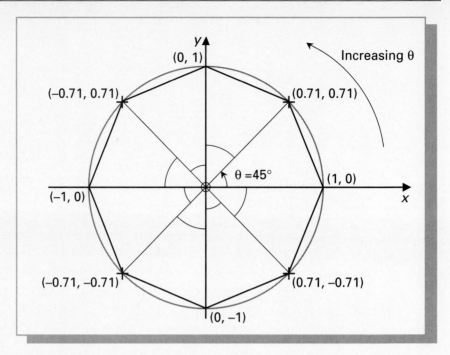

Figure 7.15 A circle: $\mathbf{r}(\theta) = \cos\theta\,\mathbf{i} + \sin\theta\,\mathbf{j}$.

In addition, equal increments in θ provide points equally spaced around the circumference. A computer can be programmed according to this method, and the smaller the interval between pairs of values of θ, the better and smoother the resulting circle.

7.5 The ellipse

The ellipse is the curve whose shape we see when we view a circle which is tilted, as shown in Figure 7.16; it is a very common shape in views of the real world, since circular objects are rarely seen head on. It is the shape of the orbits of planets around the sun, and it occurs in daily life as the cut face of a cylinder (of salami, or French bread, for instance) when sliced diagonally.

The ellipse may be envisaged as a 'squashed circle', and like a circle it can be constructed easily using pins and a loop of thread (see Figure 7.11(a) and (b) for a comparison of the two constructions). When a circle is drawn this way the pin marks its centre, but in an ellipse the two pins mark its two **focus points** or **foci**; the **diameter** of a circle is always constant, but the diameter of an ellipse has a maximum along the **major axis**, a minimum along the **minor axis**, and these lines are at right angles, cutting at its **centre**.

For the simplest graph of an ellipse we place its centre at the origin with the major axis along the x-axis and the minor axis along the y-axis. In Figure 7.17 we show such an ellipse with its major axis of length 6, and its minor axis of length 4. A vector equation for this is

$$\mathbf{r}(\theta) = 3\cos\theta\,\mathbf{i} + 2\sin\theta\,\mathbf{j}$$

A coin "head on"
is circular

Figure 7.16 A tilted circular disc appears as an ellipse.

which uses as parameter an angle θ which, in this case, is *not* the angle between each position vector and the x-axis. (To indicate the whole perimeter of an ellipse we again take values of the angle θ between $0°$ and $360°$, but we cannot show the angle on the diagram as easily as we did in the case of a circle.) In Table 7.6 we show a table of values for calculating the position vectors shown in Figure 7.18; the more values of θ that are taken, the smoother the resulting ellipse. However, we note in passing that equal increments in θ lead to decided bunching at the ends of the major axis. To overcome this rather undesirable feature, other parametric forms and methods of recursion have been developed, which you may find in other texts.

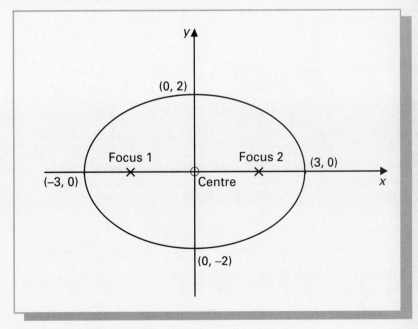

Figure 7.17 The ellipse: $\mathbf{r}(\theta) = 3\cos\theta\,\mathbf{i} + 2\sin\theta\,\mathbf{j}$.

Table 7.6 Values for $\mathbf{r}(\theta) = 3\cos\theta\,\mathbf{i} + 2\sin\theta\,\mathbf{j}$.

θ	0°	15°	30°	45°	60°	75°	90°	180°	270°
$x = 3\cos\theta$	3	2.90	2.60	2.12	1.5	0.78	0	−3	0
$y = 2\sin\theta$	0	0.52	1	1.41	1.73	1.93	2	0	−2

We complete this section by deducing the standard Cartesian equation of an ellipse. From above we have two parametric equations:

$$\begin{cases} x = 3\cos\theta \\ y = 2\sin\theta \end{cases}$$

From these we have

$$\cos\theta = \frac{x}{3} \text{ and } \sin\theta = \frac{y}{2}$$

so applying the result of Section 1.5 we can 'square and add' to get

$$\left(\frac{x}{3}\right)^2 + \left(\frac{y}{2}\right)^2 = 1$$

so that the Cartesian equation is

$$\frac{x^2}{3^2} + \frac{y^2}{2^2} = 1$$

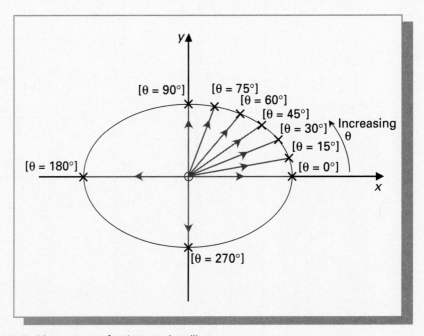

Figure 7.18 Position vectors of points on the ellipse.

that is

$$\frac{x^2}{9} + \frac{y^2}{4} = 1$$

In a similar way we obtain the Cartesian equation for a general ellipse in its standard position. If its major axis has length $2a$, and its minor axis has length $2b$, then its vector equation is

$$\mathbf{r}(\theta) = a \cos \theta \, \mathbf{i} + b \sin \theta \, \mathbf{j}$$

and its Cartesian equation is

$$\frac{x^2}{a^2} + \frac{y^2}{b^2} = 1$$

7.6 The circular helix

The only three-dimensional curve, or **space curve**, that we consider in this chapter is the **circular helix**, as it is one of the simplest to visualize. Its shape follows the curve of the thread of an ordinary screw, or a spiral staircase. In nature it exists in the tendrils of climbing plants such as the morning glory (*Ipomoea*), but more significantly for all of us it is the basic form of the strands of DNA, and its shape plays an essential part in the transmission of our genetic code from generation to generation.

A vector equation for a circular helix has its **i**- and **j**-components based on the parameter θ just as if it were a circle of radius R; its **k**-component is 'Cθ', a positive multiple of the angle. Thus a vector equation of a helix is

$$\mathbf{r}(\theta) = R \cos \theta \, \mathbf{i} + R \sin \theta \, \mathbf{j} + C\theta \mathbf{k}$$

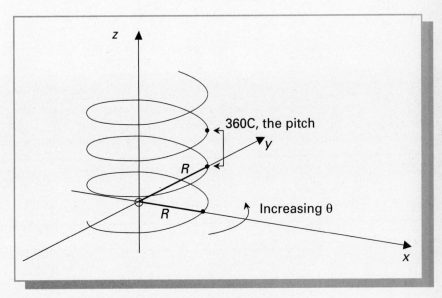

Figure 7.19 The circular helix: $\mathbf{r}(\theta) = R \cos \theta \, \mathbf{i} + R \sin \theta \, \mathbf{j} + C\theta \, \mathbf{k}$.

We see that if θ is measured in degrees, whenever the angle θ is increased by $360°$, the x- and y-coordinates of a point on the curve return to their original values; but the z-coordinate is increased by a constant distance, called the **pitch** of the helix. A sketch of this curve is shown in Figure 7.19.

In general, the identification of a vector equation for a space curve is not trivial, nor is the task of sketching such a curve. As in this case, it often simplifies matters to concentrate temporarily on two components and ignore the third: this sometimes enables us to identify an associated planar curve from which we can deduce the relevant space curve.

7.7 Summary of some principal planar curves

We now complete this chapter by including, for easy reference, a summary table of the principal features of the straight line and some planar curves. In Table 7.7 we have a list of lines and curves and their Cartesian equations when in standard position. We include also some parameters (by no means unique) which, occurring in their vector equations, can be used in order to graph the curves.

Table 7.7 Equations for lines and curves.

Curve	Cartesian equation	Standard parameters
Straight line	$y = mx + c$ m is gradient c is y-intercept	$\begin{cases} x = au + b \\ y = cu + d \end{cases}$
Parabola	$y^2 = 4ax$ 'Sideways' passing through the origin	$\begin{cases} x = au^2 \\ y = 2au \end{cases}$
Circle	$x^2 + y^2 = R^2$ Centre at origin radius R $\dfrac{x^2}{a^2} + \dfrac{y^2}{b^2} = 1$	$\begin{cases} x = R\cos\theta \\ y = R\sin\theta \end{cases}$
Ellipse	Major axis $= 2a$ Minor axis $= 2b$ Centre at origin	$\begin{cases} x = a\cos\theta \\ y = b\sin\theta \end{cases}$

Exercises

7.1 Eliminate the parameter from the parametric equations of this vector equation:

$$\mathbf{r}(u) = au^2\mathbf{i} + 2au\mathbf{j}$$

(a is any scalar number). Hence verify that this vector equation corresponds to the parabola whose Cartesian equation is

$$y^2 = 4ax$$

7.2 Consider the planar curve given by the vector equation

$$\mathbf{r}(u) = -u\mathbf{i} + \frac{1}{u}\mathbf{j}, \quad u \neq 0$$

By constructing a table of values for u, sketch this curve as u increases from -10 to 10. (Do not omit consideration of $-1 < u < 0$ and $0 < u < 1$.)

7.3 Consider the straight line which has the vector equation

$$\mathbf{r}(u) = -u\mathbf{i} + \mathbf{j} + \mathbf{k}$$

and, by identifying the components, sketch its graph as u varies from -1 to 3.

7.4 A three-dimensional curve has a vector equation

$$\mathbf{r}(\theta) = \frac{\theta}{360}\mathbf{i} + 5\cos\theta\,\mathbf{j} + 3\sin\theta\,\mathbf{k}$$

where the parameter θ is measured in degrees. Identify this curve, and describe its significant features.

Answer

7.4 An elliptical helix, whose axis is the x-axis. Major axis = 10; minor axis = 6; pitch = 1.

Part 2
Transformations:
Matrix algebra

8

Tools for transformations:
Matrices

8.1 Transformations

In Part 1, we considered the computer representation of geometrical features that are recognizably related to the vertices and edges of real-life objects. We found that we have to develop our understanding of the mathematical concepts involved so that all the information can be transmitted purely as numbers. Once this has been done we are able to communicate precise information about points, angles, lines and curves to a computer, so that details of position, direction, and length (in two and three dimensions) can be faithfully held within it. Through the theory of vectors, we are able to capture representations of three-dimensional objects by a computer. However, graphical displays on a computer screen are much more than static sketches or diagrams: we must be able to move the computer images, turn them around, alter their positions and change their proportions; only then can the potential of this medium become apparent. The manipulations we seek to perform are called **transformations**. They include **rotation** around an axis; **translation** or **shifting** in a straight line; **scaling**, which may be enlarging or contracting; **reflection** in a line or plane; and **perspective** changes where the position of the viewing point is altered. These types of transformations are indicated in Figure 8.1.

In order to apply the transformations to the 'objects inside the computer' we must form the necessary instructions in a purely numerical way. The techniques for doing this use the mathematical entities known as **matrices**, which can operate on the position vectors of the vertices of objects stored in a computer, and also react with each other. Before progressing further with the geometrical implications, we first look at what matrices are, and describe some of their useful features. Then we shall investigate how matrices can be combined using addition and multiplication, since these skills are vital to our understanding of their role within computer graphics.

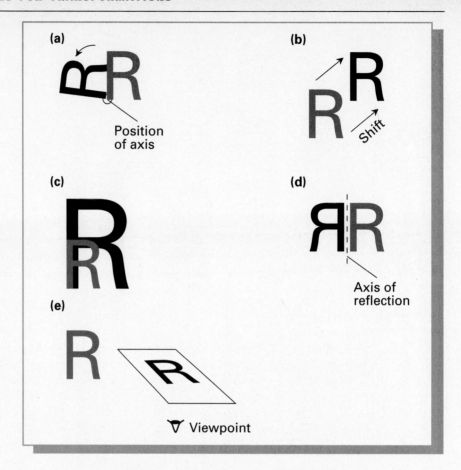

Figure 8.1 Examples of transformations: (a) rotation about an axis; (b) translation; (c) scaling (or enlargement); (d) reflection; (e) perspective changes.

8.2 Matrices

A **matrix** is formed by arranging a set of numbers into a rectangular pattern. This rectangular pattern is categorized by its **dimensions**, that is the number of (horizontal) **rows** it has, and the number of (vertical) **columns**. Thus a (3×4) matrix has 3 rows of numbers and 4 columns of numbers: the pattern is as follows

$$\begin{bmatrix} * & * & * & * \\ * & * & * & * \\ * & * & * & * \end{bmatrix}$$

There is no limit on the number of rows or columns that a matrix can have. Simple examples are illustrated in Figure 8.2. The convention is to use a capital letter for a matrix, in **bold** when printed, or underlined when written.

The numbers in a matrix are called its **elements**; they can be any numbers, whole numbers or fractions, positive or negative numbers, or zero. When a matrix is rewritten (see Figure 8.3) so that its rows and columns are interchanged, then a different

$$
\mathbf{A} = \begin{bmatrix} 1 & 6 & 3 \\ -1 & 2 & 4 \end{bmatrix} \begin{matrix} \text{Row 1} \\ \text{Row 2} \end{matrix}
$$

Col 1 Col 2 Col 3

The dimensions of A are (2 × 3)

$$
\mathbf{B} = \begin{bmatrix} 1 & 1 & 2 \\ 3 & 1 & 0 \\ 1 & -4 & 6 \\ 0 & 2 & 1 \end{bmatrix} \begin{matrix} \text{Row 1} \\ \text{Row 2} \\ \text{Row 3} \\ \text{Row 4} \end{matrix}
$$

Col 1 Col 2 Col 3

The dimensions of B are (4 × 3)

$$
\mathbf{C} = \begin{bmatrix} 1 & 6 \\ 2 & 9 \\ -3 & -2 \\ 0 & 1 \\ 1 & 0 \end{bmatrix} \begin{matrix} \text{Row 1} \\ \text{Row 2} \\ \text{Row 3} \\ \text{Row 4} \\ \text{Row 5} \end{matrix}
$$

Col 1 Col 2

The dimensions of C are (5 × 2)

$$
\mathbf{D} = \begin{bmatrix} 1 & 0 & 1 \\ 0 & 1 & 0.5 \\ 0.3 & 0 & 0.2 \end{bmatrix} \begin{matrix} \text{Row 1} \\ \text{Row 2} \\ \text{Row 3} \end{matrix}
$$

Col 1 Col 2 Col 3

The dimensions of D are (3 × 3)

Figure 8.2 The dimensions of matrices.

$$
\mathbf{A} = \begin{bmatrix} 1 & 6 & 3 \\ -1 & 2 & 4 \end{bmatrix}
$$

The dimensions of A are (2 × 3)

$$
\mathbf{A'} = \begin{bmatrix} 1 & -1 \\ 6 & 2 \\ 3 & 4 \end{bmatrix}
$$

The dimensions of A' are (3 × 2)

Figure 8.3 The transpose of a matrix. The transpose of **A** is written as **A'**.

matrix results called the **transpose** of the original. A **zero matrix** is one in which all the elements are zeros; examples are shown in Figure 8.4. You can see that there is a zero matrix for every different pair of dimensions: the overall system of matrices does not have a unique zero as the system of ordinary numbers does.

When a matrix has equal numbers of rows and columns, as **D** in Figure 8.2, then it is called a **square matrix**. We can have square matrices of varying dimensions, for example (2 × 2), (3 × 3), (4 × 4) and (5 × 5). It is useful to be able to identify the elements on the **diagonal** of a square matrix, and these are read downwards from the top left-hand corner to the bottom right-hand corner, as shown in Figure 8.5.

$$\mathbf{O}_{(3 \times 2)} = \begin{bmatrix} 0 & 0 \\ 0 & 0 \\ 0 & 0 \end{bmatrix} \quad \mathbf{O}_{(2 \times 2)} = \begin{bmatrix} 0 & 0 \\ 0 & 0 \end{bmatrix} \quad \mathbf{O}_{(2 \times 4)} = \begin{bmatrix} 0 & 0 & 0 & 0 \\ 0 & 0 & 0 & 0 \end{bmatrix}$$

Figure 8.4 Some zero matrices.

$$\mathbf{D} = \begin{bmatrix} 1 & 0 & 1 \\ 0 & 1 & 0.5 \\ 0.3 & 0 & 0.2 \end{bmatrix}$$

Figure 8.5 The diagonal of a square matrix.

$$\begin{bmatrix} 3 & 0 \\ 0 & -1 \end{bmatrix} \qquad \begin{bmatrix} 2 & 0 & 0 \\ 0 & -6 & 0 \\ 0 & 0 & 99 \end{bmatrix}$$

Figure 8.6 Examples of diagonal matrices.

$$\mathbf{I}_{(2 \times 2)} = \begin{bmatrix} 1 & 0 \\ 0 & 1 \end{bmatrix} \quad \mathbf{I}_{(3 \times 3)} = \begin{bmatrix} 1 & 0 & 0 \\ 0 & 1 & 0 \\ 0 & 0 & 1 \end{bmatrix} \quad \mathbf{I}_{(4 \times 4)} = \begin{bmatrix} 1 & 0 & 0 & 0 \\ 0 & 1 & 0 & 0 \\ 0 & 0 & 1 & 0 \\ 0 & 0 & 0 & 1 \end{bmatrix}$$

Figure 8.7 Some identity matrices.

$$\begin{bmatrix} 2 & 3 & -1 \\ 3 & 4 & 0 \\ -1 & 0 & 1 \end{bmatrix}$$

Axis of symmetry

Figure 8.8 A symmetric matrix.

If a square matrix has zeros everywhere except on its diagonal, then it is called a **diagonal matrix** (see Figure 8.6), and a diagonal matrix which has 1s all down its diagonal is called an **identity matrix**, denoted by **I**. Just as there are many zero matrices, so in Figure 8.7 we see that there are many identity matrices, each associated with particular dimensions of square matrices. If the rows and columns of a square matrix are the same, then taking its transpose leaves it unaltered; this is the property of a **symmetric matrix**, in which we can imagine an axis of symmetry through the diagonal, as indicated in Figure 8.8.

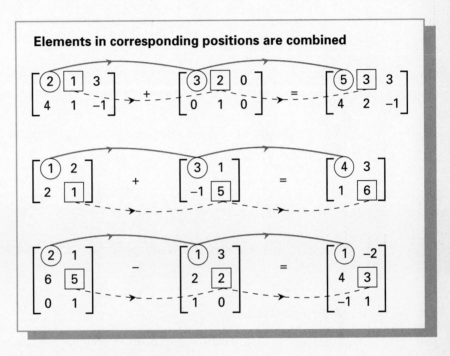

Figure 8.9 Adding and subtracting matrices.

Reversing the order of the matrices yields the same result

$$\begin{bmatrix} 6 & 4 & -1 \\ 2 & 1 & 3 \end{bmatrix} \quad + \quad \begin{bmatrix} 2 & 0 & 0 \\ 3 & 1 & 4 \end{bmatrix} \quad = \quad \begin{bmatrix} 8 & 4 & -1 \\ 5 & 2 & 7 \end{bmatrix}$$

$$\begin{bmatrix} 2 & 0 & 0 \\ 3 & 1 & 4 \end{bmatrix} \quad + \quad \begin{bmatrix} 6 & 4 & -1 \\ 2 & 1 & 3 \end{bmatrix} \quad = \quad \begin{bmatrix} 8 & 4 & -1 \\ 5 & 2 & 7 \end{bmatrix}$$

Figure 8.10 Matrix addition is commutative.

8.3 Adding and subtracting matrices

When two matrices have the same dimensions, then addition and subtraction are simple. They are performed **elementwise**, that is, each element is combined with the element in the corresponding position. Examples of adding and subtracting matrices which have the same dimensions are shown in Figure 8.9. Because order does not matter when numbers are added, so obviously order does not matter when matrices are added: matrix addition is commutative, as illustrated in Figure 8.10. But order *does* matter when either numbers or matrices are subtracted, as we show in Figure 8.11; subtraction is not a commutative operation.

We must be clear that matrices can only be added or subtracted when they have the same dimensions. If matrices have different dimensions, then it is not possible to add or subtract them.

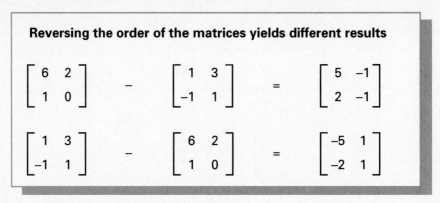

Figure 8.11 Matrix subtraction is not commutative.

8.4 Multiplying matrices

There are two ways in which matrices can be multiplied. The first involves the whole of a matrix being multiplied by a number. This is similar to the scaling of vectors met in Section 2.3.3, and the multiplication is done elementwise so that each of the elements is multiplied separately by the number in question. Some examples of this are shown in Figure 8.12.

The other form of multiplication occurs when two matrices are multiplied together and, as in the above case, the actual multiplication sign is often omitted. Because of the way in which the calculations are done, two matrices can only be multiplied together when the number of columns in the first is the same as the number of rows in the second. Thus to test whether matrices can be multiplied we first look at their dimensions. As indicated in Figure 8.13, this tells us whether the multiplication is possible, and, if it is, this also gives us the dimensions of the resulting matrix.

Having checked that the multiplication of the matrices is possible we proceed as follows. The multiplication is done by dealing with the rows of the first matrix in turn, and combining their elements with those of the columns of the second matrix. To obtain the first element in the first row of the answer, we multiply corresponding elements in the first row and the first column and add the results. To obtain the first element in the second column of the answer, we multiply corresponding ele-

(a)

$$3 \begin{bmatrix} 1 & 2 \\ 2 & 1 \end{bmatrix} = \begin{bmatrix} 3 & 6 \\ 6 & 3 \end{bmatrix}$$

(b)

$$-1 \begin{bmatrix} 1 & 0 & 1 \\ 2 & 1 & 2 \end{bmatrix} = \begin{bmatrix} -1 & 0 & -1 \\ -2 & -1 & -2 \end{bmatrix}$$

(c)

$$4 \begin{bmatrix} 1 & 0 \\ 0 & 1 \\ 1 & 1 \end{bmatrix} + 3 \begin{bmatrix} 2 & 1 \\ -1 & 0 \\ 2 & -2 \end{bmatrix}$$

$$= \begin{bmatrix} 4 & 0 \\ 0 & 4 \\ 4 & 4 \end{bmatrix} + \begin{bmatrix} 6 & 3 \\ -3 & 0 \\ 6 & -6 \end{bmatrix} = \begin{bmatrix} 10 & 3 \\ -3 & 4 \\ 10 & -2 \end{bmatrix}$$

Figure 8.12 Multiplying a matrix by a number.

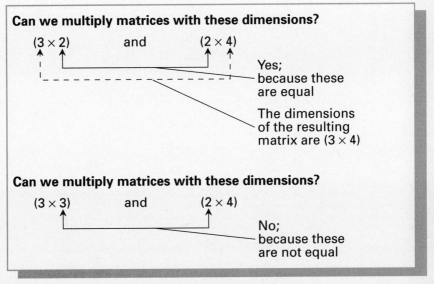

Can we multiply matrices with these dimensions?

(3×2) and (2×4)

Yes; because these are equal

The dimensions of the resulting matrix are (3×4)

Can we multiply matrices with these dimensions?

(3×3) and (2×4)

No; because these are not equal

Figure 8.13 Testing whether matrix multiplication is possible.

ments in the first row and the second column and add the results. This method is repeated for each element of the answer; in general terms, to obtain the pth element in the qth column of the answer, we multiply each element of the pth row of the first matrix by the corresponding element in the qth column of the second matrix and add the results. The way to do this is represented visually in Figure 8.14, and we note that order is very important: we deal with horizontal rows in the first

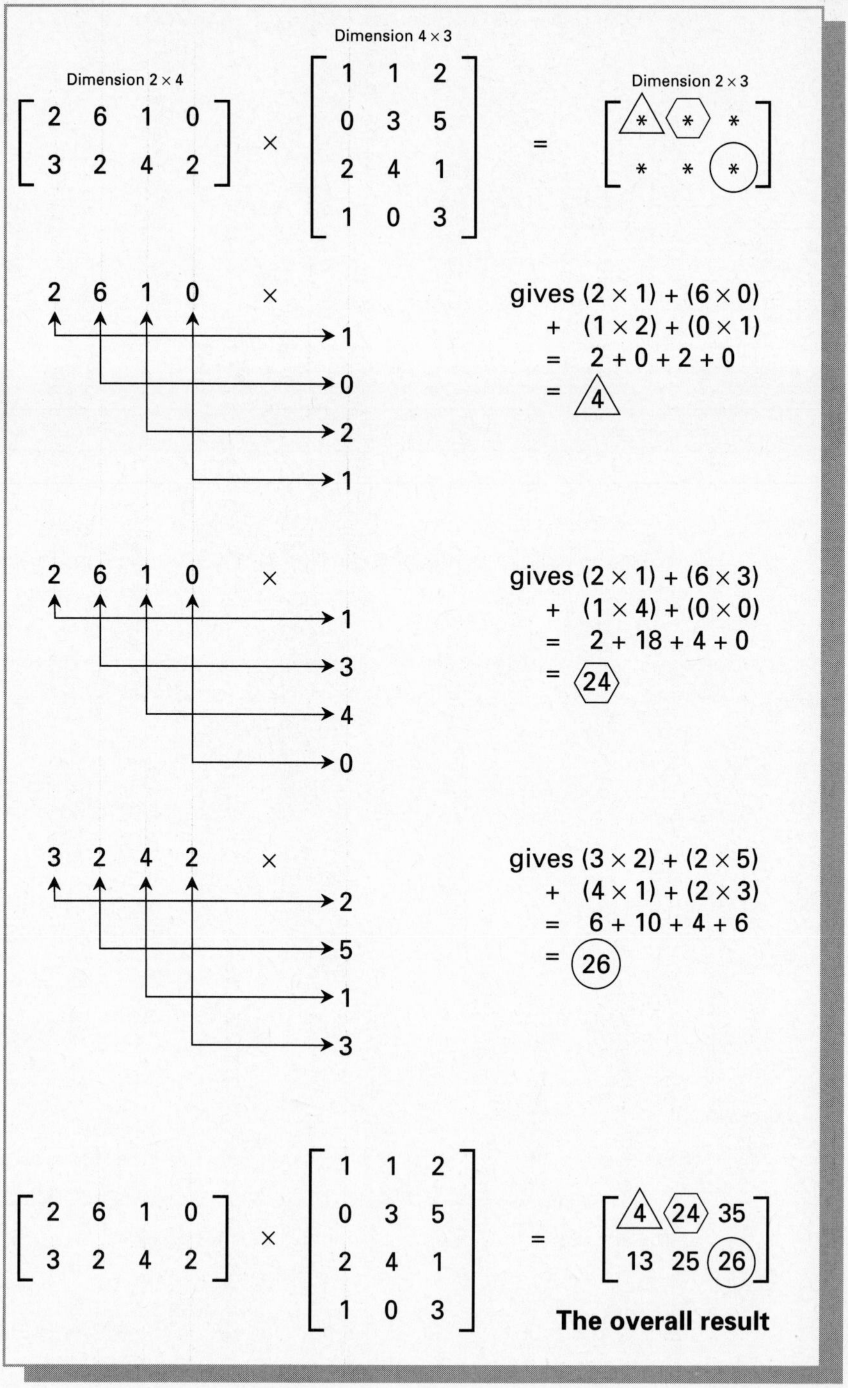

Dimension 4 × 3

Dimension 2 × 4

Dimension 2 × 3

$$\begin{bmatrix} 2 & 6 & 1 & 0 \\ 3 & 2 & 4 & 2 \end{bmatrix} \times \begin{bmatrix} 1 & 1 & 2 \\ 0 & 3 & 5 \\ 2 & 4 & 1 \\ 1 & 0 & 3 \end{bmatrix} = \begin{bmatrix} * & * & * \\ * & * & * \end{bmatrix}$$

2 6 1 0   ×

→ 1
→ 0
→ 2
→ 1

gives $(2 \times 1) + (6 \times 0)$
$+ (1 \times 2) + (0 \times 1)$
$= 2 + 0 + 2 + 0$
$= \boxed{4}$

2 6 1 0   ×

→ 1
→ 3
→ 4
→ 0

gives $(2 \times 1) + (6 \times 3)$
$+ (1 \times 4) + (0 \times 0)$
$= 2 + 18 + 4 + 0$
$= \boxed{24}$

3 2 4 2   ×

→ 2
→ 5
→ 1
→ 3

gives $(3 \times 2) + (2 \times 5)$
$+ (4 \times 1) + (2 \times 3)$
$= 6 + 10 + 4 + 6$
$= \boxed{26}$

$$\begin{bmatrix} 2 & 6 & 1 & 0 \\ 3 & 2 & 4 & 2 \end{bmatrix} \times \begin{bmatrix} 1 & 1 & 2 \\ 0 & 3 & 5 \\ 2 & 4 & 1 \\ 1 & 0 & 3 \end{bmatrix} = \begin{bmatrix} 4 & 24 & 35 \\ 13 & 25 & 26 \end{bmatrix}$$

The overall result

Figure 8.14 Multiplying two matrices.

matrix and vertical columns in the second matrix; the alternative is incorrect. To remember this, you may care to think of the first matrix as consisting of a stack of diving boards, which must be traversed horizontally before a diver can plunge vertically though the columns in the second matrix; the alternative motion of a vertical leap followed by a horizontal run is not physically feasible! As you see, the procedure for matrix multiplication is not one that is intuitively obvious, but it is well tried and tested and moreover it provides us with effective tools for the manipulation of graphical images within a computer. We need to practise and master the techniques; you may be confident that, as a form of multiplication, it does deliver the results we require.

If the dimensions of two matrices are such that it is possible to multiply them in the reverse order, as illustrated in Figure 8.15, then usually we get two different results. This is an example of a multiplication that is not commutative and we must always ensure that we multiply matrices in the appropriate order to obtain a result that corresponds to a combined transformation.

When we deal with square matrices with the same dimensions, then they have the same number of rows and columns and so they can always be multiplied together, but remember that the result may vary depending on the order in which they are taken (see again Figure 8.15). The exception to this is when we are multiplying by the identity matrix; in this case, whatever the dimensions, the original matrix is unchanged, as shown in Figure 8.16. The identity matrix acts on any square matrix with the same dimensions precisely like the number '1' acts on numbers. (Geometrically, an identity matrix corresponds to the (uninteresting) transformation that leaves everything unchanged.)

In this respect it is interesting that some square matrices have inverses, as numbers do. We are familiar with the fact that $\frac{1}{2}$ is the **inverse** of 2, and 2 is the inverse of $\frac{1}{2}$, because when we multiply them together we get '1':

$$\tfrac{1}{2} \times 2 = 2 \times \tfrac{1}{2} = 1$$

Since we can write $\frac{1}{2} = 2^{-1}$, we have

$$2^{-1} \times 2 = 2 \times 2^{-1} = 1$$

Reversing the order of the matrices usually yields different results

$$\begin{bmatrix} 2 & 1 \\ 3 & 2 \end{bmatrix} \times \begin{bmatrix} 1 & 4 \\ 2 & 6 \end{bmatrix} = \begin{bmatrix} 4 & 14 \\ 7 & 24 \end{bmatrix}$$

$$\begin{bmatrix} 1 & 4 \\ 2 & 6 \end{bmatrix} \times \begin{bmatrix} 2 & 1 \\ 3 & 2 \end{bmatrix} = \begin{bmatrix} 14 & 9 \\ 22 & 14 \end{bmatrix}$$

Figure 8.15 Matrix multiplication is not commutative.

(a)

$$\begin{bmatrix} 2 & -1 \\ 6 & 3 \end{bmatrix} \times \begin{bmatrix} 1 & 0 \\ 0 & 1 \end{bmatrix} = \begin{bmatrix} 1 & 0 \\ 0 & 1 \end{bmatrix} \times \begin{bmatrix} 2 & -1 \\ 6 & 3 \end{bmatrix} = \begin{bmatrix} 2 & -1 \\ 6 & 3 \end{bmatrix}$$

(b)

$$\begin{bmatrix} 4 & 1 & 0 \\ -1 & 2 & 3 \\ 0 & 1 & -1 \end{bmatrix} \times \begin{bmatrix} 1 & 0 & 0 \\ 0 & 1 & 0 \\ 0 & 0 & 1 \end{bmatrix} = \begin{bmatrix} 1 & 0 & 0 \\ 0 & 1 & 0 \\ 0 & 0 & 1 \end{bmatrix} \times \begin{bmatrix} 4 & 1 & 0 \\ -1 & 2 & 3 \\ 0 & 1 & -1 \end{bmatrix}$$

$$= \begin{bmatrix} 4 & 1 & 0 \\ -1 & 2 & 3 \\ 0 & 1 & -1 \end{bmatrix}$$

Figure 8.16 Multiplying by an identity matrix.

Similarly, $\frac{1}{8}$ is the inverse of 8, and 8 is the inverse of $\frac{1}{8}$, because

$$\tfrac{1}{8} \times 8 = 8 \times \tfrac{1}{8} = 1$$

and since we can write $\frac{1}{8} = 8^{-1}$, we have

$$8^{-1} \times 8 = 8 \times 8^{-1} = 1$$

In exactly the same way we can say that if two matrices multiplied together give $\mathbf{I}$, the identity matrix, that is

$$\mathbf{A} \times \mathbf{B} = \mathbf{B} \times \mathbf{A} = \mathbf{I}$$

then the matrix $\mathbf{A}$ is the **inverse** of the matrix $\mathbf{B}$, and the matrix $\mathbf{B}$ is the inverse of the matrix $\mathbf{A}$; we write

$$\mathbf{A} = \mathbf{B}^{-1} \text{ and } \mathbf{B} = \mathbf{A}^{-1}.$$

When dealing with (2×2) matrices there is a fairly easy way to find the inverse of a matrix. Some examples are shown in Figure 8.17 for you to identify the patterns for yourself. If the determinant of the (2×2) matrix has value '1' (see Section 4.2.1) then finding the inverse of the matrix involves no more than changing the elements on the diagonal, and writing the negatives of the other elements. However, if the determinant value is not '1' it is necessary also to divide by that determinant value. Graphically, the effect of an inverse matrix is to undo the transformation performed by the original matrix.

After this brief introduction to matrices we proceed, in the following chapters, to show how they are used for manipulating graphical images.

(a)

$$\begin{bmatrix} 7 & 3 \\ 2 & 1 \end{bmatrix} \times \begin{bmatrix} 1 & -3 \\ -2 & 7 \end{bmatrix} = \begin{bmatrix} 1 & 0 \\ 0 & 1 \end{bmatrix}$$

So if A = $\begin{bmatrix} 7 & 3 \\ 2 & 1 \end{bmatrix}$ then A^{-1}= $\begin{bmatrix} 1 & -3 \\ -2 & 7 \end{bmatrix}$

(b)

$$\begin{bmatrix} 3 & 4 \\ 2 & 3 \end{bmatrix} \times \begin{bmatrix} 3 & -4 \\ -2 & 3 \end{bmatrix} = \begin{bmatrix} 1 & 0 \\ 0 & 1 \end{bmatrix}$$

So if B = $\begin{bmatrix} 3 & 4 \\ 2 & 3 \end{bmatrix}$ then B^{-1} = $\begin{bmatrix} 3 & -4 \\ -2 & 3 \end{bmatrix}$

(c)

$$\begin{bmatrix} 3 & 5 \\ 2 & 4 \end{bmatrix} \times \begin{bmatrix} 4 & -5 \\ -2 & 3 \end{bmatrix} = \begin{bmatrix} 2 & 0 \\ 0 & 2 \end{bmatrix}$$

So if C = $\begin{bmatrix} 3 & 5 \\ 2 & 4 \end{bmatrix}$

then C^{-1} = $\frac{1}{2}\begin{bmatrix} 4 & -5 \\ -2 & 3 \end{bmatrix}$ = $\begin{bmatrix} 2 & -\frac{5}{2} \\ -1 & \frac{3}{2} \end{bmatrix}$

Figure 8.17 Inverses of (2 × 2) matrices.

Exercises

8.1 Evaluate where possible:

a) $\begin{bmatrix} 1 & 2 & -5 \\ 0 & 1 & 8 \end{bmatrix} + \begin{bmatrix} 3 & 2 & 1 \\ 2 & 1 & 6 \end{bmatrix}$

b) $\begin{bmatrix} 2 & 3 \\ 1 & 1 \\ 0 & 4 \\ 3 & 2 \end{bmatrix} + \begin{bmatrix} 3 & 4 \\ 2 & 3 \\ 4 & 2 \\ 1 & 1 \end{bmatrix}$

c) $\begin{bmatrix} 3 & -1 \\ -6 & 0 \end{bmatrix} + \begin{bmatrix} -1 & 5 \\ 3 & 2 \end{bmatrix}$

d) $4 \begin{bmatrix} 1 & 2 & 4 \\ 2 & 1 & 3 \end{bmatrix} - 2 \begin{bmatrix} 2 & 0 & -3 \\ 1 & 1 & 0 \end{bmatrix}$

e) $\begin{bmatrix} 5 & 3 \\ 2 & 1 \\ 0 & 1 \end{bmatrix} - \begin{bmatrix} 2 & 2 \\ 0 & 4 \end{bmatrix}$

8.2 If $A = \begin{bmatrix} 2 & -5 & 1 \\ 3 & 0 & 4 \end{bmatrix}$, $B = \begin{bmatrix} 1 & -2 & -3 \\ 0 & -1 & 5 \end{bmatrix}$, and $C = \begin{bmatrix} 1 & 0 & -2 \\ 1 & -1 & -1 \end{bmatrix}$

find the value of $3A + 4B - 2C$.

8.3 In which of the following cases can we form the products $A \times B$ and/or $B \times A$? Evaluate those products that exist

a) $A = \begin{bmatrix} 0 & 3 \\ 4 & 5 \end{bmatrix}$, $B = \begin{bmatrix} 2 & -1 \\ 3 & 2 \end{bmatrix}$

b) $A = \begin{bmatrix} 1 & -2 \\ 3 & 0 \end{bmatrix}$, $B = \begin{bmatrix} 2 & 1 \\ 3 & 6 \\ 1 & 5 \end{bmatrix}$

c) $A = \begin{bmatrix} 3 & 2 & 6 & 8 \\ 4 & -1 & 3 & 7 \end{bmatrix}$, $B = \begin{bmatrix} 2 & 3 \\ -1 & 0 \\ 0 & 1 \end{bmatrix}$

d) $A = \begin{bmatrix} 1 & -1 \\ 0 & 2 \\ 2 & 1 \end{bmatrix}$, $B = \begin{bmatrix} 0 & -1 & 0 \\ -1 & 1 & 1 \end{bmatrix}$

8.4 If $P = \begin{bmatrix} 2 & 0 \\ 0 & 4 \end{bmatrix}$, $Q = \begin{bmatrix} 1 & 1 \\ 2 & 3 \end{bmatrix}$ and $R = \begin{bmatrix} 1 & 0 \\ 0 & -3 \end{bmatrix}$

a) calculate the values of $P \times Q$, $Q \times P$, $P \times R$ and $R \times P$;

b) verify that $P \times (Q + R) = (P \times Q) + (P \times R)$;

c) verify that $P \times (Q \times R) = (P \times Q) \times R$.

8.5 Show that the matrices $\begin{bmatrix} 3 & 2 \\ 4 & 3 \end{bmatrix}$ and $\begin{bmatrix} 3 & -2 \\ -4 & 3 \end{bmatrix}$ are inverses.

8.6 Multiply together $\begin{bmatrix} 5 & 2 \\ 7 & 3 \end{bmatrix}$ and $\begin{bmatrix} 3 & -2 \\ -7 & 5 \end{bmatrix}$

and also $\begin{bmatrix} 5 & -3 \\ 2 & -1 \end{bmatrix}$ and $\begin{bmatrix} -1 & 3 \\ -2 & 5 \end{bmatrix}$.

Can you deduce what the inverse of $\begin{bmatrix} -7 & 4 \\ -2 & 1 \end{bmatrix}$ is? Verify your answer.

8.7 If $A = \begin{bmatrix} 2 & 1 & 2 \\ 3 & 5 & 7 \\ 1 & 0 & 1 \end{bmatrix}$, $B = \begin{bmatrix} -3 & 1 & 0 \\ 6 & 2 & 1 \\ 1 & -1 & 2 \end{bmatrix}$ and $I_3 = \begin{bmatrix} 1 & 0 & 0 \\ 0 & 1 & 0 \\ 0 & 0 & 1 \end{bmatrix}$

find the values of $A + B$, $A \times B$, $B \times A$, and A^2, and verify that $A \times I_3 = I_3 \times A = A$.

Answers

8.1 a) $\begin{bmatrix} 4 & 4 & -4 \\ 2 & 2 & 14 \end{bmatrix}$; b) $\begin{bmatrix} 5 & 7 \\ 3 & 4 \\ 4 & 6 \\ 4 & 3 \end{bmatrix}$; c) $\begin{bmatrix} 2 & 4 \\ -3 & 2 \end{bmatrix}$; d) $\begin{bmatrix} 0 & 8 & 22 \\ 6 & 2 & 12 \end{bmatrix}$;

e) not possible.

8.2 $\begin{bmatrix} 8 & -23 & -5 \\ 7 & -2 & 34 \end{bmatrix}$.

8.3 a) $A \times B = \begin{bmatrix} 9 & 6 \\ 23 & 6 \end{bmatrix}$, $B \times A = \begin{bmatrix} -4 & 1 \\ 8 & 19 \end{bmatrix}$; b) $A \times B$ not possible,

$B \times A = \begin{bmatrix} 5 & -4 \\ 21 & -6 \\ 16 & -2 \end{bmatrix}$; c) $A \times B$ not possible, $B \times A = \begin{bmatrix} 18 & 1 & 21 & 37 \\ -3 & -2 & -6 & -8 \\ 4 & -1 & 3 & 7 \end{bmatrix}$

d) $A \times B = \begin{bmatrix} 1 & -2 & -1 \\ -2 & 2 & 2 \\ -1 & -1 & 1 \end{bmatrix}$, $B \times A = \begin{bmatrix} 0 & -2 \\ 1 & 4 \end{bmatrix}$

8.4 a) $P \times Q = \begin{bmatrix} 2 & 2 \\ 8 & 12 \end{bmatrix}$; $Q \times P = \begin{bmatrix} 2 & 4 \\ 4 & 12 \end{bmatrix}$; $P \times R = \begin{bmatrix} 2 & 0 \\ 0 & -12 \end{bmatrix}$;

$R \times P = \begin{bmatrix} 2 & 0 \\ 0 & -12 \end{bmatrix}$ and here exceptionally, $P \times R = R \times P$.

8.6 Both products give I_2. The inverse is $\begin{bmatrix} 1 & -4 \\ 2 & -7 \end{bmatrix}$; multiply them together to see.

8.7 $\begin{bmatrix} -1 & 2 & 2 \\ 9 & 7 & 8 \\ 2 & -1 & 3 \end{bmatrix}$; $\begin{bmatrix} 2 & 2 & 5 \\ 28 & 6 & 19 \\ -2 & 0 & 2 \end{bmatrix}$; $\begin{bmatrix} -3 & 2 & 1 \\ 19 & 16 & 27 \\ 1 & -4 & -3 \end{bmatrix}$; $\begin{bmatrix} 9 & 7 & 13 \\ 28 & 28 & 48 \\ 3 & 1 & 3 \end{bmatrix}$.

Moving in a plane (1):
Scaling, reflection and rotation

9.1 Matrices as geometric operators

Matrices, as introduced in the previous chapter, are the numerical tools by which we can transform vectors. In particular, (2×2) matrices can be used as **geometric operators** to cause scaling, reflection or rotation (or any combination of these) on the two-dimensional position vectors of points in a plane.

We start by explaining how, in numerical terms, a matrix and a vector can be combined. On the Cartesian plane, we suppose we have a point P with position vector **p**, where, for example,

$$\mathbf{p} = 3\mathbf{i} + 2\mathbf{j}$$

which can of course be written as a row vector

$$\mathbf{p} = (3 \quad 2).$$

Then the matrix

$$\mathbf{M} = \begin{bmatrix} a & b \\ c & d \end{bmatrix}$$

can be applied to this row vector. We use a process similar to that used for matrix multiplication (see Section 8.4), and the result is a new position vector, $\mathbf{p}^*$, which corresponds to a transformed point P^*. In the case we are considering we have

$$\mathbf{p}^* = \mathbf{pM} = (3 \quad 2)\begin{bmatrix} a & b \\ c & d \end{bmatrix}$$

$$= (3a + 2c \quad 3b + 2d)$$

Thus, if we take the position vector of a point and **post–multiply** it by the transforming matrix (the matrix comes after the vector), we get the position vector of a new, transformed point. The particular type of transformation involved depends upon the numbers a, b, c and d, which are the elements of **M**. In the following sections we investigate some of the different possibilities.

9.2 Scaling position vectors

In Section 2.3.3, we scaled vectors by multiplying overall by a scalar number. This had the effect of altering the modulus of the vector but keeping its direction along the same line (in either a positive or negative sense). To scale in a positive sense using matrix notation we take a matrix $\mathbf{M}$ (as above) where the numbers a and d are positive and equal and the numbers b and c are both zero. Thus we have the matrix

$$\mathbf{M} = \begin{bmatrix} a & 0 \\ 0 & a \end{bmatrix}, \quad (a > 0)$$

which can be applied to the position vector $\mathbf{p} = (3 \quad 2)$ as follows:

$$(3 \quad 2) \begin{bmatrix} a & 0 \\ 0 & a \end{bmatrix} = (3a \quad 2a) = \mathbf{p}^*$$

The result is the position vector $\mathbf{p}^*$ which is the original position vector $\mathbf{p}$ scaled by the positive number a.

If the numbers a and d are both 1, then we have the matrix

$$\mathbf{M} = \begin{bmatrix} 1 & 0 \\ 0 & 1 \end{bmatrix}$$

This is the (2×2) identity matrix (see Section 8.2) and applying it to any position vector will leave that vector unchanged, as we expect from the discussion in Section 8.4.

If we take as an example the case where the numbers a and d are both 4, and apply this matrix $\mathbf{M}$ to the position vector $\mathbf{p} = (3 \quad 2)$ then we get

$$(3 \quad 2) \begin{bmatrix} 4 & 0 \\ 0 & 4 \end{bmatrix} = (12 \quad 8)$$

The result of this is shown in Figure 9.1; the scaling is **balanced** being the same in both the x-direction and the y-direction, and the net effect is an expansion along the line of the position vector. When the position vectors of all the vertices of any shape are dealt with like this, then we get a straightforward enlargement (or contraction) of the shape, with no distortion (see Figure 9.2). We see that with a balanced scaling, shape is preserved even though size is altered.

Suppose we keep the numbers b and c as zeros, but have a and d as different positive numbers. The effect of this is to create an **unbalanced** scaling, where the stretching or shrinking in the (horizontal) x-direction is different from the stretching or shrinking in the (vertical) y-direction. As an example we consider the effect on the position vector $(3 \quad 2)$ when we apply the matrix

$$\mathbf{M} = \begin{bmatrix} 2 & 0 \\ 0 & 5 \end{bmatrix}$$

we get

$$(3 \quad 2) \begin{bmatrix} 2 & 0 \\ 0 & 5 \end{bmatrix} = (6 \quad 10)$$

and we see in Figure 9.3 that this is an unbalanced stretching, greater in the vertical direction than in the horizontal direction.

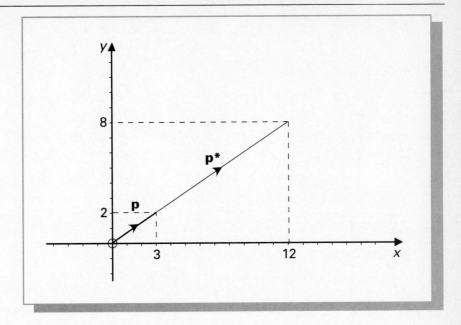

Figure 9.1 A balanced scaling by **M** = $\begin{bmatrix} 4 & 0 \\ 0 & 4 \end{bmatrix}$.

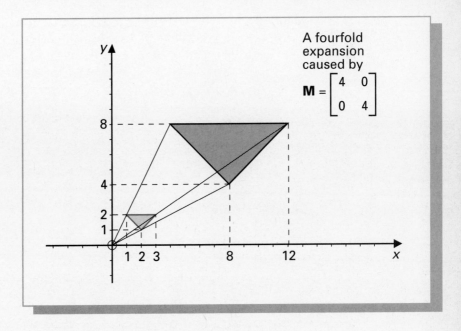

Figure 9.2 A balanced scaling preserves 'shape'.

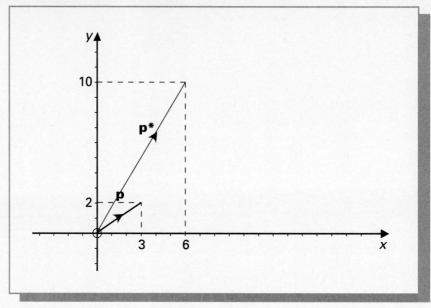

Figure 9.3 An unbalanced scaling by $\mathbf{M} = \begin{bmatrix} 2 & 0 \\ 0 & 5 \end{bmatrix}$.

In Figure 9.4 we show the effects of applying other scaling matrices, such as

(a) $\begin{bmatrix} 4 & 0 \\ 0 & 1 \end{bmatrix}$ (b) $\begin{bmatrix} 1 & 0 \\ 0 & 5 \end{bmatrix}$ (c) $\begin{bmatrix} 3 & 0 \\ 0 & 2 \end{bmatrix}$ (d) $\begin{bmatrix} 4 & 0 \\ 0 & 6 \end{bmatrix}$

to the same position vector (3   2). In each case we see that the horizontal scaling is measured by proportions along the x-axis (that is, away from the y-axis), and the vertical scaling is measured by proportions along the y-axis (that is, away

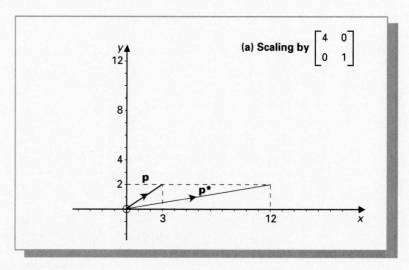

Figure 9.4 Different scaling.

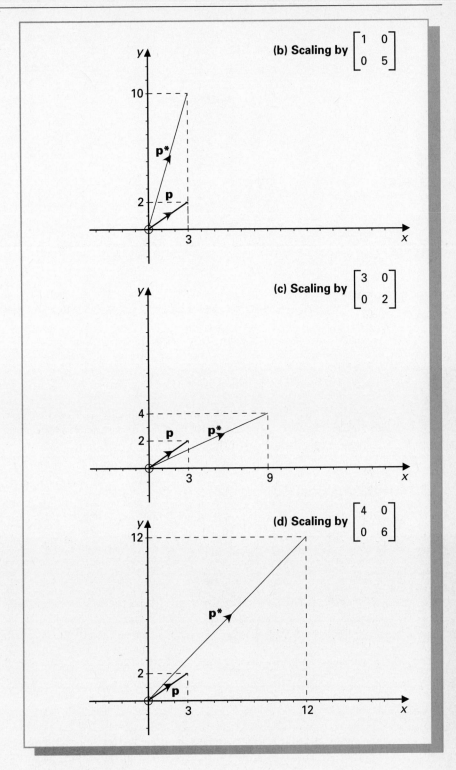

Figure 9.4 Different scaling.

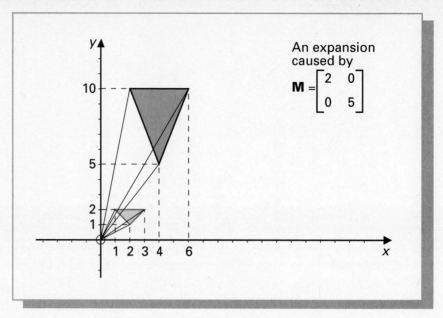

An expansion
caused by

$$\mathbf{M} = \begin{bmatrix} 2 & 0 \\ 0 & 5 \end{bmatrix}$$

Figure 9.5 An unbalanced scaling distorts shape: an expansion by $\mathbf{M} = \begin{bmatrix} 2 & 0 \\ 0 & 5 \end{bmatrix}$.

from the x-axis); these scalings are quite independent of one another. As illustrated in Figure 9.5, if we apply an unbalanced scaling to a set of vertices the result is often a considerable distortion of the original shape.

9.3 Reflecting position vectors in the axes

In the two-dimensional case, if we wish merely to reflect a position vector in the x-axis we post-multiply it by the (2×2) matrix

$$\mathbf{M} = \begin{bmatrix} 1 & 0 \\ 0 & -1 \end{bmatrix}$$

For a reflection in the y-axis we use

$$\mathbf{M} = \begin{bmatrix} -1 & 0 \\ 0 & 1 \end{bmatrix}$$

The results of applying these to the position vector $(3 \quad 2)$ are shown in Figure 9.6. The effect of the matrix

$$\mathbf{M} = \begin{bmatrix} -1 & 0 \\ 0 & -1 \end{bmatrix}$$

on any position vector is to reflect it in both axes simultaneously, as indicated in Figure 9.7. This is equivalent to a reflection in the origin, or to an overall scaling by the factor (-1) as already mentioned in Section 2.3.3.

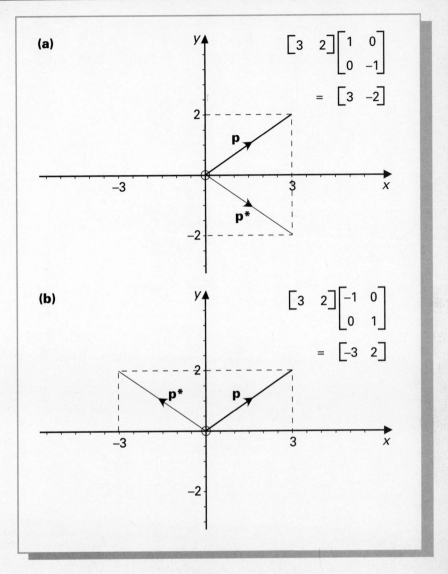

Figure 9.6 (a) Reflecting in the x-axis. (b) Reflecting in the y-azis.

In general, if we post-multiply any position vector by a matrix

$$\mathbf{M} = \begin{bmatrix} a & 0 \\ 0 & d \end{bmatrix}$$

where either or both of the numbers a and d are negative, then the effect is of a scaling combined with a reflection in the appropriate axes. To illustrate this, in Figure 9.8 we show the result of post-multiplying the position vector (3   2) by the following matrices:

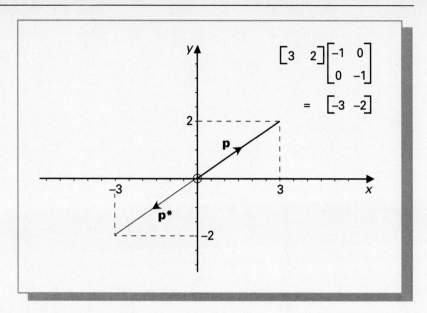

Figure 9.7 Reflecting in the origin.

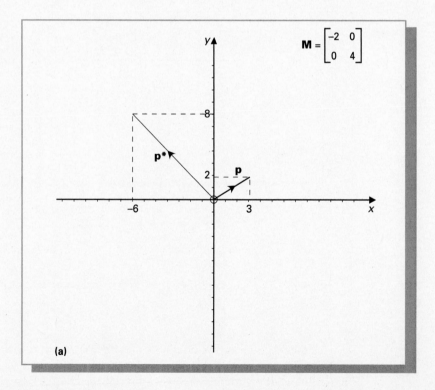

(a)

Figure 9.8 (a) Scaling and reflecting.

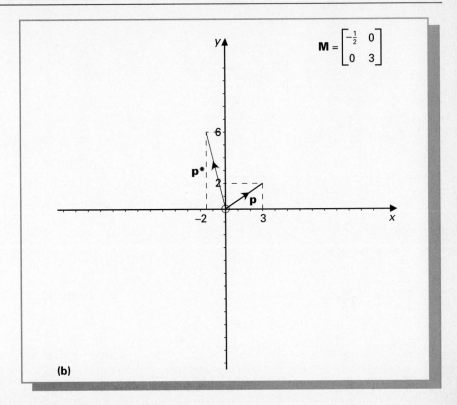

(b)

Figure 9.8 (b) Scaling and reflecting.

(a) $\begin{bmatrix} -2 & 0 \\ 0 & 4 \end{bmatrix}$ (b) $\begin{bmatrix} -\frac{1}{2} & 0 \\ 0 & 3 \end{bmatrix}$ (c) $\begin{bmatrix} 4 & 0 \\ 0 & -6 \end{bmatrix}$ (d) $\begin{bmatrix} -2 & 0 \\ 0 & -4 \end{bmatrix}$

9.4 Rotating position vectors about the origin

Just as with scaling and reflection about an axis, so also rotation about the origin in two dimensions is easily performed by post-multiplying by a (2×2) matrix that is formed in a certain way. As in the previous cases, we take the matrix

$$\mathbf{M} = \begin{bmatrix} a & b \\ c & d \end{bmatrix}$$

but before we identify general numbers a, b, c and d and the connections between them, we look at the matrices that cause rotations through one, two, three and four right angles. (By the standard convention, angles are positive when they are measured in an anticlockwise direction, as mentioned in Section 1.5.)

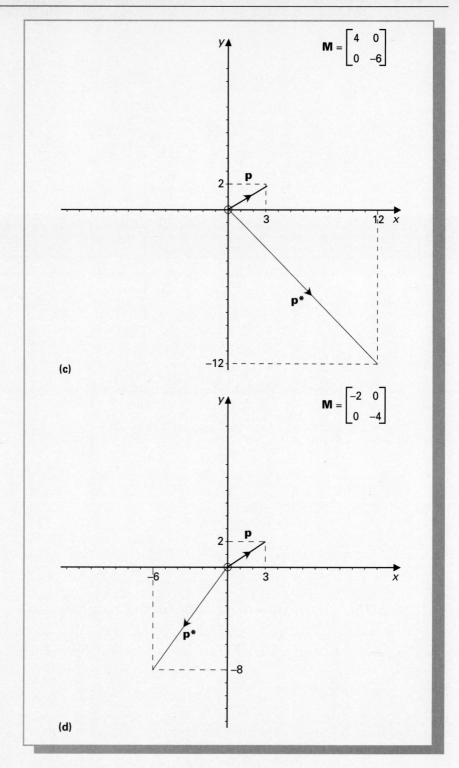

Figure 9.8 (c), and (d) Scaling and reflecting.

The matrix

$$M = \begin{bmatrix} 0 & 1 \\ -1 & 0 \end{bmatrix}$$

causes a rotation through an angle of 90°, that is $\pi/2$ radians or one right angle. When we consider the matrix

$$M = \begin{bmatrix} -1 & 0 \\ 0 & -1 \end{bmatrix}$$

then we find it causes a rotation through an angle of 180°, that is π radians or two right angles; this gives the same result as a reflection in the origin (see Section 9.3). The matrix

$$M = \begin{bmatrix} 0 & -1 \\ 1 & 0 \end{bmatrix}$$

causes a rotation through an angle of 270°, that is $3\pi/2$ radians or three right angles. If we take the matrix

$$M = \begin{bmatrix} 1 & 0 \\ 0 & 1 \end{bmatrix}$$

then we see that it causes a rotation through an angle of 360°, that is 2π radians or four right angles; since this is the identity matrix it is obvious that the net effect is that any position vector is unchanged. In Figure 9.9 we show the results of these rotation matrices acting on the position vector (3   2).

Now we come to the underlying pattern in the elements in rotation matrices, and see what connections can be made between the numbers a, b, c and d. It can be shown that when a position vector is rotated through an angle θ anticlockwise about the origin, then the matrix that causes this is

$$M = \begin{bmatrix} \cos\theta & \sin\theta \\ -\sin\theta & \cos\theta \end{bmatrix}$$

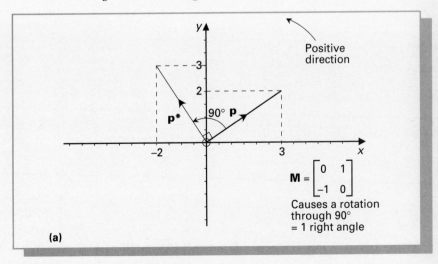

(a)

Figure 9.9 (a) Rotation through right angles.

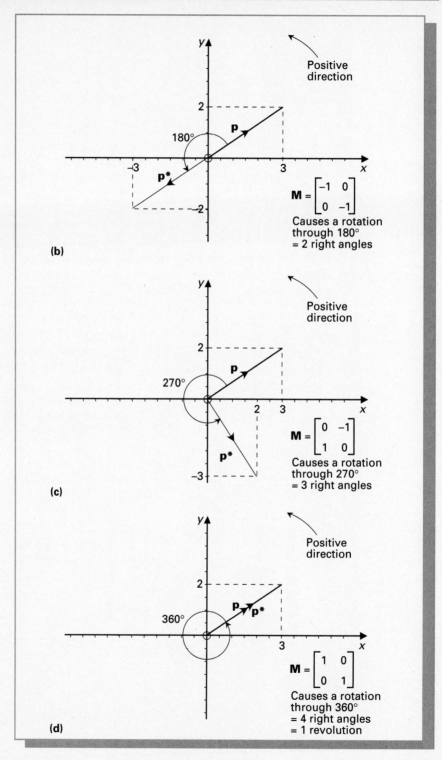

Figure 9.9 (b), (c), and (d) Rotation through right angles.

(It is quite possible to use this result without proving it; we indicate the proof in Appendix B.) Thus if we rotate the position vector (3 2) through any angle θ, we calculate the new position vector by

$$(3 \quad 2)\begin{bmatrix} \cos\theta & \sin\theta \\ -\sin\theta & \cos\theta \end{bmatrix} = (3\cos\theta - 2\sin\theta \quad 3\sin\theta + 2\cos\theta)$$

In particular, we can rotate the position vector (3 2) through 60° anticlockwise, as shown in Figure 9.10. We calculate the new position vector as follows:

$$(3 \quad 2)\begin{bmatrix} \cos 60° & \sin 60° \\ -\sin 60° & \cos 60° \end{bmatrix} = (3\cos 60° - 2\sin 60° \quad 3\sin 60° + 2\cos 60°)$$

$$\simeq ([3 \times 0.5 - 2 \times 0.8660] \quad [3 \times 0.8660 + 2 \times 0.5])$$

$$= ([1.5 - 1.732] \quad [2.598 + 1])$$

$$= (-0.23 \quad 3.60)$$

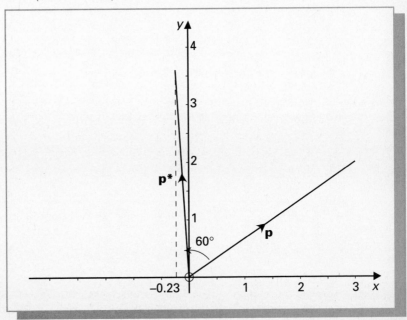

Figure 9.10 Rotating (3 2) through 60°.

9.5 Transforming polygons

In the above sections we have dealt specifically with transforming position vectors in two dimensions and we have seen how to scale them, reflect them in the axes, and rotate them about the origin; this of course gives us direct information about transforming points in a plane, since we can easily deduce coordinates from the components of position vectors. For more practical purposes, though, we are likely to be concerned with transforming lines and shapes in a plane, and whenever we are dealing just with straight lines and shapes whose edges are all straight lines (called **polygons**) the method is straightforward.

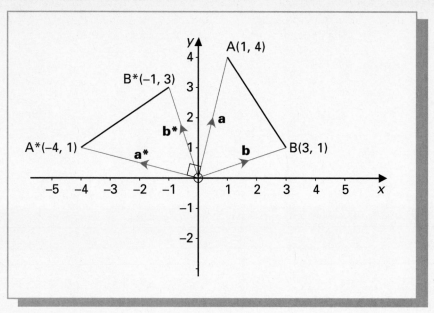

Figure 9.11 Rotating a line through 90°.

If we wish to transform a straight line, then we transform the position vectors of its end points. Joining up the points given by the 'new' position vectors gives the 'new' straight line. For example, suppose we have the line that joins the points A(1, 4) and B(3, 1), as shown in Figure 9.11, and we want to rotate it anticlockwise through 90°. The position vector of A is

$$\mathbf{a} = (1 \quad 4)$$

Post–multiplying by the appropriate rotation matrix gives

$$(1 \quad 4) \begin{bmatrix} 0 & 1 \\ -1 & 0 \end{bmatrix} = (-4 \quad 1)$$

Thus the new position vector, $\mathbf{a}^*$, is $(-4 \quad 1)$, and so the coordinates of the transformed end point A* are $(-4, 1)$. Similarly we can calculate the coordinates of B*, the other end point after transformation: they are $(-1, 3)$. In practice these calculations are usually done together, as shown here:

$$\begin{matrix} \text{position vector of A} \to (1 \quad 4) \\ \text{position vector of B} \to (3 \quad 1) \end{matrix} \begin{bmatrix} 0 & 1 \\ -1 & 0 \end{bmatrix} = \begin{matrix} (-4 \quad 1) \leftarrow \text{position vector of A*} \\ (-1 \quad 3) \leftarrow \text{position vector of B*} \end{matrix}$$

and the process is exactly the same as in the multiplication of matrices given in Section 8.4. The straight line joining A* and B* is the line AB rotated through 90° in the positive direction.

Since a polygon is any planar shape whose edges are all straight lines, we can transform any polygon by transforming all of its vertices. As as example we consider the triangle whose vertices are P(1, 3), Q(3, 0) and R(6, 4), and scale it by the matrix

$$\mathbf{M} = \begin{bmatrix} 3 & 0 \\ 0 & 2 \end{bmatrix}$$

to get a 'new' triangle with vertices P*, Q* and R*. We can deal with the three sets of calculations simultaneously, as if by matrix multiplication:

$$
\begin{array}{l}
\text{position vector of P} \rightarrow \\
\text{position vector of Q} \rightarrow \\
\text{position vector of R} \rightarrow
\end{array}
\begin{bmatrix} 1 & 3 \\ 3 & 0 \\ 6 & 4 \end{bmatrix}
\begin{bmatrix} 3 & 0 \\ 0 & 2 \end{bmatrix}
=
\begin{bmatrix} 3 & 6 \\ 9 & 0 \\ 18 & 8 \end{bmatrix}
\begin{array}{l}
\leftarrow \text{position vector of P*} \\
\leftarrow \text{position vector of Q*} \\
\leftarrow \text{position vector of R*}
\end{array}
$$

The triangles PQR and P*Q*R* are shown in Figure 9.12.

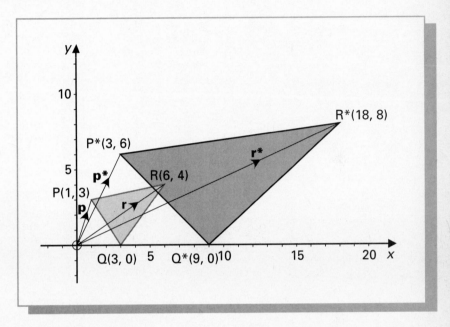

Figure 9.12 Scaling a polygon.

It is worthwhile noting that in all the transformations considered in this chapter we have not yet dealt with translations, that is the shifting of points or shapes. Any movements have occurred by virtue only of the scaling or reflection or rotation of the position vectors. In Figure 19.13 we summarize some of the transformations we have so far met, and the (2×2) matrices that perform them.

Exercises

9.1 Write down the (2×2) matrix that causes a stretching by 4 in the direction of the x-axis, and a shrinking by $\frac{1}{4}$ in the direction of the y-axis. Use this matrix as a geometric operator to transform the coordinates of the point P(1, 8).

9.2 Write down the matrix that supplies a balanced scaling by a factor of 2 about the origin. Use this matrix to transform the triangle whose vertices have coordinates A(4, 2), B(4, 4), C(2, 4), and sketch a graph of the result.

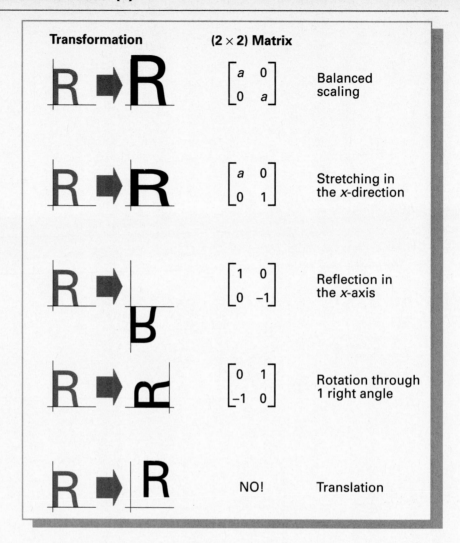

Transformation	(2 × 2) Matrix	
	$\begin{bmatrix} a & 0 \\ 0 & a \end{bmatrix}$	Balanced scaling
	$\begin{bmatrix} a & 0 \\ 0 & 1 \end{bmatrix}$	Stretching in the x-direction
	$\begin{bmatrix} 1 & 0 \\ 0 & -1 \end{bmatrix}$	Reflection in the x-axis
	$\begin{bmatrix} 0 & 1 \\ -1 & 0 \end{bmatrix}$	Rotation through 1 right angle
	NO!	Translation

Figure 9.13 Some transformations and their (2 × 2) matrices.

9.3 Repeat Exercise 9.2 using the scaling matrix $\begin{bmatrix} 3 & 0 \\ 0 & \frac{1}{2} \end{bmatrix}$, and sketch the result on a graph. Compare the graphs for Exercise 9.2 and Exercise 9.3.

9.4 Continuing with the theme of Exercise 8.6, write down the inverse of the scaling matrix

$$\begin{bmatrix} 2 & 0 \\ 0 & 5 \end{bmatrix}.$$

Can you deduce its effect as a geometric operator?

9.5 Use the reflection matrix

$$\begin{bmatrix} 1 & 0 \\ 0 & -1 \end{bmatrix}$$

to transform the triangle with vertices D(8, 1), E(7, 3) and F(6, 2). Sketch a graph of the reflected triangle, and state the axis of reflection.

9.6 Identify the transformation given by the matrix $\begin{bmatrix} 6 & 0 \\ 0 & -2 \end{bmatrix}$.

9.7 Consider the unit square with vertices H(1, 1), I(2, 1), J(2, 2), K(1, 2). Apply the transformation matrix

$$\begin{bmatrix} -3 & 0 \\ 0 & -3 \end{bmatrix}$$

to this square and graph the result. How has the area of the shape been affected by this transformation?

9.8 Let the position vector (4   5) be rotated through an angle of 30° anticlockwise about the origin. What is the transformation matrix? What is the resulting position vector?

9.9 Sketch the triangle whose vertices have coordinates (0, 0), (2, 1) and (0, 1). Rotate it through 45° anticlockwise about the origin and then calculate the coordinates of the vertices of the transformed triangle.

9.10 What is the inverse of the general rotation matrix given by $\begin{bmatrix} \cos \theta & \sin \theta \\ -\sin \theta & \cos \theta \end{bmatrix}$? Interpret this geometrically.

Answers

9.1 $\begin{bmatrix} 4 & 0 \\ 0 & \frac{1}{4} \end{bmatrix}$; new coordinates (4, 2).

9.2 $\begin{bmatrix} 2 & 0 \\ 0 & 2 \end{bmatrix}$; new vertices at A*(8, 4), B*(8, 8), C*(4, 8).

9.3 New vertices at A#(12, 1), B#(12, 2), C#(6, 2)

9.4 Inverse is $\frac{1}{10}\begin{bmatrix} 5 & 0 \\ 0 & 2 \end{bmatrix}$ or $\begin{bmatrix} 0.5 & 0 \\ 0 & 0.2 \end{bmatrix}$.

The effect is a shrinking by 0.5 in x-direction and by 0.2 in y-direction.

9.5 New vertices at D*(8, –1), E*(7, –3), F*(6, –2); reflection in the x-axis.

9.6 Stretching by a factor of 6 in x-direction, and by a factor of 2 in y-direction, with reflection in the x-axis.

9.7 New vertices at H*(−3, −3), I*(−6, −3), J*(−6, −6), K*(−3, −6); new area = old area $\times 3^2$.

9.8 $\begin{bmatrix} \cos 30° & \sin 30° \\ -\sin 30° & \cos 30° \end{bmatrix} \simeq \begin{bmatrix} 0.87 & 0.5 \\ -0.5 & 0.87 \end{bmatrix}$; (0.96   6.33).

9.9 New vertices have coordinates (0, 0), (0.71, 2.12), (−0.71, 0.71).

9.10 $\begin{bmatrix} \cos θ & -\sin θ \\ \sin θ & \cos θ \end{bmatrix}$; rotation *clockwise* through θ.

10

Moving in a plane (2):
Combining transformations; translations

10.1 Order in combining transformations

In Chapter 9 we considered simple cases of scaling, reflection and rotation in a plane. Each of these transformations can be dealt with as a matrix operation, by taking a position vector and post-multiplying it by a (2×2) matrix using the technique of multiplication given in Section 8.4. However, when manipulating an image captured in a computer we are likely to wish to orientate it and scale it in different ways, either simultaneously or sequentially; when dealing with the matrices containing the numerical instructions for the operations, we may well need to use more than one at a time. From the outset we must emphasize that the order in which different matrix operations are applied can crucially affect the result: order matters.

Let us see what occurs when we 'first reflect then rotate' an image, and compare it with the result when we 'first rotate then reflect' the same image. To describe these results we use the notation of Figure 10.1, where the four **quadrants** of the plane are numbered. As shown in Figure 10.2, we start with the image of a letter 'R' standing on the x-axis in the first quadrant. First we reflect it in the x-axis, and we get the letter upside-down; then we rotate it through 90° so that the end result is a letter 'R' lying face up in the first quadrant with its foot against the y-axis. When we apply these operations in the reverse order, the initial rotation through 90° yields a letter 'R' lying face up in the second quadrant, and the subsequent reflection in the x-axis gives a letter 'R' lying face down in the third quadrant. These two results are obviously different, which confirms that order matters.

The connection with matrices was mentioned in Section 8.4: matrix multiplication is not commutative. If we reverse the order in which two matrices are multiplied together, then almost always we obtain different results. This becomes obvious when we take the position vector of the top vertex of the letter 'R' to be $(x \quad y)$ and apply to it the matrices for reflection and rotation in different order. As we showed in Section 9.3, the matrix that causes a reflection in the x-axis is

$$\begin{bmatrix} 1 & 0 \\ 0 & -1 \end{bmatrix}$$

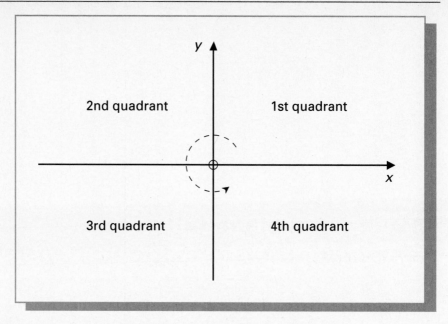

Figure 10.1 The standard numbering of the quadrants of a plane.

and from Section 9.4 the matrix that causes rotation through 90° about the origin is

$$\begin{bmatrix} 0 & 1 \\ -1 & 0 \end{bmatrix}$$

These are the matrices by which we post-multiply the position vector. We first reflect the position vector $(x \quad y)$ in the x-axis:

$$(x \quad y)\begin{bmatrix} 1 & 0 \\ 0 & -1 \end{bmatrix} = (x \quad -y)$$

To this reflected vector we apply the matrix to rotate it through 90°:

$$(x \quad -y)\begin{bmatrix} 0 & 1 \\ -1 & 0 \end{bmatrix} = (y \quad x)$$

so the transformed position vector is $(y \quad x)$. When we apply these operations in the reverse order, we first rotate through 90°:

$$(x \quad y)\begin{bmatrix} 0 & 1 \\ -1 & 0 \end{bmatrix} = (-y \quad x)$$

and then we reflect this rotated vector in the x-axis:

$$(-y \quad x)\begin{bmatrix} 1 & 0 \\ 0 & -1 \end{bmatrix} = (-y \quad -x)$$

This second transformed vector is obviously different from the first; these results can be seen to correspond exactly with the diagrams of Figure 10.2.

These two combined transformations have different matrix forms, owing to the

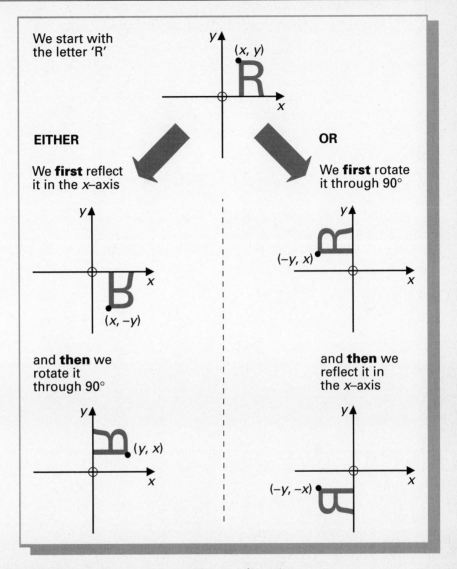

We start with the letter 'R'

(x, y)

EITHER

We **first** reflect it in the *x*–axis

$(x, -y)$

and **then** we rotate it through 90°

(y, x)

OR

We **first** rotate it through 90°

$(-y, x)$

and **then** we reflect it in the *x*–axis

$(-y, -x)$

Figure 10.2 The order matters when applying transformations.

order in which the matrices are multiplied. It is quite usual to omit the actual multiplication sign between the matrices, so multiplying them in the order 'reflect then rotate' gives:

$$\begin{bmatrix} 1 & 0 \\ 0 & -1 \end{bmatrix} \begin{bmatrix} 0 & 1 \\ -1 & 0 \end{bmatrix} = \begin{bmatrix} 0 & 1 \\ 1 & 0 \end{bmatrix}$$

Multiplying them in the order 'rotate then reflect' gives:

$$\begin{bmatrix} 0 & 1 \\ -1 & 0 \end{bmatrix} \begin{bmatrix} 1 & 0 \\ 0 & -1 \end{bmatrix} = \begin{bmatrix} 0 & -1 \\ -1 & 0 \end{bmatrix}$$

These different results refer again to the different outcomes shown in Figure 10.2.

10.2 Specific combinations of transformations

The emphasis on order in Section 10.1 applies when different types of transformations are considered. It does not apply at all when there is a sequence of two (or more) scalings, or two (or more) reflections in the axes, or two (or more) rotations in the plane about the origin. In these particular cases neither the overall result nor the matrix of the combined transformation depends on the order of operations. The following example demonstrates this.

Example 10.1 One rotation followed by another

We shall calculate the single matrix that is equivalent to a rotation about the origin through 60°, followed by another rotation about the origin through 30° (see Figure 10.3).

From Section 9.4 we know the form of a rotation matrix; thus we take first the matrix for rotation through 60°, then the matrix for rotation through 30°, and multiply them:

$$\begin{bmatrix} \cos 60° & \sin 60° \\ -\sin 60° & \cos 60° \end{bmatrix} \begin{bmatrix} \cos 30° & \sin 30° \\ -\sin 30° & \cos 30° \end{bmatrix} = \begin{bmatrix} 0.5 & 0.87 \\ -0.87 & 0.5 \end{bmatrix} \begin{bmatrix} 0.87 & 0.5 \\ -0.5 & 0.87 \end{bmatrix}$$

$$= \begin{bmatrix} 0 & 1 \\ -1 & 0 \end{bmatrix}$$

$$= \begin{bmatrix} \cos 90° & \sin 90° \\ -\sin 90° & \cos 90° \end{bmatrix}$$

as you may verify with a calculator. We should get precisely the same result if we performed the multiplication in the different order; the overall result is obviously equivalent to a single rotation through 90°.

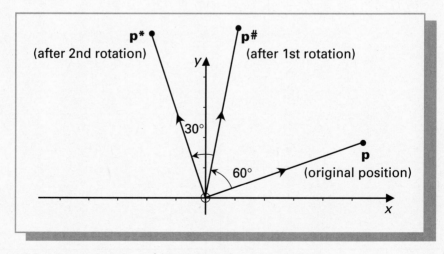

Figure 10.3 Successive rotations of 60° and 30° about the origin.

In general, when dealing with a sequence of rotations about the origin, the overall result is obtained by combining the angles of rotation. The following result, which uses formulae stated in Appendix C, holds for rotation through any two angles θ and ϕ:

$$\begin{bmatrix} \cos\theta & \sin\theta \\ -\sin\theta & \cos\theta \end{bmatrix} \begin{bmatrix} \cos\phi & \sin\phi \\ -\sin\phi & \cos\phi \end{bmatrix} = \begin{bmatrix} \cos(\theta+\phi) & \sin(\theta+\phi) \\ -\sin(\theta+\phi) & \cos(\theta+\phi) \end{bmatrix}$$

The effect of the combined matrix is illustrated in Figure 10.4.

When dealing with different transformations we remember that order matters, and we next look at some examples which involve scalings, reflections and rotations in different combinations.

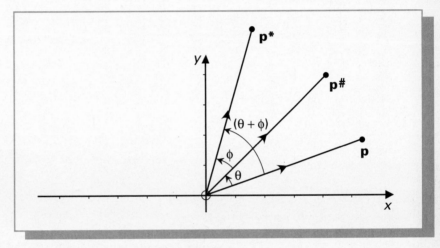

Figure 10.4 Successive rotations (the general case).

Example 10.2 A reflection followed by a rotation

We shall determine the single matrix that gives a reflection in the line '$y = x$' followed by a rotation through 60° about the origin.

From our knowledge of the standard equation of a straight line (see Section 7.1) we see that the line '$y = x$' has gradient $m = 1$, and y-intercept at zero, that is, it passes through the origin. This line is shown in Figure 10.5.

The matrix that causes a reflection in the line '$y = x$' is

$$\begin{bmatrix} 0 & 1 \\ 1 & 0 \end{bmatrix}$$

This can be illustrated by applying it to the position vector (3   4) as follows: if the result is compared with the diagram in Figure 10.5, it can be seen that the net effect is to interchange the x-component and the y-component of the vector.

$$(3 \quad 4)\begin{bmatrix} 0 & 1 \\ 1 & 0 \end{bmatrix} = (4 \quad 3)$$

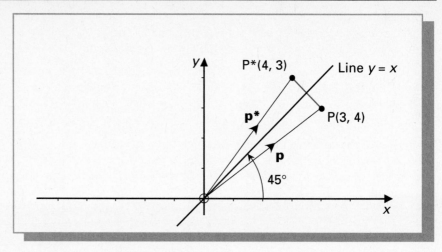

Figure 10.5 Reflection followed by rotation.

So to determine the matrix for the given combination of transformations, we multiply the matrices in order:

$$\begin{bmatrix} 0 & 1 \\ 1 & 0 \end{bmatrix} \begin{bmatrix} \cos 60° & \sin 60° \\ -\sin 60° & \cos 60° \end{bmatrix} = \begin{bmatrix} -\sin 60° & \cos 60° \\ \cos 60° & \sin 60° \end{bmatrix}$$

$$\textit{first} \text{ reflect} \qquad \textit{then} \text{ rotate} \qquad \simeq \begin{bmatrix} -0.87 & 0.5 \\ 0.5 & 0.87 \end{bmatrix}$$

If the transformations had been required in the reverse order, then we should have multiplied the matrices in the reverse order, and obtained a different overall result.

Example 10.3 A rotation followed by a scaling

We shall find the single matrix which gives a rotation through an angle θ about the origin, followed by a scaling by a factor of 3 in the x-direction and by 2 in the y-direction.

From Sections 9.4 and 9.2 we know that the individual matrices are: for the rotation

$$\begin{bmatrix} \cos \theta & \sin \theta \\ -\sin \theta & \cos \theta \end{bmatrix}$$

and for the scaling

$$\begin{bmatrix} 3 & 0 \\ 0 & 2 \end{bmatrix}$$

Thus the matrix required for the combined transformation is obtained by multiplying:

$$\begin{bmatrix} \cos \theta & \sin \theta \\ -\sin \theta & \cos \theta \end{bmatrix} \begin{bmatrix} 3 & 0 \\ 0 & 2 \end{bmatrix} = \begin{bmatrix} 3\cos \theta & 2\sin \theta \\ -3\sin \theta & 2\cos \theta \end{bmatrix}$$

$$\textit{first} \text{ rotate} \qquad \textit{then} \text{ scale}$$

Multiplying the matrices in the reverse order would give a different result; you are invited to verify this for yourself.

Example 10.4 A reflection in a line through the origin

We now determine the single matrix that will perform a reflection, not in one of the axes, but in a fixed line L inclined at an angle θ to the positive x-axis.

As indicated in Figure 10.6, the required reflection of the point P with position vector $(\mathbf{x} \quad \mathbf{y})$ is an image point P* with position vector $(\mathbf{x}^* \quad \mathbf{y}^*)$; P and P* are equidistant from the line L, and on opposite sides of it.

We follow a standard technique for this reflection, using 'known' transformations at each stage. Geometrically, we first rotate the line L and the point P through an angle θ *clockwise* about the origin, so that L is aligned along the x-axis. Then we reflect the point in the x-axis. Finally we rotate L and the points back through an angle of θ *anticlockwise* about the origin: this restores the original orientation, with P* now the required reflection of P. These stages are shown in Figure 10.7.

Using matrix operators, we have

$$\begin{bmatrix} \cos(-\theta) & \sin(-\theta) \\ -\sin(-\theta) & \cos(-\theta) \end{bmatrix}$$

to perform the initial rotation: The clockwise rotation means that we are turning through a negative angle, $(-\theta)$. Then the reflection in the x-axis requires the matrix

$$\begin{bmatrix} 1 & 0 \\ 0 & -1 \end{bmatrix}$$

and for the final rotation through the angle θ in the anticlockwise (positive) direction we have the matrix

$$\begin{bmatrix} \cos\theta & \sin\theta \\ -\sin\theta & \cos\theta \end{bmatrix}$$

To obtain the single matrix to perform the combined transformation we multiply these three matrices in the correct order:

$$\begin{bmatrix} \cos(-\theta) & \sin(-\theta) \\ -\sin(-\theta) & \cos(-\theta) \end{bmatrix} \begin{bmatrix} 1 & 0 \\ 0 & -1 \end{bmatrix} \begin{bmatrix} \cos\theta & \sin\theta \\ -\sin\theta & \cos\theta \end{bmatrix}$$

first rotate clockwise   *then* reflect   *then* rotate anticlockwise

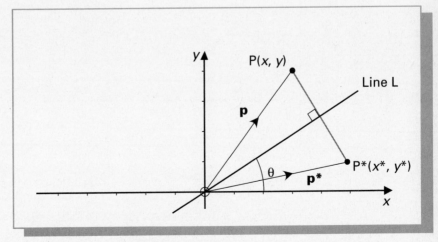

Figure 10.6 Reflection in a fixed line L.

Using the definitions for the trigonometric ratios of negative angles given in Section 1.5, this becomes

$$\begin{bmatrix} \cos\theta & -\sin\theta \\ \sin\theta & \cos\theta \end{bmatrix} \begin{bmatrix} 1 & 0 \\ 0 & -1 \end{bmatrix} \begin{bmatrix} \cos\theta & \sin\theta \\ -\sin\theta & \cos\theta \end{bmatrix}$$

Multiplying together the second pair of matrices we have

$$\begin{bmatrix} \cos\theta & -\sin\theta \\ \sin\theta & \cos\theta \end{bmatrix} \begin{bmatrix} \cos\theta & \sin\theta \\ \sin\theta & -\cos\theta \end{bmatrix}$$

Then, using the 'double angle' formulae stated in Appendix C, we have the matrix for the overall transformation:

$$\begin{bmatrix} \cos 2\theta & \sin 2\theta \\ \sin 2\theta & -\cos 2\theta \end{bmatrix}$$

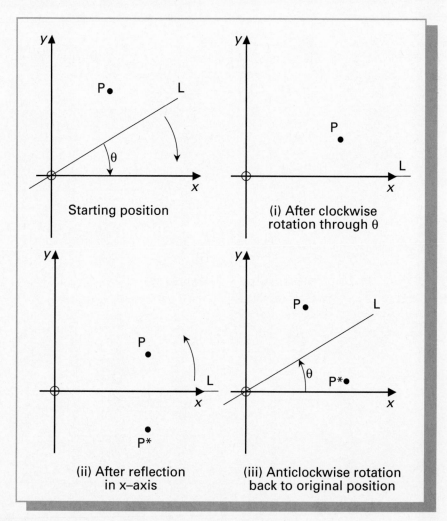

Figure 10.7 Reflection in a fixed line: three stages.

We see that the single matrix that performs the reflection in a fixed line L depends only on the angle at which the line is inclined to the x-axis.

10.3 Translations

We come now to the last of our standard transformations: **translations** also known as **shifts**. There is one way in which these can be dealt with very easily, just using vectors. For example the vector (3   4) can be interpreted as 'move 3 along and 4 up'. Thus if the position vector of the point P is (3   1) and we shift it by (3   4), we get the position vector of the transformed point P* by

$$(x^* \quad y^*) = (3 \quad 1) + (3 \quad 4) = (6 \quad 5)$$

This approach is illustrated in Figure 10.8.

The above method is based on the addition of vectors, and so it is not directly compatible with the way we deal with other transformations, using multiplication by matrices. It is highly desirable that there should be a single system in which all transformations can be described, and combined if necessary, using matrices.

Unfortunately, it is impossible to perform a two-dimensional translation by multiplying vectors by a (2×2) matrix. We can easily illustrate this by seeing what happens when we multiply the zero vector (which is the position vector of the point at the origin) by any (2×2) matrix; we get

$$(0 \quad 0) \begin{bmatrix} a & b \\ c & d \end{bmatrix} = (0 \quad 0)$$

Thus whatever the elements in the matrix, the result is always the zero vector, so the point at the origin is not moved. There is no such thing as a (2×2) matrix that can shift the point at the origin by multiplication; hence (2×2) matrices cannot cause translations in the plane.

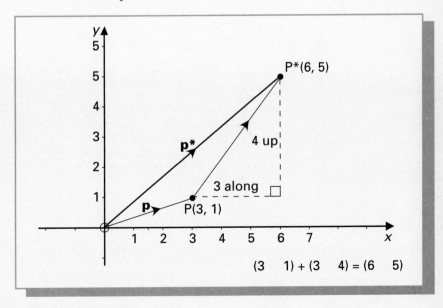

Figure 10.8 Shifting by adding vectors.

In order to be able to use matrix multiplication to perform all transformations, our idea of position vectors in two dimensions must be extended. We now introduce a third element into the position vector of every point, so that what was written $(x \quad y)$ becomes $(x \quad y \quad 1)$, called a **homogeneous vector**.

We now identify the matrix that will shift the particular homogeneous vector $(3 \quad 1 \quad 1)$ by the rule 'move 3 along and 4 up'. It is the (3×3) matrix

$$\begin{bmatrix} 1 & 0 & 0 \\ 0 & 1 & 0 \\ 3 & 4 & 1 \end{bmatrix}$$

and it will apply the shift by multiplication, as we show next. We take the homogeneous vector and post-multiply it by this shift matrix:

$$(3 \quad 1 \quad 1) \begin{bmatrix} 1 & 0 & 0 \\ 0 & 1 & 0 \\ 3 & 4 & 1 \end{bmatrix}$$

$$= (3 + 3 \quad 1 + 4 \quad 1)$$

$$= (6 \quad 5 \quad 1)$$

which is the homogeneous vector corresponding to the position vector $(6 \quad 5)$, as required.

This new system of describing and transforming points in a plane using homogeneous vectors is sometimes also called the system of **homogeneous coordinates**. We shall deal with it in more detail in the coming chapters.

10.4 (3×3) Matrices for transformations in a plane

When homogeneous vectors are used, every planar transformation can be represented by a (3×3) matrix, and the transformations can be combined as needed by multiplying the matrices. We conclude this chapter with some examples of these (3×3) matrices; you should be able to see easily how they are formed, with the original (2×2) matrix (where it existed) placed in the top left-hand segment and accompanied by similar arrangements of 0s and 1s in the final row and column.

For transforming two-dimensional homogeneous vectors we have these patterns:

1. A (3×3) **scaling** matrix that expands by a factor of 'a' in the x-direction, and a factor of 'b' in the y-direction:

$$\begin{bmatrix} a & 0 & 0 \\ 0 & b & 0 \\ 0 & 0 & 1 \end{bmatrix}$$

2. A (3×3) matrix that causes **reflection** in the x-axis:

$$\begin{bmatrix} 1 & 0 & 0 \\ 0 & -1 & 0 \\ 0 & 0 & 1 \end{bmatrix}$$

3. A (3×3) matrix that causes **reflection** in the y-axis:

$$\begin{bmatrix} -1 & 0 & 0 \\ 0 & 1 & 0 \\ 0 & 0 & 1 \end{bmatrix}$$

4. A (3×3) matrix that causes a **rotation** through an angle θ about the origin:

$$\begin{bmatrix} \cos \theta & \sin \theta & 0 \\ -\sin \theta & \cos \theta & 0 \\ 0 & 0 & 1 \end{bmatrix}$$

5. A (3×3) matrix that causes a **translation** of h units in the x-direction and k units in the y-direction:

$$\begin{bmatrix} 1 & 0 & 0 \\ 0 & 1 & 0 \\ h & k & 1 \end{bmatrix}$$

In the following chapter we shall explore more consequences of combining these transformations, and investigate the resulting patterns in the combined (3×3) matrices.

Exercises

10.1   What is the single (2×2) matrix that gives a rotation about the origin through $60°$, followed by a reflection in the line $y = x$?

10.2   What is the single (2×2) matrix that gives a scaling by a factor of 3 in the x-direction and by a factor of 2 in the y-direction, followed by a rotation about the origin through an angle θ?

10.3   What is the single (2×2) matrix that gives a scaling by a factor of 6 in the x-direction and by 2 in the y-direction, followed by a scaling by a factor of 3 in the x-direction and by 4 in the y-direction? What is the effect of the re-ordering of these two operations?

10.4   Take the triangle that has vertices at A(1, 2), B(2, 3) and C(4, 2), and reflect it in the line through the origin which is inclined at $30°$ to the (positive) x-axis. Calculate the coordinates of the vertices of the transformed triangle and sketch your result.

10.5   The triangle ABC whose vertices have position vectors A(1   0), B(0   1) and C(−1   0), is transformed by the matrix

$$\mathbf{M} = \begin{bmatrix} 3 & 2 \\ -1 & 2 \end{bmatrix}$$

to create a second triangle A*B*C*. Calculate the ratio of the areas of these two triangles. Calculate the value of the determinant of $\mathbf{M}$, and compare these answers. (Note that the result obtained here is generally true.)

10.6   Write down the (3×3) matrix that performs translations of $(+5)$ in the x-direction and $(−2)$ in the y-direction, when homogeneous vectors replace the position vectors of points in the plane. Verify the action of this matrix by applying it to the square PQRS on the the base PQ, where P has coordinates (4, 1) and Q has coordinates (7, 3). Sketch your result.

10.7 Determine the appropriate (2×2) matrix to perform the transformation indicated in each of the following cases, and calculate the coordinates of the transformed vertices. Sketch the results.

a) Take the shape in Figure 10.9 and rotate it by 30° about the origin.

b) Take the shape in Figure 10.10 and scale it by a factor of $\frac{1}{2}$ in the x-direction and by a factor of 2 in the y-direction.

10.8 Use a (3×3) matrix to shift the square in Figure 10.11 by +3 units across and 1 unit down. Write down the matrix, and the coordinates of the transformed vertices.

10.9 What (3×3) matrix will change the centre of the scene, as shown in Figure 10.12, and reflect the mountains in the lake?

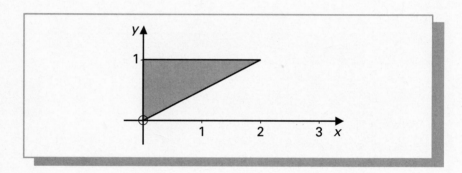

Figure 10.9 For Exercise 10.7 a.

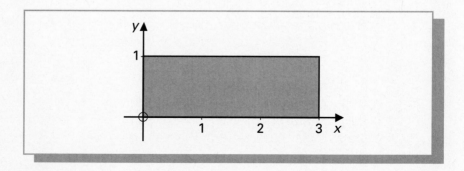

Figure 10,10 For Exercise 10.7 b.

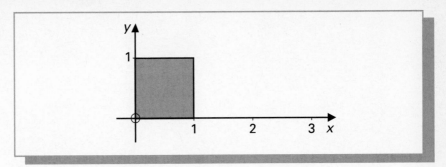

Figure 10.11 For Exercise 10.8.

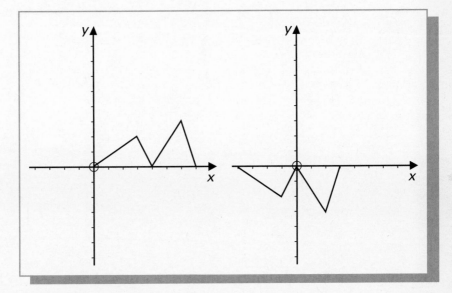

Figure 10.12 For Exercise 10.9.

Answers

10.1 $\begin{bmatrix} 0.87 & 0.5 \\ 0.5 & -0.87 \end{bmatrix}$.

10.2 $\begin{bmatrix} 3\cos\theta & 3\sin\theta \\ -2\sin\theta & 2\cos\theta \end{bmatrix}$.

10.3 $\begin{bmatrix} 18 & 0 \\ 0 & 8 \end{bmatrix}$, none.

10.4 A*(2.23, −0.13), B*(3.60, 0.23), C*(3.73, 2.46).

10.5 Area ratio = 8:1 = 8/1 = 8; value of determinant = 8; they are equal.

10.6 $\begin{bmatrix} 1 & 0 & 0 \\ 0 & 1 & 0 \\ 5 & -2 & 1 \end{bmatrix}$; R(5, 6), S(2, 4); P*(9, -1), Q*(12, 1), R*(10, 4), S*(7, 2).

10.7 a) $\begin{bmatrix} 0.87 & 0.5 \\ -0.5 & 0.87 \end{bmatrix}$; (0, 0), (1.23, 1.87), (-0.5, 0.87).

b) $\begin{bmatrix} \frac{1}{2} & 0 \\ 0 & 2 \end{bmatrix}$; (0, 0), $(1\frac{1}{2}, 0)$, $(1\frac{1}{2}, 2)$, (0, 2).

10.8 $\begin{bmatrix} 1 & 0 & 0 \\ 0 & 1 & 0 \\ 3 & -1 & 1 \end{bmatrix}$; (3, -1), (4, -1), (4, 0), (3, 0).

10.9 $\begin{bmatrix} 1 & 0 & 0 \\ 0 & -1 & 0 \\ -4 & 0 & 1 \end{bmatrix}$.

Sizing things up:
Homogeneous vectors

11.1 Simple homogeneous vectors

In the last chapter we sought a method of translating or shifting a point in two dimensions by multiplying its position vector by a matrix. This turned out not to be as straightforward as when we were dealing with rotations or scalings. It was necessary to introduce a third component into the position vector, so that what had been written $(x \quad y)$ became $(x \quad y \quad 1)$, and then the matrix multiplication was successfully applied to these new homogeneous vectors.

It is important to remember that while there are three components in these homogeneous vectors, they still represent the position vectors of points in two dimensions. Any point in two dimensions can have its position vector written as a homogeneous vector; for example, the point P with coordinates $(-2, 5)$ has a position vector $(-2 \quad 5)$, but its homogeneous vector is $(-2 \quad 5 \quad 1)$. In future (see Chapter 13) when we are dealing with the transformations of points in three dimensions, we shall introduce a fourth component to construct the homogeneous vector. The point Q with coordinates $(6, 1, -3)$, say, has position vector $(6 \quad 1 \quad -3)$ and homogeneous vector $(6 \quad 1 \quad -3 \quad 1)$.

11.2 General homogeneous vectors

It is not essential that the final component in homogeneous vectors is always a '1'. In the plane, a point with position vector $(x \quad y)$ can be represented by the homogeneous vector $(cx \quad cy \quad c)$, where 'c' is any non-zero scalar number. As an example, the point with position vector $(3 \quad 2)$ can be represented by

$$(3 \quad 2 \quad 1) \text{ if } c = 1$$

or by

$$(6 \quad 4 \quad 2) \text{ if } c = 2$$

or by

$$(9 \quad 6 \quad 3) \text{ if } c = 3$$

or by

$$(18 \quad 12 \quad 6) \text{ if } c = 6$$

or by

$$(-12 \quad -8 \quad -4) \text{ if } c = -4$$

or by

$$(1\tfrac{1}{2} \quad 1 \quad \tfrac{1}{2}) \text{ if } c = \tfrac{1}{2}, \text{ etc.}$$

There is no unique representation of a point when using homogeneous vectors.

When we are given a point by a homogeneous vector we must be able to determine the actual position vector of the 'physical' point. The calculation is straightforward: in order to interpret the homogeneous vector graphically we just 'divide all through' to make the last component equal '1' (since we have stated that $c \neq 0$, this is always possible). Then the first two components give us the position vector of the 'physical' point, as we show in the following examples.

Example 11.1   Finding two-dimensional coordinates from a homogeneous vector

We consider the homogeneous vector $(25 \quad 40 \quad 5)$, and find the coordinates of the 'physical' point it represents.

To make the final component '1' we divide all through by 5, and get $(5 \quad 8 \quad 1)$. Thus the 'physical' point has position vector $(5 \quad 8)$ and coordinates $(5, 8)$.

Example 11.2   As above, where final component is a fraction

We consider the homogeneous vector $(2 \quad -1 \quad \tfrac{1}{4})$, and find the coordinates of the physical point it represents.

To make the final component '1' we divide all through by $\tfrac{1}{4}$, which is the same as multiplying all through by 4, and we get $(8 \quad -4 \quad 1)$. Thus the 'physical' point has position vector $(8 \quad -4)$ and coordinates $(8, -4)$.

Example 11.3   As above, where final component is negative

We consider the homogeneous vector $(-2 \quad 4 \quad -3)$, and find the coordinates of the 'physical' point it represents.

To make the final component '1' we divide all through by -3, and we get $(\tfrac{2}{3} \quad -\tfrac{4}{3} \quad 1)$. Thus the 'physical' point has position vector $(\tfrac{2}{3} \quad -\tfrac{4}{3})$ and hence coordinates $(\tfrac{2}{3}, -\tfrac{4}{3})$.

Example 11.4   Finding three-dimensional coordinates from a homogeneous vector

We consider the homogeneous vector $(8 \quad 6 \quad 0 \quad 2)$, and find the coordinates of the 'physical' point it represents.

To make the final component '1' we divide all through by 2, and we get (4   3   0   1). This gives the 'physical' point in three dimensions with position vector (4   3   0), and coordinates (4, 3, 0).

When a two dimensional homogeneous vector has 'zero' as its third component, then its form is $(x \quad y \quad 0)$. This situation is significantly different from the examples dealt with above. Any homogeneous vector with coordinates $(x \quad y \quad 0)$ does not give us a 'physical' point, with an actual position that can be plotted on a plane: any homogeneous vector of the form $(x \quad y \quad 0)$ refers to a **point at infinity**. We shall be returning to this idea in Chapter 13.

11.3 Matrix operations using homogeneous vectors

In Section 10.4 we listed some of the recognizable patterns in (3×3) matrices that perform the separate transformations of scaling, reflection, rotation and translation when operating on homogeneous vectors. We now consider a general (3×3) matrix

$$\begin{bmatrix} a & b & 0 \\ c & d & 0 \\ h & k & s \end{bmatrix}$$

and identify the effects of the different groups of entries shown.

The following matrix has elements only in the upper left–hand corner:

$$\begin{bmatrix} a & b & * \\ c & d & * \\ * & * & * \end{bmatrix}$$

As discussed in Chapter 9, these elements have an effect in terms of rotation, scaling in the x- and/or y-directions (called **local scaling**), and reflection in the axes (which can be regarded as local scaling with a negative scale factor). The order in which these operations are applied affects the elements in the combined matrix, and this group of elements is termed the **rotation group**, R.

From Chapter 10 we know that when a matrix has elements in the positions indicated here

$$\begin{bmatrix} * & * & * \\ * & * & * \\ h & k & * \end{bmatrix}$$

then we have the effect of translation, or shift. The translation vector is $(h \quad k)$, and these are the **translation elements**, T.

In the general matrix shown above there is one more entry whose effect we can now identify. The entry in the bottom right-hand position shown here

$$\begin{bmatrix} * & * & * \\ * & * & * \\ * & * & s \end{bmatrix}$$

effects **overall scaling**, S. If the element s is *less than* 1 then multiplication by this matrix involves an **overall expansion**, while if the element s is *greater than* 1 then multiplication by this matrix involves an **overall contraction**. This statement may appear to be counter to intuition, but the following examples will justify it.

Example 11.5 The effect of an overall contraction

We consider the effect when the point with position vector (15   18) is transformed by the matrix

$$\begin{bmatrix} 1 & 0 & 0 \\ 0 & 1 & 0 \\ 0 & 0 & 3 \end{bmatrix}$$

The homogeneous vector is muliplied by the matrix so we have

$$(15 \quad 18 \quad 1)\begin{bmatrix} 1 & 0 & 0 \\ 0 & 1 & 0 \\ 0 & 0 & 3 \end{bmatrix} = (15 \quad 18 \quad 3)$$

Applying the method of Section 11.2, this is equivalent to

$$(15 \div 3 \quad 18 \div 3 \quad 3 \div 3) = (5 \quad 6 \quad 1)$$

which represents the 'physical' point with position vector (5   6). Thus when the element in the matrix is $s = 3 \, (> 1)$, the original position vector (15   18) is contracted and becomes (5   6); '$s = 3$' causes an overall contraction by the factor $\frac{1}{3}$.

Example 11.6 The effect of an overall expansion

We now consider the effect when the point with position vector (4   5) is transformed by the matrix

$$\begin{bmatrix} 1 & 0 & 0 \\ 0 & 1 & 0 \\ 0 & 0 & \frac{1}{2} \end{bmatrix}$$

The homogeneous vector is multiplied by the matrix, so we have

$$(4 \quad 5 \quad 1)\begin{bmatrix} 1 & 0 & 0 \\ 0 & 1 & 0 \\ 0 & 0 & \frac{1}{2} \end{bmatrix} = (4 \quad 5 \quad \tfrac{1}{2})$$

Using the method of Section 11.2 again, this is equivalent to

$$(4 \div \tfrac{1}{2} \quad 5 \div \tfrac{1}{2} \quad \tfrac{1}{2} \div \tfrac{1}{2}) = (8 \quad 10 \quad 1)$$

which represents the 'physical' point with position vector (8   10). Thus when the element in the matrix is $s = \frac{1}{2} \, (< 1)$, the original position vector (4   5) is expanded and becomes (8   10); '$s = \frac{1}{2}$' causes an overall expansion by the factor 2.

In Chapter 10 we discussed how the result of a sequence of transformations depends on the order in which they are applied, and, equivalently, on the order in which the matrices are multiplied. This remains true when we are dealing with these (3×3) matrices with which we multiply the homogeneous vectors. It is only in certain specific cases that we can identify the entries in a combined matrix immediately;

only when the order of operations is *first* Rotation group, *then* Translation elements, and *finally* overall Scaling can all the appropriate entries be placed in the matrix exactly where they would be expected. When the operations are in this order then matrix multiplication gives

$$
\begin{bmatrix} a & b & 0 \\ c & d & 0 \\ 0 & 0 & 1 \end{bmatrix} \times \begin{bmatrix} 1 & 0 & 0 \\ 0 & 1 & 0 \\ h & k & 1 \end{bmatrix} \times \begin{bmatrix} 1 & 0 & 0 \\ 0 & 1 & 0 \\ 0 & 0 & s \end{bmatrix} = \begin{bmatrix} a & b & 0 \\ c & d & 0 \\ h & k & s \end{bmatrix}
$$

Rotation group   Translation   overall Scaling
elements

It can easily be verified that multiplying the three matrices together in any different order gives a different result, and one that is not immediately recognizable. For the recognizable pattern to result it is essential that the order is 'Rotation group, Translation elements, overall Scaling', that is 'R–T–S', for which the phrase 'Return–To–Sender' may be a useful reminder!

We complete this chapter with an example that indicates how recognition of the R–T–S order can considerably shorten a set of calculations.

Example 11.7 Reflection, then translation, then scaling

We shall transform the point with coordinates $(2, 4)$ by first reflecting it in the x-axis, then translating it by the vector $(5 \quad 6)$ and finally by reducing the overall scale to $\frac{1}{8}$ of the original.

To perform this transformation we need the homogeneous vector corresponding to this point, that is $(2 \quad 4 \quad 1)$. Then, rather than multiply by three separate matrices one after another, we notice that the order of the given operations is 'reflect (Rotation group), Translate, then overall Scale'. As this is in the recognizable order we can write down the single matrix immediately, and so we need just one calculation:

$$
(2 \quad 4 \quad 1) \begin{bmatrix} 1 & 0 & 0 \\ 0 & -1 & 0 \\ 5 & 6 & 8 \end{bmatrix} = (2 + 5 \quad -4 + 6 \quad 8)
$$

$$
= (7 \quad 2 \quad 8)
$$

$$
= (7 \div 8 \quad 2 \div 8 \quad 8 \div 8) \text{ using Section 11.2}
$$

$$
= (\tfrac{7}{8} \quad \tfrac{1}{4} \quad 1)
$$

$$
= (0.875 \quad 0.25 \quad 1)
$$

Thus the 'physical' coordinates of the transformed point are $(0.88, 0.25)$.

The methods used in the examples so far are easily extended so that they can be applied in the future to position vectors in three dimensions.

Exercises

11.1 Consider the matrices **R**, **T** and **S** that follow. **R** contains a 'rotation group' of elements, **T** contains only 'translation elements' and **S** contains only an element for overall scaling:

$$R = \begin{bmatrix} 3 & 7 & 0 \\ 2 & 5 & 0 \\ 0 & 0 & 1 \end{bmatrix}, T = \begin{bmatrix} 1 & 0 & 0 \\ 0 & 1 & 0 \\ 4 & 6 & 1 \end{bmatrix}, S = \begin{bmatrix} 1 & 0 & 0 \\ 0 & 1 & 0 \\ 0 & 0 & 9 \end{bmatrix}$$

Using matrix multiplication, evaluate the combined matrix (**R T**), and then the combined matrix (**RT**)**S**. Show that in your result you have the original elements in their expected positions. (You will arrive at the same result if you calculate **R**(**TS**), since matrix multiplication is **associative**.)

Now evaluate the products (**T R**)**S** and **R**(**S T**), and show that in neither case do you achieve a result where all the elements in the combined matrix immediately indicate the separate transformations.

11.2 Write down the (2×2) matrix **M** that represents a rotation about the origin through an angle $\pi/2$. Calculate $\mathbf{M}^2$, $\mathbf{M}^3$, and $\mathbf{M}^4$, and identify the geometric results of multiplying by these matrices.

11.3 Represent in matrix form each step in the following sequence of transformations:

a) a reflection in the x-axis;

b) a rotation clockwise about the origin through $\pi/3$;

c) a reflection in the y-axis.

Express the result of these three transformations, in this order, by a single (2×2) matrix, and illustrate its action on the straight line with end points $(1, 4)$ and $(3, 2)$.

11.4 Represent as a (3×3) matrix each of the following transformations:

a) expansion by a factor of 2 in the x-direction;

b) rotation through an angle of $+\pi/4$ about the origin;

c) reflection in the y-axis;

d) translation through $(-1 \quad 3)$;

e) overall expansion by 2.

When these transformations are applied successively, in the order given, determine the single matrix that effects the combined result. Use the combined matrix to transform the coordinates of the corners of the square ABCD with coordinates $(0, 0)$, $(1, 0)$, $(0, 1)$, $(1, 1)$ respectively. Plot the result on a graph.

Answers

11.1 $(\mathbf{R\ T})\mathbf{S} = \mathbf{R}(\mathbf{T\ S}) = \begin{bmatrix} 3 & 7 & 0 \\ 2 & 5 & 0 \\ 4 & 6 & 9 \end{bmatrix}$, $(\mathbf{T\ R})\mathbf{S} = \begin{bmatrix} 3 & 7 & 0 \\ 2 & 5 & 0 \\ 24 & 58 & 9 \end{bmatrix}$,

$$\mathbf{R}(\mathbf{S\ T}) = \begin{bmatrix} 3 & 7 & 0 \\ 2 & 5 & 0 \\ 36 & 54 & 9 \end{bmatrix}.$$

11.2 $M = \begin{bmatrix} 0 & 1 \\ -1 & 0 \end{bmatrix}$; $M^2 = \begin{bmatrix} -1 & 0 \\ 0 & -1 \end{bmatrix}$; $M^3 = \begin{bmatrix} 0 & -1 \\ 1 & 0 \end{bmatrix}$; $M^4 = \begin{bmatrix} 1 & 0 \\ 0 & 1 \end{bmatrix}$.

M^2, M^3, M^4 respectively: rotation through $+\pi$, $+3\pi/2$ and $+2\pi$ ($\equiv$ identity).

11.3 a) $\begin{bmatrix} 1 & 0 \\ 0 & -1 \end{bmatrix}$; b) $\begin{bmatrix} 0.50 & -0.87 \\ 0.87 & 0.50 \end{bmatrix}$; c) $\begin{bmatrix} -1 & 0 \\ 0 & 1 \end{bmatrix}$.

The combined matrix is $\begin{bmatrix} -0.50 & -0.87 \\ 0.87 & -0.50 \end{bmatrix}$.

The transformed line has end points $(2.98, -2.87)$ and $(0.24, -3.61)$.

11.4 a) $\begin{bmatrix} 2 & 0 & 0 \\ 0 & 1 & 0 \\ 0 & 0 & 1 \end{bmatrix}$; b) $\begin{bmatrix} 0.71 & 0.71 & 0 \\ -0.71 & 0.71 & 0 \\ 0 & 0 & 1 \end{bmatrix}$; c) $\begin{bmatrix} -1 & 0 & 0 \\ 0 & 1 & 0 \\ 0 & 0 & 1 \end{bmatrix}$;

d) $\begin{bmatrix} 1 & 0 & 0 \\ 0 & 1 & 0 \\ -1 & 3 & 1 \end{bmatrix}$; e) $\begin{bmatrix} 1 & 0 & 0 \\ 0 & 1 & 0 \\ 0 & 0 & \frac{1}{2} \end{bmatrix}$; Combined: $\begin{bmatrix} -1.41 & 1.41 & 0 \\ 0.71 & 0.71 & 0 \\ -1 & 3 & \frac{1}{2} \end{bmatrix}$.

$A^*(-2, 6)$, $B^*(-4.82, 8.82)$, $C^*(-0.58, 7.42)$, $D^*(-3.4, 10.24)$.

Useful manoeuvres:
'Non-standard' rotations and reflections;
the viewing transformation

12.1 Standard and non-standard

In Chapters 9 and 10 we considered types of (2×2) matrices that cause different transformations in two dimensions. In particular, in Sections 9.3 and 9.4 we dealt with what we shall take to be **standard reflections** (in an axis) and **standard rotations** (about the origin). In addition to these, in Example 10.4 we used a combination of matrices to cause what we shall call a **non-standard reflection**, a reflection in a line through the origin which was not one of the axes. In the sections that now follow, we deal with other non-standard two-dimensional transformations, for example a rotation about a point other than the origin, and a reflection in a line which does not even pass through the origin. Finally we shall discuss what is meant in the world of computer graphics by the **viewing transformation** from one plane to another, and construct the matrix that performs this.

12.2 Rotation about an arbitrary point

As shown in Figure 12.1, there is an (arbitrary) point in a plane, $C(h, k)$, which is to be the **centre of rotation**. Under the transformation considered, every point in the plane is to be rotated through an angle of θ anticlockwise about C. In particular the point P is to be rotated through θ to the position P*.

This non-standard rotation is performed by following a sequence of known standard transformations. First we apply the transformation that shifts the centre to the origin; next we rotate all the points in the plane through θ about the origin; and finally we shift the centre back to its original position. The overall result of this sequence of transformations is precisely the required rotation about C. Especially because we are dealing with translations here, it is necessary to deal with homogeneous vectors, and so all these transformations in the plane will be performed by (3×3) matrices (see Section 11.3). The matrices are as follows. The matrix to shift C to the origin is

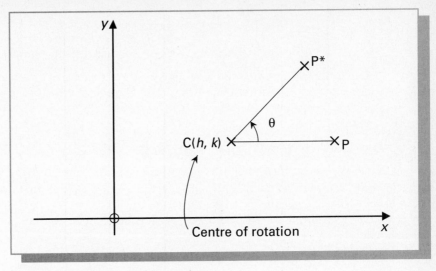

Figure 12.1 Rotation about an arbitary point.

$$\mathbf{T} = \begin{bmatrix} 1 & 0 & 0 \\ 0 & 1 & 0 \\ -h & -k & 1 \end{bmatrix}$$

and the matrix to cause a rotation through an angle of θ about the origin is

$$\mathbf{R} = \begin{bmatrix} \cos\theta & \sin\theta & 0 \\ -\sin\theta & \cos\theta & 0 \\ 0 & 0 & 1 \end{bmatrix}$$

The matrix that undoes the effect of $\mathbf{T}$, and shifts the centre back to its original position, can be seen to be

$$\begin{bmatrix} 1 & 0 & 0 \\ 0 & 1 & 0 \\ h & k & 1 \end{bmatrix}$$

and as applying this immediately after $\mathbf{T}$ would leave things unchanged, this matrix is the inverse of $\mathbf{T}$, called $\mathbf{T}^{-1}$ (this idea was discussed in Section 8.4). Thus the sequence of matrices to perform this non-standard rotation is given by

$$\mathbf{M} = \mathbf{T}\,\mathbf{R}\,\mathbf{T}^{-1}$$

and we have

$$\mathbf{M} = \begin{bmatrix} 1 & 0 & 0 \\ 0 & 1 & 0 \\ -h & -k & 1 \end{bmatrix} \begin{bmatrix} \cos\theta & \sin\theta & 0 \\ -\sin\theta & \cos\theta & 0 \\ 0 & 0 & 1 \end{bmatrix} \begin{bmatrix} 1 & 0 & 0 \\ 0 & 1 & 0 \\ h & k & 1 \end{bmatrix}$$

first shift to O   *then* rotate   *then* shift back

When these matrices are multiplied together, $\mathbf{T}$ by $\mathbf{R}$ and then the result by $\mathbf{T}^{-1}$, say, the result is:

$$\mathbf{M} = \begin{bmatrix} \cos\theta & \sin\theta & 0 \\ -\sin\theta & \cos\theta & 0 \\ h(1-\cos\theta)+k\sin\theta & k(1-\cos\theta)-h\sin\theta & 1 \end{bmatrix}$$

This looks cumbersome and it is unnecessary to memorize it. It may be quoted, or else calculations can be done easily from the initial matrices, as we show in the following example.

Example 12.1 Applying a specific rotation

We will find the single matrix $\mathbf{M}$ that will cause all the points in the plane to be rotated through an angle of 90° about the point C(4, 3), as shown in Figure 12.2. Then we will look in particular at the result of applying $\mathbf{M}$ to the point P(6, 3).

We can deal with this in one of two ways. On the one hand we can multiply the following three matrices:

$$\begin{bmatrix} 1 & 0 & 0 \\ 0 & 1 & 0 \\ -4 & -3 & 1 \end{bmatrix} \begin{bmatrix} \cos 90° & \sin 90° & 0 \\ -\sin 90° & \cos 90° & 0 \\ 0 & 0 & 1 \end{bmatrix} \begin{bmatrix} 1 & 0 & 0 \\ 0 & 1 & 0 \\ 4 & 3 & 1 \end{bmatrix}$$

which is quite straightforward in this case once we obtain the values '$\cos 90° = 0$' and '$\sin 90° = 1$' from a calculator. Alternatively we can use these trigonometric values, and also the values of '$h = 4$' and '$k = 3$' that are given, and insert them all directly into the combined matrix $\mathbf{M}$, as written above. In this latter case, we have

$$h(1-\cos\theta) + k\sin\theta = 4(1-0) + (3 \times 1)$$

$$= (4 \times 1) + (3 \times 1)$$

$$= 4 + 3$$

$$= 7$$

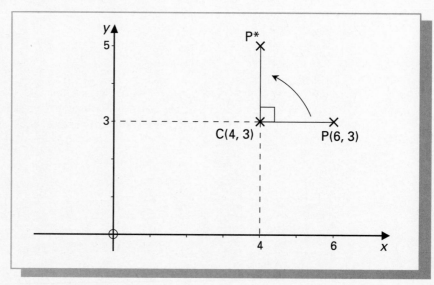

Figure 12.2 Rotation through 90° about C.

and

$$k(1 - \cos\theta) - h\sin\theta = 3(1 - 0) - (4 \times 1)$$

$$= (3 \times 1) - (4 \times 1)$$

$$= 3 - 4$$

$$= -1$$

In either case, we can calculate the resulting single matrix to be

$$\mathbf{M} = \begin{bmatrix} 0 & 1 & 0 \\ -1 & 0 & 0 \\ 7 & -1 & 1 \end{bmatrix}$$

We illustrate this result by applying $\mathbf{M}$ to the point P(6, 3), shown in Figure 12.2. The homogeneous vector is (6   3   1), so we multiply as follows:

$$(6 \quad 3 \quad 1) \begin{bmatrix} 0 & 1 & 0 \\ -1 & 0 & 0 \\ 7 & -1 & 1 \end{bmatrix} = (-3 + 7 \quad 6 - 1 \quad 1)$$

$$= (4 \quad 5 \quad 1)$$

The coordinates of the transformed point P* are (4, 5), and it is obvious from Figure 12.2 that we have performed the required rotation through 90°.

12.3 Reflection in an arbitrary line

Since we have already dealt with plane reflections in the two axes, and in any line that passes through the origin, we are here dealing with the general case and shall assume that the fixed line which is to be the axis of reflection does not pass through the origin. As shown in Figure 12.3, we take it to be the line L, with y-intercept at (0, k) and inclined at an angle θ to the direction of the positive x-axis. After reflection the point P will be transformed to P*; P and P* are equidistant from the line L and on opposite sides of it.

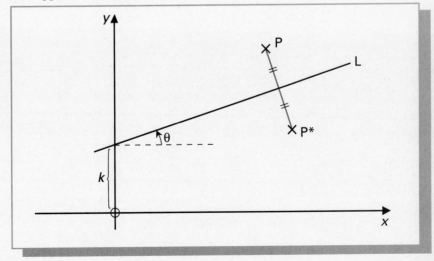

Figure 12.3 Reflection in an arbitrary line.

As with the other non-standard transformations, we achieve the result by applying a sequence of simpler transformations. There are five stages involved here. First we apply the transformation that moves all points up or down (in the direction of the y-axis) so that L passes through the origin; next we rotate all points through $(-\theta)$ about the origin, making L lie along the x-axis; next we perform a reflection in the x-axis. Then we 'undo' these transformations: we rotate through $(+\theta)$ about the origin, so that L is in its original orientation and finally we shift in the direction of the y-axis so that L is back in its original position. As in the earlier example we use homogeneous vectors throughout, and the transforming matrices are (3×3) even though all the operations are being done within the plane. The matrices now follow. The matrix to shift up/down so that L passes through the origin is

$$
\mathbf{T} = \begin{bmatrix} 1 & 0 & 0 \\ 0 & 1 & 0 \\ 0 & -k & 1 \end{bmatrix}
$$

The matrix that rotates the line L so that it lies along the direction of the x-axis is

$$
\mathbf{R} = \begin{bmatrix} \cos(-\theta) & \sin(-\theta) & 0 \\ -\sin(-\theta) & \cos(-\theta) & 0 \\ 0 & 0 & 1 \end{bmatrix}
$$

which becomes, using results from Section 1.5,

$$
\mathbf{R} = \begin{bmatrix} \cos\theta & -\sin\theta & 0 \\ \sin\theta & \cos\theta & 0 \\ 0 & 0 & 1 \end{bmatrix}
$$

The matrix that causes a reflection in the x-axis is

$$
\mathbf{X} = \begin{bmatrix} 1 & 0 & 0 \\ 0 & -1 & 0 \\ 0 & 0 & 1 \end{bmatrix}
$$

In order to undo the effect of $\mathbf{R}$ we have the inverse of $\mathbf{R}$ which causes a rotation through an angle $(+\theta)$ about the origin, namely

$$
\mathbf{R}^{-1} = \begin{bmatrix} \cos\theta & \sin\theta & 0 \\ -\sin\theta & \cos\theta & 0 \\ 0 & 0 & 1 \end{bmatrix}
$$

and to undo the effect of $\mathbf{T}$ we have its inverse $\mathbf{T}^{-1}$ which shifts everything back into its original position:

$$
\mathbf{T}^{-1} = \begin{bmatrix} 1 & 0 & 0 \\ 0 & 1 & 0 \\ 0 & k & 1 \end{bmatrix}
$$

Thus the sequence of matrices needed to perform this non–standard reflection is

$$
\mathbf{M} = \mathbf{T}\,\mathbf{R}\,\mathbf{X}\,\mathbf{R}^{-1}\,\mathbf{T}^{-1}
$$

When these matrices are multiplied together (remembering to maintain this given order) the result is

$$\mathbf{M} = \begin{bmatrix} \cos^2\theta - \sin^2\theta & 2\sin\theta \cdot \cos\theta & 0 \\ 2\sin\theta \cdot \cos\theta & \sin^2\theta - \cos^2\theta & 0 \\ -2k \cdot \sin\theta \cdot \cos\theta & -k\sin^2\theta + k\cos^2\theta + k & 1 \end{bmatrix}$$

and by applying the formulae for double angles, stated in Appendix C, we simplify this to:

$$\mathbf{M} = \begin{bmatrix} \cos 2\theta & \sin 2\theta & 0 \\ \sin 2\theta & -\cos 2\theta & 0 \\ -k\sin 2\theta & k + k\cos 2\theta & 1 \end{bmatrix}$$

We shall use this matrix in the example which follows.

Example 12.2 Applying a specific reflection

We now determine the single matrix that causes all the points in the plane to be reflected in the line with Cartesian equation $y = \frac{1}{2}x + 2$. Then we apply this matrix to reflect the triangle with vertices at A(2, 4), B(4, 6) and C(2, 6) in the line.

The line with Cartesian equation $y = \frac{1}{2}x + 2$ is shown in Figure 12.4: as we explained in Section 7.1, it has gradient $\frac{1}{2}$, and it cuts the y-axis at the point where $y = 2$.

From the diagram we see that the value of k is 2; since the value of the gradient is $\frac{1}{2}$ it means that '$\tan \theta = \frac{1}{2}$' so from a calculator we can obtain $\theta \approx 26.57°$. Thus $2\theta \approx 53.13°$, and hence $\cos 2\theta = 0.6$ and $\sin 2\theta = 0.8$. We put these values into the matrix $\mathbf{M}$ which gives

$$\mathbf{M} = \begin{bmatrix} 0.6 & 0.8 & 0 \\ 0.8 & -0.6 & 0 \\ -1.6 & 3.2 & 1 \end{bmatrix}$$

To reflect the given triangle in the line, we first convert the position vectors of its vertices into homogeneous vectors, and then multiply them by the matrix M (this is the method used in Section 9.5.). Thus we have:

$$\begin{matrix} A \\ B \\ C \end{matrix} \begin{bmatrix} 2 & 4 & 1 \\ 4 & 6 & 1 \\ 2 & 6 & 1 \end{bmatrix} \begin{bmatrix} 0.6 & 0.8 & 0 \\ 0.8 & -0.6 & 0 \\ -1.6 & 3.2 & 1 \end{bmatrix} = \begin{bmatrix} 2.8 & 2.4 & 1 \\ 5.6 & 2.8 & 1 \\ 4.4 & 1.2 & 1 \end{bmatrix} \begin{matrix} A* \\ B* \\ C* \end{matrix}$$

The transformed triangle A*B*C*, with vertices at (2.8, 2.4), (5.6, 2.8) and (4.4, 1.2), is shown in Figure 12.4. It is clearly the result of the reflection in the given line.

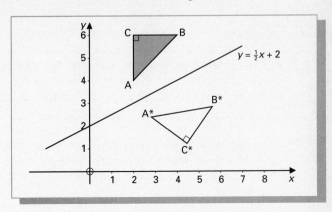

Figure 12.4 Reflection in a given line.

12.4 The viewing transformation

One of the skills of graphical work is to be selective in the reproduction of images. It is unlikely that the whole of an object, taking up the entire screen display, will be a satisfactory representation for many purposes. It is more likely that attention will be paid to just part of an object, positioned in a particular section of the screen, and to do this we employ what is known as the **viewing transformation**.

We imagine that we are considering a simplified, two-dimensional view of a real object, for instance the front of a house; if the whole of this appears in the entire display screen, then we have the situation shown in Figure 12.5. The bottom (horizontal) and left (vertical) edges of the screen are interpreted as the x- and y-axes respectively, and the coordinates on the screen are **normalized** so that they all lie between 0 and 1. Thus while positions on the 'real' house might be measured in metres, horizontally and vertically from some point chosen to be an origin, the coordinates of corresponding points on the screen will usually all be positive numbers less than one.

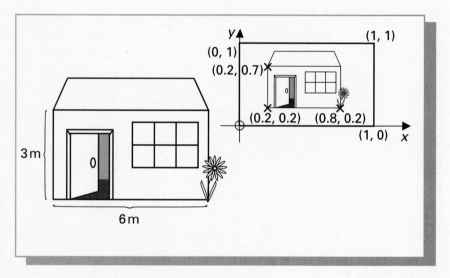

Figure 12.5 An object and its image on a viewing screen.

Instead of viewing a whole object, it is usual to focus on just part of it, and this is termed the viewing **window**. For real applications of this technique it is obvious that many different shapes of window will be used; however, for our present purposes we shall concentrate on **rectangular windows**. Sometimes the entire screen will be used to display the contents of a window, but sometimes just part of the screen, called a **viewport**, will be used for the display; these two situations are illustrated in Figure 12.6.

Before coming to the calculations by which 'real' measurements taken from a window on an object can be transformed to give us coordinates on an image in a

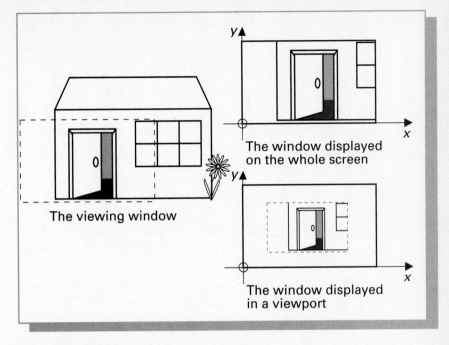

Figure 12.6 The window and the viewport.

viewport, let us consider the illustrations in Figure 12.7(a) and (b). As each window defines the area of interest on the object, and every viewport is an area whose position on the viewing screen is defined, we see that it is quite possible to have different windows appearing in the same viewport and also the same window appearing in different viewports.

We now consider the viewing transformation itself: by this we take the coordinates of points on that part of the object in a designated window, and transform them to give the coordinates of the corresponding points in the appropriate viewport on the screen. As with all the non-standard transformations, we employ a sequence of simple operations, each of which is performed by one of the matrices we have already met. There are three operations in the sequence. First we have the 'window shift', when we shift the lower left corner of the window to the origin on the object; next we scale the window dimensions to the dimensions of the viewport, and imagine the two origins to be coincident; finally we have the 'viewport shift', when we shift the lower left corner of the viewport from the screen origin to its proper position. We use the coordinates and dimensions shown in Figure 12.8, and see that the matrices are as follows. The window shift is given by

$$\mathbf{W} = \begin{bmatrix} 1 & 0 & 0 \\ 0 & 1 & 0 \\ -a & -b & 1 \end{bmatrix}$$

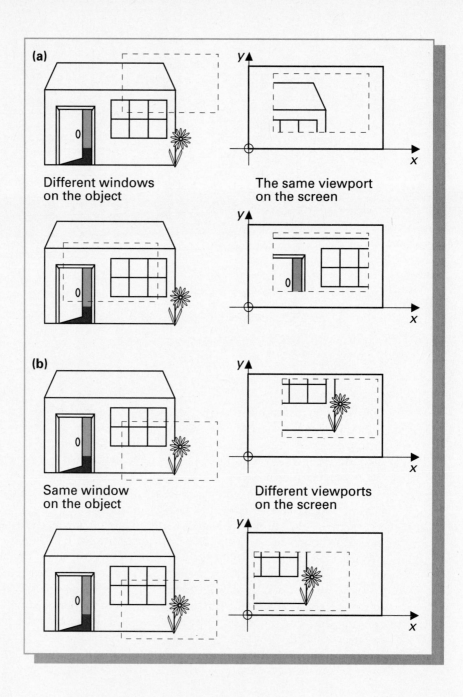

Figure 12.7 (a) Different windows, same viewport.
(b) Same window, different viewports.

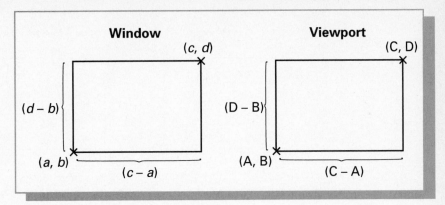

Figure 12.8 Notation for the viewing transformation.

The scaling involves a factor of $\dfrac{(C - A)}{(c - a)}$ in the x-direction, and $\dfrac{(D - B)}{(d - b)}$ in the y-direction, so the matrix for local scaling is

$$S = \begin{bmatrix} \dfrac{(C - A)}{(c - a)} & 0 & 0 \\ 0 & \dfrac{(D - B)}{(d - b)} & 0 \\ 0 & 0 & 1 \end{bmatrix}$$

The viewport shift is given by

$$V = \begin{bmatrix} 1 & 0 & 0 \\ 0 & 1 & 0 \\ A & B & 1 \end{bmatrix}$$

Multiplying these matrices in order we get

$$M = W\,S\,V$$

which is the matrix which performs this viewing transformation.

We complete this chapter with an example to illustrate the viewing transformation.

Example 12.3 Applying a viewing transformation

Part of a picture of some faces (the 'object') is to be displayed on part of a screen whose coordinate system has been normalized in the standard way. We shall describe the three transformations to transform the window shown in Figure 12.9 to the viewport indicated. In addition we shall use matrix methods to calculate the coordinates of the labelled point where it appears on the screen.

The three transformations are: first we shift the point H to the origin on the object; next we scale the dimensions in the x- and y-directions; and lastly we shift from the origin on the image to the point K.

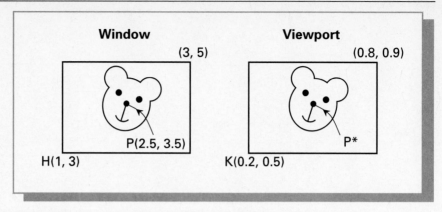

Figure 12.9 The viewing transformation from picture to screen.

The matrix for the window shift is

$$W = \begin{bmatrix} 1 & 0 & 0 \\ 0 & 1 & 0 \\ -1 & -3 & 1 \end{bmatrix}$$

The scaling matrix is

$$S = \begin{bmatrix} \dfrac{0.8 - 0.2}{3 - 1} & 0 & 0 \\ 0 & \dfrac{0.9 - 0.5}{5 - 3} & 0 \\ 0 & 0 & 1 \end{bmatrix}$$

$$= \begin{bmatrix} 0.3 & 0 & 0 \\ 0 & 0.2 & 0 \\ 0 & 0 & 1 \end{bmatrix}$$

The matrix for the viewport shift is

$$V = \begin{bmatrix} 1 & 0 & 0 \\ 0 & 1 & 0 \\ 0.2 & 0.5 & 1 \end{bmatrix}$$

When we multiply these three matrices together (remembering that order matters) we get

$$M = W\,S\,V$$

$$= \begin{bmatrix} 0.3 & 0 & 0 \\ 0 & 0.2 & 0 \\ -0.1 & -0.1 & 1 \end{bmatrix}$$

The point P has coordinates (2.5, 3.5) so its homogeneous vector is (2.5 3.5 1). We multiply this by the matrix M and obtain:

$$(2.5 \quad 3.5 \quad 1) \begin{bmatrix} 0.3 & 0 & 0 \\ 0 & 0.2 & 0 \\ -0.1 & -0.1 & 1 \end{bmatrix} = (0.65 \quad 0.6 \quad 1)$$

Thus the coordinates of P* in the viewport are (0.65, 0.6)

When the window or the viewport are not rectangular then more involved methods, beyond our present scope, are employed to perform the viewing transformation.

Exercises

12.1 Write down the sequence of three (3×3) matrices that will cause a rotation through $\pi/4$ anticlockwise, in the x–y plane, about the point with coordinates $(3, 1)$. Consider the triangle PQR, where the vertices have coordinates $(6, 1)$, $(8, 2)$ and $(7, 3)$ respectively, and calculate the new coordinates of its vertices after it has been so rotated.

12.2 The quadrilateral KLMN whose vertices have coordinates K(4, 1), L(5, 2), M(6, 4) and N(4$\frac{1}{2}$, 3) is reflected in the line $y = 2x - 1$. Use matrix methods to calculate the coordinates of the transformed vertices.

12.3 Part of a picture of a field of daisies (the 'object') is to be displayed on part of a screen as indicated in Figure 12.10. The coordinate system on the screen has been 'normalized' in the standard way. Describe the sequence of transformations that will transform the window shown to the viewport indicated, and give the matrix for each. Calculate the coordinates of the labelled point where it appears on the screen.

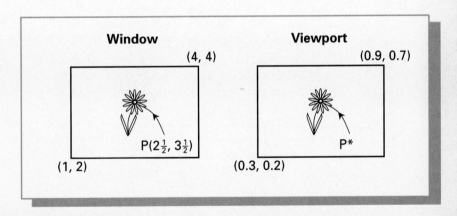

Figure 12.10 For Exercise 12.3.

Answers

12.1 $\begin{bmatrix} 1 & 0 & 0 \\ 0 & 1 & 0 \\ -3 & -1 & 1 \end{bmatrix}$, $\begin{bmatrix} 0.71 & 0.71 & 0 \\ -0.71 & 0.71 & 0 \\ 0 & 0 & 1 \end{bmatrix}$, $\begin{bmatrix} 1 & 0 & 0 \\ 0 & 1 & 0 \\ 3 & 1 & 1 \end{bmatrix}$; P*(5.13, 3.13), Q*(5.84, 5.26), R*(4.42, 5.26).

12.2 K*(−0.8, 3.4), L*(−0.6, 4.8), M*(0.4, 6.8), N*(0.5, 5).

12.3 (0.6, 0.58).

Into the third dimension:
Moving along rays, points at infinity, and three-dimensional transformations

13.1 Geometrical insights using homogeneous vectors

Homogeneous vectors were introduced in Chapter 10 to facilitate the application of graphical transformations, especially translations. In Section 11.2 we gave examples to show how there is no unique set of components for a homogeneous vector that corresponds to the position vector of any point in the Cartesian plane: $(12 \quad 6 \quad 3)$, $(8 \quad 4 \quad 2)$, $(2 \quad 1 \quad \frac{1}{2})$ and $(4 \quad 2 \quad 1)$ all represent the same 'physical' point. However, when the third component is '1' we can immediately identify the coordinates of the 'physical' point. Thus the homogeneous vector $(4 \quad 2 \quad 1)$ above tells us that the position vector of the 'physical' point is $(4 \quad 2)$ and hence its coordinates are $(4, 2)$; more generally the homogeneous vector $(X \quad Y \quad 1)$ gives the position vector of the 'physical' point as $(X \quad Y)$, and its coordinates (X, Y).

In effect, so that we can perform all the required two-dimensional transformations by matrix multiplication, we have introduced a third component into the position vectors; these are now of the form $(x \quad y \quad z)$, though when we are considering the coordinates of the 'physical' points we require that $z = 1$. Hence, in a sense, results of two-dimensional transformations can be considered as being in three dimensions, but lying in the plane $z = 1$. This 'physical plane', containing the 'physical point' with position vector $(4 \quad 2 \quad 1)$, is shown in Figure 13.1.

It is interesting to consider how points with coordinates such as P$(4 \quad 2 \quad 1)$ and Q$(12 \quad 6 \quad 3)$, which represent the same 'physical' point, are related graphically, since this will also help us to understand what is meant by a 'point at infinity'. As illustrated in Figure 13.2, P is already a point on the plane $z = 1$, whereas Q is lying in the plane $z = 3$. When we consider the position vector from the origin to P, and extend it outwards for a (potentially) unlimited distance, we have what is termed a **ray**. This ray through P cuts the plane $z = 3$ at precisely the point Q. You will easily see that the points with vectors $(8 \quad 4 \quad 2)$ and $(2 \quad 1 \quad \frac{1}{2})$ are also located on this ray, but situated in different z-planes. All the points with homogeneous vectors $(4c \quad 2c \quad c)$, where c is any non-zero number, are located on this ray: their position vectors lie along the ray. Thus in seeking to find the 'physical' point corresponding to any homogeneous vector, we move along this ray from the origin until we intersect with the plane $z = 1$; this point of intersection is the 'physical' point.

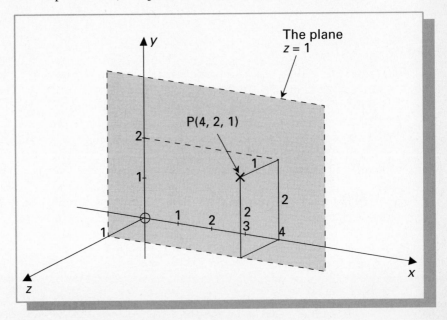

Figure 13.1 The 'physical' point on the plane $z = 1$.

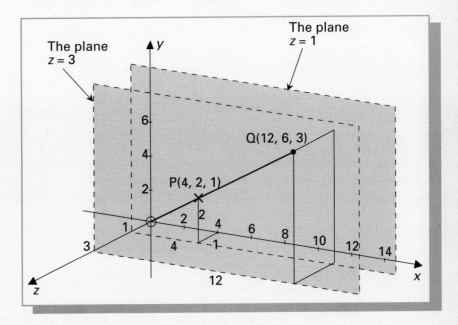

Figure 13.2 Points along a ray from O.

13.2 Completing consideration of (3 × 3) matrices

In Section 11.3, we omitted any reference to matrices for two-dimensional transformations that have the elements indicated here

$$\begin{bmatrix} * & * & p \\ * & * & q \\ * & * & * \end{bmatrix}$$

We can now, briefly, satisfy curiosity about these two remaining elements p and q; the particular type of transformation they cause is not used in computer graphics, but the sort of calculations involved will soon be seen (in the context of three-dimensional perspective) to be very important. The effect of these two remaining elements p and q in the general transformation matrix can be described using the ideas of rays. When a homogeneous vector is multiplied by a matrix in which they occur, it is transformed so that it lies along a different ray, *and* its end point is situated in a different z-plane. Then in order to appreciate the 'physical' point that results we move back along the transformed vector to the $z = 1$ plane. The way in which the calculations are done (though not the end result) bears a strong resemblance to the way in which we deal with **perspective** in three dimensions.

We take the matrix

$$\begin{bmatrix} 1 & 0 & p \\ 0 & 1 & q \\ 0 & 0 & 1 \end{bmatrix}$$

and determine its effect on the point P(2, 3). We note that in terms of its rotation group, translation elements and overall scaling this matrix is as straightforward as possible: there are no changes caused by these elements. We apply now it to the homogeneous vector associated with P, which is (2 3 1):

$$(2 \quad 3 \quad 1) \times \begin{bmatrix} 1 & 0 & p \\ 0 & 1 & q \\ 0 & 0 & 1 \end{bmatrix} = (2 \quad 3 \quad 2p + 3q + 1)$$

The x- and y-coordinates are unchanged, but we have changed the z-coordinate; the transformed point is no longer in the plane $z = 1$, but in the plane $z = 2p + 3q + 1$. In order to obtain the 'physical' point we move back along the ray onto the plane $z = 1$. As in Section 11.2, we do this arithmetically by dividing each coordinate by $(2p + 3q + 1)$ so that the last coordinate becomes '1'. We obtain:

$$(2 \quad 3 \quad 2p + 3q + 1) \equiv \left(\frac{2}{2p + 3q + 1} \quad \frac{3}{2p + 3q + 1} \quad 1 \right)$$

so the coordinates of the transformed point, on the plane $z = 1$, are

$$\left(\frac{2}{2p + 3q + 1}, \frac{3}{2p + 3q + 1} \right)$$

In the example that follows we show that the effect obtained by taking a (3 × 3) matrix where the p and q entries are not zero, and applying it to homogeneous vectors which correspond to points in a plane, can be quite unexpected.

Example 13.1 Transforming back into the physical plane

The straight line PQ has end points with coordinates P(2, 3) and Q(6, 7). Using homogeneous vectors we shall transform this line and find its image under multiplication by the matrix

$$\mathbf{M} = \begin{bmatrix} 1 & 0 & 1 \\ 0 & 1 & 1 \\ 0 & 0 & 1 \end{bmatrix}$$

The homogeneous vectors are P(2 3 1) and Q(6 7 1); as previously, we multiply them by **M** in a single calculation:

$$\begin{array}{c} P \\ Q \end{array} \begin{bmatrix} 2 & 3 & 1 \\ 6 & 7 & 1 \end{bmatrix} \times \begin{bmatrix} 1 & 0 & 1 \\ 0 & 1 & 1 \\ 0 & 0 & 1 \end{bmatrix} = \begin{bmatrix} 2 & 3 & 6 \\ 6 & 7 & 14 \end{bmatrix} \begin{array}{c} P^* \\ Q^* \end{array}$$

The transformed points P* and Q* are in different z-planes, so to obtain the 'physical' points we move back onto the plane $z = 1$:

$$P^*(2 \quad 3 \quad 6) \equiv \left(\frac{2}{6} \quad \frac{3}{6} \quad \frac{6}{6} \right) = \left(\frac{1}{3} \quad \frac{1}{2} \quad 1 \right) P^{\#}$$

$$Q^*(6 \quad 7 \quad 14) \equiv \left(\frac{6}{14} \quad \frac{7}{14} \quad \frac{14}{14} \right) = \left(\frac{3}{7} \quad \frac{1}{2} \quad 1 \right) Q^{\#}$$

Thus the coordinates of the image points $P^{\#}$ and $Q^{\#}$ in the plane $z = 1$ are $P^{\#}(\frac{1}{3}, \frac{1}{2})$ and $Q^{\#}(\frac{3}{7}, \frac{1}{2})$ and the results of this transformation are shown in Figure 13.3.

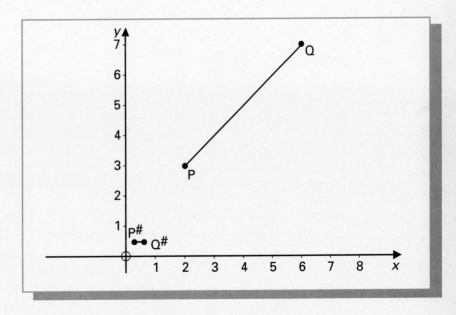

Figure 13.3 The result of applying 'elements p and q' in two dimensions.

13.3 Points at infinity

In all the calculations performed so far on homogeneous vectors we have been very careful to ensure that the last entry is non-zero: we have only dealt with $(x \quad y \quad h)$ when $h \neq 0$. But the special case where the last entry is zero (that is, $h = 0$) is very useful and important: homogeneous vectors of the form $(x \quad y \quad 0)$ give us **points at infinity**. The concept of a point at infinity is fundamental in the consideration of parallel lines. For instance, the sun is so far away from the earth that it can be thought of as a 'point at infinity', and the rays of light that reach us from the sun are effectively parallel. 'Points at infinity' are the idea used when we consider parallel lines continuing for so far into the distance that they appear to converge; an illustration commonly given is that railway lines appear to meet at a point in the far distance. In particular, a point at infinity is used in the calculation for the **vanishing point** which occurs in perspective constructions involving parallel lines.

However, before considering three-dimensional implications of points at infinity we first look in more detail at points at infinity in two dimensions. All the homogeneous vectors $(cX \quad cY \quad c)$, where $c \neq 0$, represent the same 'physical' point (X, Y); but what happens if we consider the homogeneous vector $(X \quad Y \quad h)$ and then, while X and Y remain fixed, we let the number h get smaller and smaller until it is nearly indistinguishable from zero? 'In the limit', as h goes on getting smaller, we (almost) reach the point with coordinates $(X \quad Y \quad 0)$, that is, a point at infinity. Using the technique of Section 11.2 we now investigate a pattern to see what graphical meaning we can give to this point. We take different homogeneous vectors with their first components the same, namely 3 and 2; when the third component is $h = 1$ we have

$$(3 \quad 2 \quad 1),$$

$h = \frac{1}{2}$ gives

$$(3 \quad 2 \quad \tfrac{1}{2}) \equiv (6 \quad 4 \quad 1)$$

$h = \frac{1}{4}$ gives

$$(3 \quad 2 \quad \tfrac{1}{4}) \equiv (12 \quad 8 \quad 1)$$

$h = \frac{1}{8}$ gives

$$(3 \quad 2 \quad \tfrac{1}{8}) \equiv (24 \quad 16 \quad 1)$$

$h = \frac{1}{10}$ gives

$$(3 \quad 2 \quad \tfrac{1}{10}) \equiv (30 \quad 20 \quad 1)$$

$h = \frac{1}{50}$ gives

$$(3 \quad 2 \quad \tfrac{1}{50}) \equiv (150 \quad 100 \quad 1)$$

$h = \frac{1}{100}$ gives

$$(3 \quad 2 \quad \tfrac{1}{100}) \equiv (300 \quad 200 \quad 1)$$

$h = \frac{1}{1000}$ gives

$$(3 \quad 2 \quad \tfrac{1}{1000}) \equiv (3000 \quad 2000 \quad 1)$$

and so on. We see that the coordinates of these 'physical' points, lying in the plane $z = 1$, all satisfy the relationship '$y = \frac{2}{3}x$', so that they all lie on the straight line shown in Figure 13.4. This straight line passes through the point where $x = 0$ and $y = 0$ in the plane $z = 1$ and has gradient $\frac{2}{3}$. As the value of h decreases, so the points on this line get further from $(0, 0)$ in this plane. It is reasonable to say that as h becomes indistinguishable from zero, so the coordinates of the corresponding point become infinitely far from $(0, 0)$ and we get a point at infinity, $(3 \quad 2 \quad 0)$. This is the point at infinity along the direction of the line $y = \frac{2}{3}x$ as indicated, in the first quadrant.

At either end of every (infinitely long) line in the plane there is a point at infinity. It is the point whose homogeneous vector has its third component zero, and the first two components satisfy the Cartesian equation of the line; some examples are indicated in Figure 13.5. In general the homogeneous vector $(X \quad Y \quad 0)$ is the point at infinity in the direction specified by the pair of direction cosines

$$\begin{cases} \cos \alpha = \dfrac{X}{\sqrt{X^2 + Y^2}} \\[3mm] \cos \beta = \dfrac{Y}{\sqrt{X^2 + Y^2}} \end{cases}$$

as described in Example 2.4. It is important to recognize that all lines pointing in a particular direction have the same point at infinity.

In computer graphics work, the most commonly used points at infinity are for lines in the directions of the axes. For two-dimensional work we note that $(1 \quad 0 \quad 0)$ is the point at infinity for lines in the direction of the positive x-axis and $(-1 \quad 0 \quad 0)$ is the point at infinity for lines in the direction of the negative x-axis. Other points at infinity include: $(0 \quad 1 \quad 0)$ for lines in the direction of the positive y-axis, $(0 \quad -1 \quad 0)$ for lines in the direction of the negative y-axis, $(1 \quad 1 \quad 0)$ for lines in the direction of the line $y = x$ (in the first quadrant), and so on.

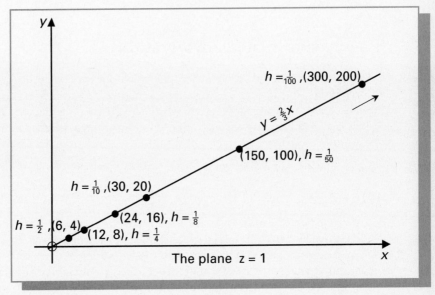

Figure 13.4 Approaching the point at infinity along the line $y = \frac{2}{3}x$, as h gets smaller.

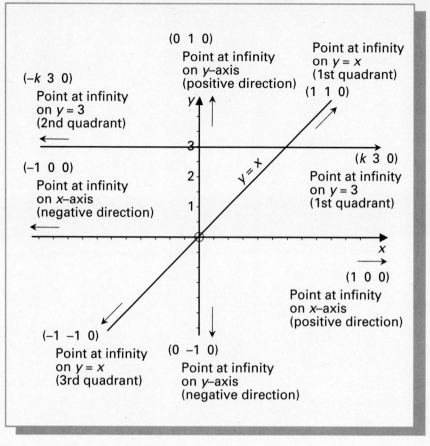

Figure 13.5 Some points at infinity.

13.4 Three-dimensional transformations

We can now extend our knowledge of two-dimensional transformations to the three-dimensional case. We start by gathering the results in Section 11.3 and Section 13.2 into the 'do everything' matrix for two-dimensional transformations. This is a (3×3) matrix which acts on the homogeneous vectors of two-dimensional position vectors:

$$\begin{bmatrix} a & b & p \\ c & d & q \\ h & k & s \end{bmatrix}$$

and its elements form the rotation group $\{a, b, c, d\}$, the translation elements $\{h, k\}$, the element for overall scaling $\{s\}$, and those for moving along a ray $\{p, q\}$.

When we proceed to consider the transformations of three-dimensional objects, each point has its 'physical' position described by three coordinates (see Sections 1.4 and 3.3), as shown in Figure 13.6. The coordinates of the point P shown are (X, Y, Z), and its position vector **OP** is $(X \quad Y \quad Z)$ or $X\mathbf{i} + Y\mathbf{j} + Z\mathbf{k}$ in component

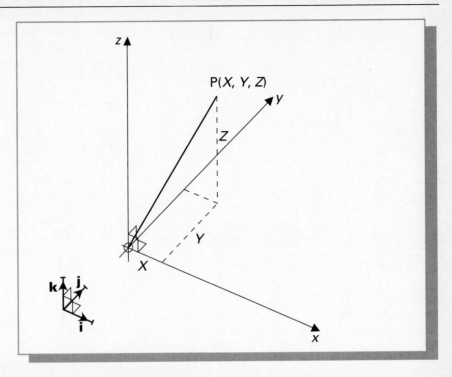

Figure 13.6 A point in three dimensions.

form. We can apply the standard transformations of local scaling (in the x-, y- or z-direction), reflection (in the y–z, z–x or x–y plane), and rotation (about an axis) by multiplying each of the 'physical' position vectors by a (3×3) matrix; the methods are completely analogous to those used for two dimensions. However, in order to be able to deal with translation and overall scaling, we must introduce homogeneous vectors for three dimensions. We have the same basic idea as before: the 'physical' position vector $(X \quad Y \quad Z)$ has a homogeneous vector $(X \quad Y \quad Z \quad 1)$. As in Section 11.2, whenever the final component is a '1' then we can immediately identify the 'physical' coordinates (X, Y, Z) of the point in question. If the final component is not '1' (but not zero either) then we obtain the 'physical' coordinates by dividing through by that last component; for example, the homogeneous vector $(2 \quad 6 \quad 4 \quad 2)$ is equivalent to $(1 \quad 3 \quad 2 \quad 1)$ by dividing through by 2, and the coordinates of the 'physical' point in space are therefore $(1, 3, 2)$.

Having developed the homogeneous vectors for three dimensions, we can perform all the standard transformations by multiplying by a (4×4) matrix. The 'do everything' (4×4) matrix is written

$$\begin{bmatrix} a & b & c & p \\ d & e & f & q \\ g & i & j & r \\ h & k & \ell & s \end{bmatrix}$$

and, as in the (3×3) case, groups of elements have different functions. These are briefly described in Figure 13.7 and summarized in Section 13.5. The elements p,

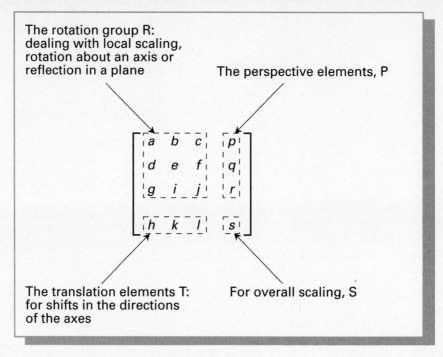

Figure 13.7 The 'do everything' (4 × 4) matrix.

q and r, and the perspective transformations they produce, will be dealt with more fully in the next two chapters.

13.5 Some specific (4 × 4) matrices

We complete this chapter by describing some simple (4 × 4) matrices and the standard three-dimensional transformations they produce. We note that, as with planar transformations, we deal with successive transformations of a point by the successive multiplications of its homogeneous vector by appropriate matrices: the order of these multiplications is all-important. As in the two-dimensional case, non-standard transformations are performed by combinations of simpler transformations; for example, rotation about a general axis is carried out by a sequence of translations and rotations, and reflection in an arbitrary plane is performed by a sequence of translations, rotations and reflection. The methods are straightforward extensions of those already employed in Chapter 12.

13.5.1 Local scaling

Local scaling, in the direction of an axis, is performed using a diagonal matrix as shown here. The result scales in any or all of the x-, y- or z-directions, depending on the values of a, e and j.

$$(x \quad y \quad z \quad 1) \begin{bmatrix} a & 0 & 0 & 0 \\ 0 & e & 0 & 0 \\ 0 & 0 & j & 0 \\ 0 & 0 & 0 & 1 \end{bmatrix} = (ax \quad ey \quad jz \quad 1)$$

13.5.2 Reflections in the coordinate planes

The matrix required to perform a single such reflection is a simplified version of a matrix for local scaling.

For a reflection in the *y–z* plane only the *x*-coordinate changes, so the form of the matrix is:

$$
\begin{bmatrix}
-1 & 0 & 0 & 0 \\
0 & 1 & 0 & 0 \\
0 & 0 & 1 & 0 \\
0 & 0 & 0 & 1
\end{bmatrix}
$$

For a reflection in the *z–x* plane only the *y*-coordinate changes, so the form of the matrix is:

$$
\begin{bmatrix}
1 & 0 & 0 & 0 \\
0 & -1 & 0 & 0 \\
0 & 0 & 1 & 0 \\
0 & 0 & 0 & 1
\end{bmatrix}
$$

For a reflection in the *x–y* plane only the *z*-coordinate changes, so the form of the matrix is:

$$
\begin{bmatrix}
1 & 0 & 0 & 0 \\
0 & 1 & 0 & 0 \\
0 & 0 & -1 & 0 \\
0 & 0 & 0 & 1
\end{bmatrix}
$$

13.5.3 Rotations about the coordinate axes

For each of these we use the trigonometric ratios (sine and cosine) of the angle of rotation.

When we rotate a point about the *x*-axis, through an angle θ, its *x*-coordinate is unaltered. Thus the first row and the first column in this matrix do not involve θ. For rotation about the *x*-axis the form of the matrix is:

$$
\begin{bmatrix}
1 & 0 & 0 & 0 \\
0 & \cos\theta & \sin\theta & 0 \\
0 & -\sin\theta & \cos\theta & 0 \\
0 & 0 & 0 & 1
\end{bmatrix}
$$

In a rotation through an angle ψ about the *z*-axis the *z*-cordinates of points are unchanged, and so the third row and the third column of the matrix will not involve ψ. A matrix for rotation about the *z*-axis is:

$$
\begin{bmatrix}
\cos\psi & \sin\psi & 0 & 0 \\
-\sin\psi & \cos\psi & 0 & 0 \\
0 & 0 & 1 & 0 \\
0 & 0 & 0 & 1
\end{bmatrix}
$$

When we rotate a point about the *y*-axis through an angle ϕ, then the *y*-coordinates are unchanged, and so it is the second row and the second column of the matrix that do not involve ϕ. There is an important difference to be noted in the pattern of the signs of the 'sin φ' terms in this case: this change is necessary to preserve the right-handed rotation convention (see Section 3.3). To rotate about the y-axis we have a matrix of this form:

$$\begin{bmatrix} \cos\phi & 0 & -\sin\phi & 0 \\ 0 & 1 & 0 & 0 \\ \sin\phi & 0 & \cos\phi & 0 \\ 0 & 0 & 0 & 1 \end{bmatrix}$$

13.5.4 Translation

The matrix for this transformation is just as we would expect, and gives the following result:

$$(x \quad y \quad z \quad 1)\begin{bmatrix} 1 & 0 & 0 & 0 \\ 0 & 1 & 0 & 0 \\ 0 & 0 & 1 & 0 \\ h & k & \ell & 1 \end{bmatrix}$$

$$= (\ (x + h) \quad (y + k) \quad (z + \ell) \quad 1)$$

13.5.5 Overall scaling

The final element, s, in the matrix governs overall scaling. When s < 1 then there is overall expansion, and when s > 1 there is overall contraction. The calculation follows this pattern:

$$(x \quad y \quad z \quad 1)\begin{bmatrix} 1 & 0 & 0 & 0 \\ 0 & 1 & 0 & 0 \\ 0 & 0 & 1 & 0 \\ 0 & 0 & 0 & s \end{bmatrix} = (x \quad y \quad z \quad s)$$

$$\equiv \left(\frac{x}{s} \quad \frac{y}{s} \quad \frac{z}{s} \quad 1\right)$$

13.5.6 In conclusion

It is a straightforward matter to demonstrate the action of each of the above matrices by applying it to a given point, for instance the point with coordinates (1, 1, 1) whose homogeneous vector is (1 1 1 1). The results may be calculated, and also displayed graphically. The exercises provide practice with the necessary manipulations.

As stated above, matrices that perform perspective transformations are considered later, in Chapters 14 and 15.

Exercises

13.1 Identify the coordinates in the 'physical plane' that are associated with these homogeneous vectors: a) (92 −44 4); b) (−19 21 5); c) (6 −11 0.4).

13.2 Identify the direction of each of these points at infinity: a) (6 8 0); b) (13 −7 0); c) (−5 3 0).

13.3 Give the coordinates of the points at infinity along the following lines, in the directions indicated:

a) $y = 4x$, in the 1st quadrant;

b) $y = \frac{1}{2}x$, in the 3rd quadrant;

c) $y = \frac{-x}{9}$, in the 4th quadrant.

13.4 Take the triangle PQR, where the vertices have coordinates P(1, 2), Q(2, 2), R(2, 1), and transform it using the matrix

$$\mathbf{M} = \begin{bmatrix} 1 & 0 & 3 \\ 0 & 1 & 1 \\ 0 & 0 & 1 \end{bmatrix}$$

to obtain the triangle P*Q*R*. Then move this result back onto the 'physical plane', $z = 1$, and obtain the coordinates of the vertices of the resulting triangle P#Q#R#.

13.5 Write down the separate (4×4) matrices which would produce each of the following transformations:

a) shift +0.5 in the x-direction, 0 in the y-direction and −0.2 in z-direction;

b) scale the z-coordinates to be half as large;

c) scale both the x-and y-coordinates to be twice as large;

d) rotate through an angle of $\pi/4$ about the x-axis;

e) rotate through an angle of $\pi/3$ about the y-axis;

f) reflect in the x–y plane, and then scale overall by a factor of 3;

g) rotate through an angle of π about the line passing through the points $(0, 0, 0)$ and $(1, 0, 1)$.

13.6 Provide a sketch of the line $y = 2z$ in the plane $x = 0$, and hence calculate the angle made between the plane $y = 2z$ and the plane $z = 0$.

Use this result to determine the matrix transformation which performs a reflection in the plane $y = 2z$, and calculate the coordinates of the point F*, which is the reflection of F(6, 2, 5) in this plane.

13.7 Calculate the single matrix which performs translations in the x-, y- and z-directions of −1, −1 and −1 respectively, followed by, successively, a +30° rotation about the x-axis and a +45° rotation about the y-axis. Apply this transformation to the unit cube with vertices at $(0, 0, 0)$, $(1, 0, 0)$, $(0, 1, 0)$, $(0, 0, 1)$, and state the coordinates of the vertices of the image formed.

13.8 We can define a **tilt** to be the transformation caused by first rotating about the x-axis and then rotating about the y-axis.

a) If the angle of rotation about the x-axis is θ, and the angle of rotation about the y-axis is ϕ, determine the general tilting matrix.

b) Determine the tilting matrix when $\theta = \phi = \pi/4$.

c) Does the order of performing the rotations matter?

Answers

13.1 a) $(23, -11)$; b) $(-3.8, 4.2)$; c) $(15, -27.5)$.

13.2 a) Along line $y = (4/3)x$, in 1st quadrant; b) along line $y = (-7/13)x$, in 4th quadrant; c) along line $y = (-3/5)x$, in 2nd quadrant.

13.3 a) $(1 \quad 4 \quad 0)$; b) $(-2 \quad -1 \quad 0)$; c) $(9 \quad -1 \quad 0)$.

13.4 $P^*(1 \quad 2 \quad 6)$, $Q^*(2 \quad 2 \quad 9)$, $R^*(2 \quad 1 \quad 8)$.

$P^{\#}(\frac{1}{6}, \frac{1}{3})$, $Q^{\#}(\frac{2}{9}, \frac{2}{9})$, $R^{\#}(\frac{1}{4}, \frac{1}{8})$.

13.5 a) $\begin{bmatrix} 1 & 0 & 0 & 0 \\ 0 & 1 & 0 & 0 \\ 0 & 0 & 1 & 0 \\ 0.5 & 0 & -0.2 & 1 \end{bmatrix}$; b) $\begin{bmatrix} 1 & 0 & 0 & 0 \\ 0 & 1 & 0 & 0 \\ 0 & 0 & \frac{1}{2} & 0 \\ 0 & 0 & 0 & 1 \end{bmatrix}$; c) $\begin{bmatrix} 2 & 0 & 0 & 0 \\ 0 & 2 & 0 & 0 \\ 0 & 0 & 1 & 0 \\ 0 & 0 & 0 & 1 \end{bmatrix}$

d) $\begin{bmatrix} 1 & 0 & 0 & 0 \\ 0 & 0.71 & 0.71 & 0 \\ 0 & -0.71 & 0.71 & 0 \\ 0 & 0 & 0 & 1 \end{bmatrix}$; e) $\begin{bmatrix} \frac{1}{2} & 0 & -0.87 & 0 \\ 0 & 1 & 0 & 0 \\ 0.87 & 0 & \frac{1}{2} & 0 \\ 0 & 0 & 0 & 1 \end{bmatrix}$;

f) $\begin{bmatrix} 1 & 0 & 0 & 0 \\ 0 & 1 & 0 & 0 \\ 0 & 0 & -1 & 0 \\ 0 & 0 & 0 & \frac{1}{3} \end{bmatrix}$; g) $\begin{bmatrix} 0 & 0 & 1 & 0 \\ 0 & -1 & 0 & 0 \\ 1 & 0 & 0 & 0 \\ 0 & 0 & 0 & 1 \end{bmatrix}$

13.6 $26.57°$; $\begin{bmatrix} 1 & 0 & 0 & 0 \\ 0 & 0.6 & 0.8 & 0 \\ 0 & 0.8 & -0.6 & 0 \\ 0 & 0 & 0 & 1 \end{bmatrix}$; $F^*(6, 5.2, -1.4)$.

13.7 $\begin{bmatrix} 0.71 & 0 & -0.71 & 0 \\ 0.35 & 0.87 & 0.35 & 0 \\ 0.61 & -0.5 & 0.61 & 0 \\ -1.67 & -0.37 & -0.26 & 1 \end{bmatrix}$

New coordinates: $(-1.67, -0.37, -0.26)$, $(-0.96, -0.37, -0.97)$,

$(-1.32, 0.5, 0.09)$, $(-1.06, -0.87, 0.35)$.

13.8 a) $\begin{bmatrix} \cos\phi & 0 & -\sin\phi & 0 \\ \sin\theta\sin\phi & \cos\theta & \sin\theta\cos\phi & 0 \\ \sin\phi\cos\theta & -\sin\theta & \cos\theta\cos\phi & 0 \\ 0 & 0 & 0 & 1 \end{bmatrix}$; b) $\begin{bmatrix} 0.71 & 0 & -0.71 & 0 \\ 0.5 & 0.71 & 0.5 & 0 \\ 0.5 & -0.71 & 0.5 & 0 \\ 0 & 0 & 0 & 1 \end{bmatrix}$

c) Yes.

14

Points of view:
Projection and single point perspective

14.1 Projection from three dimensions onto a plane

At the end of the last chapter we dealt with transforming three-dimensional objects using matrices. As explained, we identify points by their homogeneous vectors, and we multiply by (4×4) matrices to produce scalings, reflections, rotations and translations. We must remember that the objects and their transformed images are all three dimensional: they can be held inside the computer in numerical form, in terms of the coordinates of their points, but of course they cannot be viewed directly. In this form they do not have solid reality, but they exist inside the computer as electronic states of the hardware. If we wish to visualize these objects and images then the usual method is by means of the computer screen, as we indicated informally in Figure 1.3. The standard technique is to view a **projected image** or **projection** on the two-dimensional screen which we assume to be a planar surface.

We are all very familiar with the concept of representing three-dimensional images on a surface: in sketching, painting pictures, perhaps studying technical drawing or art appreciation, and understanding photographs and slides. Sometimes we might be prepared to say of an image on a page that it 'looks three dimensional'. In considering the images in Figure 14.1, some people might say that the one on the left 'is two dimensional' whereas the one on the right 'is three dimensional', but of course neither of them is three dimensional as they are both drawn on a two-dimensional page. The way they differ is that the right-hand image is drawn using perspective techniques to provide depth cues, but both are two-dimensional projections of a cube. The considerable conceptual difference between a truly three-dimensional image and a two-dimensional image can be highlighted by contrasting a statue of a woman with a painting of that woman: they are completely different forms of images.

The most straightforward way of considering a two-dimensional 'screen image' of a three-dimensional object is to imagine what might be thought of, naively, as similar to the shadow cast by the object onto the screen. We assume that a translucent screen is in a fixed position, in front of or behind the object when viewed from a given direction. The screen, which is the **plane of projection**, or the **viewing plane**, is usually taken to be one of the coordinate planes; the **viewing point** is from a fixed direction defined with respect to the coordinate axes.

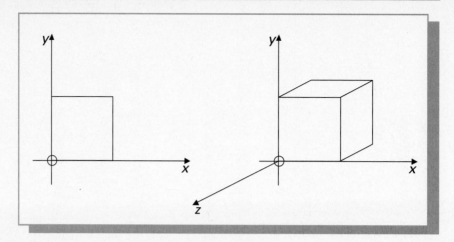

Figure 14.1 Different two-dimensional images of a cube.

To illustrate the idea of projection we next focus on one of the simplest types, called **orthographic projection**. This is a 'parallel plane projection', and is the projection most commonly used for the graphics needed in engineering drawing and in architectural plans. Its matrix happens to be the most straightforward to apply.

14.2 Orthographic projection

This projection delivers a planar image of a three-dimensional object, and we shall show its effect when any one of the three coordinate planes is the viewing plane. The object we shall deal with is a simplified model of a barn, as shown in Figure 14.2. In order to obtain an orthographic projection of an object, whenever possible we arrange for one of its plane faces to be set parallel to one of the coordinate

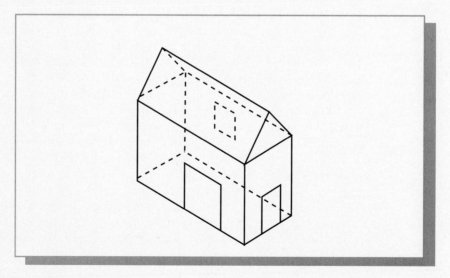

Figure 14.2 The model of a barn.

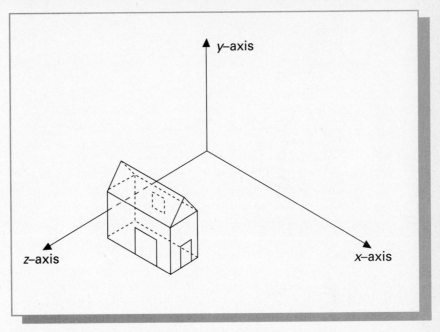

Figure 14.3 The plane faces of the barn arranged parallel to the coordinate planes.

planes; for this object, the barn, we can arrange for plane faces to be set parallel to all three of the coordinate planes (see Figure 14.3).

Consistent with other computer graphics applications, we arrange for the x- and

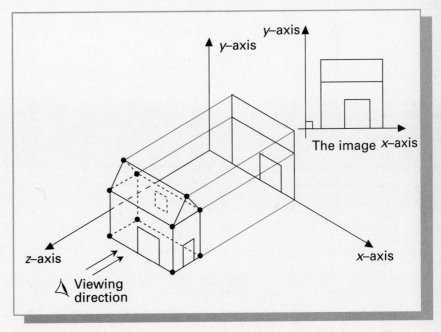

Figure 14.4 The barn projected onto the x–y plane, i.e. 'z=0', showing the 'projectors'.

z-axes to lie in the horizontal plane, with the y-axis vertically upwards. In Figure 14.4 we show the result of projecting the barn onto the x–y plane (that is the plane $z = 0$). The viewing point is (infinitely far away) along the positive z-axis, and so the **projectors**, the notional lines that join points on the barn to the corresponding points on its planar image, are parallel lines. The two-dimensional image does not show all the parts of the barn, and we see that much information is lost in the projection transformation; for example there is no information about the front door in this particular projection.

Figures 14.5 and 14.6 show the results of projecting the barn onto the plane $x = 0$ from a point infinitely far away along the positive x-axis, and onto the plane $y = 0$ from a point infinitely far away along the positive y-axis. Here, too, projection leads to significant amounts of information being lost; the window and side door do not appear in the first case, and neither the doors nor the window appear in the second case. Since the viewing points are all 'at infinity', in every case the projectors are parallel (the projectors are analogous to the sun's rays, and the projected image corresponds to a shadow of the barn).

The matrices that produce these transformations are clearly ones that keep unchanged two of the three coordinate values, but equally clearly they make the third coordinate zero and thus lose all the information carried by it. These matrices now follow.

For projection onto the x–y plane, where $z = 0$, the matrix is

$$\begin{bmatrix} 1 & 0 & 0 & 0 \\ 0 & 1 & 0 & 0 \\ 0 & 0 & 0 & 0 \\ 0 & 0 & 0 & 1 \end{bmatrix}$$

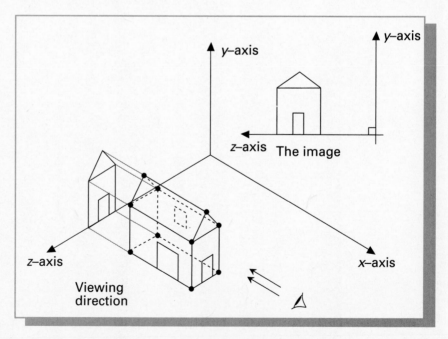

Figure 14.5 The barn projected onto the y–z plane, i.e. '$x = 0$', showing the projectors.

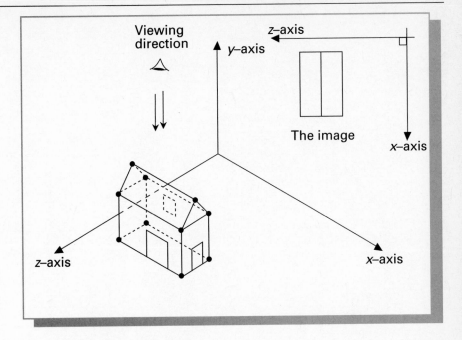

Figure 14.6 The barn projected onto the z–x plane, i.e. 'y = 0' (projectors not shown since barn is touching this plane).

We see that the third column contains only zeros, so the z-coordinate of every position vector becomes zero when multiplied by this matrix, as shown here:

$$(X \quad Y \quad Z \quad 1) \begin{bmatrix} 1 & 0 & 0 & 0 \\ 0 & 1 & 0 & 0 \\ 0 & 0 & 0 & 0 \\ 0 & 0 & 0 & 1 \end{bmatrix} = (X \quad Y \quad 0 \quad 1).$$

The physical coordinates of the transformed point are $(X, Y, 0)$; but in the plane of projection $z = 0$ the point has coordinates (X, Y).

For projection onto the y–z plane, that is the plane where $x = 0$, the matrix is

$$\begin{bmatrix} 0 & 0 & 0 & 0 \\ 0 & 1 & 0 & 0 \\ 0 & 0 & 1 & 0 \\ 0 & 0 & 0 & 1 \end{bmatrix}$$

Here the first column contains only zeros, so it is the x-coordinate of each position vector which becomes zero on multiplication.

Similarly for projection onto the z–x plane, where $y = 0$, we have the following matrix which makes the y-coordinate of each position vector zero on multiplication:

$$\begin{bmatrix} 1 & 0 & 0 & 0 \\ 0 & 0 & 0 & 0 \\ 0 & 0 & 1 & 0 \\ 0 & 0 & 0 & 1 \end{bmatrix}$$

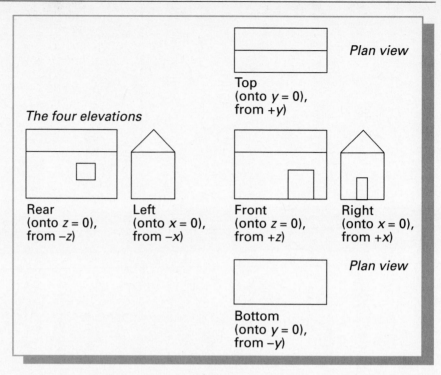

Figure 14.7 The six standard projections of the barn.

As we see from the diagrams, under any single orthographic projection we lose considerable information. Thus if we wish to display information about all aspects of an object we must use **multiple projections**. There are six standard projections of an object used for this purpose: onto the three coordinate planes, from positive and negative points at infinity respectively. These six projections taken together contain all the information relating to the surface of an object; by convention they are displayed in the arrangement shown in Figure 14.7.

14.3 The need for perspective

The orthographic projections of the last section are informative, but limited in their realism. For example, under orthographic projection the size of planar images is unaffected by the relative distances of the objects, which we illustrate in Figure 14.8; this is contrary to our expectation for realistic representation. When we aim for a 'realistic' two-dimensional representation of a three-dimensional object or scene we employ **depth cues** of different types, to give the impression of relative distances. For example a distant object might be partially obscured by a nearer one; the size of an object would be reduced as its distance away from the viewing point increased; non-uniform foreshortening would occur in a tilted object. Other depth cues involve the enhanced clarity of nearby objects and the perception that colour

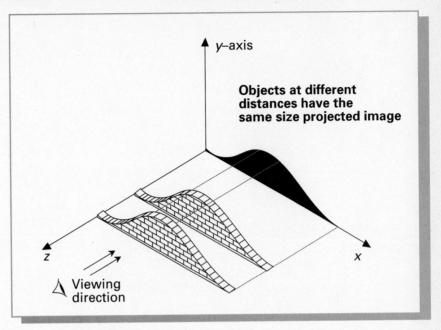

Figure 14.8   Objects at different distances from the screen have the same size projected image.

intensity fades with distance, although the means of realizing these last two effects is well outside the scope of this book.

In a great deal of graphical work (for animation and simulation as well as for virtual reality) the prime intention is to present an image that is as realistic as possible, so the viewer's sense of depth perception must be enhanced. The most easily managed type of depth cues for this purpose are those that depend on the techniques of **perspective**. When perspective has been used, lines that are parallel appear to converge to **vanishing points** and as a consequence the size of an object appears to be reduced according to its distance from the viewing point, and foreshortening occurs according to orientation and distance.

Projection and perspective are separate processes: projection acts on a three-dimensional object and produces a two-dimensional image, while perspective, like rotation, reflection, translation or scaling, is a transformation that acts on a three-dimensional object to give us a three-dimensional image. However, unlike these others, perspective is a transformation that always distorts the shape of objects. For example, under perspective a rectangle can be transformed to a trapezium shape, and a circle can be transformed to an ellipse (see Figure 14.9); but when a three-dimensional perspective image is projected onto a two-dimensional screen, this distortion of shapes helps our perception of depth. Thus perspective views are widely used; in fact for the general appreciation of realistic two-dimensional images of our three-dimensional experience, informed as we are both by artists' work since medieval times and now by photographs and films, perspective views are essential and standard.

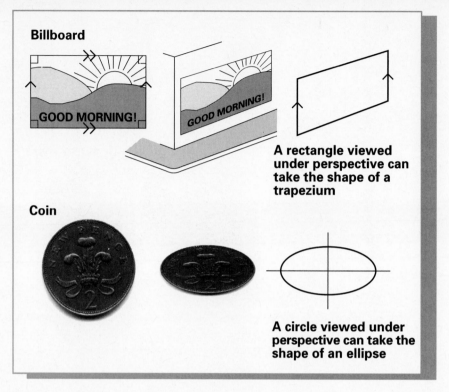

Figure 14.9 The modification of shapes under perspective views.

As we indicated in Section 13.4, it is the top three entries in the last column of a (4×4) matrix that are involved in a perspective transformation. Thus when we have a matrix

$$
\begin{bmatrix}
a & b & c & p \\
d & e & f & q \\
g & i & j & r \\
h & k & \ell & s
\end{bmatrix}
$$

and not all of the values p, q, r are zero, then this matrix will perform a transformation involving perspective. We now proceed to investigate the simplest form of perspective, and then to combine it with an orthographic projection to give us a **perspective-projection** which may be viewed on a two-dimensional screen.

14.4 Single point perspective

When the transforming matrix has just one non-zero entry among the top three positions of its final column then it produces a **single point perspective**. The following matrix, where $r \neq 0$, is the simplest one we can write; it produces a single point perspective with the viewing point on the z-axis:

$$
\begin{bmatrix}
1 & 0 & 0 & 0 \\
0 & 1 & 0 & 0 \\
0 & 0 & 1 & r \\
0 & 0 & 0 & 1
\end{bmatrix}
$$

Of course there are similar matrices that will produce single point perspectives with viewing points on the x-axis (when $q = r = 0$, but $p \neq 0$), or on the y-axis (when $p = r = 0$, but $q \neq 0$).

When we apply the above matrix to a general homogeneous vector we get

$$
(X \quad Y \quad Z \quad 1)
\begin{bmatrix}
1 & 0 & 0 & 0 \\
0 & 1 & 0 & 0 \\
0 & 0 & 1 & r \\
0 & 0 & 0 & 1
\end{bmatrix}
$$

$$
= (X \quad Y \quad Z \quad rZ+1)
$$

$$
\equiv \left(\frac{X}{rZ+1} \quad \frac{Y}{rZ+1} \quad \frac{Z}{rZ+1} \quad 1 \right)
$$

so we see that the physical coordinates of the image point are $(X/(rZ+1)$, $Y/(rZ+1)$, $Z/(rZ+1))$. These coordinates give the transformed point in three dimensions. In the section that follows we apply a projection so that we can view this point on a viewing plane: this will give us more understanding of the perspective transformation, and in addition we shall identify the value of r geometrically.

14.5 Perspective-projection

We take the homogeneous vector corresponding to the coordinates of the point transformed by perspective as above, and project them onto the plane $z = 0$ using the matrix from Section 14.2. We get

$$
\left(\frac{X}{rZ+1} \quad \frac{Y}{rZ+1} \quad \frac{Z}{rZ+1} \quad 1 \right)
\begin{bmatrix}
1 & 0 & 0 & 0 \\
0 & 1 & 0 & 0 \\
0 & 0 & 0 & 0 \\
0 & 0 & 0 & 1
\end{bmatrix}
$$

$$
= \left(\frac{X}{rZ+1} \quad \frac{Y}{rZ+1} \quad 0 \quad 1 \right)
$$

thus the physical coordinates, in three dimensions, of the transformed point are $(X/(rZ+1)$, $Y/(rZ+1)$, $0)$. When the image point is viewed on the viewing plane $z = 0$, then the only relevant coordinates are the first two, namely $(X/(rZ+1)$, $Y/(rZ+1))$.

Instead of first multiplying by the perspective matrix, and then by the projection matrix, we can obtain the same result by multiplying by the single matrix formed by these two multiplied together. The single matrix that will produce the combined perspective-projection in this case is given by

$$
\begin{bmatrix} 1 & 0 & 0 & 0 \\ 0 & 1 & 0 & 0 \\ 0 & 0 & 1 & r \\ 0 & 0 & 0 & 1 \end{bmatrix} \times \begin{bmatrix} 1 & 0 & 0 & 0 \\ 0 & 1 & 0 & 0 \\ 0 & 0 & 0 & 0 \\ 0 & 0 & 0 & 1 \end{bmatrix} = \begin{bmatrix} 1 & 0 & 0 & 0 \\ 0 & 1 & 0 & 0 \\ 0 & 0 & 0 & r \\ 0 & 0 & 0 & 1 \end{bmatrix}
$$

We take care to multiply these matrices in the correct order: perspective first, then projection. The projection must always be done last since it causes information to be irretrievably lost.

For the orthographic projections of Section 14.2 we arranged the three-dimensional object (the barn) so that all its vertices had positive coordinates, in x, y and z. When the above perspective-projection is applied to an object in this position, the essential features are shown in Figure 14.10: the viewing point is positioned at z_c on the positive part of the z-axis and the number r is negative. A typical point on an object is P(X, Y, Z) which has its perspective-projection P*(X^*, Y^*) on the viewing plane $z = 0$. All perspective-projections are based on the idea that an object, or scene, is viewed from a single eye point, so we can imagine diverging lines drawn from the eye to the object which extend to meet the viewing plane. This corresponds with the way we view real objects since, as people, we are always at a particular position within a scene and not looking in from 'the outside'. This arrangement of perspective-projection has some features in common with a film projector, which directs light from a point source (the viewing point), past a film (the object), onto a screen (the viewing plane).

However, at this stage we follow the usual convention for computer graphics professionals and regard the object as being on the 'other side' of the viewing plane from the viewing point (the calculations are unaltered by this convention). The

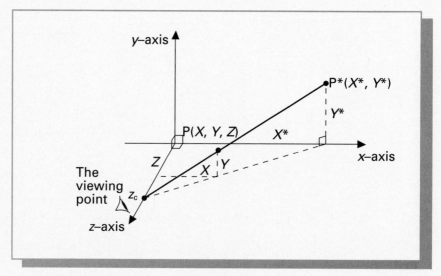

Figure 14.10 Projection of a point in three dimensions onto a two-dimensional viewing plane. $z_c = -1/r$ and since r is taken to be a negative number, so z_c is positive, as shown.

viewing point is still taken to be on the positive z-axis, and the viewing plane is still the plane $z = 0$; but every vertex on the object has a negative z-coordinate. This situation is illustrated in Figure 14.11(a): the viewing point is at $(0, 0, z_c)$ and a typical point on the object is P(X, Y, Z), where Z is a negative number. P is transformed under perspective-projection to the point P* with coordinates (X^*, Y^*) on the viewing plane. In this case we imagine diverging lines drawn from the eye, which cut the viewing plane before they reach the object; this corresponds with envisaging an object being 'inside the computer' but viewed in two dimensions on the computer screen, as indicated in Figure 14.11(b).

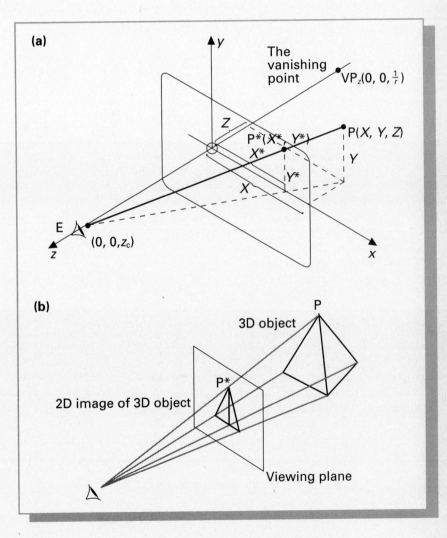

Figure 14.11 (a) and (b) The object the 'other side' of the viewing plane.

The value of z_c (at the viewing point) is related to the value of r in the matrix: in fact $z_c = -1/r$, since r is negative this does give us a point on the positive z-axis. Using the matrix we obtained above (but bearing in mind that Z is here a negative number) we know that

$$X^* = \frac{X}{rZ + 1}$$

and

$$Y^* = \frac{Y}{rZ + 1}$$

similar △s and Appendix D

Anyone familiar with the theory of similar triangles will be able to verify the relationships between these coordinates geometrically; we indicate this in Appendix D. We note that although these equations connecting the projected coordinates with the original coordinates have here been formed using negative values of Z, in fact the equations remain true whether the object is in front of or behind the viewing plane, with Z positive or negative.

We suppose now that we change the position of the point P. As P recedes from the viewing point so it gets further from the viewing plane and its z-coordinate (still negative) is larger in size. Since r is negative this makes the value of $(rZ + 1)$ increase, and so overall the values of X^* and Y^* decrease. This certainly corresponds with our idea that the perspective image of a more distant object should be smaller. In addition we note that if $Z = 0$ then $X^* = X$ and $Y^* = Y$, so that all points in the viewing plane remain unaltered by the perspective-projection. Thus when the front face of the barn is in the plane $z = 0$ it remains undistorted by this transformation, while the images of the other faces change in size and/or shape, as shown in Figure 14.12.

Let us now consider what happens under a perspective transformation to lines which 'go off into the distance' and have a point at infinity in the sense described

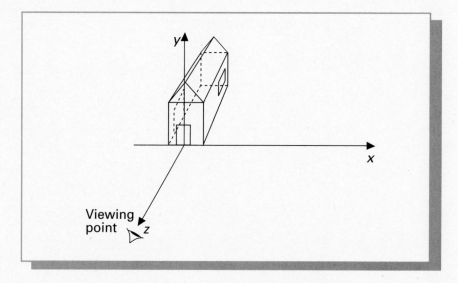

Figure 14.12 The front face of the barn is in the viewing plane and so is undistorted.

in Section 13.3. Just as in two dimensions, all lines that have the same gradient and so go in the same direction have the same point at infinity; for the lines parallel to the z-axis this is the point given by $(0 \quad 0 \quad 1 \quad 0)$. We apply the perspective transformation to this point:

$$(0 \quad 0 \quad 1 \quad 0) \begin{bmatrix} 1 & 0 & 0 & 0 \\ 0 & 1 & 0 & 0 \\ 0 & 0 & 1 & r \\ 0 & 0 & 0 & 1 \end{bmatrix} = (0 \quad 0 \quad 1 \quad r)$$

$$\equiv (0 \quad 0 \quad \tfrac{1}{r} \quad 1)$$

Thus the physical coordinates of the image of this point at infinity are $(0, 0, 1/r)$, and this is known as VP_z, the **principal vanishing point** of lines parallel to the z-axis. It is rather surprising that a point at infinity, by definition unattainable, has an ordinary, finite image point. All the lines parallel to the z-axis, approaching from the positive z-direction, have the same point at infinity; thus all of them when transformed pass through this same principal vanishing point. VP_z is the point to which these parallel lines appear to converge when we apply perspective. Geometrically, as shown in Figure 14.13, this vanishing point lies on the z-axis as far 'behind' the viewing plane as the viewing point is in front of it: it is the reflection of the viewing point in the viewing plane.

When the vanishing point VP_z $(0, 0, 1/r)$ is projected onto the plane $z = 0$, the coordinates of its image on the plane are $(0, 0)$. Thus, under this combined perspective-projection, the origin $O(0, 0)$ is the vanishing point of all lines originally

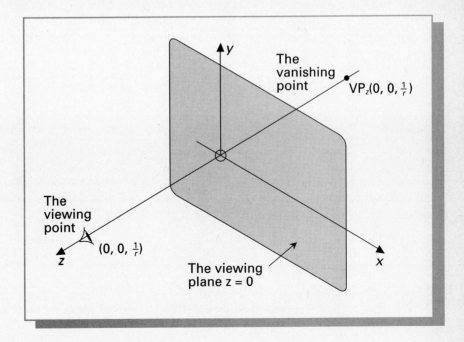

Figure 14.13 The vanishing point VP_z.

parallel to the z-axis. This fact is used in the example that follows, where we construct a single point perspective-projection of a cube.

Just before proceeding we note that all the above discussions and results can easily be adapted to deal with single point perspective-projections in the x- and y-directions. Using a viewing point on the x-axis at $(x_c, 0, 0)$, where $x_c = -1/p$, with the viewing plane $x = 0$, then the principal vanishing point VP_x is at $(1/p, 0, 0)$. When projected onto the viewing plane the vanishing point has coordinates $(0, 0)$. There are similar results for perspective-projection in the y-direction.

14.6 Tunnel perspective

We now use the above results to construct, without any further calculations, a two-dimensional image of a cube under single point perspective-projection. The cube is shown in Figure 14.14(a), and it is important that we recognize clearly how we are viewing it: the end result depends upon the precise details of the viewing arrangement. The cube is placed so that every edge is parallel to a coordinate axis; the z-axis passes through the centre of its front face and its front face is in the viewing plane $z = 0$. The eye, positioned on the positive z-axis, is looking directly and centrally onto the front face of the cube.

To construct the required image we see how different parts of the cube are transformed. The front face, ABCD, is in the viewing plane and so will remain undistorted. The edges AE, BF, CG and DH are segments of lines parallel to the positive z-axis, thus they all have the same point at infinity given by $(0 \ \ 0 \ \ 1 \ \ 0)$. We have already noted that the vanishing point on the viewing plane corresponding to this point at infinity is the origin, $O(0, 0)$. Thus each of the transformed edges will pass through O in the viewing plane. A, B, C and D are unchanged, so the vertices of the back face E, F, G and H are transformed to E*, F*, G* and H* where the lines E*A, F*B, G*C and H*D (extended) all pass through O. The image of the cube under this perspective-projection is shown in Figure 14.14(b).

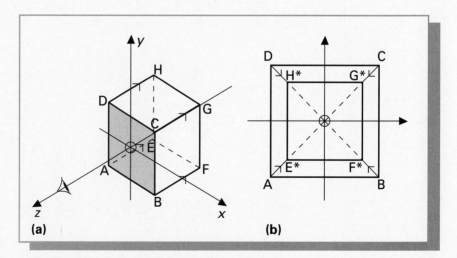

Figure 14.14 (a) The viewing arrangement of the cube.
(b) The perspective-projection of the cube.

14.7 To improve realism

Section 14.6 gives us the simplest example of a perspective-projection, but it is not the most informative view of a cube. The depth cues in tunnel perspective, which is based on the use of single point perspective with a single vanishing point, are not immediately obvious. In the next chapter we introduce modifications to the perspective transformation which will allow us to produce more realistic views. These are based on ways in which we naturally obtain alternative views of a real object, by moving it to one side or turning it around. Additionally these new transformations can employ two or three vanishing points; they are known as two point perspective and three point perspective.

Exercises

All these questions relate to the same single point perspective transformation, with viewing point at the point X(20, 0, 0).

14.1 There is a cube whose base is the square ABCD, where the coordinates are A(0, 0, 0), B(0, 0, 3), C(3, 0, 3) and D(3, 0, 0). This cube is first transformed by the single point perspective transformation with viewing point at X(20, 0, 0), and then the result is projected onto the viewing plane $x = 0$.

a) Write down the coordinates of E, F, G and H, the other vertices of the cube

b) Write down the matrix of the perspective transformation.

c) Calculate the coordinates of the vertices of the image of the cube when transformed by perspective.

d) Write down the matrix of the orthographic projection.

e) Calculate the vertices of the planar shape, as projected onto the viewing plane.

14.2 Under the single point perspective transformation viewed from the point X(20, 0, 0) find in homogeneous form the images of

a) the origin,

b) the viewing point,

c) the vanishing point.

Are any of these **invariant** (that is, unchanged) under this transformation?

14.3 a) Draw a sketch to illustrate that the line joining the points M(2, 3, 4) and N(5, 3, 4) is parallel to the x-axis.

b) This line is subjected to a single point perspective transformation viewed from the point X(20, 0, 0); what are the coordinates of the transformed points M* and N*?

c) Write down the vector equation of the line through M* and N*: that is

'$\mathbf{r}(u) = ...$'

d) Verify that the vanishing point of the transformation lies on the line M*N*.

(Note that *all* lines that are originally parallel to the x-axis will appear, after the perspective transformation, to pass through the vanishing point.)

Answers

14.1 a) E(0, 3, 0), F(0, 3, 3), G(3, 3, 3), H(3, 3, 0); b) $\begin{bmatrix} 1 & 0 & 0 & -\frac{1}{20} \\ 0 & 1 & 0 & 0 \\ 0 & 0 & 1 & 0 \\ 0 & 0 & 0 & 1 \end{bmatrix}$

c) A*(0, 0, 0), B*(0, 0, 3), C*(3.53, 0, 3.53), D*(3.53, 0, 0), E*(0, 3, 0), F*(0, 3, 3), G*(3.53, 3.53, 3.53), H*(3.53, 3.53, 0);

d) $\begin{bmatrix} 0 & 0 & 0 & 0 \\ 0 & 1 & 0 & 0 \\ 0 & 0 & 1 & 0 \\ 0 & 0 & 0 & 1 \end{bmatrix}$;

e) $A^{\#}$(0, 0, 0), $B^{\#}$(0, 0, 3), $C^{\#}$(0, 0, 3.53), $D^{\#}$(0, 0, 0), $E^{\#}$(0, 3, 0), $F^{\#}$(0, 3, 3), $G^{\#}$(0, 3.53, 3.53), $H^{\#}$(0, 3.53, 0).

14.2 a) (0 0 0 1); b) (20 0 0 1); c) (–20 0 0 1).

The origin is invariant.

14.3 b) M*(2.22, 3.33, 4.44), N*(6.67, 4, 5.33).

c) $\mathbf{r}(u) = (2.22 + 4.45u)\mathbf{i} + (3.33 + 0.67u)\mathbf{j} + (4.44 + 0.89u)\mathbf{k}$.

15

A greater sense of perspective:
Two point and three point perspective

15.1 Improving perspective

In Section 14.6 we investigated tunnel perspective. Because the cube was placed centrally, with one face directly visible situated in the viewing plane, and because we used single point perspective with the viewing point on the central axis of the cube, our single vanishing point gave a very limited sense of depth perception. In order to obtain more realistic views than this we now explore alternative ways of positioning the object.

For the sake of simplicity, we continue our investigation of perspective with the assumption that the viewing plane is fixed and is identical with the x–y plane, that is, the plane $z = 0$. The viewing point is also considered fixed, on the positive z-axis: the object alone is free to be moved. This corresponds with how we might naturally obtain improved views of an object by turning it around in our hands, inspecting it at different distances and from different angles. Of course there is another way of obtaining improved views of objects or scenes: this is to regard the object as fixed and vary the viewing point, which corresponds with how we might ourselves move around a larger object or travel through a scene. When a viewing point is moved along a path through a scene we obtain a **fly through**, but we shall not be dealing here with this technique.

We now deal with the improved viewpoints that can be obtained by moving the object. These movements result in changes in the position of the object which can be described as translations and/or rotations, thus they can be implemented by the matrices we discussed in earlier chapters. The effects of applying these transformations to a cube before a perspective-projection is performed are explored in the following sections; we obtain different levels of realism in the images. In general we find that more realistic images result when we arrange that more faces are directly visible from the viewing point.

15.2 Translation then single point perspective

Suppose we apply a single translation to the centred cube we dealt with in Section

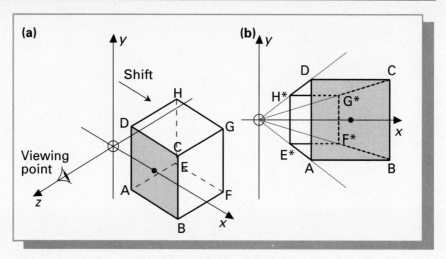

Figure 15.1 (a) The centred cube shifted along the x-axis.
(b) The single point perspective-projection of the shifted cube.

14.6 (Figure 14.14(a)); we move it along the positive x-axis to a position shown in Figure 15.1(a). All the faces of the cube are still parallel with the coordinate planes, but the cube is no longer placed centrally with respect to the viewing point on the z-axis; two faces are now directly visible. We apply the method of Section 14.6 to construct the perspective-projection of this cube in the viewing plane $z = 0$. The front face is still in the viewing plane and so remains undistorted; the origin is the vanishing point of lines parallel to the z-axis so we draw in the image lines AE*, BF*, CG* and DH* so that extended they pass through O. The result of this combined transformation is shown in Figure 15.1(b); we obviously have here a more realistic image than before, but not yet one that is completely convincing for all purposes.

The realism is improved further if we apply a diagonal shift to the cube (moving it in both the x- and y-directions) before applying a single point perspective. Thus we move the cube to a position shown in Figure 15.2(a), so that three faces are directly visible from the viewing point on the z-axis. We apply the same perspective-projection as before, and by the same construction we obtain the image shown in Figure 15.2(b). We can agree that this is a significant improvement.

Example 15.1 Applying translation, then single point perspective

We here use numerical methods rather than construction to apply translation then single point perspective-projection to a cube. We take the unit cube ABCDEFGH with a vertex at the origin, as shown in Figure 15.3(a). We shall apply a translation of 5 units in the x-direction and 5 units in the y-direction (so that three faces are directly visible from the viewing point on the z-axis). After this we shall perform a perspective-projection onto the plane $z = 0$ from a viewing point at $(0, 0, 8)$, to obtain the two-dimensional image in Figure 15.3(b).

We first obtain the matrix for the overall transformation by multiplying the translation matrix by the perspective-projection matrix (see Sections 13.5.4 and 14.5). We note that $z_c = -1/r$, so

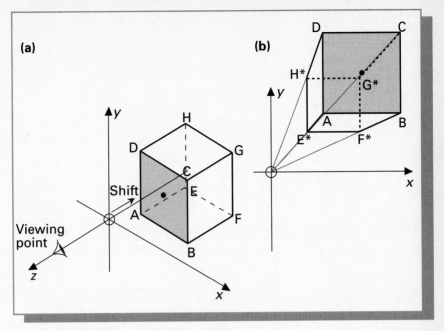

Figure 15.2 (a) The centred cube shifted diagonally.
(b) The single point perspective–projection of the shifted cube.

$$r = \frac{-1}{z_c} = \frac{-1}{8} = -0.125$$

gives us the entry in the matrix. We get

$$
\begin{bmatrix} 1 & 0 & 0 & 0 \\ 0 & 1 & 0 & 0 \\ 0 & 0 & 1 & 0 \\ 5 & 5 & 0 & 1 \end{bmatrix}
\times
\begin{bmatrix} 1 & 0 & 0 & 0 \\ 0 & 1 & 0 & 0 \\ 0 & 0 & 0 & -0.125 \\ 0 & 0 & 0 & 1 \end{bmatrix}
=
\begin{bmatrix} 1 & 0 & 0 & 0 \\ 0 & 1 & 0 & 0 \\ 0 & 0 & 0 & -0.125 \\ 5 & 5 & 0 & 1 \end{bmatrix}
$$

translation   perspective-projection   combined transformation.

This combined matrix is now applied to the homogeneous vectors corresponding to the vertices of the cube:

$$
\begin{array}{c}
A \\ B \\ C \\ D \\ E \\ F \\ G \\ H
\end{array}
\begin{bmatrix}
0 & 0 & 0 & 1 \\
1 & 0 & 0 & 1 \\
1 & 1 & 0 & 1 \\
0 & 1 & 0 & 1 \\
0 & 0 & -1 & 1 \\
1 & 0 & -1 & 1 \\
1 & 1 & -1 & 1 \\
0 & 1 & -1 & 1
\end{bmatrix}
\times
\begin{bmatrix}
1 & 0 & 0 & 0 \\
0 & 1 & 0 & 0 \\
0 & 0 & 0 & -0.125 \\
5 & 5 & 0 & 1
\end{bmatrix}
=
\begin{bmatrix}
5 & 5 & 0 & 1 \\
6 & 5 & 0 & 1 \\
6 & 6 & 0 & 1 \\
5 & 6 & 0 & 1 \\
5 & 5 & 0 & 1.125 \\
6 & 5 & 0 & 1.125 \\
6 & 6 & 0 & 1.125 \\
5 & 6 & 0 & 1.125
\end{bmatrix}
\begin{array}{c}
A^* \\ B^* \\ C^* \\ D^* \\ E^* \\ F^* \\ G^* \\ H^*
\end{array}
$$

We divide by the final component in each image vector to obtain the physical coordinates of

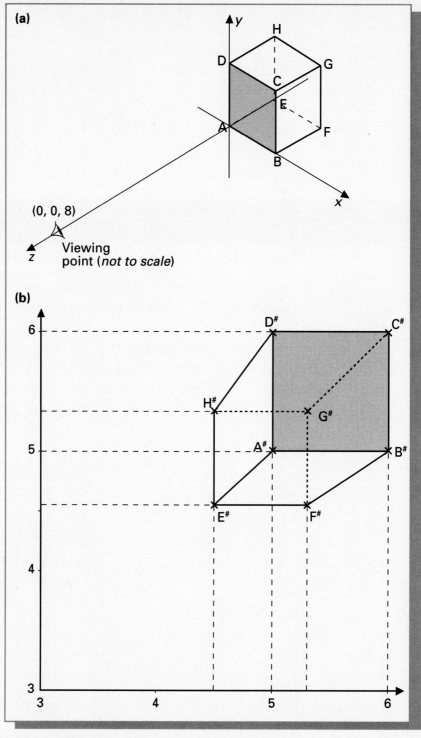

Figure 15.3 (a) The unit cube with a vertex at the origin.
(b) Translation then perspective-projection (see Example 15.1).

the image points; since they are all in the viewing plane $z = 0$ we write them as

$$A^{\#}(5, 5)$$
$$B^{\#}(6, 5)$$
$$C^{\#}(6, 6$$
$$D^{\#}(5, 6)$$
$$E^{\#}(5 \div 1.125, 5 \div 1.125) \simeq (4.44, 4.44)$$
$$F^{\#}(6 \div 1.125, 5 \div 1.125) \simeq (5.33, 4.44)$$
$$G^{\#}(6 \div 1.125, 6 \div 1.125) \simeq (5.33, 5.33)$$
$$H^{\#}(5 \div 1.125, 6 \div 1.125) \simeq (4.44, 5.33)$$

In Figure 15.3(b) these points are plotted on a two-dimensional graph, and joined by edges corresponding to those on the cube. Although we are using an exaggerated scale here we see that this gives a fairly good representation of three-dimensional depth.

15.3 Rotation then single point perspective, giving two point perspective

We return once more to consider the centred cube of Figure 14.14(a). Suppose we rotate it through an angle ϕ about the y-axis: this will reveal two faces to a viewing point on the z-axis (see Figure 15.4(a)), so when we subsequently apply a perspective-projection onto the viewing plane $z = 0$ we anticipate seeing some depth cues. However, the projected image, shown in Figure 15.4(b), is not as informative as we might have hoped. The front vertical edge is longest, as expected, and the visible faces have been distorted, but as an image of a cube it is not immediately convincing.

We can investigate what is happening by constructing the matrix for the combined transformation: we multiply together the matrix for rotation about the y-axis (see Section 13.5.3) and the matrix for a single point perspective-projection onto the viewing plane $z = 0$ where the viewing point is on the z-axis. The result is given by

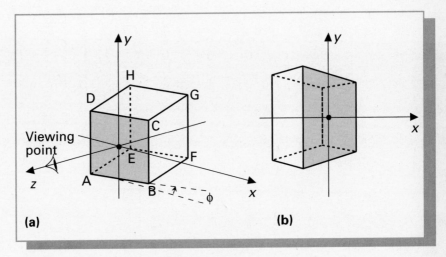

Figure 15.4 (a) The centred cube rotated through ϕ.
(b) The result of rotation then single point perspective-projection.

$$
\begin{bmatrix} \cos\phi & 0 & -\sin\phi & 0 \\ 0 & 1 & 0 & 0 \\ \sin\phi & 0 & \cos\phi & 0 \\ 0 & 0 & 0 & 1 \end{bmatrix} \times \begin{bmatrix} 1 & 0 & 0 & 0 \\ 0 & 1 & 0 & 0 \\ 0 & 0 & 0 & r \\ 0 & 0 & 0 & 1 \end{bmatrix} = \begin{bmatrix} \cos\phi & 0 & 0 & -r\sin\phi \\ 0 & 1 & 0 & 0 \\ \sin\phi & 0 & 0 & r\cos\phi \\ 0 & 0 & 0 & 1 \end{bmatrix}
$$

$\qquad$ rotation about y-axis $\qquad$ perspective-projection $\quad$ combined transformation

We recognize that this matrix for the combined transformation is exhibiting a new pattern: there are two non-zero entries above the '1' in the last column. This indicates that we have generated quite naturally a **two point perspective**. With this perspective we have two vanishing points to aid the realism of the image, but since our rotation gave us only two directly visible faces we cannot achieve a really worthwhile image with this. Instead we shall investigate a two point perspective in more detail, and to better effect, in the next section.

15.4 Rotation, translation then single point perspective, giving improved two point perspective

If we rotate a cube from its position in Figure 15.3(a) and then translate it, we make three of its faces directly visible; this combination of transformations is used to yield a good impression of three-dimensional depth. Thus we shall now apply rotation followed by translation and then a single point perspective, and project the result onto a viewing plane. We find that this also is equivalent to a two point perspective-projection.

We take the unit cube shown in Figure 15.3(a) and first rotate it about the y-axis (we take $\phi = 30°$ for illustration) to reveal a second face, then shift it down (3 units in the negative y-direction) which allows a third (top) face to become visible. After this we apply a perspective-projection onto the plane $z = 0$, with a viewing point on the z-axis at $(0, 0, 4)$. Noting that $r = -1/4 = -0.25$, we take the transformations in the appropriate order and multiply the matrices as follows:

$$
\begin{bmatrix} \cos 30° & 0 & -\sin 30° & 0 \\ 0 & 1 & 0 & 0 \\ \sin 30° & 0 & \cos 30° & 0 \\ 0 & 0 & 0 & 1 \end{bmatrix} \times \begin{bmatrix} 1 & 0 & 0 & 0 \\ 0 & 1 & 0 & 0 \\ 0 & 0 & 1 & 0 \\ 0 & -3 & 0 & 1 \end{bmatrix} \times \begin{bmatrix} 1 & 0 & 0 & 0 \\ 0 & 1 & 0 & 0 \\ 0 & 0 & 0 & -0.25 \\ 0 & 0 & 0 & 1 \end{bmatrix}
$$

$\qquad\qquad$ rotation $\qquad\qquad\qquad$ translation $\qquad\qquad$ perspective-projection

To two decimal place accuracy we calculate that the single matrix for the combined transformation is:

$$
\begin{bmatrix} 0.87 & 0 & 0 & 0.13 \\ 0 & 1 & 0 & 0 \\ 0.5 & 0 & 0 & -0.22 \\ 0 & -3 & 0 & 1 \end{bmatrix}
$$

The two non-zero entries above the '1' in the last column tell us that, as in Section 15.3, this is a situation involving two point perspective.

As before, we use this matrix to multiply the homogeneous vectors corresponding to the vertices of the cube:

$$
\begin{array}{c}
\text{A} \\ \text{B} \\ \text{C} \\ \text{D} \\ \text{E} \\ \text{F} \\ \text{G} \\ \text{H}
\end{array}
\begin{bmatrix}
0 & 0 & 0 & 1 \\
1 & 0 & 0 & 1 \\
1 & 1 & 0 & 1 \\
0 & 1 & 0 & 1 \\
0 & 0 & -1 & 1 \\
1 & 0 & -1 & 1 \\
1 & 1 & -1 & 1 \\
0 & 1 & -1 & 1
\end{bmatrix}
\times
\begin{bmatrix}
0.87 & 0 & 0 & 0.13 \\
0 & 1 & 0 & 0 \\
0.5 & 0 & 0 & -0.22 \\
0 & -3 & 0 & 1
\end{bmatrix}
=
\begin{bmatrix}
0 & -3 & 0 & 1 \\
0.87 & -3 & 0 & 1.13 \\
0.87 & -2 & 0 & 1.13 \\
0 & -2 & 0 & 1 \\
-0.5 & -3 & 0 & 1.22 \\
0.37 & -3 & 0 & 1.35 \\
0.37 & -2 & 0 & 1.35 \\
-0.5 & -2 & 0 & 1.22
\end{bmatrix}
\begin{array}{c}
\text{A*} \\ \text{B*} \\ \text{C*} \\ \text{D*} \\ \text{E*} \\ \text{F*} \\ \text{G*} \\ \text{H*}
\end{array}
$$

We obtain the physical coordinates of the image, now projected onto the plane $z = 0$, in the standard way. They are:

$$A^{\#}(0, -3)$$
$$B^{\#}(0.87 \div 1.13, -3 \div 1.13) \simeq (0.80, -2.65)$$
$$C^{\#}(0.87 \div 1.13, -2 \div 1.13) \simeq (0.80, -1.80)$$
$$D^{\#}(0, -2)$$
$$E^{\#}(-0.5 \div 1.22, -3 \div 1.22) \simeq (-0.41, -2.46)$$
$$F^{\#}(0.37 \div 1.35, -3 \div 1.35) \simeq (0.27, -2.22)$$
$$G^{\#}(0.37 \div 1.35, -2 \div 1.35) \simeq (0.27, -1.48)$$
$$H^{\#}(-0.5 \div 1.22, -2 \div 1.22) \simeq (-0.41, -1.64)$$

In Figure 15.5 we show the two-dimensional result of this transformation: the impression of depth that it gives is very satisfactory.

Since this transformation involves two point perspective we expect that there will be two principal vanishing points. In the combined matrix above there are entries in the positions of 'p' and 'r', so we shall be able to determine VP_x and VP_z. VP_x and VP_z are defined as in Section 14.5: they are the images of points at infinity in the directions of the x- and z-axes, and also the points to which lines parallel with the x-, or z-, axes appear to converge after the perspective transformation has been applied. To determine their projections on the viewing plane we calculate the images of $(1 \quad 0 \quad 0 \quad 0)$ and $(0 \quad 0 \quad 1 \quad 0)$ under the combined matrix, as follows

$$
\begin{bmatrix}
1 & 0 & 0 & 0 \\
0 & 0 & 1 & 0
\end{bmatrix}
\times
\begin{bmatrix}
0.87 & 0 & 0 & 0.13 \\
0 & 1 & 0 & 0 \\
0.5 & 0 & 0 & -0.22 \\
0 & -3 & 0 & 1
\end{bmatrix}
=
\begin{bmatrix}
0.87 & 0 & 0 & 0.13 \\
0.5 & 0 & 0 & -0.22
\end{bmatrix}
$$

Dividing each of the resulting vectors by its final component, we obtain the coordinates of the principal vanishing points on the viewing plane:

$$VP_x (0.87 \div 0.13, 0) \simeq (6.69, 0)$$

$$VP_z (0.5 \div (-0.22), 0) \simeq (-2.27, 0).$$

These points are plotted in Figure 15.6, and we see that they do indeed give us the expected points of convergence for the parallel edges of the image.

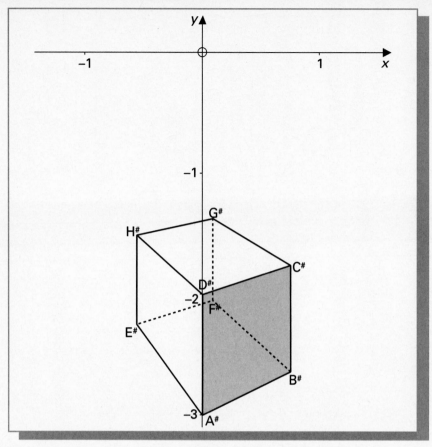

Figure 15.5 Rotation, translation then perspective-projection (see Section 15.4).

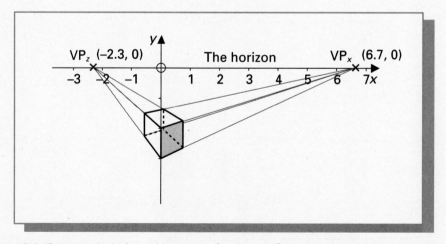

Figure 15.6 The two principal vanishing points for the transformation shown in Figure 15.5.

15.5 Two rotations, translation then single point perspective, giving three point perspective

In very rare circumstances a **three point perspective** is considered necessary, with three principal vanishing points. In this case, a realistic view can be obtained by a sequence of transformations similar to the following. First, we apply a rotation about the y-axis, then a rotation about the x-axis. The object is then shifted away from all axes by a translation. Finally a perspective-projection is performed, from a viewing point on the z-axis, onto the viewing plane $z = 0$. We have already considered the matrices which perform each of these transformations, and the method of multiplying them together (in the correct order) and then applying the result to the homogeneous vectors of points on the object is exactly the same as we have used in previous sections. If depth perception in all three dimensions is important, then this combination of matrices yields an effective perspective-projection.

15.6 The three types of perspective-projection

As we have seen, a two-dimensional image is displayed in single point perspective when the transforming matrix has a single non-zero entry in one of the top three positions in the last column. A typical matrix has the form

$$\begin{bmatrix} * & * & 0 & 0 \\ * & * & 0 & 0 \\ * & * & 0 & r \\ * & * & 0 & 1 \end{bmatrix}$$

A single point perspective-projection yields one principal vanishing point; the effect obtained is indicated in Figure 15.7.

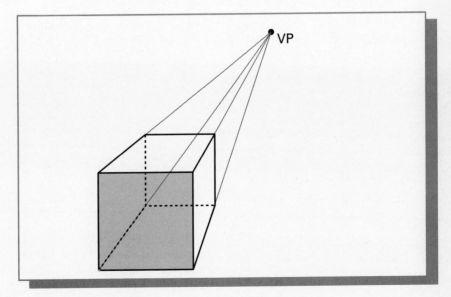

Figure 15.7 Single point perspective.

Two non-zero entries in the top three of the last column give two point perspective, in which two principal vanishing points occur. A transformation matrix such as

$$\begin{bmatrix} * & * & 0 & p \\ * & * & 0 & 0 \\ * & * & 0 & r \\ * & * & 0 & 1 \end{bmatrix}$$

leads to an image such as that illustrated in Figure 15.8. Lines parallel to the axes in the horizontal plane converge to meet in the two principal vanishing points, while vertical lines remain unaltered. For many purposes, when only horizontal distances are significant, this effect is quite satisfactory for our appreciation of three-dimensional depth.

When all the entries in the last column of a transforming matrix are non-zero then the resulting image is represented in three point perspective, with three principal vanishing points. Thus a transforming matrix of the form

$$\begin{bmatrix} * & * & 0 & p \\ * & * & 0 & q \\ * & * & 0 & r \\ * & * & 0 & 1 \end{bmatrix}$$

is useful for situations where all three dimensions are significantly involved in our appreciation of depth and distance. An example might be when we consider a large building whose height tapers away above us just as much as the horizontal lines on its facades taper into the distance. This effect is shown in Figure 15.9, where we see that distortion is involved in the vertical direction as well as the horizontal; for most purposes this degree of perspective is usually unnecessary.

15.7 Vanishing points and trace points

When dealing with perspective views it is often helpful to be able to identify and calculate the principal vanishing points, which can be used as aids in simple constructions.

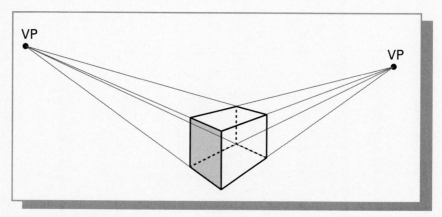

Figure 15.8 Two point perspective.

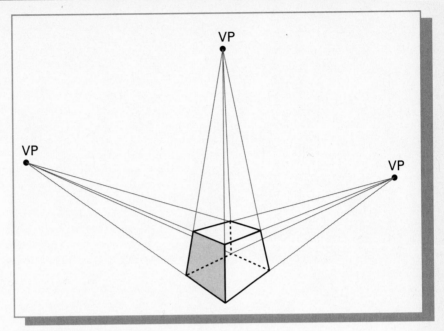

Figure 15.9 Three point perspective.

We concentrate here on two point perspective, which is the most commonly used form. We suppose there is no distortion in the y-direction, assumed to be vertical; then the two principal vanishing points are VP_x and VP_z, which are the points of apparent convergence for the sets of lines parallel to the x-axis and z-axis respectively. As in Section 15.4, all the lines on the object that were originally parallel to the x-axis will, after the transformation, converge to VP_x, and all the lines that were originally parallel to the z-axis will converge to VP_z. The straight line joining VP_x and VP_z is called the **horizon**. These features are displayed in Figure 15.6. Since the viewing point is on the z-axis, the horizon here lies along the x-axis.

In Section 15.4 we showed how to calculate the coordinates of the projections of the principal vanishing points. Other vanishing points arise from sets of lines that are parallel to each other and lying in planes parallel to the x–z plane; all have their own vanishing points which lie on the horizon (an example is shown in Figure 15.10). The exact positions of these vanishing points can be calculated by determining the projected images of the points at infinity in the appropriate directions.

However, if we consider a plane that is set at an angle to the x–z plane, then the perspective-projection of any set of parallel lines within that plane will converge to a point known as a **trace point**. Trace points can lie either above or below the horizon, and they too can be very useful when a two-dimensional perspective image is being constructed; a trace point is shown in Figure 15.11. The coordinates of a trace point are easily calculated by the expected method, that is, as the projected image of a particular point at infinity.

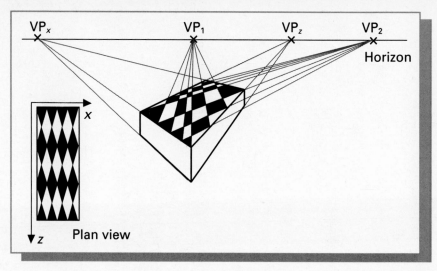

Figure 15.10 Two point perspective of patterned table top: the vanishing points lie on the horizon.

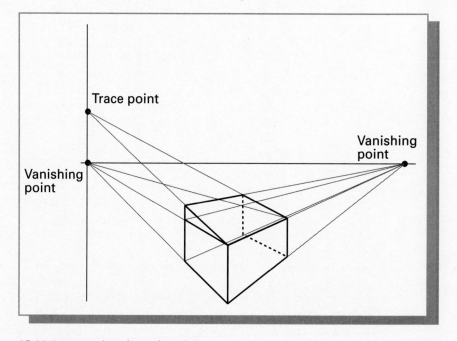

Figure 15.11 A trace point, above the origin.

Exercises

15.1 Consider the cube whose centre is at the origin as shown in Figure 15.12. To obtain a realistic view of it projected on the x–y plane, shift it 8 units in each of the x- and y-directions, and then project it onto the plane $z = 0$ from a viewing point at $(0, 0, 12)$. Write down the single matrix that performs the combined transformation, and sketch the projected view that results.

15.2 An object is rotated about the y-axis through an angle of 45°, and then subjected to a single point perspective-projection onto the plane $z = 0$, with a viewing point at $(0, 0, 8)$. Determine the single matrix which will perform this transformation, and verify that this is equivalent to a two point perspective-projection.

15.3 Consider the unit cube on the base formed by $P(0, 0, 0)$, $Q(1, 0, 0)$, $R(1, 0, -1)$, $S(0, 0, -1)$, which is to be viewed from a point along the positive z-axis. Apply a rotation about the y-axis through an angle of 60° (to reveal the left-hand face), then a translation of 2 units in the positive y-direction (to reveal the underneath face). Project the result onto the plane $z = 0$, using single point perspective viewed from $(0, 0, 2.5)$. Calculate the coordinates of the transformed vertices, and make a sketch of the result in the viewing plane. What are the coordinates of the principal vanishing points?

Answers

15.1
$$\begin{bmatrix} 1 & 0 & 0 & 0 \\ 0 & 1 & 0 & 0 \\ 0 & 0 & 0 & -\frac{1}{12} \\ 8 & 8 & 0 & 1 \end{bmatrix}$$

15.2
$$\begin{bmatrix} 0.71 & 0 & 0 & 0.09 \\ 0 & 1 & 0 & 0 \\ 0.71 & 0 & 0 & -0.09 \\ 0 & 0 & 0 & 1 \end{bmatrix}$$

The transformation in 15.2 is equivalent to a two point perspective-projection, since there are two non-zero entries above the '1' in the last column.

15.3 $(0, 2)$, $(0.37, 1.49)$, $(-0.24, 1.29)$, $(-0.72, 1.67)$, $(0, 3)$, $(0.37, 2.23)$, $(-0.24, 1.94)$, $(-0.72, 2.5)$. $VP_x (1.45, 0)$, $VP_z (-4.33, 0)$.

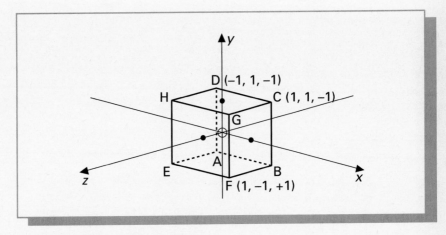

Figure 15.12 A cube centred at the origin.

Part 3
Space curves and surfaces: *Differentiation*

16

Slopes of lines and planar curves: *Gradient functions*

16.1 Lines and curves

In almost all the work covered in previous chapters we have been concentrating on straight lines, and how they can be manipulated for different graphical effects. The exception was in Chapter 7, where some specific two- and three-dimensional curves were considered: we looked at their Cartesian equations and also at ways of describing them using different parameters. Obviously, to make further progress in computer graphics, we must now address more general curves, and also surfaces both planar and non-planar.

Curves and surfaces are important components of all real graphical applications. We can think, for instance, of fabric folds in a computer animation, or the bodywork of a car in design work, or the surfaces of interior organs in a surgical training package. We shall focus on curves first, because when we can deal with curves then the step to surfaces is fairly straightforward.

There are different ways of approaching the general idea of a curve, in two or three dimensions. One possibility, introduced in Chapter 7, is to think of any curve as a (potentially infinite) collection of points in sequence. It is not feasible to attempt to store the coordinates of every such point in a computer, but a finite set of the points can be selected and their coordinates stored. Then an approximation to the curve can be constructed by joining the given points. If they are joined by straight line segments then equally spaced points can yield distortions, so it is usual to increase the density of points where a curve gets 'tighter' with its **radius of curvature** decreasing, as shown in Figure 16.1. This method can be much improved by joining the given points by standard curves (as we shall see in Chapter 18) rather than straight lines.

An alternative method can be used to deal with curves whose **analytical** form (the Cartesian equation or vector equation) is known. In this case we can use the equation as in Chapter 7; the storage is compact – for example we need only store the coordinates of the centre and the length of its radius to define a circle or sphere

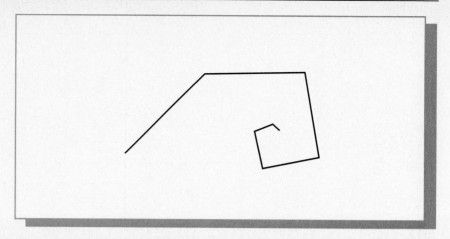

Figure 16.1 Curve of increasing radius of curvature approximated by straight line segments.

completely; precision is increased – all the information is included in the equation; and the coordinates of the intermediate points, for interpolation, can easily by calculated. This case has an important additional advantage, in that we are able to calculate from the analytical form such curve properties as the slopes of tangents. As before, when we use the parametric form of a curve we can obtain the position vectors of specific points by varying the value of the parameter. These points, and hence the curve itself, may then be transformed by any of the standard transformation matrices.

We now consider in more detail one of the principal advantages of knowing the analytical form of a curve: the ability it gives us to determine the slope at any point on the curve. With this skill we shall be able to find tangents and normals to curves and surfaces: these are essential for dealing with, among other things, the realistic depiction of the reflection of light from three-dimensional objects. We first review what we know about the slope or gradient of a line.

16.2 Slope of a straight line from its Cartesian equation

In Section 7.1 we considered the general Cartesian equation of a straight line

$$y = mx + c$$

and we identified the number m with the gradient of the line and c as the y-intercept. In fact, as defined in Example 1.3, the slope or gradient of a straight line is given by

$$m = \frac{\text{difference in } y}{\text{difference in } x}$$

as illustrated in Figure 16.2. Thus using the notation in the diagram we can write

$$m = \frac{y_1 - y}{x_1 - x}$$

We now consider the particular straight line given by

$$y = 2x + 4$$

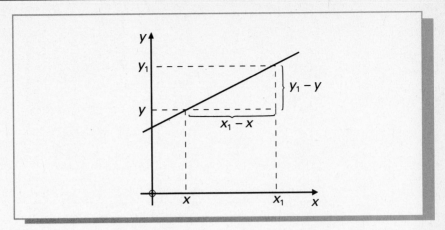

Figure 16.2 Gradient of a straight line.

We use here exactly the same technique as in Section 5.2 to determine corresponding values of x and y: we place our choice of x-values in the first row of a table, and then calculate each corresponding value of y. Thus we obtain the values in Table 16.1.

Table 16.1 Values of coordinates of points on the straight line $y = 2x + 4$.

x	-3	-2	-1	0	1	2	3
$2x$	-6	-4	-2	0	2	4	6
$+4$	$+4$	$+4$	$+4$	$+4$	$+4$	$+4$	$+4$
$y = 2x + 4$	-2	0	2	4	6	8	10

The pairs of values of x and y are then taken to be the coordinates of points, which we join up to display the line shown in Figure 16.3.

For this straight line as for all others, the gradient does not change as we move along it. Thus we can find the gradient of the entire line by calculating the gradient of the line segment between the points (1, 6) and (3, 10) as shown in Figure 16.3. Thus

$$m = \frac{10 - 6}{3 - 1} = \frac{4}{2} = 2$$

This positive gradient indicates an 'uphill' line (see Example 1.3), and the size of the gradient is $\underline{2}$, where the equation was $y = \underline{2}x + 4$; no coincidence!

16.3 Slope of a curve from its Cartesian equation

Finding the slope of a curve starts from finding the slope of a straight line, where that line is a **chord** across the curve (see Figure 16.4(a)). However, this idea is not

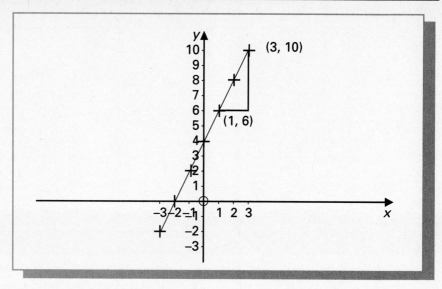

Figure 16.3 Graph of the line $y = 2x + 4$.

sufficient by itself, since intuitively we can see that the slope of a curve is related rather to the slope of a **tangent** to the curve (see again Figure 16.4(a)). A **tangent line** is one that just touches the curve, and is placed symmetrically against it.

To find the slope of the curve in Figure 16.4(a) at P we start by considering another point P_1 on the curve and join it to P by a straight line, PP_1. The slope of PP_1 is given by

$$\text{slope } PP_1 = \frac{y_1 - y}{x_1 - x} = \frac{P_1 Q_1}{P Q_1}$$

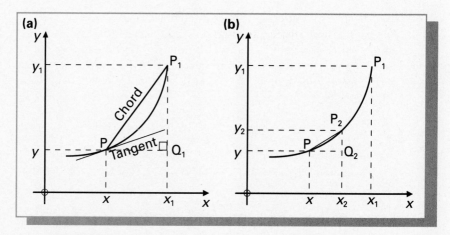

Figure 16.4 (a) Tangent and chord to a curve.
(b) Chord approximating to the tangent with P_2 close to P.

Of course the slope of PP_1 is not the same as the slope of the curve at P. However, if we consider a point P_2 which is closer to P on the curve as in Figure 16.4(b) and repeat the process, we obtain a straight line PP_2 with the slope given by

$$\text{slope } PP_2 = \frac{y_2 - y}{x_2 - x} = \frac{P_2 Q_2}{PQ_2}$$

It is clear from Figure 16.4(b) that the slope of PP_2 is closer to the slope of the curve at P, and if we take further points P_3, P_4, ..., P_n getting closer and closer to P on the curve, then the slopes of PP_3, PP_4,..., PP_n become closer and closer to the slope of the curve at P. What we are describing is a **limiting process** and it proceeds until the P_n point is almost indistinguishable from P. When P_n is only a minute distance away from P in both the x- and y-directions, then we denote these distances by 'δx' and 'δy'. Thus the slope of PP_n is given by

$$\text{slope } PP_n = \frac{P_n Q_n}{PQ_n} = \frac{\delta y}{\delta x}$$

We here have a fraction with an 'almost zero' quantity δy on the top and an 'almost zero' quantity δx on the bottom. But still the value of the gradient $\delta y / \delta x$ has a meaning, and in the limit as δx approaches zero, we say that $\delta y / \delta x \simeq dy/dx$. By this process, called **differentiation**, we have arrived at the **gradient function** or **derivative** of a curve, since dy/dx (which we say as 'dee-wy by dee-ex') is the name given to the gradient of a tangent of a curve. Geometrically when δx is almost zero, then P_n is (almost) coincident with P, and the chord PP_n is (almost identical with) the tangent line at P. We need to make a great 'leap of faith' to believe that this gives a reasonable answer. You may justify this by referring to any standard calculus textbook (look it up under 'differentiation from first principles').

We have arrived at a method of calculating the numerical value of the gradient of any tangent to a curve, which is then defined to be the gradient of the curve itself at that point. We shall see in the following section that the methods of these calculations follow straightforward patterns and in Appendix E we include a step-by-step 'differentiation from first principles' of the curve given by the equation $y = x^2$ with the result $dy/dx = 2x$

16.4 Practical rules for differentiation

We now discuss the gradient functions or derivatives of some functions that are commonly used for computer graphics.

16.4.1 Constants

The simplest graph is for a function that does not vary at all, and hence stays as a constant number, C, for all values of x. This function can be written

$$y = C$$

and an example is plotted in Figure 16.5. Its gradient m is clearly zero so

$$m = \frac{dy}{dx} = 0$$

This result is shown as the first row in Table 16.3 in Section 16.4.5.

16.4.2 A general straight line

As in Section 16.2 we know that every straight line has an equation of the form $y = mx + c$, and that the value of 'm' gives us the gradient of the line. Thus for any such straight line, $dy/dx = m$. In particular, for the straight line $y = x$ shown in Figure 16.6 we have

$$y = 1 \times x + 0$$

so that $m = 1$. Thus for the function $y = x$ we have $dy/dx = 1$. This result appears in the second row of Table 16.3.

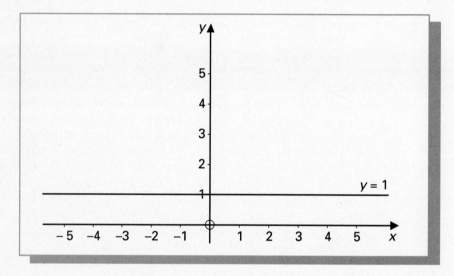

Figure 16.5 Graph of the straight line $y = 1$ with zero derivative.

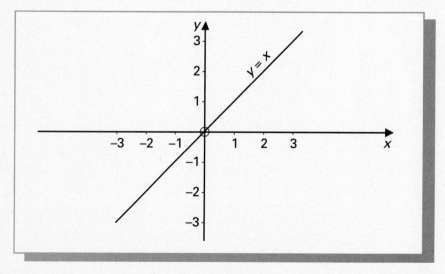

Figure 16.6 Graph of the straight line given by $y = x$.

16.4.3 The function $y = x^2$

The third row of Table 16.3 gives the result obtained by differentiation from first principles in Appendix E. The result is that when we have the curve given by

$$y = x^2$$

then the derivative is

$$\frac{dy}{dx} = 2x$$

We now consider this result at specific points on the curve between the values $x = -2$ and $x = 2$. Evaluating the function at a number of points produces Table 16.2, and the values from the table are plotted to give the curve in Figure 16.7.

Table 16.2 Values of x and y for the curve $y = x^2$.

x	−2.0	−1.5	−1.0	−0.5	0	0.5	1.0	1.5	2.0
$y = x^2$	4.0	2.25	1.0	0.25	0	0.25	1.0	2.25	4.0

Inspecting this curve we see that at the point A at the bottom of the curve, where $x = 0$, the direction of the curve is along the x-axis, and it thus has zero slope here. At the point B given by $x = 1$, it can be seen that the curve is sloping in the positive, uphill direction, that is from bottom left to top right. At the point C where $x = -1$, the slope is negative or downhill, from top left to bottom right. We will see that these slopes can be obtained from the derivative and that the numerical values of the slopes at points B and C can be calculated.

From what has been said previously we regard the derivative, $2x$, to be the slope of the curve. We can check this out in the particular cases. First at $x = 0$,

$$m = \frac{dy}{dx} = 2 \times 0 = 0$$

The slope is thus zero, which is confirmed when we look at the bottom of the graph

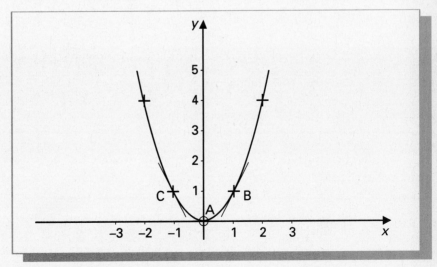

Figure 16.7 Graph of the function $y = x^2$.

in Figure 16.7. We next consider the point, B, where $x = 1$. Here

$$m = \frac{dy}{dx} = 2 \times 1 = 2$$

which corresponds to the positive gradient on the graph in Figure 16.7. We consider further the point C, corresponding to $x = -1$, then

$$m = \frac{dy}{dx} = 2 \times (-1) = -2$$

which gives the negative gradient which can also be seen from the graph.

16.4.4 The function $y = x^n$

When we differentiate different powers of x, we obtain the following results:

for $\quad y = x^2$, $\qquad \dfrac{dy}{dx} = 2x$ (see above)

for $\quad y = x^3$, $\qquad \dfrac{dy}{dx} = 3x^2$

for $\quad y = x^4$, $\qquad \dfrac{dy}{dx} = 4x^3$

for $\quad y = x^5$, $\qquad \dfrac{dy}{dx} = 5x^4$

There is an obvious pattern developing here, and it can be shown that it is always true that

for $\quad y = x^n$, $\qquad \dfrac{dy}{dx} = nx^{n-1}$

as shown in Table 16.3. Negative powers are also allowed, so that for example, when $n = -1$,

for $\quad y = x^{-1}$, $\qquad \dfrac{dy}{dx} = (-1)\, x^{-1-1}$

$$= -x^{-2}$$

Since a negative power means 'an inverse', we have

$$x^{-1} = \frac{1}{x} \text{ and } x^{-2} = \frac{1}{x^2}$$

Thus the above result can be rewritten:

for $\quad y = \dfrac{1}{x}$, $\qquad \dfrac{dy}{dx} = -\dfrac{1}{x^2}$

To illustrate the case when n is a fraction, we consider $n = \frac{1}{2}$. Then

for $\quad y = x^{1/2}$, $\qquad \dfrac{dy}{dx} = \dfrac{1}{2} x^{-1/2}$

As already seen in Section 7.3, the power $\frac{1}{2}$ corresponds to the square root so that, in combination with the negative power, we have

for $\quad y = \sqrt{x}$ $\qquad \dfrac{dy}{dx} = \dfrac{1}{2}\dfrac{1}{x^{1/2}} = \dfrac{1}{2\sqrt{x}}$

16.4.5 Table of derivatives

We can put the above results together to form a table of the most commonly used derivatives.

Table 16.3 Derivatives of commonly used functions.

y	$\dfrac{dy}{dx}$
C, constant	0
x	1
x^2	$2x$
x^n	nx^{n-1}
$\sin x$	$\cos x$
$\cos x$	$-\sin x$

The last two rows of Table 16.3 are concerned with the trigonometric functions sine and cosine introduced in Section 1.5. These quantities have previously been defined in terms of the sides of a right-angled triangle for a particular value of an angle. Different values of the angle give different values for the sine and cosine; thus as discussed in Section 7.2 they can each be thought of as functions of the angle. For the derivatives of these functions given in Table 16.3 it is essential that the angle is measured in radians (see Section 1.5).

16.4.6 Combinations of functions

Other functions could have been added to Table 16.3 but they are not widely used in the early stages of computer graphics and can be found when needed from the many books on calculus. It is, however, important to be able to find the derivative of combinations of functions. This then allows us to find the slopes of a wide range of curves with many practical applications. Combinations of functions of the type discussed in Sections 16.4.1 to 16.4.4 are very widely used for curves and for surfaces, as we shall see. Some combinations, such as $x^4 + 3x^3 + 5x + 2$ for example, are called **polynomials**. Simple rules apply to differentiating these combinations of functions:

1. The individual parts may be differentiated separately, that is we can differentiate 'term by term'.

2. Multiplying factors can be 'taken through' the differentiation.

3. Constant terms have zero derivative.

Let us first use these simple rules to differentiate $y = x^4 + 3x^3 + 5x + 2$. Dealing on a term-by-term basis we get immediately that

$$\frac{dy}{dx} = 4x^{4-1} + 3 \times 3\ x^{3-1} + 5 \times 1 + 0$$

$$= 4x^3 + 9x^2 + 5$$

As another example we consider the function $y = x^2 + 1$. We differentiate according to the above rules, and we obtain

$$\frac{dy}{dx} = 2x + 0$$
$$= 2x$$

In fact this is precisely the same gradient as we get by differentiating the curve function $y = x^2$. We can see the geometric meaning of this result by looking at the curves shown in Figures 16.7 and 16.8. The curve '$y = x^2 + 1$' in Figure 16.8 only differs from the curve '$y = x^2$' in Figure 16.7 by being raised by 1 unit, and its slope is clearly not changed by this translation.

Finally we take the curve whose function is $y = x^2 - 10x + 24$ and we consider the gradients of the tangents to this curve at the points where $x = 0$, $x = 4$, $x = 5$, $x = 6$ and $x = 10$. To get a feeling for this curve we start out by sketching it, using a 'table of values' (Table 16.4) similar to Tables 16.1 and 16.2. We choose values of x, then calculate the corresponding y-values. The coordinates of points are read from the table and the corresponding graph is shown in Figure 16.9 on which we show also the five tangent lines at the stated points. We find the gradients of these tangents by first differentiating the curve function

$$y = x^2 - 10x + 24$$

Table 16.4 Values of x and y for the function $y = x^2 - 10x + 24$.

x	0	1	2	3	4	5	6	7	8	9	10
x^2	0	1	4	9	16	25	36	49	64	81	100
$-10x$	-0	-10	-20	-30	-40	-50	-60	-70	-80	-90	-100
$+24$	$+24$	$+24$	$+24$	$+24$	$+24$	$+24$	$+24$	$+24$	$+24$	$+24$	$+24$
$y = x^2 - 10x + 24$	24	15	8	3	0	-1	0	3	8	15	24

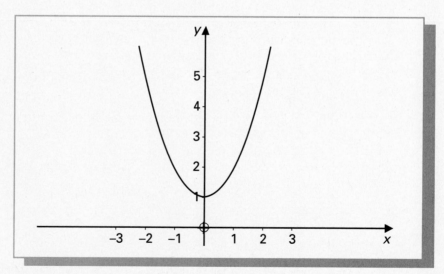

Figure 16.8 Graph of the function $y = x^2 + 1$.

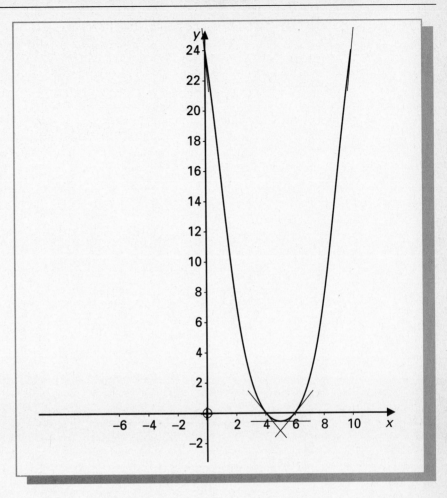

Figure 16.9 Graph of the function $y = x^2 - 10x + 24$, showing tangents at the points having values of $x = 0, 4, 5, 6, 10$

to give

$$\frac{dy}{dx} = 2x - (10 \times 1) + 0$$

That is

$$\frac{dy}{dx} = 2x - 10$$

For the point where $x = 0$, we substitute this value and obtain

$$\frac{dy}{dx} = (2 \times 0) - 10 = -10$$

Thus the gradient of the tangent to this curve where $x = 0$ is '−10'. That is shown, as expected, as a steep 'downhill' line on the graph. Similar calculations give the gradients of the tangents for the other values of x.

16.5 Slope of a straight line from its vector equation

In the previous sections we have focused on differentiating functions of lines and curves when they are given using Cartesian coordinates. However, we know that for practical applications in computer graphics we are much more likely to need the equations of lines and curves using parameters. We now complete this chapter by showing how the techniques of differentiation can be used to find the gradient of a straight line given by its vector (parametric) equation. Using information from Section 6.1, we know that the vector equation of a straight line passing through points whose position vectors are $\mathbf{a}$ and $\mathbf{b}$ can be given by

$$\mathbf{r}(u) = \mathbf{a} + u(\mathbf{b} - \mathbf{a})$$

where u is a parameter. As an illustration we take $\mathbf{a} = (1 \quad 2)$ and $\mathbf{b} = (4 \quad 3)$, and we calculate the gradient of this line, shown in Figure 16.10.

The equation of the line is

$$\mathbf{r}(u) = (1 \quad 2) + u[(4 \quad 3) - (1 \quad 2)]$$
$$= (1 \quad 2) + u(3 \quad 1)$$
$$= (1 + 3u \quad \quad 2 + u)$$

In component terms we have

$$\mathbf{r}(u) = (1 + 3u)\mathbf{i} + (2 + u)\mathbf{j}$$

and from this we can obtain the gradient of the line. The $\mathbf{i}$-component is $x = 1 + 3u$, so that

$$\frac{dx}{du} = 0 + (3 \times 1) = 3$$

The $\mathbf{j}$-component is $y = 2 + u$ so that

$$\frac{dy}{du} = 0 + 1 = 1$$

Since $\mathbf{i}$ and $\mathbf{j}$ are constant vectors, the tangent vector (in this case the straight line itself) is denoted by

$$\frac{d\mathbf{r}}{du} = \frac{dx}{du}\mathbf{i} + \frac{dy}{du}\mathbf{j}$$

Thus here the tangent vector is

$$\frac{d\mathbf{r}}{du} = 3\mathbf{i} + \mathbf{j}$$

which of course can also be written

$$\frac{d\mathbf{r}}{du} = (3 \quad 1)$$

The gradient of the tangent vector is given by

$$\frac{dy}{dx} = \frac{dy/du}{dx/du}$$

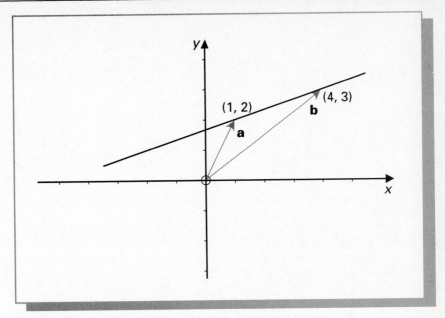

Figure 16.10 Straight line given by the vector equation $\mathbf{r}(u) = \mathbf{a} + u(\mathbf{b} - \mathbf{a})$.

and so in this case

$$\frac{\mathrm{d}y}{\mathrm{d}x} = \frac{1}{3}$$

This method, described above for a straight line, works equally well to enable us to find the tangent vector to a planar curve whose equation is given in vector form.

Finally we note that using this format the gradient function $\mathrm{d}y/\mathrm{d}x$ depends on both $\mathrm{d}y/\mathrm{d}u$ and $\mathrm{d}x/\mathrm{d}u$. Since

$$\frac{\mathrm{d}y}{\mathrm{d}x} = \frac{\mathrm{d}y/\mathrm{d}u}{\mathrm{d}x/\mathrm{d}u}$$

if $\mathrm{d}y/\mathrm{d}u = 0$ we have $\mathrm{d}y/\mathrm{d}x = 0$; thus the tangent is parallel to the x-axis. Alternatively, if $\mathrm{d}x/\mathrm{d}u = 0$ then $\mathrm{d}y/\mathrm{d}x$ is 'infinitely large' (so large that it can be given no precise value) and so the tangent is parallel to the y-axis. The representation of a straightforward geometric feature of a vertical tangent by an infinitely large quantity is unfortunate since such quantities cannot be dealt with by a computer. In fact the parametric representation of slopes of curves is an improvement on the Cartesian representation, since a vertical slope is given by a finite value of $\mathrm{d}y/\mathrm{d}u$ together with $\mathrm{d}x/\mathrm{d}u = 0$.

Here we have introduced the basic ideas of differentiation, so that we can now calculate the slopes of general curves. This is an important technique in computer graphics. In future chapters we shall be extending it both to find the tangent of curves in space, and also to find the slopes along surfaces.

Exercises

16.1 Using the x-values $x = 1$, $x = 2$ and $x = 3$ in each case, plot the graphs of the straight lines whose Cartesian equations are:

a) $y = x$, b) $y = x - 1$, c) $y = \frac{1}{2}x + 3$

16.2 On a two-dimensional graph, sketch the straight lines whose Cartesian equations are:

a) $y = 4x + 1$ b) $y = \frac{1}{2}x + 3$ c) $y = x - 7$

d) $y = -x + 2$ e) $y = -\frac{1}{2}x - 1$ f) $y = -3x$.

16.3 For each of the straight lines in Exercise 16.2, write down (i) its gradient and (ii) its 'y-intercept'.

16.4 Write down the Cartesian equations of the straight lines with the following gradients and y-intercepts:

a) $2; 1$ b) $\frac{1}{4}; -3$ c) $0.8; 2.2$

16.5 Differentiate the following functions, and hence write down the gradient function of each:

a) $y = 3x + 2$ b) $y = 4x^2 - 2x + 9$ c) $y = x^3 - 27$

d) $y = \frac{1}{2}x^2 + 4x$ e) $y = 6x^4 + 3x^2 - 5$ f) $y = (x - 4)^2$

16.6 Find the value of the slopes of the following functions at the points indicated:

a) $y = 4x^2 + 9x - 1$, when $x = 2$

b) $y = x^3 - 3x^2$, when $x = -3$

c) $y = t^{3/2} + t^{1/2} - t^{-1/2}$, when $t = 1$

16.7 a) If $y = \sin \theta + 2 \cos \theta$, determine $dy/d\theta$, and calculate its value when $\theta = \pi/4$.

b) If $z = \cos \theta - \frac{1}{2} \sin \theta$, determine $dz/d\theta$, and calculate its value when $\theta = 3\pi/4$.

c) If $x = 3 \sin \theta$ and $y = 4 \cos \theta$, write down $dx/d\theta$ and $dy/d\theta$, and hence evaluate dy/dx when $\theta = \pi/3$.

16.8 Determine a vector equation of the straight line that passes through each of the following pairs of points, using the form $\mathbf{r}(u) = x(u)\mathbf{i} + y(u)\mathbf{j}$. (Answers may vary).

a) $(0, 0)$ and $(2, 2)$

b) $(-1, 0)$ and $(3, 5)$

c) $(-2, 1)$ and $(2, -2)$

In each case also calculate dx/du and dy/du and hence write down the 'tangent vector' to each line. What is the gradient of each tangent?

Answers

16.1 The lines will pass through the points with these coordinates:

a) $(1, 1)$, $(2, 2)$, $(3, 3)$; b) $(1, 0)$, $(2, 1)$, $(3, 2)$;

c) $(1, 3\frac{1}{2})$, $(2, 4)$.

16.3 a) (i) 4 (ii) 1; b) (i) $\frac{1}{2}$ (ii) 3; c) (i) 1 (ii) -7;

d) (i) -1 (ii) 2; e) (i) $-\frac{1}{2}$ (ii) -1; f) (i) -3 (ii) 0.

16.4 a) $y = 2x + 1$; b) $y = \frac{1}{4}x - 3$ or $4y = x - 12$; c) $y = 0.8x + 2.2$ or $5y = 4x + 11$.

16.5 a) $\frac{dy}{dx} = 3$; b) $\frac{dy}{dx} = 8x - 2$; c) $\frac{dy}{dx} = 3x^2$;

d) $\frac{dy}{dx} = x + 4$; e) $\frac{dy}{dx} = 24x^3 + 6x$; f) $\frac{dy}{dx} = 2x - 8$.

16.6 a) 25; b) 45 c) $2\frac{1}{2}$.

16.7 a) -0.71; b) -0.35; c) -2.31.

16.8 a) $\mathbf{r}(u) = 2u\mathbf{i} + 2u\mathbf{j}$. $\frac{dx}{du} = 2$, $\frac{dy}{du} = 2$. $(2 \quad 2)$. Gradient is 1.

b) $\mathbf{r}(u) = (-1 + 4u)\mathbf{i} + 5u\mathbf{j}$. $\frac{dx}{du} = 4$, $\frac{dy}{du} = 5$. $(4 \quad 5)$. Gradient is $5/4$.

c) $\mathbf{r}(u) = (-2 + 4u)\mathbf{i} + (1 - 3u)\mathbf{j}$. $\frac{dx}{du} = 4$, $\frac{dy}{du} = -3$. $(4 \quad -3)$. Gradient is $-3/4$.

Slopes of space curves:
Tangents and normals

17.1 Space curves

In the previous chapter we dealt with straight lines and curves drawn in the x–y plane, principally those given by Cartesian equations. There we saw that their slope is given by differentiating the formula that describes the curve. However, as we showed in Chapter 7, describing curves by their Cartesian equations is not the best way for computer graphics: vector equations with parameters are preferred. Thus, as was seen in two dimensions, a circle of radius R can be given by

$$\mathbf{r}(\theta) = R \cos \theta \, \mathbf{i} + R \sin \theta \, \mathbf{j}$$

and in three dimensions a circular helix of radius R can be given by

$$\mathbf{r}(\theta) = R \cos \theta \, \mathbf{i} + R \sin \theta \, \mathbf{j} + C\theta \mathbf{k}$$

The helix is clearly a curve passing through three-dimensional space, and the circle is a curve lying in a particular plane in three-dimensional space. Thus we may call these curves **space curves**. They can form the basis of tracks or fly throughs, or have related graphical features attached to them as in Figure 17.1 where the helix has been extended to form a helical tube: clearly the shape of the outside of this tube is related to the slope of the basic helix.

In this chapter we shall deal with the task of finding the slopes of general curves in space. Subsequently we shall also calculate the slopes of normals to curves, and extend these ideas to normals of surfaces, which are essential for 'lighting models'.

17.2 The tangent vector to a space curve

A **continuous** space curve (that is, one in which there are no gaps) is illustrated in Figure 17.2, and two neighbouring points P and P_1 are shown on it. Such a curve can be named '$\mathbf{r}(u)$', and we remember that, using this notation, $\mathbf{r}(u)$ is the position vector of the point P on the curve for any particular value of the parameter u. Since P and P_1 are neighbouring points on the curve, if P has position vector $\mathbf{r}(u)$

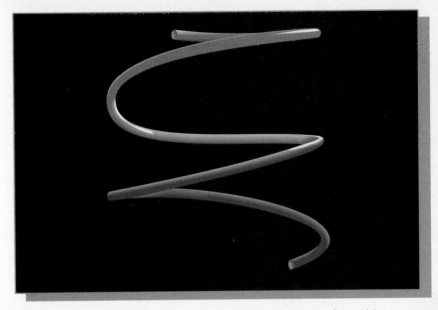

Figure 17.1 A tube based on a helix *(source: Matthew Holton, University of Teesside).*

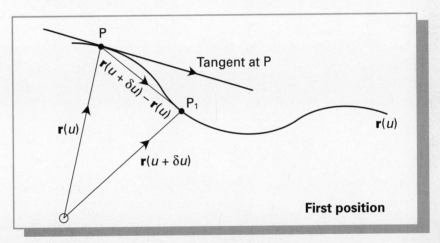

Figure 17.2 Neighbouring points on a space curve (first position).

then P_1 has position vector $\mathbf{r}(u + \delta u)$: the use of the same $\mathbf{r}$ indicates that P_1 is on the same curve and the original value of the parameter being increased by the small amount δu means that P_1 is near to P.

The position vectors of P and P_1 are shown in Figure 17.2, and we see that we can also draw in the vector $\mathbf{PP}_1$. Since these three vectors form a triangle, by the rule for adding vectors we have

$$\mathbf{r}(u + \delta u) = \mathbf{r}(u) + \mathbf{PP}_1$$

and hence

$$\mathbf{PP}_1 = \mathbf{r}(u + \delta u) - \mathbf{r}(u)$$

Now in a similar way to that shown in Figure 16.4, the point P_1 can be moved closer to the point P by making δu smaller (see Figure 17.3). This causes the vector $\mathbf{PP_1}$ to lie more in the direction of the space curve. By taking P_1 closer and closer to P, the vector $\mathbf{PP_1}$ becomes closer and closer to the direction of the tangent to the curve at P.

If we consider only the vector $\mathbf{PP_1}$ given by $\mathbf{r}(u+\delta u) - \mathbf{r}(u)$ as δu gets smaller and smaller then we would finish up with a vector $\mathbf{PP_1}$ which was itself nearly zero: this would tell us nothing, in particular nothing about the direction of the tangent. We need a quantity that gives us the tangent but does not have zero length. This is achieved by multiplying $\mathbf{PP_1}$ by the scalar quantity $(1/\delta u)$, to obtain

$$\frac{1}{\delta u}\left(\mathbf{r}(u+\delta u) - \mathbf{r}(u)\right) = \frac{\mathbf{r}(u+\delta u) - \mathbf{r}(u)}{\delta u}$$

As δu tends to zero, the top and the bottom of this fraction tend to zero, but their ratio tends to a finite quantity that is the derivative of the vector form of the curve and is denoted by $d\mathbf{r}(u)/du$, or $d\mathbf{r}/du$. This quantity is a tangent vector $\mathbf{t}$ to the space curve at the point P. As expected, it is a vector quantity since a tangent is a straight line that has direction. For most purposes only the direction of this tan-

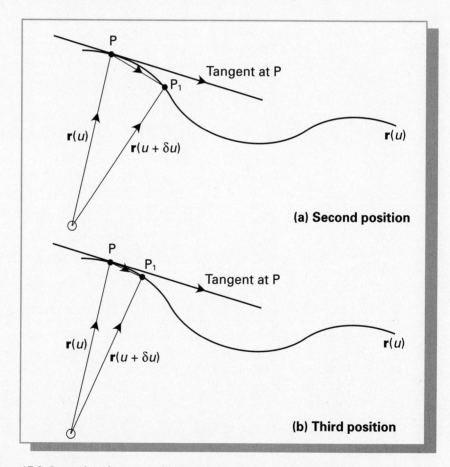

(a) **Second position**

(b) **Third position**

Figure 17.3 P_1 moving closer to P: (a) second position; (b) third position.

gent is important, and so we shall often use merely the tangent vector of length '1', that is the **unit tangent** to the curve given by $\hat{\mathbf{t}} = \mathbf{t}\ /|\mathbf{t}|$.

17.3 Tangents and normals for curves in a plane

In practice, the calculation of a specific tangent vector is usually carried out from the vector equation of the curve when it is given in component form. Once we have a vector that is a tangent to the curve at any point, then we are in a position to investigate whether we can determine a normal to that curve, and whether this normal is unique. We now illustrate the techniques involved by means of two examples, based on a parabola and an ellipse similar to those discussed in Sections 7.3 and 7.5.

Example 17.1 A parabola

We consider the parabola with equation

$$\mathbf{r}(u) = 3u^2\mathbf{i} + 4u\mathbf{j}$$

and determine its tangents and normals for particular parameter values.

So that we can sketch the curve, we construct Table 17.1 based on our chosen values of the parameter u:

Table 17.1 Values for components of $\mathbf{r}(u) = 3u^2\mathbf{i} + 4u\mathbf{j}$.

u	−4	−3	−2	−1	0	1	2	3	4
$3u^2$	48	27	12	3	0	3	12	27	48
$4u$	−16	−12	−8	−4	0	4	8	12	16

As in Section 7.3, we now plot points on this curve and join them to display the parabola shown in Figure 17.4.

To find the tangent vector at any point on this parabola, we apply the techniques for differentiation discussed in Section 16.4.4. The parabola equation is

$$\mathbf{r}(u) = 3u^2\mathbf{i} + 4u\mathbf{j}$$

and, as in Section 16.5, we differentiate $\mathbf{r}$ by differentiating the $\mathbf{i}$- and $\mathbf{j}$-components term by term (remembering that $\mathbf{i}$ and $\mathbf{j}$ are constant vectors). The $\mathbf{i}$-component is

$$x = 3u^2, \text{ so } dx/du = 6u$$

the $\mathbf{j}$-component is

$$y = 4u, \text{ so } dy/du = 4$$

Then

$$\frac{d\mathbf{r}}{du} = \frac{dx}{du}\mathbf{i} + \frac{dy}{du}\mathbf{j}$$

so that in this case we have

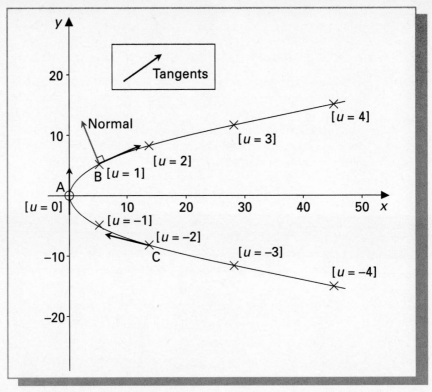

Figure 17.4 Tangent vectors to a parabola.

$$\frac{dr}{du} = 6u\mathbf{i} + 4\mathbf{j}$$

which is the form of the tangent vector at any general point on the parabola. To simplify the notation we are calling a general tangent vector **t** and we have

$$\frac{dr}{du} = \mathbf{t} = 6u\mathbf{i} + 4\mathbf{j}$$

We now check that this formula for **t** gives us the appropriate tangents to the parabola for any particular value of u which we choose. If we take $u = 0$, then

$$\mathbf{t} = 0\mathbf{i} + 4\mathbf{j}, \text{ so } \mathbf{t} = 4\mathbf{j}$$

This is the vector pointing along the direction of the y-axis at A, shown in Figure 17.4, and is clearly a tangent to the curve at A. For this value of u we can see that the magnitude of the tangent vector is 4, and so the unit vector here is

$$\hat{\mathbf{t}} = \frac{4\mathbf{j}}{4} = \mathbf{j}, \text{ along the } y\text{-axis.}$$

If we take another value of the parameter, $u = 1$ say, then we have

$$\mathbf{t} = (6 \times 1)\mathbf{i} + 4\mathbf{j}$$

so that

$$t = 6i + 4j$$

This tangent vector is plotted by proceeding 6 units in the direction of i and 4 units in the direction of j so that its gradient is $4/6 = 2/3$; it is clearly in the correct direction for the tangent to the parabola at the point B as shown in Figure 17.4. The magnitude of this tangent vector is

$$|t| = \sqrt{(6^2 + 4^2)} = \sqrt{36 + 16} = \sqrt{52}$$

so the unit tangent at the point B is given by

$$\hat{t} = \frac{1}{\sqrt{52}}(6i + 4j)$$

that is

$$\hat{t} \simeq 0.83i + 0.55j$$

If we want the vector equation of this tangent line, then we use the method of Section 6.1. The line passes through B which has position vector $(3i + 4j)$, and its direction is given by $(6i + 4j)$, thus its vector equation is

$$r(v) = (3i + 4j) + v(6i + 4j)$$

$$= (3 + 6v)i + (4 + 4v)j$$

We have used a different letter for the parameter needed in the equation of this line, to avoid confusion with that used in the equation of the curve itself.

We now take yet another value of the original parameter. When $u = -2$ on the parabola, we have

$$t = (6 \times -2)i + 4j$$

so that

$$t = -12i + 4j$$

This tangent vector is plotted by proceeding 12 units in the direction of negative i, and 4 units in the direction of j. This is shown in Figure 17.4 as the correct direction for the tangent line at the point C, with gradient $4/-12 = 1/-3$. We now perform the same calculations as before. The magnitude of this vector is

$$\sqrt{((-12)^2 + 4^2)} = \sqrt{(144 + 16)} = \sqrt{160}$$

so the unit tangent at the point C is given by

$$\hat{t} = \frac{1}{\sqrt{160}}(-12i + 4j)$$

that is

$$\hat{t} \simeq -0.95i + 0.32j$$

Finally, to determine the vector equation of this tangent line we note that it passes through the point C whose position vector is $(12i - 8j)$, and its direction is given by $(-12i + 4j)$, hence by the method of Section 6.1 again, its vector equation is

$$r(v) = (12i - 8j) + v(-12i + 4j)$$

that is

$$r(v) = (12 - 12v)i + (-8 + 4v)j$$

using an alternative parameter, v, as before.

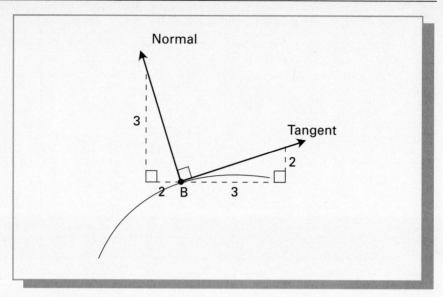

Figure 17.5 The normal to B on the parabola.

As shown above, at any point on the curve we can calculate the gradient of the tangent. Then since tangents and normals are perpendicular by definition, we can deduce the gradient of a normal at any point, and hence, if we want, the vector equation of the normal. We illustrate this by again considering the tangent at the point B. We have already seen that the gradient of this tangent is 2/3. So, since the parabola lies in the *x*–*y* plane, we can use the result from Example 1.5, and show that the gradient of the normal to the parabola in the *x*–*y* plane is –3/2. Within the plane of a planar curve there is only one normal to the curve at any point. Hence, as indicated in Figure 17.5, the normal has direction $(2\mathbf{i} - 3\mathbf{j})$. Since it passes through the point B whose position vector is $(3\mathbf{i} + 4\mathbf{j})$, we can immediately use the method of Section 6.1 as before to write down the vector equation for this line

$$\mathbf{r}(w) = (3\mathbf{i} + 4\mathbf{j}) + w(2\mathbf{i} - 3\mathbf{j})$$

Hence the equation of the normal, in terms of a different alternative parameter *w*, is

$$\mathbf{r}(w) = (3 + 2w)\mathbf{i} + (4 - 3w)\mathbf{j}$$

Example 17.2   An ellipse

We consider the ellipse with equation

$$\mathbf{r}(\theta) = 2\cos\theta\,\mathbf{i} + \sin\theta\,\mathbf{j}$$

and determine its tangents and normals for particular parameter values.

As in Section 17.1 we begin by constructing a table (Table 17.2) based upon our choice of values of the parameter θ. Since we shall be using differentiation it is essential that θ, a variable angle, is measured in radians. The other figures in the table are accurate to two places of decimals, which gives us plenty of accuracy for the scale we are using. As before, we now sketch the ellipse by plotting these values and joining up the points with a curve, as shown in Figure 17.6.

Table 17.2 Values of components of $\mathbf{r}(\theta) = 2 \cos \theta\, \mathbf{i} + \sin \theta\, \mathbf{j}$.

θ	0	$\pi/4$	$\pi/2$	$3\pi/4$	π	$5\pi/4$	$3\pi/2$	$7\pi/4$	2π
$2 \cos \theta$	2	1.41	0	−1.41	−2	−1.41	0	1.41	2
$\sin \theta$	0	0.71	1	0.71	0	−0.71	−1	−0.71	0

To find the tangent vector at any point on this ellipse, we differentiate the equation of the curve term by term (since $\mathbf{i}$ and $\mathbf{j}$ are constant vectors). From the equation

$$\mathbf{r}(\theta) = 2 \cos \theta\, \mathbf{i} + \sin \theta\, \mathbf{j}$$

we have that the $\mathbf{i}$-component, x, is $2 \cos \theta$, and the $\mathbf{j}$-component, y, is $\sin \theta$. From these we use the standard derivatives from Table 16.3 to obtain

$$\frac{dx}{d\theta} = -2 \sin \theta \text{ and } \frac{dy}{d\theta} = \cos \theta$$

Thus a tangent vector at a general point on the ellipse is here given by

$$\mathbf{t} = \frac{d\mathbf{r}}{d\theta} = -2 \sin \theta\, \mathbf{i} + \cos \theta\, \mathbf{j}$$

We now consider the tangents to the ellipse for particular values of the parameter θ. For the value $\theta = 0$ we have

$$\mathbf{t} = -2 \sin 0\, \mathbf{i} + \cos 0\, \mathbf{j}$$

so here

$$\mathbf{t} = 0\mathbf{i} + 1\mathbf{j}$$

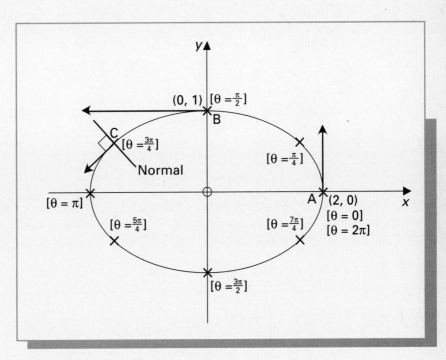

Figure 17.6 Tangents and normal to an ellipse.

taking values from a calculator if necessary, that is

$$\mathbf{t} = \mathbf{j}$$

The tangent in this case is a unit vector, so here we have $\hat{\mathbf{t}} = \mathbf{j}$. This tangent vector is plotted on Figure 17.6 at the point A which has coordinates $(2, 0)$; it is clearly in the correct direction.

If we take the parameter value $\theta = \pi/2$, then we have

$$\mathbf{t} = -2 \sin \pi/2 \; \mathbf{i} + \cos \pi/2 \; \mathbf{j}$$

that is

$$\mathbf{t} = -2\mathbf{i} + 0\mathbf{j}$$

so we get

$$\mathbf{t} = -2\mathbf{i}$$

which is a tangent vector at this point. This vector is in the direction of the negative x-axis, which is clearly consistent with the tangent to the ellipse drawn at the point B$(0, 1)$. The magnitude of the vector is 2, so the unit tangent to the ellipse at the point B is given by $\hat{\mathbf{t}} = -\mathbf{i}$.

We now take yet another value of the parameter: when $\theta = 3\pi/4$ we have

$$\mathbf{t} = -2 \sin 3\pi/4 \; \mathbf{i} + \cos 3\pi/4 \; \mathbf{j}$$

which, when simplified using a calculator, becomes

$$\mathbf{t} \simeq -1.41\mathbf{i} - 0.71\mathbf{j}$$

This tangent vector is plotted by proceeding 1.41 units in the direction of negative $\mathbf{i}$, and 0.71 units in the direction of negative $\mathbf{j}$. This is shown in Figure 17.6 as the appropriate direction for the tangent line at the point C. The gradient of this line is $-0.71/-1.41$ using our approximations; in fact it is exactly $\frac{1}{2}$. The magnitude of this tangent vector is

$$\sqrt{(-1.41)^2 + (-0.71)^2} \simeq \sqrt{2 + \tfrac{1}{2}} \simeq 1.58$$

Thus the unit tangent at the point C is given by

$$\hat{\mathbf{t}} \simeq \frac{1}{1.58} (-1.41\mathbf{i} - 0.71\mathbf{j})$$

that is

$$\hat{\mathbf{t}} \simeq -0.89\mathbf{i} - 0.45\mathbf{j}$$

If we want the vector equation of this tangent line, we note that it passes through the point C whose position vector is $(-1.41\mathbf{i} + 0.71\mathbf{j})$, and its direction is given by $(-1.41\mathbf{i} - 0.71\mathbf{j})$, thus its equation is

$$\mathbf{r}(v) = (-1.41\mathbf{i} + 0.71\mathbf{j}) + v(-1.41\mathbf{i} - 0.71\mathbf{j})$$

that is

$$\mathbf{r}(v) = (-1.41 - 1.41v)\mathbf{i} + (0.71 - 0.71v)\mathbf{j}$$

where we introduce v as the parameter for the tangent line. If it is more convenient, this may be factorized to:

$$\mathbf{r}(v) = -1.41(1 + v)\mathbf{i} + 0.71(1 - v)\mathbf{j}$$

This ellipse, like the parabola of Example 17.1, is a curve which lies in the two-dimensional x–y plane. In this plane, at every point on the curve there is only one normal which may be drawn. In this example we return to the tangent at the point C: we stated above that the gradient of this tangent is $\frac{1}{2}$, so the gradient of the normal in this plane is –2, see Example 1.5. Thus the direction of this normal is given by the vector $(\mathbf{i} - 2\mathbf{j})$. Since it passes through the point C which has position vector $(-1.41\mathbf{i} + 0.71\mathbf{j})$ we can write down the vector equation of the normal as:

$$\mathbf{r}(w) = (-1.41\mathbf{i} + 0.71\mathbf{j}) + w(\mathbf{i} - 2\mathbf{j})$$

that is

$$\mathbf{r}(w) = (-1.41 + w)\mathbf{i} + (0.71 - 2w)\mathbf{j}$$

where this time we use w as the parameter for the line.

17.4 Tangents and normals in three dimensions

For any space curve, defined in three dimensions, we can apply the methods of differentiation to determine the tangent at any point, exactly as we did in Section 17.3 above. We take the component form of the vector equation of the curve, and differentiate it term by term with respect to the parameter. This will always give us a tangent vector, provided that the curve is continuous. By straightforward means we can then find the direction of the tangent vector, and a unit tangent vector. We can also determine the vector equation of the tangent line if it is needed.

However, if we seek a normal to a space curve, we find that there is no single normal vector, but rather a **normal plane** to the curve at any point. All that we require of a normal vector is that it is perpendicular to a tangent vector; but we see that for any given tangent vector there are an unlimited number of vectors normal to it: these all lie in the plane that is normal to the curve, as shown in Figure 17.7. In three dimensions as in two this perpendicularity is guaranteed if we ensure that the scalar product of vectors is zero (see Section 3.2).

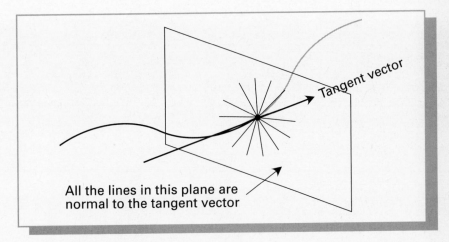

Figure 17.7 Normal plane to a space curve.

To illustrate these features on a space curve, we now consider a circular helix, of the type first introduced in Section 7.6.

Example 17.3 A helix

We consider the helix with equation

$$r(\theta) = 2 \cos \theta i + 2 \sin \theta j + 0.3\theta k$$

which can be visualized as lying coiled around the outside of a cylinder of radius 2, as shown in Figure 17.8. Increasing the parameter θ causes a cyclic progression around the cylinder, with the i- and j-components returning to their original values after every additional 2π. But increases in θ simultaneously cause movement along the length of the cylinder in the direction of k, and we see that in this case the pitch of the helix is the distance $0.6\pi \simeq 1.88$.

To find a tangent vector at any point on this helix we apply the standard techniques of differentiation. The vector equation of the curve is

$$r(\theta) = 2 \cos \theta i + 2 \sin \theta j + 0.3\theta k$$

so the i-component is

$$x = 2 \cos \theta \text{ and hence } \frac{dx}{d\theta} = -2 \sin \theta$$

the j-component is

$$y = 2 \sin \theta \text{ and hence } \frac{dy}{d\theta} = 2 \cos \theta$$

the k-component is

$$z = 0.3\theta \text{ and hence } \frac{dz}{d\theta} = 0.3$$

Combining these as in Section 17.3 gives us a tangent vector t at a general point on the curve

$$t = \frac{dr}{d\theta} = -2 \sin \theta i + 2 \cos \theta j + 0.3k$$

We next check that for some specific values of θ this formula does give us the expected tangents. If we take the value $\theta = 0$, then we first find the position vector of the point with this parameter, which is

$$r = 2 \cos 0 i + 2 \sin 0 j + (0.3 \times 0)k$$

which simplifies to

$$r = 2i$$

and gives us the point A in Figure 17.8. At this point, the tangent vector is

$$t = -2 \sin 0 i + 2 \cos 0 j + 0.3k$$

which simplifies to

$$t = 2j + 0.3k$$

This is definitely consistent with the tangent vector drawn in at A. Its direction is plotted by proceeding 2 units in the direction of j and 0.3 units in the direction of k, and it does not vary in the direction of i .

For another example we take the value $\theta = 3\pi/2$. The position vector of the point with this parameter is

$$\mathbf{r} = 2 \cos 3\pi/2\,\mathbf{i} + 2 \sin 3\pi/2\,\mathbf{j} + (0.3 \times 3\pi/2)\mathbf{k}$$

which simplifies to

$$\mathbf{r} \simeq -2\mathbf{j} + 1.41\mathbf{k}$$

This is the point is marked B on the helix. At B a tangent vector is

$$\mathbf{t} = -2 \sin 3\pi/2\,\mathbf{i} + 2 \cos 3\pi/2\,\mathbf{j} + 0.3\mathbf{k}$$

that is

$$\mathbf{t} = 2\mathbf{i} + 0.3\mathbf{k}$$

This is plotted by proceeding 2 units in the direction of $\mathbf{i}$, and 0.3 units in the direction of $\mathbf{k}$. We see that this is quite consistent with the direction of the tangent drawn on the helix at B, which does not vary at all in the direction of $\mathbf{j}$.

Suppose we are looking for a normal to the helix at B; then we are seeking a vector that has a zero scalar product when multiplied by $(-2\mathbf{i} + 0.3\mathbf{k})$. By trial and error we can verify that there are many possibilities, including those illustrated here:

$$(-2\mathbf{i} + 0\mathbf{j} + 0.3\mathbf{k}) \cdot (3\mathbf{i} + 0\mathbf{j} + 20\mathbf{k}) = -6 + 0 + 6 = 0$$

$$(-2\mathbf{i} + 0\mathbf{j} + 0.3\mathbf{k}) \cdot (-3\mathbf{i} + 0\mathbf{j} - 20\mathbf{k}) = +6 + 0 - 6 = 0$$

$$(-2\mathbf{i} + 0\mathbf{j} + 0.3\mathbf{k}) \cdot (9\mathbf{i} + 5\mathbf{j} + 60\mathbf{k}) = -18 + 0 + 18 = 0,$$

and

$$(-2\mathbf{i} + 0\mathbf{j} + 0.3\mathbf{k}) \cdot (-1.5\mathbf{i} - 3\mathbf{j} - 10\mathbf{k}) = +3 + 0 - 3 = 0$$

Thus we see that there is no unique normal vector to this curve: there are very many vectors that are normal to the tangent we started with and they all lie in the normal plane at the point B, which is illustrated in Figure 17.8.

When we are dealing with curves drawn in a plane, then at any point on the curve a single normal can be drawn; but for a curve in space we have a normal plane at any point. However when we deal with a plane in space, or any other surface, then at each point there is a unique normal to that surface; we shall return to these ideas in Chapter 20.

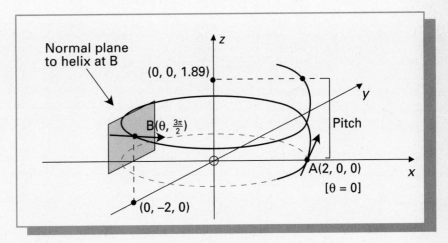

Figure 17.8 Tangents to a helix, and a normal plane.

Exercises

In Exercises 17.1 – 17.9, take each of the vector equations and plot their curves by calculating components for appropriate values of the parameters, using a 'table of values'. In Exercises 17.1, 17.2 and 17.3, eliminate the parameter in order to obtain the Cartesian equation, and so verify the shape of the curve.

17.1. $\mathbf{r}(u) = 3u\mathbf{i} + (6u - 1)\mathbf{j}$

17.2. $\mathbf{r}(u) = 2u\mathbf{i} + 8u^2\mathbf{j}$

17.3. $\mathbf{r}(\theta) = 2\cos\theta\,\mathbf{i} + \sin\theta\,\mathbf{j}$

17.4. $\mathbf{r}(u) = \mathbf{i} + u\mathbf{j} + \mathbf{k}$

17.5. $\mathbf{r}(u) = 2\mathbf{i} + u\mathbf{j} + u\mathbf{k}$

17.6. $\mathbf{r}(u) = 2u\mathbf{i} - \mathbf{j} + (3u + 1)\mathbf{k}$

17.7. $\mathbf{r}(u) = u\mathbf{i} + u\mathbf{j} + (u + 1)\mathbf{k}$

17.8. $\mathbf{r}(u) = u\mathbf{i} + u^2\mathbf{j} + 3\mathbf{k}$

17.9 $\mathbf{r}(\theta) = \cos\theta\,\mathbf{i} + \sin\theta\,\mathbf{j} + \theta\mathbf{k}$

In Exercises 17.10 – 17.14, find the unit tangent vector to the curves at the given value of each parameter.

17.10. $\mathbf{r}(u) = (1 - u)\mathbf{i} + 2u\mathbf{j}$, at $u = 1$

17.11. $\mathbf{r}(\theta) = 2\cos\theta\,\mathbf{i} + 2\sin\theta\,\mathbf{j}$, at $\theta = \pi/2$

17.12. $\mathbf{r}(\theta) = 4\cos\theta\,\mathbf{i} + \sin\theta\,\mathbf{j}$, at $\theta = 0$

17.13. $\mathbf{r}(u) = \cos u\,\mathbf{i} + \sin u\,\mathbf{j} + 2u\mathbf{k}$, at $u = 2\pi$

17.14. $\mathbf{r}(u) = u\mathbf{i} + u^2\mathbf{j} + u^3\mathbf{k}$, at $u = 3$

17.15 Consider the two-dimensional curve given by the vector equation

$$\mathbf{r}(u) = (u + 1)\mathbf{i} + u^2\mathbf{j}$$

a) Write down a general form of a tangent vector to this curve, and a general form of a normal vector to this curve. For the point on the curve where the parameter takes the value $u = 2$, write down the unit tangent vector and the unit normal vector.

b) What is the position vector of the point on the curve where $u = 2$? Use this to write down vector equations of the lines that are tangent and normal to the curve at this point.

Answers

17.1 $y = 2x - 1$ (a straight line).

17.2 $y = 2x^2$ (a parabola).

17.3 $\dfrac{x^2}{4} + y^2 = 1$ (an ellipse).

17.4 (A straight line, parallel to the y-axis, through $(1, 1, 1)$).

17.10 $-0.45\mathbf{i} + 0.89\mathbf{j}$.

17.11 $-\mathbf{i}$.

17.12 $\mathbf{j}$.

17.13 $0.45\mathbf{j} + 0.89\mathbf{k}$.

17.14 $0.04\mathbf{i} + 0.22\mathbf{j} + 0.98\mathbf{k}$.

17.15 a) $\mathbf{t} = \mathbf{i} + 2u\mathbf{j}$; $\mathbf{n} = 2u\mathbf{i} - \mathbf{j}$; $0.24\mathbf{i} + 0.97\mathbf{j}$; $0.97\mathbf{i} - 0.24\mathbf{j}$.

b) $3\mathbf{i} + 4\mathbf{j}$; tangent line $\mathbf{r}(v) = (3 + v)\mathbf{i} + (4 + 4v)\mathbf{j}$; normal line: $\mathbf{r}(w) = (3 + 4w)\mathbf{i} + (4 - w)\mathbf{j}$, ($v$ and w are used as parameters since these are different lines).

18

Curve fitting:
Interpolation and shape functions

18.1 Lines and curves from real objects

In this chapter we consider lines and curves as parts of real objects. We consider them not merely from the mathematical point of view, but also with regard to the ways they help us visualize realistic objects in two and three dimensions. The lines, circles, parabolas and ellipses that we have introduced previously provide a library of basic geometric entities, called **primitives**. However, they rarely occur in an exact form in the real world, even though they can approximate to the shapes of actual objects, like a stretched string or the outline of a coin. Real objects such as boats, cars, aeroplanes, shoes or bottles use greater varieties of shapes than these and thus require to be described by more flexible methods.

The simplest technique for defining a real shape consists of plotting a sequence of points, as in Figure 18.1(a). The points shown here clearly suggest the outline of a small boat, though not one we would want to entrust our lives to. What is lacking is the completion of the outline; the gaps betwen the points need to be filled in. The complete outline of the boat cannot be described by a single mathematical expression, and probably the boat was originally designed without any explicit reference to mathematics. However, an unbroken outline can easily be produced, and the simplest way to do this is by joining up the points with straight lines as shown in Figure 18.1(b). We know from Chapter 6 that straight lines have simple mathematical formulae.

The diagram of Figure 18.1(b) still lacks realism. An improved, smoother shape can be produced by joining up the points with curves instead of lines: either the curves of Chapter 7 or more involved curves known as splines. The simple outline of Figure 18.1(b) could form the basis of a more fully developed computer graphics image such as that in Figure 18.2 (note that the ribs of the boat are parabolas).

As introduced in Section 7.3, filling the gaps between points is called interpolation, and in the rest of this chapter we focus on two straightforward forms of this process. When we determine a line or a curve that passes through every one of a

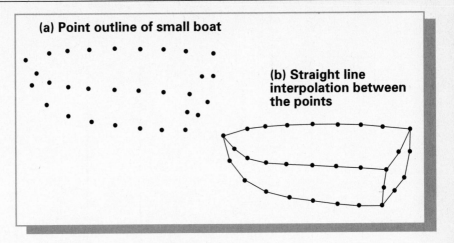

(a) Point outline of small boat

(b) Straight line interpolation between the points

Figure 18.1 (a) Point outline of a small boat.
(b) Straight line interpolation between the points.

given set of points this is known as **curve fitting**, and the overall technique we describe is called **piecewise polynomial approximation**. When we have as our objective a smooth, continuous curve, then we must pay special attention to the fitted curve at the points where the segments of lines or curves meet. In Figure 18.3(a) we show the effects obtained by joining up a set of points using segments of straight lines and arcs of curves under different conditions. In each case we have a continuous curve (with no gaps), but for any particular result account must also be taken of the gradients at the joins: a curve that is smooth overall cannot have any

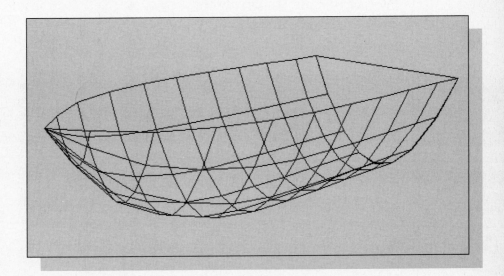

Figure 18.2 Computer graphics image of a small boat (*source: Matthew Holton, University of Teesside*).

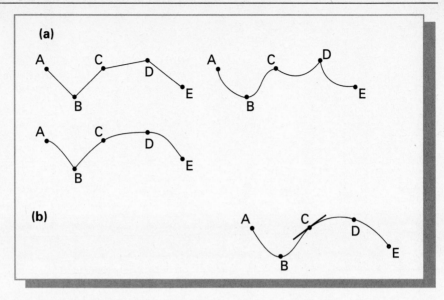

Figure 18.3 (a) Different curves fitted to a set of points.
(b) An overall smooth curve fitted to the points; the tangents at C have equal gradients.

abrupt changes in gradient. If we wish to join up the given points by a smooth continuous curve, then we need (at least) to match up the tangents at the joins, and one result is the curve shown in Figure 18.3(b).

There is an alternative procedure known as **curve fairing**, where the 'best' smooth curve (in some sense) is drawn to match the data points. However, when we have a curve which fairs the data, then it is possible that it does not touch all of the data points. This can happen when a draughtsman uses a flexible guide for drawing curves, or when calculations are done for a **curve of best fit**, or when certain types of spline curves are used; a simple example is shown in Figure 18.4.

18.2 Linear interpolation

As already indicated, linear interpolation is the process where we fill in the gap between two given points in an outline by a straight line, called the linear **interpolant**. We start this task simply, by supposing that we have been given just the position vectors, $\mathbf{a}$ and $\mathbf{b}$ say, of two points A and B. We have no other information

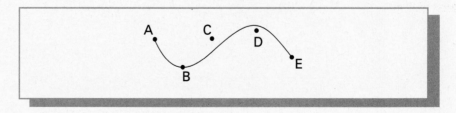

Figure 18.4 An example of curve fairing.

about the points, and no conditions concerning gradients to deal with. Using the method of Section 6.1, with a parameter u which takes the values 0 and 1 at the given points, we write down a vector equation for the straight line from A to B. This equation is

$$\mathbf{r}(u) = \mathbf{a} + u(\mathbf{b} - \mathbf{a})$$

which we rearrange as follows

$$\mathbf{r}(u) = \mathbf{a} + u\mathbf{b} - u\mathbf{a}$$

$$\mathbf{r}(u) = \mathbf{a} - u\mathbf{a} + u\mathbf{b}$$

$$\mathbf{r}(u) = (1 - u)\mathbf{a} + u\mathbf{b}$$

From this form we can easily determine the position vector of any point intermediate between A and B, since, as in Section 6.1, the intermediate points correspond to parameter values between 0 and 1. Thus the mid-point of AB corresponds to the parameter value $[u = \frac{1}{2}]$; $[u = 0.1]$ gives a point near to A and $[u = 0.9]$ gives a point near to B. As in Chapter 6, we use square brackets to emphasize that we are dealing here with values of the parameter, and not actual coordinates; the points are shown in Figure 18.5.

It is possible for the parameter to take different ranges of values. As an alternative to the above situation we can have the values of the parameter increasing from $[u = -1]$ at A to $[u = +1]$ at B: this case is indicated in Figure 18.6. Here we use the method of Section 6.3 to write down a vector equation of the line through AB. The equation is

$$\mathbf{r}(u) = \mathbf{a} + \frac{u - [-1]}{+1 - [-1]}(\mathbf{b} - \mathbf{a})$$

which we simplify as follows

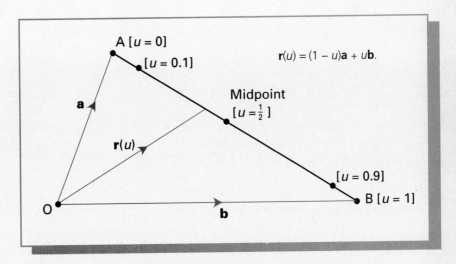

Figure 18.5 Linear interpolation between points A and B; the parameter takes value from 0 to 1.

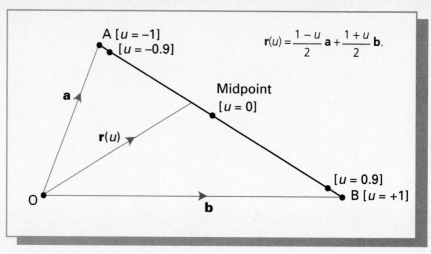

Figure 18.6 Linear interpolation between points A and B; the parameter takes values from −1 to +1.

$$\mathbf{r}(u) = \mathbf{a} + \frac{u+1}{2}(\mathbf{b} - \mathbf{a})$$

$$\mathbf{r}(u) = \mathbf{a} + \frac{u+1}{2}\mathbf{b} - \frac{u+1}{2}\mathbf{a}$$

$$\mathbf{r}(u) = \mathbf{a} - \frac{u+1}{2}\mathbf{a} + \frac{u+1}{2}\mathbf{b}$$

$$\mathbf{r}(u) = (1 - \frac{u+1}{2})\mathbf{a} + \frac{u+1}{2}\mathbf{b}$$

$$\mathbf{r}(u) = \left(\frac{2 - [u+1]}{2}\right)\mathbf{a} + \frac{u+1}{2}\mathbf{b}$$

that is

$$\mathbf{r}(u) = \frac{1-u}{2}\mathbf{a} + \frac{1+u}{2}\mathbf{b}$$

In this case taking $[u = 0]$ gives the position vector of the mid-point of the line segment, $[u = -0.9]$ gives a point near to A and $[u = +0.9]$ gives a point near to B, as shown.

For the two cases above we see that we have different but equivalent vector equations for the same line, depending on the range chosen for the parameter. However, in each equation $\mathbf{r}(u)$ is the sum of two terms: (a linear expression in u) × one position vector, plus (another linear expression in u) × the other position vector. In the first equation these expressions are $(1 - u)$ and (u), and in the second equation they are $(1 - u)/2$ and $(1 + u)/2$; the general name for these is **weight functions**, but when they take the values 0 and 1 at the data points they are called **shape functions**.

Example 18.1 The linear interpolant between two points

In the *x–y* plane we take the points A and B whose coordinates are (2, 5) and (5, 3), and we write down a vector equation for the line that passes through them, using a parameter *u* which takes values between 0 and 1. We use this equation to determine the coordinates of the midpoint M of AB, and the points corresponding to $[u = 0.1]$ and $[u = 0.9]$.

A has position vector $(2\mathbf{i} + 5\mathbf{j})$ and B has position vector $(5\mathbf{i} + 3\mathbf{j})$, so we can immediately write down the equation of the straight line as

$$\mathbf{r}(u) = (1 - u)(2\mathbf{i} + 5\mathbf{j}) + u(5\mathbf{i} + 3\mathbf{j})$$

At the midpoint of AB we know that $[u = 0.5]$, so we calculate $\mathbf{r}(0.5)$:

$$\mathbf{r}(0.5) = (1 - 0.5)(2\mathbf{i} + 5\mathbf{j}) + 0.5(5\mathbf{i} + 3\mathbf{j})$$
$$= 0.5(2\mathbf{i} + 5\mathbf{j}) + 0.5(5\mathbf{i} + 3\mathbf{j})$$
$$= 1\mathbf{i} + 2.5\mathbf{j} + 2.5\mathbf{i} + 1.5\mathbf{j}$$
$$= 3.5\mathbf{i} + 4\mathbf{j}$$

Thus the coordinates of the midpoint of AB are (3.5, 4); this corresponds with the result obtained using the method of Example 1.2.

When $[u = 0.1]$ we get

$$\mathbf{r}(0.1) = (1 - 0.1)(2\mathbf{i} + 5\mathbf{j}) + 0.1(5\mathbf{i} + 3\mathbf{j})$$
$$= 0.9(2\mathbf{i} + 5\mathbf{j}) + 0.1(5\mathbf{i} + 3\mathbf{j})$$
$$= 1.8\mathbf{i} + 4.5\mathbf{j} + 0.5\mathbf{i} + 0.3\mathbf{j}$$
$$= 2.3\mathbf{i} + 4.8\mathbf{j}$$

so the coordinates of the point corresponding to the parameter value $[u = 0.1]$ are (2.3, 4.8). Similarly when $[u = 0.9]$ we get

$$\mathbf{r}(0.9) = (1 - 0.9)(2\mathbf{i} + 5\mathbf{j}) + 0.9(5\mathbf{i} + 3\mathbf{j})$$
$$= 0.1(2\mathbf{i} + 5\mathbf{j}) + 0.9(5\mathbf{i} + 3\mathbf{j})$$
$$= 0.2\mathbf{i} + 0.5\mathbf{j} + 4.5\mathbf{i} + 2.7\mathbf{j}$$
$$= 4.7\mathbf{i} + 3.2\mathbf{j}$$

so the point where the parameter value is $[u = 0.9]$ has coordinates (4.7, 3.2). These points on the line AB are shown in Figure 18.7(a).

Example 18.2 The linear interpolant using different shape functions

We take the same points A(2, 5) and B(5, 3) and again write down a vector equation for the linear interpolant; this time the parameter *u* takes values between −1 and +1. Using this equation we again calculate the coordinates of the midpoint of AB, and also of the points corresponding to $[u = -0.9]$ and $[u = +0.9]$.

Since we know the position vectors of A and B we write down the vector equation immediately:

$$\mathbf{r}(u) = \frac{1 - u}{2}(2\mathbf{i} + 5\mathbf{j}) + \frac{1 + u}{2}(5\mathbf{i} + 3\mathbf{j})$$

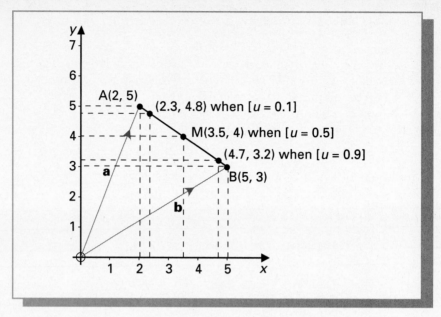

Figure 18.7 (a) Using $\mathbf{r}(u) = (1-u)\mathbf{a} + u\mathbf{b}$ to find the coordinates of points on AB.

For the midpoint of AB we take $[u = 0]$ and get

$$\mathbf{r}(0) = \frac{1-0}{2}(2\mathbf{i} + 5\mathbf{j}) + \frac{1+0}{2}(5\mathbf{i} + 3\mathbf{j})$$

$$= \tfrac{1}{2}(2\mathbf{i} + 5\mathbf{j}) + \tfrac{1}{2}(5\mathbf{i} + 3\mathbf{j})$$

$$= 3\tfrac{1}{2}\mathbf{i} + 4\mathbf{j}$$

as in Example 18.1, and as expected.

When $[u = -0.9]$ we get

$$\mathbf{r}(-0.9) = \frac{1 - [-0.9]}{2}(2\mathbf{i} + 5\mathbf{j}) + \frac{1 + [-0.9]}{2}(5\mathbf{i} + 3\mathbf{j})$$

$$= 0.95(2\mathbf{i} + 5\mathbf{j}) + 0.05(5\mathbf{i} + 3\mathbf{j})$$

$$= 1.9\mathbf{i} + 4.75\mathbf{j} + 0.25\mathbf{i} + 0.15\mathbf{j}$$

$$= 2.15\mathbf{i} + 4.9\mathbf{j}$$

so the coordinates of the point corresponding to the parameter value $[u = -0.9]$ are $(2.15, 4.9)$. Similarly when $[u = +0.9]$ we get

$$\mathbf{r}(+0.9) = \frac{1 - [+0.9]}{2}(2\mathbf{i} + 5\mathbf{j}) + \frac{1 + [+0.9]}{2}(5\mathbf{i} + 3\mathbf{j})$$

$$= 0.05(2\mathbf{i} + 5\mathbf{j}) + 0.95(5\mathbf{i} + 3\mathbf{j})$$

$$= 0.1\mathbf{i} + 0.25\mathbf{j} + 4.75\mathbf{i} + 2.85\mathbf{j}$$

$$= 4.85\mathbf{i} + 3.1\mathbf{j}$$

so the point where the parameter value is $[u = +0.9]$ has coordinates $(4.85, 3.1)$. These points on the line AB are shown in Figure 18.7(b).

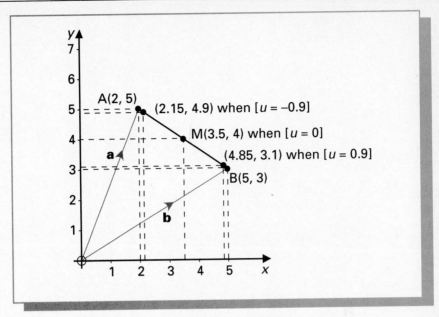

Figure 18.7 (b) Using $\mathbf{r}(u) = \dfrac{1-u}{2}\mathbf{a} + \dfrac{1+u}{2}\mathbf{b}$ to find the coordinates of points on AB.

18.3 Quadratic interpolation

As discussed above, with linear interpolation we use straight line segments to fill the gaps between pairs of points in an outline. Since the result of this is often less than satisfactory for realistic outlines, we improve on it by interpolating with an arc of a curve. The simplest way of doing this is to consider the given points three at a time, and to construct an arc of a quadratic curve (perhaps a parabola, circle or ellipse, see Section 7.7) to join them. This is done by **quadratic interpolation**.

We start with three points A, B and C, with position vectors **a**, **b** and **c** respectively, shown in Figure 18.8(a). If we join these up with two straight line segments by the method of Section 18.2 we get the result shown in Figure 18.8(b). However it is clearly better for most realistic outlines to join them with a curve, as in Figure 18.8(c). Just as for linear interpolation, quadratic interpolation formulae are written using shape functions, which vary according to the parameter values being used. Thus in general we have:

$$\mathbf{r}(u) = M_1(u)\mathbf{a} + M_2(u)\mathbf{b} + M_3(u)\mathbf{c}$$

where $M_1(u)$, $M_2(u)$ and $M_3(u)$ are shape functions. For quadratic interpolation the shape functions involve squared terms like 'u^2' and expressions like '$u^2 + 3u + 2$', and the overall result is an arc of a quadratic curve fitting the points.

If A corresponds to the parameter value $[u = 0]$, B to $[u = \frac{1}{2}]$, and C to $[u = 1]$, then the following vector equation gives us an interpolating quadratic curve:

$$\mathbf{r}(u) = 2(\tfrac{1}{2} - u)(1 - u)\mathbf{a} + 4u(1 - u)\mathbf{b} + 2u(u - \tfrac{1}{2})\mathbf{c}$$

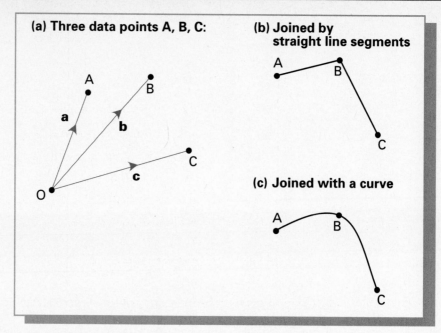

(a) Three data points A, B, C:

(b) Joined by straight line segments

(c) Joined with a curve

Figure 18.8 (a) Three data points, A, B, C, (b) joined by straight line segments or (c) joined with a curve.

This curve is indicated in Figure 18.9, and by substituting parameter values into the particular shape functions in the equation we can verify that it does pass through A, B and C. Thus when $[u = 0]$

$$\mathbf{r}(0) = 2 \times \tfrac{1}{2} \times 1\mathbf{a} + 4 \times 0 \times 1\mathbf{b} + 2 \times 0 \times (-\tfrac{1}{2})\mathbf{c}$$

$$= \mathbf{a}$$

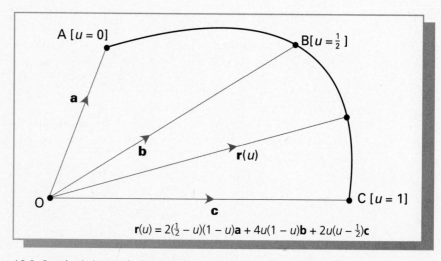

A $[u = 0]$ B$[u = \tfrac{1}{2}]$

$\mathbf{a}$

$\mathbf{b}$ $\mathbf{r}(u)$

O $\mathbf{c}$ C $[u = 1]$

$$\mathbf{r}(u) = 2(\tfrac{1}{2} - u)(1 - u)\mathbf{a} + 4u(1 - u)\mathbf{b} + 2u(u - \tfrac{1}{2})\mathbf{c}$$

Figure 18.9 Quadratic interpolation between points A and B; the parameter takes values 0, $\tfrac{1}{2}$ and 1 at the data points.

so the curve does indeed pass through A. When $[u = \frac{1}{2}]$

$$\mathbf{r}(\tfrac{1}{2}) = 2 \times 0 \times \tfrac{1}{2}\mathbf{a} + 4 \times \tfrac{1}{2} \times \tfrac{1}{2}\mathbf{b} + 2 \times \tfrac{1}{2} \times 0\mathbf{c}$$

$$= \mathbf{b}$$

so the curve also passes through B. When $[u = 1]$

$$\mathbf{r}(1) = 2 \times (-\tfrac{1}{2}) \times 0\mathbf{a} + 4 \times 1 \times 0\mathbf{b} + 2 \times 1 \times \tfrac{1}{2}\mathbf{c}$$

$$= \mathbf{c}$$

so the curve passes through C too, as expected.

Alternatively, if A is to have parameter value $[u = -1]$, with B having parameter $[u = 0]$ and C having parameter $[u = 1]$, then a quadratic interpolation formula is

$$\mathbf{r}(u) = -\tfrac{1}{2}u(1 - u)\mathbf{a} + (1 - u)(1 + u)\mathbf{b} + \tfrac{1}{2}u(1 + u)\mathbf{c}$$

We can verify that this curve too passes through the points A, B and C. When $[u = -1]$

$$\mathbf{r}(-1) = -\tfrac{1}{2} \times (-1) \times 2\mathbf{a} + 2 \times 0\mathbf{b} + \tfrac{1}{2} \times (-1) \times 0\mathbf{c}$$

$$= \mathbf{a}$$

which is the position vector of A. When $[u = 0]$

$$\mathbf{r}(0) = -\tfrac{1}{2} \times 0 \times 1\mathbf{a} + 1 \times 1\mathbf{b} + \tfrac{1}{2} \times 0 \times 1\mathbf{c}$$

$$= \mathbf{b}$$

which is the position vector of B. And when $[u = 1]$

$$\mathbf{r}(1) = -\tfrac{1}{2} \times 1 \times 0\mathbf{a} + 0 \times 2\mathbf{b} + \tfrac{1}{2} \times 1 \times 2\mathbf{c}$$

$$= \mathbf{c}$$

which is the position vector of C, as expected. These facts are indicated in Figure 18.10.

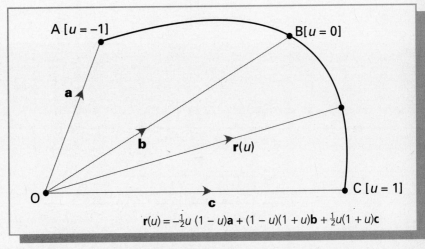

$$\mathbf{r}(u) = -\tfrac{1}{2}u(1 - u)\mathbf{a} + (1 - u)(1 + u)\mathbf{b} + \tfrac{1}{2}u(1 + u)\mathbf{c}$$

Figure 18.10 Quadratic interpolation between points A, B and C: the parameter takes values −1, 0 and +1 at the data points.

Example 18.3   A quadratic interpolant between three points

A quadratic curve is to pass through the points A(4, 2), B(2, 3) and C(1, 5). Using a parameter which takes values $[u = 0]$, $[u = 0.5]$ and $[u = 1]$ at these three points, we write down the vector equation of a quadratic curve which interpolates between them. We calculate the coordinates of the point on this curve where $[u = 0.2]$, and show it on a diagram.

Since the position vectors of A, B and C are $(4\mathbf{i} + 2\mathbf{j})$, $(2\mathbf{i} + 3\mathbf{j})$ and $(\mathbf{i} + 5\mathbf{j})$ respectively, we combine them with the shape functions from the first interpolation formula from Section 18.3 to give

$$\mathbf{r}(u) = 2(\tfrac{1}{2} - u)(1 - u)(4\mathbf{i} + 2\mathbf{j}) + 4u(1 - u)(2\mathbf{i} + 3\mathbf{j}) + 2u(u - \tfrac{1}{2})(\mathbf{i} + 5\mathbf{j})$$

Then when $[u = 0.2]$, we calculate

$$\mathbf{r}(0.2) = 2 \times 0.3 \times 0.8(4\mathbf{i} + 2\mathbf{j}) + 4 \times 0.2 \times 0.8(2\mathbf{i} + 3\mathbf{j}) + 2 \times 0.2 \times (-0.3)(\mathbf{i} + 5\mathbf{j})$$

$$= 0.48(4\mathbf{i} + 2\mathbf{j}) + 0.64(2\mathbf{i} + 3\mathbf{j}) + (-0.12)(\mathbf{i} + 5\mathbf{j})$$

$$= 1.92\mathbf{i} + 0.96\mathbf{j} + 1.28\mathbf{i} + 1.92\mathbf{j} - 0.12\mathbf{i} - 0.60\mathbf{j}$$

$$= 3.08\mathbf{i} + 2.28\mathbf{j}$$

Thus this point has coordinates (3.08, 2.28), as shown in Figure 18.11(a).

In addition, we can show further interpolated points to indicate the **generation** of the curve between A, B and C as the value of u increases. If we take the values of u at intervals of 0.1, then we obtain the points plotted in Figure 18.11(b). We have here taken the sequence $u = 0$, 0.1, 0.2, 0.3, 0.4, 0.5, 0.6, 0.7, 0.8, 0.9, 1; this may be written more shortly as '0 (0.1) 1', which means 'start at 0 and to go by increments of 0.1 to 1'.

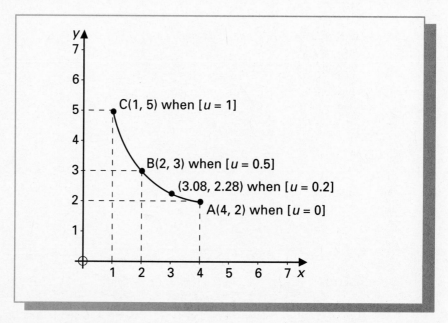

Figure 18.11 (a) The coordinates of the point where $[u = 0.2]$ on the curve joining A, B and C.

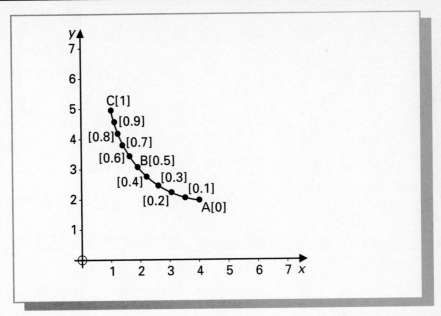

Figure 18.11 (b) The generation of the curve joining A, B and C as the value of u increases.

18.4 Uniqueness

At this point let us clarify whether there are a number of different interpolated lines and curves which can be drawn between given points; where there is only one the interpolation is unique.

When we interpolate between two data points with a straight line it is always unambiguously defined: it is the only straight line between the points and is thus unique. This is so irrespective of the shape functions used, or the parameter range.

However, between any three given points there are many quadratic curves that can be interpolated. As an example, in Figure 18.12 we see three points which are lying on the circle Γ and also on the two parabolas Π and Σ; so any one of these curves can be considered as a quadratic interpolant between the points. Thus a quadratic interpolant is not a unique curve, and in fact the nature of the curve depends on the shape functions that are used. If a particular quadratic interpolant is required then it is essential that more information be given to us. The aspect of the overall shape could be specified, or the gradients at particular points could be given.

Exercises

18.1 Determine the position vectors a_1, a_2, and a_3 that correspond to the points on the circle

$$\mathbf{r}(\theta) = 2\cos\theta\,\mathbf{i} + 2\sin\theta\,\mathbf{j},$$

where the angle θ takes values $-15°$, $-5°$ and $5°$.
Give your answers correct to three decimal places, and then verify by Pythagoras' Theorem that the radius of the circle is 2.00, correct to two decimal places. (These position vectors are used in (a), (b), (c) below.)

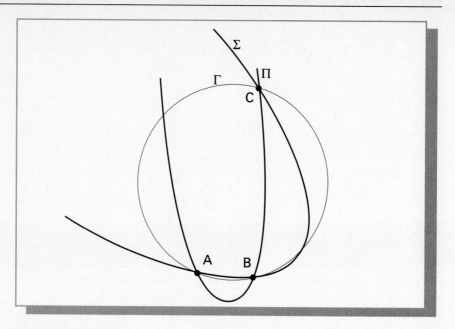

Figure 18.12 Different quadratic curves joining three points.

a) Write down the linear interpolation formula $\ell(u)$, between the points with position vectors $\mathbf{a}_2$ and $\mathbf{a}_3$, where u takes values between -1 and 1. Evaluate $\ell(0)$, and hence determine the discrepancy with the circle radius at this midpoint on the chord.

b) Calculate the angle between the chords given by the linear interpolation formulae between the points with position vectors $\mathbf{a}_1$ and $\mathbf{a}_2$, and $\mathbf{a}_2$ and $\mathbf{a}_3$.

c) Write down the quadratic interpolation formula $\mathbf{q}(u)$ between $\mathbf{a}_1$, $\mathbf{a}_2$ and $\mathbf{a}_3$ where the parameter takes the values -1, 0 and 1 at the given points, and simplify your equation. By substituting values for u, check that the curve fits these points. Evaluate $\mathbf{q}(\frac{1}{2})$, and hence determine the discrepancy with the circle radius at this point.

18.2 Consider the unit circle given by

$$\mathbf{r}(\theta) = \cos\theta\,\mathbf{i} + \sin\theta\,\mathbf{j}$$

and calculate the position vectors of the points P_1, P_2, P_3, P_4 and P_5 on the circle, where the parameter takes values 0, $\pi/8$, $\pi/4$, $3\pi/8$ and $\pi/2$ respectively. Show these points on a diagram.

a) Write down the linear interpolation formulae joining the points P_1 and P_3, and P_3 and P_5. Calculate the angle betwen these chords, where they join. Repeat this for the chords P_2P_3 and P_3P_4.

b) In terms of quadratic shape functions where the parameters take values -1, 0 and 1 at the given points, write down quadratic interpolation formulae that pass through

(i) P_1, P_2 and P_3 ('$\mathbf{r}(u)$')

(ii) P_3, P_4 and P_5 ('$\mathbf{r}(v)$')

By substituting suitable values of the parameters used, check that the curves actually fit the points. At the join, P_3, determine a tangent to each interpolant curve, and hence the angle between the curves.

Answers

18.1 $\mathbf{a}_1 = 1.93\mathbf{i} - 0.52\mathbf{j}$; $\mathbf{a}_2 = 1.99\mathbf{i} - 0.17\mathbf{j}$; $\mathbf{a}_3 = 1.99\mathbf{i} + 0.17\mathbf{j}$.

a) $\ell(u) = 1.99\mathbf{i} + 0.17u\mathbf{j}$; $\ell(0) = 1.99\mathbf{i}$;   discrepancy ≈ 0.01;   b) $9.90°$;

c) $\mathbf{q}(u) = (-0.03u^2 + 0.03u + 1.99)\mathbf{i} + (0.002u^2 + 0.35u - 0.17)\mathbf{j}$

$\mathbf{q}(\tfrac{1}{2}) = 1.9995\mathbf{i} - 0.0005\mathbf{j}$;   no apparent discrepancy.

18.2 $\mathbf{p}_1 = \mathbf{i}$; $\mathbf{p}_2 = 0.92\mathbf{i} + 0.38\mathbf{j}$; $\mathbf{p}_3 = 0.71\mathbf{i} + 0.71\mathbf{j}$; $\mathbf{p}_4 = 0.38\mathbf{i} + 0.92\mathbf{j}$; $\mathbf{p}_5 = \mathbf{j}$.

a) $P_1 \rightarrow P_3$: $\mathbf{m}(u) = (0.85 - 0.15u)\mathbf{i} + (0.35 + 0.35u)\mathbf{j}$;

$P_3 \rightarrow P_5$: $\mathbf{n}(u) = (0.35 - 0.35u)\mathbf{i} + (0.85 + 0.15u)\mathbf{j}$; $0.785^c \approx 45°$.

$P_2 \rightarrow P_3$: $\mathbf{h}(u) = (0.82 - 0.11u)\mathbf{i} + (0.55 + 0.16u)\mathbf{j}$;

$P_3 \rightarrow P_4$: $\mathbf{k}(u) = (0.55 - 0.16u)\mathbf{i} + (0.82 + 0.11u)\mathbf{j}$; $0.39^c \approx 22.4°$.

b) $\mathbf{r}(v) = (-0.07v^2 - 0.15v + 0.92)\mathbf{i} + (-0.03v^2 + 0.35v + 0.38)\mathbf{j}$

At P_3, tangent given by $\mathbf{r}(1) = -0.29\mathbf{i} + 0.29\mathbf{j}$.

$\mathbf{r}(w) = (-0.03w^2 - 0.35w + 0.38)\mathbf{i} + (-0.07w^2 + 0.15w + 0.92)\mathbf{j}$

At P_3, tangent given by $\mathbf{r}(-1) = -0.30\mathbf{i} + 0.29\mathbf{j}$. Angle is $0.02405^c \approx 1.38°$.

19

Planes and surfaces: *Biparametric forms, sweeps and revolutions*

19.1 Surface formulae and two parameters

We shall now build on all our work with lines and curves and proceed to consider surfaces, in particular the vector equations for surfaces. We start with the plane, which is 'flat' and is the simplest form of surface, and then we shall look at two particular ways of generating more general surfaces. With just one exception, we shall use parameters throughout to describe surfaces. While single parameters were needed for lines and curves in previous chapters, when dealing with any surface we need two parameters: surfaces use **biparametric forms**.

We begin by studying plane surfaces because, although they themselves have limited use, their vector equations form the basis for the most common description of a general surface. This description involves **plane facets**, which we introduce in Section 19.5.

19.2 Vector equations of planes

There are different types of equations by which planes can be defined. These equations supply compact and complete formulae which are essential for all the information about a plane to be stored and manipulated within a computer, for graphical purposes. For both straight lines and curves we found that vector equations involving parameters are the most fruitful; they are similarly useful for planes, and lead us to straightforward methods for determining points, lines and distances on the plane. (There is another way of defining a plane in three dimensions, where no parameters are involved; this is known as the **implicit form**, which we deal with briefly in Section 19.8.)

19.3 The vector equation of a plane, given two vectors in the plane

We recognize that a plane is completely defined if we are given the directions of two vectors that lie in it. Such vectors may always be moved, without altering magnitude or direction, so that they start from the same point (this idea was discussed in Section 2.1). In Figure 19.1 we show a plane S defined by the vectors **a** and **b** contained in it; each vector starts from the point C whose position vector is **c** . We suppose that P, with position vector **r** , is a variable point in the plane and that the vector from C to P is **x**: then **x** can be expressed in terms of **a** and **b** as follows. We apply a scale factor to **a** changing it to u**a** (shorter or longer as appropriate), and similarly we apply a scale factor to **b** so that it becomes v**b** ; then by the triangle rule for addition we have

$$x = u\mathbf{a} + v\mathbf{b}$$

In this way any vector in the plane can be expressed in terms of the given **a** and **b**, using two scalars u and v. Moreover, from the triangle shown we have

$$\mathbf{c} + \mathbf{x} = \mathbf{r}$$

that is

$$\mathbf{r} = \mathbf{x} + \mathbf{c}$$

Thus, using the above formula for **x**,

$$\mathbf{r} = u\mathbf{a} + v\mathbf{b} + \mathbf{c}$$

which is the equation of the position vector of a general point on the plane, and hence is a vector equation of the plane. We note that this vector equation involves the two scalars u and v: these are the parameters for the equation of the plane. For the equation of the plane we use the notation

$$S(u, v) = u\mathbf{a} + v\mathbf{b} + \mathbf{c}$$

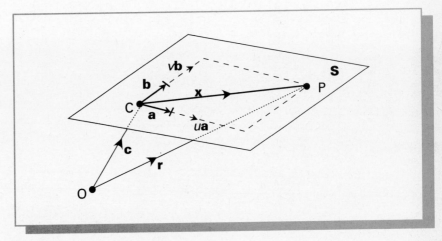

Figure 19.1 Two vectors given in the plane **S**.

to emphasize the fact that two parameters are being used: different values of u and v yield different points (or lines) in the plane.

Example 19.1   A plane through two vectors, which includes the origin

We shall find the parametric form of the equation of the plane in three dimensions which includes the vectors $\mathbf{a} = 3\mathbf{i}$ and $\mathbf{b} = 4\mathbf{j}$, and passes through the origin.

Using the above formula the plane is given by

$$\mathbf{S}(u,\, v) = u(3\mathbf{i}) + v(4\mathbf{j}) + \mathbf{0}$$

that is

$$\mathbf{S}(u,\, v) = 3u\mathbf{i} + 4v\mathbf{j}$$

Thus we see that this plane is precisely the standard two-dimensional x–y coordinate plane, defined by the vectors $\mathbf{i}$ and $\mathbf{j}$. However, in terms of the standard $(x,\, y)$ coordinates we have here $x = 3u$ and $y = 4v$, so the parameters u and v do not themselves indicate measurements along the $\mathbf{i}$ and $\mathbf{j}$ directions (see Figure 19.2). When $[u = 1]$ and $[v = 1]$ we have the point with coordinates $(3, 4)$; but when we increase v by 1 then $[u = 1]$ and $[v = 2]$, so we have the point with coordinates $(3, 8)$.

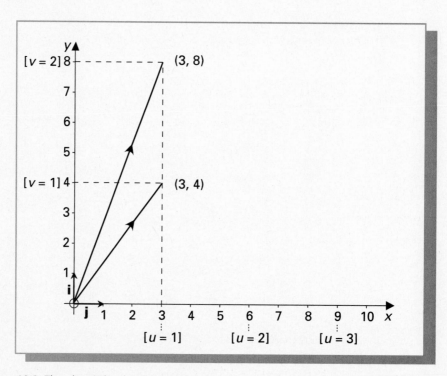

Figure 19.2 The plane $\mathbf{S}(u,\, v) = 3u\mathbf{i} + 4v\mathbf{j}$.

Example 19.2 A plane through two vectors, which includes a given point

Using parameters u and v as in Section 19.3, we determine an equation of the plane which contains vectors parallel to $\mathbf{a} = (3\mathbf{i} + 2\mathbf{j})$ and $\mathbf{b} = (\mathbf{j} + 2\mathbf{k})$, and passes through the point with position vector $\mathbf{c} = (\mathbf{i} + \mathbf{j} + \mathbf{k})$. In addition we find the coordinates of the point in this plane where $[u = 2]$ and $[v = 1]$.

From the result of Section 19.3 we write

$$S(u, v) = u(3\mathbf{i} + 2\mathbf{j}) + v(\mathbf{j} + 2\mathbf{k}) + (\mathbf{i} + \mathbf{j} + \mathbf{k})$$

We multiply out the brackets and group the components to get the equation of the plane:

$$S(u, v) = (3u + 1)\mathbf{i} + (2u + v + 1)\mathbf{j} + (2v + 1)\mathbf{k}$$

If the point P on this plane has parameter values $[u = 2, v = 1]$ then the position vector of P is

$$\mathbf{r} = S(2, 1) = (3 \times 2 + 1)\mathbf{i} + (2 \times 2 + 1 + 1)\mathbf{j} + (2 \times 1 + 1)\mathbf{k}$$

that is

$$\mathbf{r} = 7\mathbf{i} + 6\mathbf{j} + 3\mathbf{k}$$

and so the coordinates of P are $(7, 6, 3)$.

19.4 The vector equation of a plane, given two unit vectors in the plane

When the vectors whose directions define a plane are unit vectors, $\hat{\mathbf{a}}$ and $\hat{\mathbf{b}}$ say, then from Section 19.3 a vector equation of the plane is

$$S(u, v) = u\hat{\mathbf{a}} + v\hat{\mathbf{b}} + \mathbf{c}$$

using again the scalars u and v as parameters. The advantage of this way of describing the plane is that the values of the scalars can now be used to measure distances along the directions of the unit vectors. The following examples illustrate this.

Example 19.3 A plane through unit vectors, passing through the origin

We write down the parametric form of the equation of the plane in three dimensions which includes the unit vectors $\hat{\mathbf{a}} = \mathbf{i}$ and $\hat{\mathbf{b}} = \mathbf{j}$ and passes through the origin.

From the result of Section 19.4 above, an equation of this plane is

$$S(u, v) = u\mathbf{i} + v\mathbf{j} + 0$$

that is

$$S(u, v) = u\mathbf{i} + v\mathbf{j} + 0\mathbf{k}$$

It is clear that this is precisely the standard x–y plane, and here the parameters $[u, v]$ are completely equivalent to the standard (x, y) coordinates. Thus, because we began with unit vectors in the plane, the parameters themselves can be used to measure distances in the plane, in the directions of $\mathbf{i}$ and $\mathbf{j}$.

Example 19.4   Another plane where the parameters correspond to distances

We find an equation of the plane which contains the vectors $\mathbf{a} = \mathbf{i}$ and $\mathbf{b} = \mathbf{j} + \mathbf{k}$, and passes through the origin, so that the parameters correspond to distances in the plane along the directions of $\mathbf{a}$ and $\mathbf{b}$.

We first obtain the unit vectors in the plane: $\mathbf{a} = \mathbf{i}$ is a unit vector already, so $\hat{\mathbf{a}} = \mathbf{i}$. To calculate $\hat{\mathbf{b}}$, we divide $\mathbf{b}$ by its modulus. Since

$$\mathbf{b} = 1\mathbf{j} + 1\mathbf{k}$$

we have

$$|\mathbf{b}| = \sqrt{(1^2 + 1^2)} = \sqrt{2}$$

and so

$$\hat{\mathbf{b}} = \frac{1}{\sqrt{2}} \ (\mathbf{j} + \mathbf{k})$$

We use $\hat{\mathbf{a}}$, $\hat{\mathbf{b}}$ and $\mathbf{c} = 0$ in the formula of Section 19.4 to obtain an equation of this plane:

$$\mathbf{S}(u, v) = u\mathbf{i} + v(\frac{1}{\sqrt{2}}(\mathbf{j} + \mathbf{k}))$$

that is

$$\mathbf{S}(u, v) = u\mathbf{i} + \frac{v}{\sqrt{2}}\mathbf{j} + \frac{v}{\sqrt{2}}\mathbf{k}$$

Using this equation, we next verify that the parameters will measure distances in the plane in the direction of one of the given vectors. For example, we consider the following points: P given by $[u = 1, v = 2]$ and Q given by $[u = 4, v = 2]$. As their values of v are the same, the parametric distance between them is the difference in u, that is $(4 - 1) = 3$. We now calculate the actual (geometric) distance between them. The position vector of P is

$$\mathbf{r} = \mathbf{S}(1, 2) = 1\mathbf{i} + \frac{2}{\sqrt{2}}\mathbf{j} + \frac{2}{\sqrt{2}}\mathbf{k}$$

that is

$$\mathbf{r} = \mathbf{i} + \sqrt{2}\,\mathbf{j} + \sqrt{2}\,\mathbf{k}$$

thus the coordinates of P are $(1, \sqrt{2}, \sqrt{2})$. By similar means we calculate the coordinates of Q to be $(4, 2/\sqrt{2}), 2/\sqrt{2})$, that is $(4, \sqrt{2}, \sqrt{2})$. So, using Pythagoras' Theorem, the actual distance between P and Q is

$$\sqrt{(4 - 1)^2 + (\sqrt{2} - \sqrt{2})^2 + (\sqrt{2} - \sqrt{2})^2} = 3$$

Thus in this case the parametric distance is the actual distance between the points, measured along the direction of $\mathbf{a}$.

19.5 The vector equation of a plane, given three points in the plane

A plane is completely described by defining two vectors which lie in it, and it is also completely described by defining three points that lie in it; in fact these conditions are equivalent. When we are given three points, they can be joined by straight lines to give a **triangular plane facet**. Vectors can be drawn from one vertex of this facet along two of its sides, thus we immediately have the situation of Section 19.3 where we are given two vectors in a plane. The ideas of triangular plane facets can be extended to give approximations for any surface; their study provides many practical uses in the field of **polygonal modelling**.

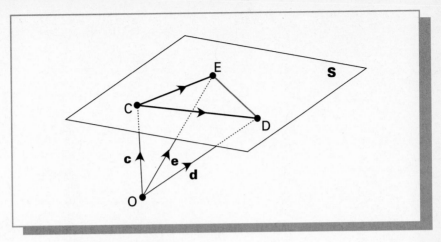

Figure 19.3 Three points in the plane **S**.

We now consider a plane surface S defined by the three points C, D and E whose position vectors are **c**, **d** and **e** respectively (see Figure 19.3). From the triangles of vectors shown, we have immediately that the vector from C to D is given by

$$\mathbf{CD} = (\mathbf{d} - \mathbf{c})$$

and the vector from C to E is given by

$$\mathbf{CE} = (\mathbf{e} - \mathbf{c})$$

Thus we replace **a** and **b** in the equation of Section 19.3 to give a vector equation for this plane as

$$S(u, v) = u(\mathbf{d} - \mathbf{c}) + v(\mathbf{e} - \mathbf{c}) + \mathbf{c}$$

where u and v are parameters, as before.

If we take the unit vectors along the directions from C to D and from C to E, then new parameters, u^* and v^*, can be used which measure distances along the directions of the vectors **CD** and **CE**. For this we have the equation

$$S(u^*, v^*) = u^* \frac{\mathbf{d} - \mathbf{c}}{|\mathbf{d} - \mathbf{c}|} + v^* \frac{\mathbf{e} - \mathbf{c}}{|\mathbf{e} - \mathbf{c}|} + \mathbf{c}$$

Example 19.5   A plane through three given points

We determine a vector equation of the plane that passes through the points C(1, 3, 2), D(2, 5, 4) and E(3, 2, 1).

We begin with the position vectors for C, D and E, and from these we obtain the vectors **CD** and **CE**. The position vectors are: for C

$$(1\mathbf{i} + 3\mathbf{j} + 2\mathbf{k})$$

for D

$$(2\mathbf{i} + 5\mathbf{j} + 4\mathbf{k})$$

and for E

$$(3i + 2j + 1k)$$

Then we have

$$CD = (2i + 5j + 4k) - (1i + 3j + 2k)$$
$$= (1i + 2j + 2k)$$

and also

$$CE = (3i + 2j + 1k) - (1i + 3j + 2k)$$
$$= (2i - 1j - 1k)$$

Using the result of Section 19.5 we now obtain an equation of the plane, with parameters u and v:

$$S(u, v) = u(1i + 2j + 2k) + v(2i - 1j - 1k) + (1i + 3j + 2k)$$

which we simplify to

$$S(u, v) = (u + 2v + 1)i + (2u - v + 3)j + (2u - v + 2)k$$

19.6 Parameter lines and parameter planes

With any parametrized version of an equation of a plane we can always substitute in particular values of the parameters to obtain particular points on the plane. We consider the equation of the plane in Section 19.3:

$$S(u, v) = ua + vb + c$$

Taking $[u = 0]$ and $[v = 0]$ gives

$$S(0, 0) = 0a + 0b + c = c$$

which is the position vector of the point C. If we take $[u = 1]$ and $[v = 0]$ we get

$$S(1, 0) = 1a + 0b + c = a + c$$

which is the position vector of α, at the other end of the vector a. Similarly if we take $[u = 0]$ and $[v = 1]$ we get the position vector of β, which is the point at the other end of the vector b. These points are shown in Figure 19.4. In general we use square brackets to enclose parameter values, where necessary, so that $[0, 1]$ is taken to mean $[u = 0, v = 1]$.

What happens if we fix the value of one parameter, but leave the other parameter free to vary? If we take $v = 0$, but u is free to vary, we have

$$S(u, 0) = ua + 0b + c = ua + c$$

This is the position vector of a point in the plane somewhere along the line of the vector a, and so gives us the line in the direction of a. When we take $[u = 0]$ but leave v free to vary, then we get the position vector of a variable point along the line of the vector b, that is we get the line in the direction of b.

We illustrate these findings on a graph which is called the **parameter plane** as shown in Figure 19.5. We must note that this parametric plane is not the same as the 'real' geometric plane $S(u, v)$; it is an idealized version, a plot of the parameter

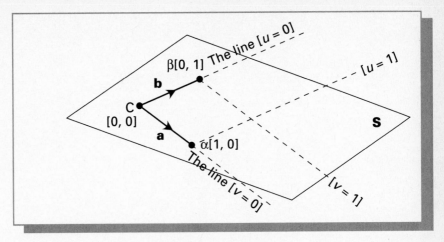

Figure 19.4 Parametric coordinates and lines in the plane $\mathbf{S}(u, v) = u\mathbf{a} + u\mathbf{b} + \mathbf{c}$.

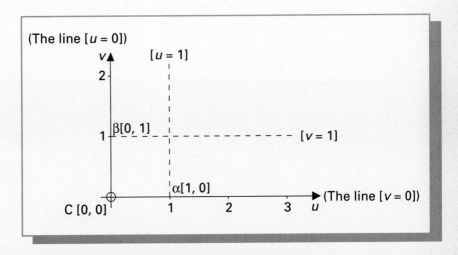

Figure 19.5 The parametric plane for $\mathbf{S}(u, v) = u\mathbf{a} + v\mathbf{b} + \mathbf{c}$.

values that define $\mathbf{S}(u, v)$. The parameters are considered to be the variables on perpendicular axes: $[u = 0, v = 0]$ represents the point C; $[u = 1, v = 0]$ represents the point α; $[u = 0, v = 1]$ represents the point β. In terms of their **parametric coordinates** we say that C is $[0, 0]$, α is $[1, 0]$ and β is $[0, 1]$. When we fix just one parameter we obtain **parametric lines**. For $[v = 0]$ but u variable, we get the u-axis on the parameter plane, which represents the direction of the vector $\mathbf{a}$; and $[v = 1]$ (or any other fixed number) with u variable yields a line parallel to the u-axis, representing a vector parallel to $\mathbf{a}$. Similarly, with $[u = 0]$ but v variable, we have the v-axis, representing the vector $\mathbf{b}$; while $[u = 1]$ (or another fixed number) yields a line parallel to the v-axis, representing a vector parallel to $\mathbf{b}$.

Example 19.6 A plane shape bounded by parameter lines

Using parameters u and v as in Section 19.3, we first identify the plane containing the vectors $\mathbf{a} = \mathbf{i}$ and $\mathbf{b} = \mathbf{j} + \mathbf{k}$ which passes through the origin. Then we consider that part of the plane bounded by the parameter lines $[u = 0]$ and $[u = 3]$, and $[v = 0]$ and $[v = 4]$, and sketch the result.

The equation of the plane is

$$S(u, v) = u\mathbf{i} + v(\mathbf{j} + \mathbf{k})$$

that is

$$S(u, v) = u\mathbf{i} + v\mathbf{j} + v\mathbf{k}$$

We take $[u = 0]$ but leave v variable and get

$$S(0, v) = 0\mathbf{i} + v\mathbf{j} + v\mathbf{k}$$

This is an equation in one parameter which represents a straight line, so we write it as

$$\mathbf{r}_1(v) = 0\mathbf{i} + v\mathbf{j} + v\mathbf{k}$$

From this we take the parametric equations

$$\begin{cases} x = 0 \\ y = v \\ z = v \end{cases}$$

which we combine (as in Section 5.2) to get the Cartesian equation of this line, which is

$$y = z \text{ in the plane } x = 0$$

Thus the line given by $\mathbf{r}_1$ has gradient 1 in the y–z plane, as shown in Figure 19.6. The range

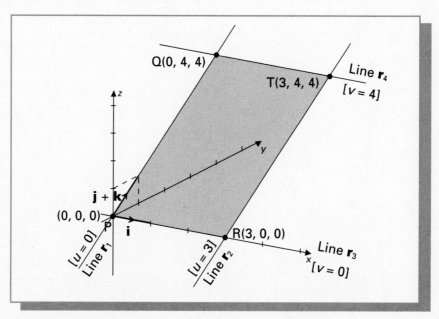

Figure 19.6 The plane containing $\mathbf{a} = \mathbf{i}$ and $\mathbf{b} = \mathbf{j} + \mathbf{k}$.

of the parameter v is from 0 to 4, so one end of this boundary line is the point P with position vector $(0\mathbf{i} + 0\mathbf{j} + 0\mathbf{k})$, that is coordinates $(0, 0, 0)$. At the other end of the line is the point Q with position vector $(0\mathbf{i} + 4\mathbf{j} + 4\mathbf{k})$ and coordinates $(0, 4, 4)$.

We next take $[u = 3]$, leaving v variable again, and we get

$$\mathbf{S}(3, v) = 3\mathbf{i} + v\mathbf{j} + v\mathbf{k}$$

This is an equation of a straight line, so we write it as

$$\mathbf{r}_2(v) = 3\mathbf{i} + v\mathbf{j} + v\mathbf{k}$$

It has the following parametric equations:

$$\begin{cases} x = 3 \\ y = v \\ z = v \end{cases}$$

As before we combine these and get the line $y = z$ in the plane $x = 3$; that is the straight line with gradient 1 in the plane $x = 3$ shown in Figure 19.6. At one end of this boundary, the parameter v takes value 0, so we have the point R$(3, 0, 0)$; at the other end the value of v is 4 so we have the point T$(3, 4, 4)$.

Next we take $[v = 0]$, and leave u variable. This gives

$$\mathbf{S}(u, 0) = u\mathbf{i} + 0\mathbf{j} + 0\mathbf{k}$$

This again involves just one parameter and represents the straight line $\mathbf{r}_3 = u\mathbf{i}$, which is the x-axis. The range of values of u is from 0 to 3. Thus at one end of this boundary we have the point with position vector $0\mathbf{i}$ and coordinates $(0, 0, 0)$: the point P once more. At the other end is the point with position vector $3\mathbf{i}$ and coordinates $(3, 0, 0)$: the point R once more.

We obtain the fourth boundary line by taking $[v = 4]$, and leaving u variable. We have the equation

$$\mathbf{S}(u, 4) = u\mathbf{i} + 4\mathbf{j} + 4\mathbf{k}$$

which, as in the previous cases, can be written as the equation of a straight line:

$$\mathbf{r}_4(u) = u\mathbf{i} + 4\mathbf{j} + 4\mathbf{k}$$

We consider the parametric equations

$$\begin{cases} x = u \\ y = 4 \\ z = 4 \end{cases}$$

which show that on this line $y = z = 4$ always, but x varies: this is a line through $(0, 4, 4)$ parallel to the x-axis, as shown. At one end of this boundary $[u = 0]$, giving the point with coordinates $(0, 4, 4)$: Q again. At the other end we have $[u = 3]$, giving the point with coordinates $(3, 4, 4)$: T again.

The bounded part of the given plane is shown in Figure 19.6, and in Figure 19.7 we show the corresponding information on a parameter plane. There the line $\mathbf{r}_1$ corresponds to the line $[u = 0]$, $\mathbf{r}_2$ corresponds to $[u = 3]$, $\mathbf{r}_3$ corresponds to $[v = 0]$, and $\mathbf{r}_4$ corresponds to $[v = 4]$.

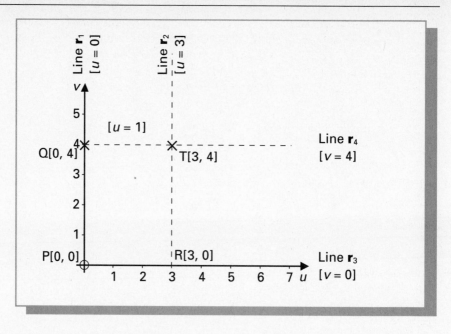

Figure 19.7 The parametric plane for $\mathbf{S}(u, v) = u\mathbf{i} + v(\mathbf{j} + \mathbf{k})$

19.7 Plotting a plane

As shown in all the previous examples, any vector equation that is biparametric, where the shape functions are linear, represents a plane surface. We now demonstrate how a plane can always be constructed from such an equation. To do this we investigate the following:

$$\mathbf{S}(u, v) = (1 + u + v)\mathbf{i} + 2v\mathbf{j} + 2\mathbf{k}$$

where we first take specific values of v and determine the resulting lines in the plane.
    When $[v = 0]$ we have

$$\mathbf{S}(u, 0) = (1 + u + 0)\mathbf{i} + (2 \times 0)\mathbf{j} + 2\mathbf{k}$$

which, as in Example 19.6, yields the equation of a straight line:

$$\mathbf{r}_1(u) = (1 + u)\mathbf{i} + 2\mathbf{k}$$

We now take specific values of u to give us points on this line: $[u = 0]$ gives us the point P with coordinates $(1, 0, 2)$; $[u = 1]$ gives us the point Q$(2, 0, 2)$. The line $\mathbf{r}_1$ that corresponds to $[v = 0]$ thus passes through P and Q, as shown in Figure 19.8.
    When $[v = 1]$, we have

$$\mathbf{S}(u, 1) = (1 + u + 1)\mathbf{i} + (2 \times 1)\mathbf{j} + 2\mathbf{k}$$

which yields the equation of the straight line

$$\mathbf{r}_2(u) = (u + 2)\mathbf{i} + 2\mathbf{j} + 2\mathbf{k}$$

As before, we take specific values of u to find the coordinates of particular points on this line; $[u=0]$ gives the point R(2, 2, 2), and $[u=1]$ gives the point T(3, 2, 2). The line $\mathbf{r}_2$, corresponding to $[v=1]$, thus passes through the points R and T as shown in the diagram.

We next consider the other parameter, keeping u fixed while allowing v to vary. We take $[u=0]$ and get:

$$\mathbf{S}(0, v) = (1 + 0 + v)\mathbf{i} + (2 \times v)\mathbf{j} + 2\mathbf{k}$$

which is the equation of a straight line

$$\mathbf{r}_3 = (1 + v)\mathbf{i} + 2v\mathbf{j} + 2\mathbf{k}$$

For particular points on this line we need specific values of v: when $[v=0]$ we have the point (1, 0, 2), which is P again; when $[v=1]$ we have the point (2, 2, 2), which is R again. Thus the line $\mathbf{r}_3$, corresponding to $[u=0]$, passes through P and R.

Finally we take $[u=1]$. The original equation becomes

$$\mathbf{S}(1, v) = (1 + 1 + v)\mathbf{i} + (2 \times v)\mathbf{j} + 2\mathbf{k}$$

from which we get the equation of a straight line

$$\mathbf{r}_4 = (2 + v)\mathbf{i} + 2v\mathbf{j} + 2\mathbf{k}$$

When $[v=0]$ we get the point (2, 0, 2), that is Q; and when $[v=1]$ we get the point (3, 2, 2), that is T. So the line $\mathbf{r}_4$, corresponding to $[u=1]$, passes through Q and T.

Referring to Figure 19.8 we see that our original vector equation gives a plane surface that contains the points P, Q, R and T, which actually are the vertices of a parallelogram.

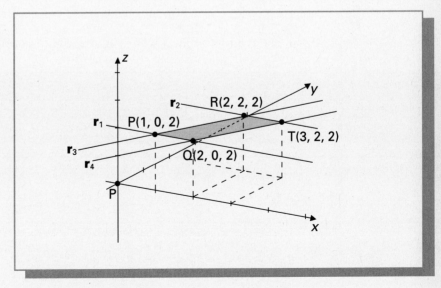

Figure 19.8 Plotting the plane $\mathbf{S}(u,v) = (1 + u + v)\mathbf{i} + 2v\mathbf{j} + 2\mathbf{k}$.

19.8 The implicit form of the equation of a plane

This form of the equation of a plane is very commonly met in more mathematical texts, and it leads to the standard Cartesian equation of a plane. However, while it is easily visualized, it is not 'user friendly' for computer graphics purposes since it does not involve parameters. We include it here out of interest, so that the underlying concepts are appreciated.

A plane in three dimensions is shown in Figure 19.9(a); C, with position vector **c**, is a fixed point in the plane, and **n** is a vector normal to the plane. This normal to the plane is in a fixed direction, and it is normal to every vector that lies in the plane. We suppose that P, with position vector **r**, is another point in the plane: P can vary all over the plane. From Figure 19.9(b) we see that **x**, the vector from C to P, lies wholly within the plane, thus it is normal to **n**, and their scalar product is zero:

$$\mathbf{x} \cdot \mathbf{n} = 0$$

Moreover, from the triangle of vectors shown, we have

$$\mathbf{x} = \mathbf{r} - \mathbf{c}$$

and so

$$(\mathbf{r} - \mathbf{c}) \cdot \mathbf{n} = 0.$$

Multiplying out the brackets gives

$$\mathbf{r} \cdot \mathbf{n} - \mathbf{c} \cdot \mathbf{n} = 0$$

and hence

$$\mathbf{r} \cdot \mathbf{n} = \mathbf{c} \cdot \mathbf{n}$$

This is the implicit form of the equation of the plane; parameters are not involved.

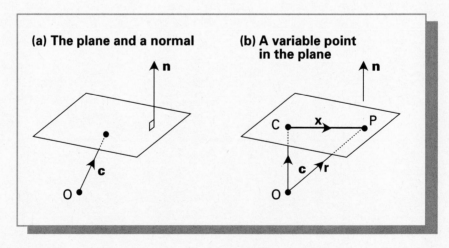

Figure 19.9 (a) The plane and a normal. (b) A variable point in the plane.

19.9 Generating a swept surface

In the two final sections of this chapter we consider some simple forms of non-planar surfaces. We begin by looking at a type of surface that is generated by moving a segment of line or curve or polygon along a predefined track, which can be straight or curved. As the line (or curve, or polygon) segment sweeps along the track a surface is produced, called a **swept surface**.

Illustrations of swept surfaces are indicated in Figure 19.10. In (a) the moving segment is three sides of a rectangle, which sweeps along a straight-line track at right angles to its own plane; the resulting surface has the form of gutter. In (b) the moving segment is a circle that sweeps along a curve; we see that this swept surface can be interpreted as a hosepipe (see also the helical tube, Figure 17.1). It is clear from these examples that to define any point on a swept surface it is sufficient to identify the values of just two parameters. For example, to specify the position of the point P on the gutter we need only know the length u around the moving segment and the length v along the track, each from an agreed origin. Similarly, to specify the position of the point Q on the hosepipe we need only know the angle θ at the centre of the circle and the length v along the curve, where each again is measured from an agreed origin. These surfaces, and all swept surfaces, are biparametric. Another example of a swept surface is the parabolic channel of Figure 19.10(c): a shaded version is shown in Figure 19.10(d).

It is straightforward to perform a simple sweep translation, such as a sweep along a track parallel to the positive z-axis, using a translation matrix. We take the vector equation of the moving segment and obtain from it the general position vector of a point, using one parameter, u; using a homogeneous vector, this is

$$(x(u) \quad y(u) \quad z(u) \quad 1)$$

Then to sweep this along a straight track of length L in the direction of $\mathbf{k}$, we multiply it by the translation matrix as follows

$$(x(u) \quad y(u) \quad z(u) \quad 1) \begin{bmatrix} 1 & 0 & 0 & 0 \\ 0 & 1 & 0 & 0 \\ 0 & 0 & 1 & 0 \\ 0 & 0 & vL & 1 \end{bmatrix}$$

where v is the second parameter which takes values between 0 and 1. The result of this multiplication yields the vector of a general point on the surface, namely

$$(x(u) \quad y(u) \quad z(u) + vL \quad 1)$$

Thus the vector equation of the surface in three dimensions is:

$$\mathbf{S}(u, v) = x(u)\mathbf{i} + y(u)\mathbf{j} + (z(u) + vL)\mathbf{k}$$

which of course employs two parameters.

Sweeps parallel to the other axes can be performed similarly; sweeps in different directions involve further modifications to the matrix.

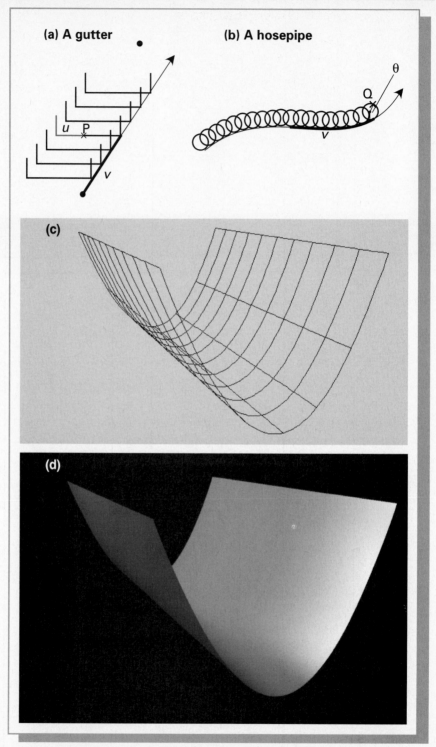

Figure 19.10 Swept surfaces: (a) a gutter; (b) a hosepipe; (c) a parabolic channel; (d) a shaded version of (c) (*source for (c) and (d): Matthew Holton, University of Teesside*).

19.10 Generating a surface of revolution

Strictly speaking, a sweep transformation can involve any or all of the following: translation, scaling and rotation. However, when a sweep involves rotation, purely, then we call the result a **surface of revolution**. Many everyday objects involve surfaces of revolution, among them barrels, bollards, tumblers, tubes, bowls, balls, cones and cotton reels; the way these surfaces can be formed is shown in Figure 19.11.

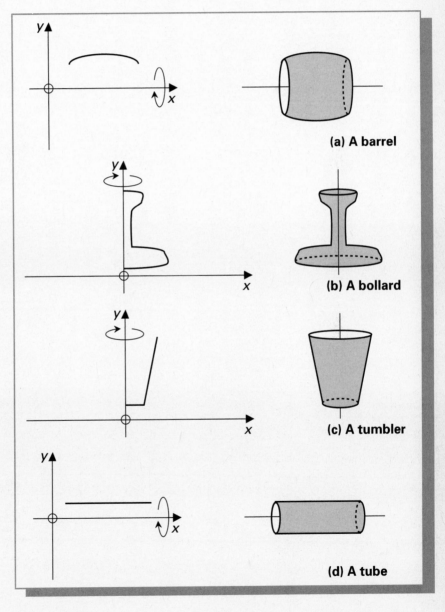

Figure 19.11 Surfaces of revolution (a) a barrel, (b) a bollard, (c) a tumbler, (d) a tube.

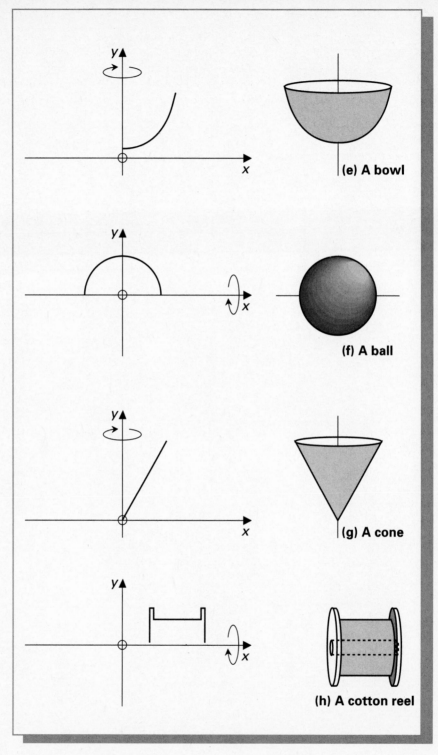

Figure 19.11   (e) a bowl, (f) a ball, (g) a cone and (h) a cotton reel.

Obviously surfaces of revolution are biparametric, and we now show how two parameters can identify any point on one such surface. We take the curved surface of a flower-pot on its side (which in formal language is the curved surface of a truncated cone), and, as shown in Figure 19.12(a), we view our shape with its axis along the x-axis. The moving line segment which **generates** the surface is a straight line in the x–y plane whose vector equation we take to be

$$\mathbf{r}(u) = x(u)\mathbf{i} + y(u)\mathbf{j}$$

We now deduce the position vector of a general point on the surface of this shape. We suppose that P is a point on the line segment with parameter u, that is P has position vector $(x(u) \quad y(u))$. When this line is rotated through an angle θ about the x-axis, the point P moves to the position Q; it is no longer in the x–y plane. Referring to Figure 19.12(a) and (b) we see that the $\mathbf{i}$-component of P is unaltered by the rotation; the $\mathbf{j}$-component was $y(u)$ and is now $y(u) \cos \theta$; the $\mathbf{k}$-component is $y(u) \sin \theta$. Thus the position vector of Q, a general point on the surface, uses the original parameter u, and the parameter θ which is the angle of rotation: the position vector of Q is

$$(x(u) \quad y(u) \cos \theta \quad y(u) \sin \theta)$$

Alternatively, we can obtain this result by matrix multiplication as follows. The position vector of the original point P is $(x(u) \quad y(u))$ in the x–y plane, but regarded as a point in three dimensions, it is $(x(u) \quad y(u) \quad 0)$. We write this as a homogeneous vector, and multiply by the appropriate rotation matrix (see Section 13.5.3):

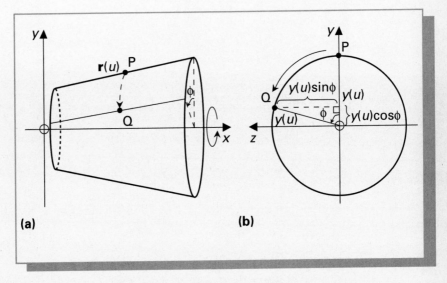

(a)　　　　　　　　　　　　　　　　**(b)**

Figure 19.12 (a) The surface of rotation (the z-axis is up out of the page).
(b) An end-on view, through P (the x-axis is up out of the page).

$$(x(u) \quad y(u) \quad 0 \quad 1) \begin{bmatrix} 1 & 0 & 0 & 0 \\ 0 & \cos\theta & \sin\theta & 0 \\ 0 & -\sin\theta & \cos\theta & 0 \\ 0 & 0 & 0 & 1 \end{bmatrix}$$

Thus we get the homogeneous vector of the rotated point Q:

$$(x(u) \quad y(u)\cos\theta \quad y(u)\sin\theta \quad 1)$$

which is equivalent to the position vector

$$(x(u) \quad y(u)\cos\theta \quad y(u)\sin\theta)$$

in three dimensions, as obtained above. The vector equation of this surface is

$$\mathbf{S}(u, \theta) = x(u)\mathbf{i} + y(u)\cos\theta\,\mathbf{j} + y(u)\sin\theta\,\mathbf{k}$$

which as expected employs two parameters.

The technique of multiplying the generalized position vector on the moving curve by the rotation matrix can be applied to find the vector equation of any surface of revolution. In particular we can use it to find a vector equation of the surface of a sphere, using notation that is compatible with that usually used for latitude and longitude (see also Example 20.3). As seen in Figure 19.13, the surface of a sphere can be generated by rotating a semi-circle about the z-axis. If the radius of the semi-circle is R, then a modified form of its equation is

$$\mathbf{r}(\phi) = R\sin\phi\,\mathbf{i} + R\cos\phi\,\mathbf{j}$$

where ϕ, the parameter, is the angle between the vector and the z-axis (compare this with Section 7.4.2).

Thus the position vector of a general point on the semi-circle in the x–z plane is

$$(R\sin\phi \quad R\cos\phi)$$

or, in the standard three dimensions, it is

$$(R\sin\phi \quad 0 \quad R\cos\phi)$$

which becomes, as a homogeneous vector,

$$(R\sin\phi \quad 0 \quad R\cos\phi \quad 1)$$

For rotation through an angle θ about the z-axis (see Section 13.5.3) the matrix is

$$\begin{bmatrix} \cos\theta & \sin\theta & 0 & 0 \\ -\sin\theta & \cos\theta & 0 & 0 \\ 0 & 0 & 1 & 0 \\ 0 & 0 & 0 & 1 \end{bmatrix}$$

and when this is multiplied by the above homogeneous vector we get

$$(R\cos\theta\sin\phi \quad R\sin\theta\sin\phi \quad R\cos\phi \quad 1)$$

Thus a vector equation of the surface of a sphere is

$$\mathbf{S}(\theta, \phi) = R\cos\theta\sin\phi\,\mathbf{i} + R\sin\theta\sin\phi\,\mathbf{j} + R\cos\phi\,\mathbf{k}$$

with two parameters as expected.

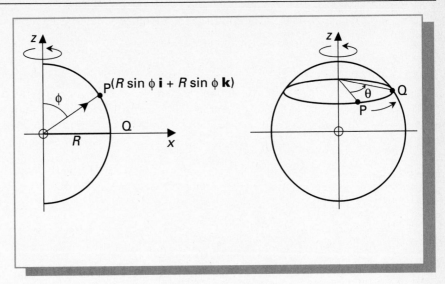

Figure 19.13 The surface of a sphere formed by rotation.

Exercises

19.1 Use the implicit form, involving scalar products, to write down the equation of the plane that passes through the point A(1, 2, 6) and that is normal to the vector $\mathbf{i} + 3\mathbf{j} - \mathbf{k}$. Then, by evaluating the scalar products, write down its equation in component terms, using the variables x, y and z.

19.2 Write down the parametric form, $\mathbf{S}(u, v)$, of the equation of the plane that contains the vectors $\mathbf{a} = \mathbf{i}$ and $\mathbf{b} = 2\mathbf{j}$. Write down the connection between the parameters u and v and more familiar concepts on the coordinate plane.

19.3 Write down the parametric form of the equation of the plane that contains the vectors $\mathbf{a} = \mathbf{i}$ and $\mathbf{b} = \mathbf{i} + \mathbf{j}$, so that the parameters indicate actual measurements along the $\mathbf{a}$ and $\mathbf{b}$ directions. Sketch the figure bounded by the parameter lines $[u = 0]$ and $[u = 2]$, $[v = 0]$ and $[v = 4]$. Indicate this same figure in parameter space also, and calculate the position vector whose parameters are $[1, 1]$.

19.4 Write down a parametric form of the equation of the plane that passes through the points P(1, 2, 0), Q(2, 0, 3) and R(0, 4, 2), so that the parameters measure actual distances in particular directions and each takes the value zero at Q.

19.5 Consider the line segment with end points H(1, 1, 0) and K(6, 2, 0) lying in the x–y plane. Rotating this line about the x-axis yields a conical surface. Determine a parametric form, $\mathbf{r}(u)$, for the equation of the line HK, and hence a parametric form, $\mathbf{S}(u, \phi)$, for the equation of the conical surface. What are the coordinates of P, the point on the surface where $u = \frac{1}{2}$ and $\phi = \pi/3$?

19.6 Using the parametric equations for an ellipse, write down a parametric form for the surface of an **ellipsoid of revolution** (like a rugby ball, or American football) with major axis 4 and minor axis 2.

19.7   A circle of radius 2, centred at $(6, 5)$ has parametric equations

$$\begin{cases} x = 6 + 2 \cos\phi \\ y = 5 + 2 \sin\phi, \quad 0 \le \phi \le 2\pi. \end{cases}$$

By rotating this circle about the x-axis write down $\mathbf{S}(\phi, \theta)$, the parametric form for the equation of the surface of a **torus** (like a rubber quoit, or a doughnut ring) of cross-sectional diameter 4 and overall diameter 16. What are the coordinates of T, the point on the surface at which $\theta = \pi/4$ and $\phi = \pi/2$?

Answers

19.1 $\mathbf{r} \cdot (1 \quad 3 \quad -1) = 1$; $x + 3y - z = 1$.

19.2 $\mathbf{S}(u, v) = u\mathbf{i} + 2v\mathbf{j}$; u gives x-coord, v gives $\frac{1}{2}$ y-coord.

19.3 $\mathbf{S}(u, v) = (u + \frac{v}{\sqrt{2}})\mathbf{i} + \frac{v}{\sqrt{2}}\mathbf{j}$; $1.71\mathbf{i} + 0.71\mathbf{j}$.

19.4 $\mathbf{S}(u, v) = (2 - 0.27u - 0.44v)\mathbf{i} + (0.53u + 0.87v)\mathbf{j} + (3 - 0.80u - 0.22v)\mathbf{k}$.

19.5 $\mathbf{r}(u) = [(1 + 5u) \quad (1 + u) \quad 0]$;

   $\mathbf{S}(u, \phi) = ((1 + 5u) \quad (1 + u)\cos\phi \quad (1 + u)\sin\phi), 0 \le \phi \le 2\pi$; $(3.5, 0.75, 1.3)$.

19.6 $\mathbf{S}(\phi, \theta) = (4\cos\phi \quad \sin\phi\cos\theta \quad \sin\phi\sin\theta), 0 \le \phi \le \pi, 0 \le \theta \le 2\pi$.

19.7 $\mathbf{S}(\phi, \theta) = ((6 + 2\cos\phi) \quad (5 + 2\sin\phi)\cos\theta \quad (5 + 2\sin\phi)\sin\theta), 0 \le \phi \le 2\pi$,
   $0 \le \theta \le 2\pi$. $(7.41, 0, 6.41)$.

20

Wire frame surfaces, surface tangents and normals:
Partial differentiation

20.1 General surfaces

In the last chapter we discussed how vector equations of simple surfaces need two parameters; we investigated this property in detail for plane surfaces, and for swept surfaces and surfaces of revolution. This fact is true for all surfaces: it can be shown that the position vector of a point on a general surface in space can be expressed using precisely two parameters, and for this we shall continue to use the notation $S(u, v)$.

In the real world there are few complete surfaces that are as relatively simple and symmetrical as the swept surfaces and surfaces of revolution we have already met. One of the traditional ways of viewing a more complicated surface, for design purposes, is by means of a framework of lines within the surface. Sometimes these lines are constructed as sets of parallel slices through the object which yield a framework of perpendicular lines (these are related to the orthographic projections of Section 14.2). Such a situation is shown in Figure 20.1. However, a better method involves constructing a framework of lines within a surface from the fundamental parametric vector equation of the surface. This form of framework, or **wire frame** is very valuable for visualization. It is one of the commonest and most easily produced representations of a surface in computer graphics; it can be straightforwardly manipulated by a computer, and it is an intrinsic part of many computer graphics packages. As an additional advantage it allows the direct calculation of vectors that are tangent to surfaces, and the surface normals that are needed for the realistic lighting of images. Thus we next investigate how a wire frame representation of a general surface can be obtained from its vector equation.

20.2 Forming a wire frame surface

To construct a wire frame surface we start by considering the position vector of a point on a general surface: this is $S(u, v)$, in terms of the parameters u and v. To

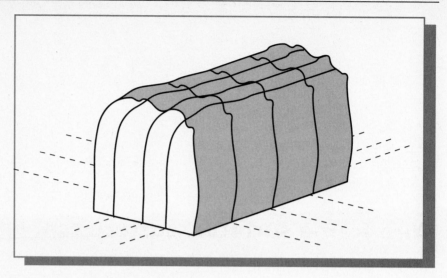

Figure 20.1 Two sets of parallel slices, yielding a framework of mutually perpendicular lines.

generate a wire frame version of the surface from this we vary the values of u and v as we now show, so that the point moves over the surface in a controlled way.

First we keep one of the parameters fixed, for example v can be kept at a constant value v_1 so that $v = v_1$. The position vector thus becomes $S(u, v_1)$, and depends on one variable parameter only. Thus, as noted in Section 19.1, it represents a curve in space, and taking successive values of u corresponds to moving along the curve. Next we take a different fixed value for v; we take $v = v_2$ where v_2 is a constant whose value is close to v_1. This gives us $S(u, v_2)$ which represents another space curve, and since v_1 and v_2 are close (and as long as the formula $S(u, v)$ is well-behaved) $S(u, v_2)$ and $S(u, v_1)$ are neighbouring curves. We show these curves in Figure 20.2, and already they look as if they are part of a surface. We proceed to take further fixed values of v, v_3, v_4, v_5 etc., all of which are close to each other, and so we get a set of neighbouring curves, $S(u, v_3)$, $S(u, v_4)$, $S(u, v_5)$ and so on, which all lie in the surface. If we could take all the intermediate values of v between v_1 and v_5 then all these neighbouring curves would be packed so closely together that they would effectively form the continuous surface; however, if we take separate values of v, then this set of separate **v-parametric curves** (with v fixed in each) can be seen in sequence on the surface, shown in Figure 20.2.

As an alternative way of generating the surface we next keep the parameter u fixed for each of a succession of constant values, and allow v to vary. We take $u = u_1$, a fixed constant; then the position vector becomes $S(u_1, v)$. Since this now depends on one variable parameter only, as before we see that it represents a curve in space. If we take a sequence of fixed values for u, u_2, u_3, u_4, u_5, etc., all close to one another, then the corresponding space curves are $S(u_2, v)$, $S(u_3, v)$, $S(u_4, v)$, $S(u_5, v)$ and so on. These neighbouring curves are shown in Figure 20.3. If all the intermediate values between u_1 and u_5 could be taken, then we should have the complete surface between these curves; when separate values are taken then we have a set of separate **u-parametric curves** (with u fixed in each).

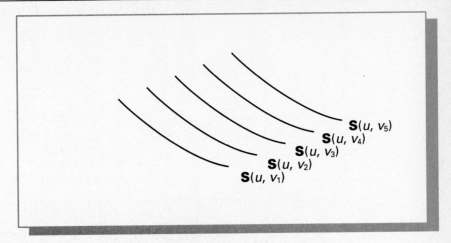

Figure 20.2 A set of *v*-parametric curves in a surface.

In Figure 20.4(a) we show both sets of parameter curves on the same diagram. We see that they cross the surface in different directions, and form an organized grid, even though they are unlikely to be at right angles to each other; this grid is the wire frame representation of the surface. Despite the many advantages of this form of representation of a surface there are certain limitations to the technique: by no means can it give any image the appearance of solidity, and confusion can arise when the back of an image is as visible as its front. However it gives the easiest form of surface description (colour shading or grey scale, pixel by pixel, which we show in Figure 20.4(b), is much more involved) and hence it is an invaluable tool in computer graphics work.

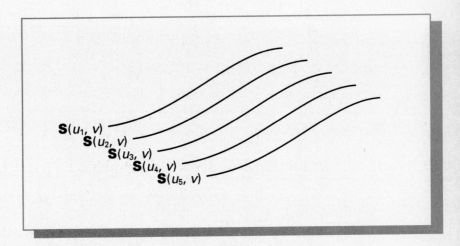

Figure 20.3 A set of *u*-parametric curves in a surface.

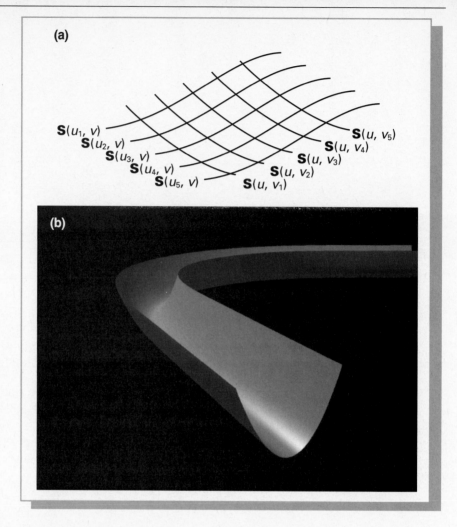

(a)

$S(u_1, v)$

$S(u_2, v)$

$S(u_3, v)$

$S(u_4, v)$

$S(u_5, v)$

$S(u, v_5)$

$S(u, v_4)$

$S(u, v_3)$

$S(u, v_2)$

$S(u, v_1)$

(b)

Figure 20.4 (a) A wire frame surface.
(b) A surface in grey scale *(source: Matthew Holton, University of Teesside)*.

20.3 Curved surfaces from vector equations

In this section we include several examples of sketching general curved surfaces from the vector form of their equations. In each case we proceed by fixing one parameter at a time: in this way we identify the parametric curves on each surface and so generate the surface. Essentially our approach to each surface is via its wire frame representation.

Example 20.1 The parabolic channel

We wish to identify and sketch the surface given by the vector equation

$$S(u, v) = u\mathbf{i} + v\mathbf{j} + (u + v^2)\mathbf{k}$$

Before beginning we note that the existence of two parameters means we expect to get a surface; it will not be a plane, as we had in Section 19.7, because the formula includes a squared term, v^2.

We consider the parametric equations:

$$\begin{cases} x = u \\ y = v \\ z = u + v^2 \end{cases}$$

and we first take some fixed values for u, while allowing v to vary. It is usually best to take simple parameter values initially, so we consider $[u = 0]$, $[u = 1]$ and $[u = 2]$ in turn.

When $[u = 0]$ we have

$$\begin{cases} x = 0 \\ y = v \\ z = v^2 \end{cases}$$

The value of x remains at zero, so this parameter curve lies in the plane where $x = 0$. By combining the last two equations we eliminate v and obtain the equation $z = y^2$ in this plane. Comparing this with the equation given in Section 7.3 (and Figure 7.5(a)) we see that we have here a parabola whose vertex is at the origin and where all the values of z are positive. This is shown in Figure 20.5.

When $[u = 1]$ we have

$$\begin{cases} x = 1 \\ y = v \\ z = 1 + v^2 \end{cases}$$

Since the value of x remains at 1 this parameter curve lies in the plane $x = 1$. The y-values are the same as when $[u = 0]$; the z-values are 1 greater than when $[u = 0]$. Thus this curve is also a parabola. It lies in the plane $x = 1$, its vertex lifted up by 1 unit in the z-direction compared with the $[u = 0]$ curve.

By exactly the same reasoning, the parameter value $[u = 2]$ gives a parabola in the plane $x = 2$ whose vertex is lifted by 2 units from the position of the $[u = 0]$ curve. All three parameter curves are shown in Figure 20.5. When dealt with similarly, other values of u will also give parabolas, each in a different plane of constant x and each lifted appropriately.

The other information needed for the wire frame description of this surface is obtained by taking some fixed values for v, while allowing u to vary. As before, we start with simple values and consider $[v = 0]$, $[v = 1]$ and $[v = 2]$ in turn.

When $[v = 0]$ we have

$$\begin{cases} x = u \\ y = 0 \\ z = u \end{cases}$$

The value of y remains at zero, so this parameter curve lies in the plane where $y = 0$. We combine the first and last equations, thereby eliminating u, and get $x = z$ in this plane. By comparison with Section 7.1 (and Figure 7.1) we identify this as the straight line with gradient 1 which passes through the origin. We show this line in Figure 20.5: it is the line that joins the vertices of the parabolas we found above.

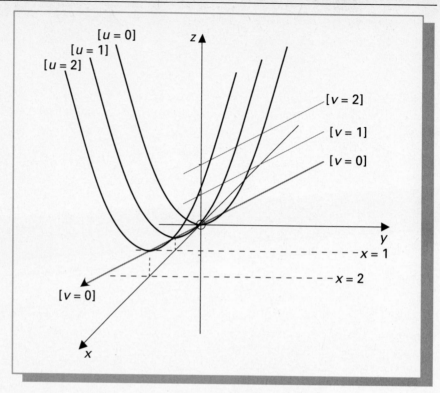

Figure 20.5 Constructing a wire frame representation of the surface
$\mathbf{S}(u, v) = u\mathbf{i} + v\mathbf{j} + (u + v^2)\mathbf{k}$.

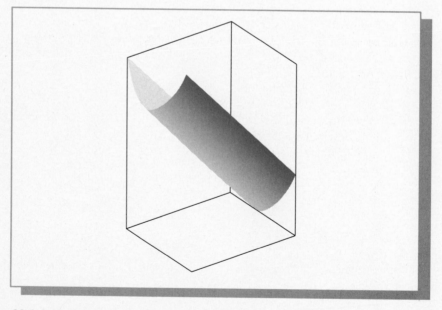

Figure 20.6 An improved visualization of the surface $\mathbf{S}(u, v) = u\mathbf{i} + v\mathbf{j} + (u + v^2)\mathbf{k}$
(source: John Dormand, University of Teesside).

When $[v = 1]$ we have

$$\begin{cases} x = u \\ y = 1 \\ z = u + 1 \end{cases}$$

Since the value of y remains at 1, this parameter curve lies in the plane $y = 1$. The first and third equations combine to give us $z = x + 1$, in this plane. We recognize this too as a straight line: it has gradient 1 and its z-intercept is 1. Thus we have here a parameter line that is parallel to that given by $[v = 0]$, and lies along the side of the parabolas.

We can deal with $[v = 2]$ similarly: the result is a straight line in the plane $y = 2$, with gradient 1 and z-intercept 2. This parameter line is parallel to the others, and like them it lies along the sides of the parabolas. These three v-parameter lines are shown in Figure 20.5.

From even the limited number of parameter values that we have considered it is clear that the surface under consideration is like a steeply sloping channel of parabolic cross-section. With u in the range from -3 to $+3$ and v in the range from -2 to $+2$, we show this surface in grey scale with hidden line removal, in Figure 20.6. This technique is beyond our scope, but the foundations of it lie with surface normals, which follow later in this chapter.

Example 20.2 The parabolic bowl

We consider the vector equation

$$\mathbf{S}(r, \theta) = r \cos \theta \, \mathbf{i} + r \sin \theta \, \mathbf{j} + r^2 \mathbf{k}$$

and apply the techniques of Example 20.1 in order to sketch the surface it represents.

We first consider the parametric equations:

$$\begin{cases} x = r \cos \theta \\ y = r \sin \theta \\ z = r^2 \end{cases}$$

and we start by taking some fixed values for r and letting θ vary; we take $[r = 0]$, $[r = 1]$ and $[r = 2]$.

When $[r = 0]$:

$$\begin{cases} x = 0 \\ y = 0 \\ z = 0 \end{cases}$$

which gives us the point at the origin.

When $[r = 1]$:

$$\begin{cases} x = \cos \theta \\ y = \sin \theta \\ z = 1 \end{cases}$$

z takes only the value 1, so this parameter curve lies in the plane $z = 1$. From Table 7.7 we identify the curve as a circle of radius 1, centred on the point $(x = 0, y = 0)$ in this plane.

When $[r = 2]$:

$$\begin{cases} x = 2 \cos \theta \\ y = 2 \sin \theta \\ z = 4 \end{cases}$$

z takes only the value 4, so this parameter curve lies in the plane $z = 4$. It also is a circle: it has

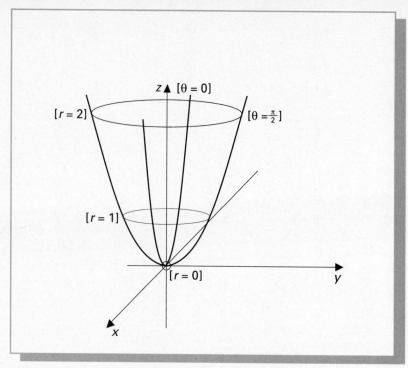

Figure 20.7 Constructing a wire frame representation of the surface
$$\mathbf{S}(r,\theta) = r\cos\theta\,\mathbf{i} + r\sin\theta\,\mathbf{j} + r^2\mathbf{k}.$$

radius 2 and is centred on $(x = 0, y = 0)$ in this plane. These three parameter curves (the first is just a point) are shown in Figure 20.7.

Next we take some fixed values for the parameter θ, and let r vary. We here consider $[\theta = 0]$ and $[\theta = \pi/2]$.

When $[\theta = 0]$:

$$\begin{cases} x = r\cos 0 = r \\ y = r\sin 0 = 0 \\ z = r^2 \end{cases}$$

As in Example 20.1, we see that this parameter curve is the parabola $z = x^2$ in the plane $y = 0$. Its vertex is at the origin and all the values of z are positive.

When $[\theta = \pi/2]$:

$$\begin{cases} x = r\cos \pi/2 = 0 \\ y = r\sin \pi/2 = r \\ z = r^2 \end{cases}$$

This parameter curve is another parabola with its vertex at the origin. It lies in the plane $x = 0$, and all the values of z on it are positive. These two θ-parameter curves are shown in Figure 20.7. Other values of θ will also be found to produce parameter curves that are parabolas; they will all have their vertices at the origin, but they will lie in different planes that contain the z-axis.

From the parameter curves in the wire frame representation in Figure 20.7 we can see that the surface we are dealing with here is a bowl of parabolic cross–section. It is similar in shape to the satellite dish discussed in Section 7.3, and an improved visualization is shown in Figure 20.8.

Figure 20.8 An improved visualization of the surface $S(r, \theta) = r\cos\theta\,\mathbf{i} + r\sin\theta\,\mathbf{j} + r^2\mathbf{k}$ (*source: Matthew Holton, University of Teesside*).

Example 20.3 The sphere

Here we revisit the spherical surface of radius R given by

$$\mathbf{S}(\theta, \phi) = R\cos\theta\,\sin\phi\,\mathbf{i} + R\sin\theta\,\sin\phi\,\mathbf{j} + R\cos\phi\,\mathbf{k}$$

which was constructed as a surface of revolution in Section 19.10. We briefly identify the parameter curves associated with this equation, and hence show how a wire frame surface for this sphere is formed.

As in the previous examples we write down the parametric equations

$$\begin{cases} x = R\cos\theta\,\sin\phi \\ y = R\sin\theta\,\sin\phi \\ z = R\cos\phi \end{cases}$$

and then identify specific parameter lines by taking fixed values for the parameters in turn.

We first consider fixed values for the parameter ϕ, while the parameter θ varies. We take $[\phi = 0]$, $[\phi = \pi/2]$ and $[\phi = \pi]$ in turn. $[\phi = 0]$ gives us

$$x = 0;\ y = 0;\ z = R$$

which is the point at $(0, 0, R)$ on the z-axis. $[\phi = \pi/2]$ gives us

$$x = R\cos\theta;\ y = R\sin\theta;\ z = 0$$

which, using Table 7.7, we recognize as a circle of radius R in the plane $z = 0$. $[\phi = \pi]$ gives us

$$x = 0;\ y = 0;\ z = -R$$

which is the point at $(0, 0, -R)$ on the z-axis. These features asociated with the fixed values of ϕ are shown in Figure 20.9. In addition we can consider any intermediate fixed value for ϕ, which we call $[\phi = \alpha]$, say. When $[\phi = \alpha]$ we have

$$x = R\cos\theta\sin\alpha; \; y = R\sin\theta\sin\alpha; \; z = R\cos\alpha$$

We can rewrite these as

$$x = (R\sin\alpha)\cos\theta; \; y = (R\sin\alpha)\sin\theta; \; z = (R\cos\alpha)$$

and as α is a fixed value we use Table 7.7 to recognize that this gives us a circle of radius $(R\sin\alpha)$ in the plane of $z = (R\cos\alpha)$. Thus in Figure 20.9 we show the circular parameter curve for α, which is any fixed value of ϕ.

We next consider fixed values for the parameter θ, while the parameter ϕ varies. We take $[\theta = 0]$ and $[\theta = \pi/2]$ in turn. For $[\theta = 0]$ we have

$$x = R\sin\phi; \; y = 0; \; z = R\cos\phi$$

which (using Table 7.7 again) we see to be a circle of radius R in the plane $y = 0$. For $[\theta = \pi/2]$ we have

$$x = 0; \; y = R\sin\phi; \; z = R\cos\phi$$

which by the same method is a circle of radius R in the plane $x = 0$. These two circles, parameter curves when θ is kept fixed, are shown in Figure 20.9.

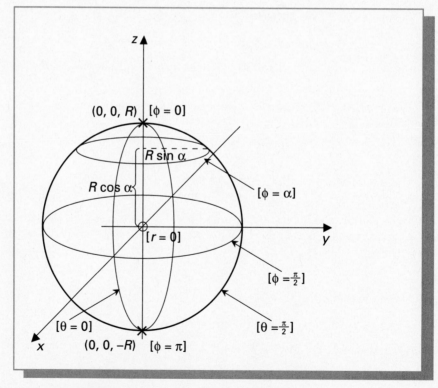

Figure 20.9 Constructing a wire frame representation of the surface
$\mathbf{S}(\theta, \phi) = R\cos\theta\sin\phi \, \mathbf{i} + R\sin\theta\sin\phi \, \mathbf{j} + R\cos\theta \, \mathbf{k}$.

With just the few parameter values we have considered here, the wire frame version of a sphere is readily appreciated. We see that the ϕ-parameter curves correspond to circles of latitude on the globe of the world (the angle of latitude at any point in the northern hemisphere is in fact $(90 - \phi)$; the θ-parameter curves are the meridians of longitude (the angle of longitude is θ, when measured from the agreed zero through Greenwich). This is an everyday example, vital for geographers and navigators among others, which illustrates the fact that any point on a surface can be specified by just two parameters.

20.4 Partial differentiation

As mentioned above, a wire frame representation of a surface gives us a direct way to determine vectors that are tangential or normal to that surface. The methods of differentiation, introduced in Chapter 16, were used in Chapter 17 for calculating tangent vectors and normal planes to space curves. Now we develop these ideas and use methods of partial differentiation applied to the parameter curves, to calculate tangents and normals to surfaces.

From the discussion of Section 20.2 it is clear that for any surface we can identify two sets of parameter curves. For example, when we considered the general surface given by $S(u, v)$ and kept one parameter fixed, $v = v_1$, we obtained $S(u, v_1)$, one of the set of v-parameter curves. $S(u, v_1)$ represents a space curve, and as u varies we know that $S(u, v_1)$ is the position vector of a point which moves along that curve. As in Section 17.2 we need to be able to differentiate the space curve $S(u, v_1)$ and get dS/du, a tangent vector; this tangent vector will obviously also be a tangent to the surface $S(u, v)$, along the parameter curve. The only problem is that since the surface formula $S(u, v)$ involves two variables, strictly speaking the derivative dS/du does not exist, so we must extend our idea of differentiation.

In general, when one parameter is kept fixed and the other is allowed to vary we can always differentiate with respect to the variable parameter; this is the process called **partial differentiation**. The notation we use for this involves '∂' (curly 'd'). Some examples, applying the rules of Section 16.4.5, will make the ideas clear: the first two involve just simple formulae and the third involves the vector equation of a surface.

Example 20.4 A function of *x* and *y*

We suppose that z is a function of two variables x and y which has the formula

$$z = xy + x^2 + y^3$$

On the one hand we can consider that (temporarily) y is a fixed number, and apply partial differentiation with respect to x; we get

$$\frac{\partial z}{\partial x} = y + 2x + 0 = y + 2x$$

On the other hand we can consider that (temporally) x is a fixed number and apply partial differentiation with respect to y:

$$\frac{\partial z}{\partial y} = x + 0 + 3y^2 = x + 3y^2$$

There is a partial derivative of z corresponding to each of its independent variables.

Example 20.5 A function of *u* and *v*

We consider a formula where *s* is a function of two variables, *u* and *v*:

$$s = 3u + 2v - uv$$

We may consider *v* to be fixed and obtain the partial derivative with respect to *u*

$$\frac{\partial s}{\partial u} = 3 + 0 - v = 3 - v$$

or we may consider *u* to be fixed and obtain the partial derivative with respect to *v*

$$\frac{\partial s}{\partial v} = 0 + 2 - u = 2 - u$$

Again we can calculate a partial derivative of *s* with respect to each of its independent variables.

Example 20.6 A vector function of *u* and *v*

The following formula gives the position vector for a point on a surface, since there are two parameters in the components:

$$\mathbf{S} = 3u\mathbf{i} + 2v\mathbf{j} + uv\mathbf{k}$$

We can apply partial differentiation as in the previous examples, and the method corresponds to that used in Section 16.5. We take *v* to be a fixed number, and differentiate with respect to *u*:

$$\frac{\partial \mathbf{S}}{\partial u} = 3\mathbf{i} + 0\mathbf{j} + v\mathbf{k} = 3\mathbf{i} + v\mathbf{k}$$

Alternatively we take *u* to be a fixed number, and differentiate with respect to *v*:

$$\frac{\partial \mathbf{S}}{\partial v} = 0\mathbf{i} + 2\mathbf{j} + u\mathbf{k} = 2\mathbf{j} + u\mathbf{k}$$

20.5 Surface tangents and surface normals

Example 20.6 above demonstrates exactly the technique needed for calculating tangents to surfaces. When we have the vector form for a surface, given by $\mathbf{S}(u, v)$ where *u* and *v* are the parameters, then calculating the partial derivatives $\partial \mathbf{S}/\partial u$ and $\partial \mathbf{S}/\partial v$ gives us tangent vectors to the surface, along the parameter curves. As shown in Figure 20.10, we have tangents to the *v*-parameter curves (where *v* is fixed and *u* variable) given by

$$\mathbf{t}_u = \frac{\partial \mathbf{S}}{\partial u}$$

and tangents to the *u*-parameter curves (where *u* is fixed and *v* variable) given by

$$\mathbf{t}_v = \frac{\partial \mathbf{S}}{\partial v}$$

Just as with tangents to space curves (see Section 17.2) the magnitude of a **surface tangent** is not unique since it depends on the parametrization used. Thus, as with space curves, it is usually only the direction of the tangents that is of interest, so we often need to calculate the unit vectors $\hat{\mathbf{t}}_u$ and $\hat{\mathbf{t}}_v$.

In order to determine the normal to a surface at any point, we first need two surface tangents at that point. These surface tangents together define the **tangent plane** to the surface at that point, and, by definition, the **surface normal** is normal to this tangent plane, see Figure 20.11(a). Thus the normal vector we seek is perpendicular to both the tangent vectors, and so using the methods of Section 4.2 this

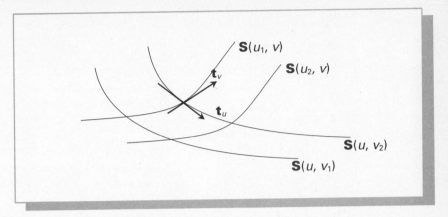

Figure 20.10 Tangents to parameter curves.

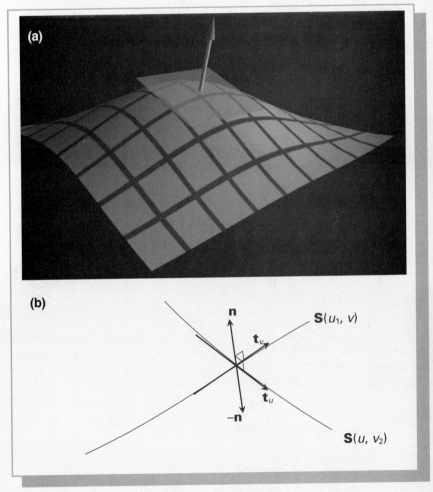

Figure 20.11 (a) A surface normal (*source: Matthew Holton, University of Teesside*)
(b) The normals to a surface .

normal is constructed as the cross product of the two tangent vectors. Thus for a surface given by $S(u, v)$, as above, a normal vector $\mathbf{n}$ at any point is calculated as

$$\mathbf{n} = \mathbf{t}_u \times \mathbf{t}_v$$

and the unit normal vector $\hat{\mathbf{n}}$ can be determined in the usual way. If $\mathbf{n}$ is a normal to the surface then we can easily see from Figure 20.11(b) that the vector $-\mathbf{n}$ (which goes in the opposite direction) is also a normal to that surface. If we seek to calculate just any normal to a given surface, then the sign ($+$ or $-$) of $\mathbf{n}$ is irrelevant, and so the order of multiplication ($\mathbf{t}_u \times \mathbf{t}_v$) or ($\mathbf{t}_v \times \mathbf{t}_u$) is also immaterial. However, if we are calculating normals in order to deal with reflections of light, for example, or other surface features, then the direction of the normal is very important. In addition, in more advanced work it can happen that a surface is to be constructed from a set of normal vectors; in this case, too, all the normals must point in the same direction, so their direction is very important.

To illustrate the value of partial differentiation we conclude this chapter by returning to some of the wire frame surfaces of Section 20.3, and calculating their surface tangents and surface normals.

Example 20.7 Tangents and normals to the surface of the parabolic channel

We consider the surface given by

$$S(u, v) = u\mathbf{i} + v\mathbf{j} + (u + v^2)\mathbf{k}$$

which we met in Example 20.1, and we now calculate its surface tangents along the parameter curves. In addition we calculate both the unit surface tangents, and the unit surface normals, at the point P where $[u = 1, v = 1]$.

To find its surface tangents, we start by determining its partial derivatives:

$$\begin{cases} \dfrac{\partial S}{\partial u} = 1\mathbf{i} + 0\mathbf{j} + (1 + 0)\mathbf{k} = \mathbf{i} + \mathbf{k} \\[2mm] \dfrac{\partial S}{\partial v} = 0\mathbf{i} + 1\mathbf{j} + (0 + 2v)\mathbf{k} = \mathbf{j} + 2v\mathbf{k} \end{cases}$$

Thus we have these vectors which are tangents to the surface along the parameter curves:

$$\begin{cases} \mathbf{t}_u = \mathbf{i} + \mathbf{k} \\ \mathbf{t}_v = \mathbf{j} + 2v\mathbf{k} \end{cases}$$

As shown in Figure 20.12, $\mathbf{t}_u$ has a fixed direction up the channel, and the direction of $\mathbf{t}_v$ is around the curve of each parabola; so these surface tangents are also tangents to the parameter curves in the wire frame of the surface, as expected.

Where the parameters have values $[u = 1, v = 1]$ the point P on the surface has position vector

$$\mathbf{r} = S(1, 1) = 1\mathbf{i} + 1\mathbf{j} + (1 + 1^2)\mathbf{k}^2$$

so its coordinates are $(1, 1, 2)$. Using these same parameter values we see that at P there are the specific tangent vectors

$$\begin{cases} \mathbf{t}_u = \mathbf{i} + \mathbf{k} \\ \hat{\mathbf{t}}_v = \mathbf{j} + 2\mathbf{k} \end{cases}$$

from which we can obtain the unit tangents

$$\begin{cases} \hat{\mathbf{t}}_u = \dfrac{\mathbf{t}_u}{|\mathbf{t}_u|} = \dfrac{1}{\sqrt{2}}(\mathbf{i}+\mathbf{k}) \\[2mm] \hat{\mathbf{t}}_v = \dfrac{\mathbf{t}_v}{|\mathbf{t}_v|} = \dfrac{1}{\sqrt{5}}(\mathbf{j}+2\mathbf{k}) \end{cases}$$

We now use the tangents to calculate the surface normal, **n**, at P:

$$\mathbf{n} = \mathbf{t}_u \times \mathbf{t}_v$$

$$= (\mathbf{i}+\mathbf{k}) \times (\mathbf{j}+2\mathbf{k})$$

To evaluate this, as in Section 4.2 we set the components of the vectors into the determinant pattern

$$\begin{vmatrix} \mathbf{i} & \mathbf{j} & \mathbf{k} \\ 1 & 0 & 1 \\ 0 & 1 & 2 \end{vmatrix}$$

and we get

$$\mathbf{n} = (0 \times 2 - 1 \times 1)\mathbf{i} - (1 \times 2 - 0 \times 1)\mathbf{j} + (1 \times 1 - 0 \times 0)\mathbf{k}$$

$$= -\mathbf{i} - 2\mathbf{j} + \mathbf{k}$$

A unit normal is

$$\hat{\mathbf{n}} = \frac{\mathbf{n}}{|\mathbf{n}|} = \frac{1}{\sqrt{6}}(-\mathbf{i} - 2\mathbf{j} + \mathbf{k})$$

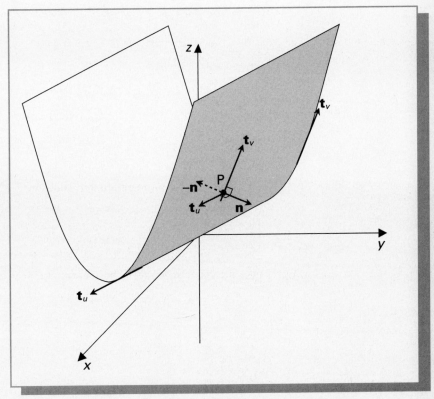

Figure 20.12 The directions of surface tangents and normal on the parabolic channel.

and the pair of unit normals are given by

$$\pm \frac{1}{\sqrt{6}} (-\mathbf{i} - 2\mathbf{j} + \mathbf{k})$$

that is

$$\frac{1}{\sqrt{6}} (-\mathbf{i} - 2\mathbf{j} + \mathbf{k})$$

or

$$\frac{1}{\sqrt{6}} (\mathbf{i} + 2\mathbf{j} - \mathbf{k})$$

Both the normals at P are also shown in Figure 20.12.

Example 20.8   Tangents and normals to the surface of the parabolic bowl

We consider the surface given by

$$\mathbf{S}(r, \theta) = r \cos\theta \, \mathbf{i} + r \sin\theta \, \mathbf{j} + r^2 \mathbf{k}$$

which we met in Example 20.2. We use the same procedures as in Example 20.7 above to determine the surface tangents along the parameter curves, and also the particular surface tangents and surface normals at the point Q where $[r = 1, \theta = \pi/2]$.

For the surface tangents we start by finding the partial derivatives (using Table 16.3 if needed):

$$\begin{cases} \dfrac{\partial \mathbf{S}}{\partial r} = 1 \cos\theta \, \mathbf{i} + 1 \sin\theta \, \mathbf{j} + 2r\mathbf{k} = \cos\theta \, \mathbf{i} + \sin\theta \mathbf{j} + 2r\mathbf{k} \\[2mm] \dfrac{\partial \mathbf{S}}{\partial \theta} = r \, (-\sin\theta) \, \mathbf{i} + r\cos\theta \mathbf{j} + 0\mathbf{k} = -r\sin\theta \, \mathbf{i} + r\cos\theta \mathbf{j} \, . \end{cases}$$

Thus we have tangent vectors along the parameter curves:

$$\begin{cases} \mathbf{t}_r = \cos\theta \, \mathbf{i} + \sin\theta \mathbf{j} + 2r\mathbf{k} \\[2mm] \mathbf{t}_\theta = -r\sin\theta \, \mathbf{i} + r\cos\theta \mathbf{j} \end{cases}$$

Where the parameters have values $[r = 1, \theta = \pi/2]$ the point Q on the surface has position vector

$$\mathbf{r} = \mathbf{S}(1, \pi/2) = 1 \cos\pi/2 \, \mathbf{i} + 1 \sin\pi/2 \mathbf{j} + 1^2 \mathbf{k}$$

$$= 0\mathbf{i} + 1\mathbf{j} + 1\mathbf{k}$$

and so its coordinates are $(0, 1, 1)$. Using these same parameter values we see that surface tangents at Q are

$$\begin{cases} \mathbf{t}_r = \cos\pi/2 \, \mathbf{i} + \sin\pi/2 \mathbf{j} + (2 \times 1)\mathbf{k} = \mathbf{j} + 2\mathbf{k} \\[2mm] \mathbf{t}_\theta = (-1 \sin\pi/2)\mathbf{i} + (1 \cos\pi/2)\mathbf{j} = -\mathbf{i} \end{cases}$$

For a surface normal at Q we take the cross product of these two tangent vectors:

$$\mathbf{n} = \mathbf{t}_\theta \times \mathbf{t}_r = (-\mathbf{i}) \times (\mathbf{j} + 2\mathbf{k})$$

Using the determinant pattern

$$\begin{vmatrix} \mathbf{i} & \mathbf{j} & \mathbf{k} \\ -1 & 0 & 0 \\ 0 & 1 & 2 \end{vmatrix}$$

we get

$$n = (0 \times 2 - 1 \times 0)\mathbf{i} - ((-1) \times 2 - 0 \times 0)\mathbf{j} + ((-1) \times 1 - 0 \times 0)\mathbf{k}$$

$$= 2\mathbf{j} - \mathbf{k}$$

The directions of the vectors we have calculated are indicated on Figure 20.13. As expected, the surface tangents at Q lie along the directions of the parameter curves and the surface normal is at right angles to both of them.

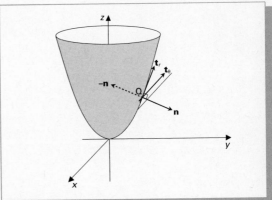

Figure 20.13 The directions of surface tangents and normal on the parabolic bowl.

Exercises

20.1 a) If $r = x^2 y + y^3 x$, determine $\dfrac{\partial r}{\partial x}$ and $\dfrac{\partial r}{\partial y}$.

b) If $S = 3x^2 y + 2y^2 z - zx$, determine $\dfrac{\partial S}{\partial x}$, $\dfrac{\partial S}{\partial y}$ and $\dfrac{\partial S}{\partial z}$.

20.2 Sketch the wire frame representation of the surface given by

$$\mathbf{S}(u, v) = u\mathbf{i} + (u + v)\mathbf{j} - v^2\mathbf{k}$$

By partial differentiation, find tangent vectors along the parameter lines. Determine specific tangents at the point on the surface where $[u = 2, v = 0]$, and calculate also the surface normals at this point. Indicate the directions of these tangents and normals on your sketch.

20.3 Sketch a wire frame representation for each of the following surfaces, using parameter lines where u and v separately take constant values. In addition, calculate the partial derivative with respect to each parameter, and hence determine tangent vectors along the parameter lines for each surface. Finally, calculate tangent vectors and surface normals when the parameters have the values indicated.

a) $\mathbf{S}(u, v) = u\mathbf{i} + v\mathbf{j} + (u^2 + v)\mathbf{k}$; $[u = 0, v = 0]$

b) $\mathbf{S}(u, v) = u\mathbf{i} + v\mathbf{j} + (u^2 + v^2)\mathbf{k}$; $[u = 0, v = 1]$

c) $\mathbf{S}(u, v) = u\mathbf{i} + (u^2 - v^2)\mathbf{j} + v\mathbf{k}$; $[u = 1, v = 0]$

Answers

20.1 a) $2xy + y^3$, $x^2 + 3y^2 x$; b) $6xy - z$, $3x^2 + 4yz$, $2y^2 - x$.

20.2 $\mathbf{j} - 2v\mathbf{k}$, $\mathbf{i} + \mathbf{j}$; $\mathbf{j}$, $\mathbf{i} + \mathbf{j}$, $\pm\mathbf{k}$.

20.3 a) $\mathbf{j} + \mathbf{k}$, $\mathbf{i} + 2u\mathbf{k}$; $\mathbf{j} + \mathbf{k}$, $\mathbf{i}$, $\pm(\mathbf{j} - \mathbf{k})$; b) $\mathbf{j} + 2v\mathbf{k}$, $\mathbf{i} + 2u\mathbf{k}$; $\mathbf{j} + 2\mathbf{k}$, $\mathbf{i}$, $\pm(2\mathbf{j} - \mathbf{k})$;

c) $-2v\mathbf{j} + \mathbf{k}$, $\mathbf{i} + 2u\mathbf{j}$; $\mathbf{k}$, $\mathbf{i} + 2\mathbf{j}$, $\pm(-2\mathbf{i} + \mathbf{j})$.

21

Piecewise surfaces:
Quadrilateral patches

21.1 Dividing up a surface

All the surfaces met in previous chapters have been relatively simple, and thus limited in their application. However, most real objects have surfaces that are far too complicated to be described in their entirety by a single mathematical formula. For instance the real surfaces of objects such as opera houses, ships' hulls, highways or hats have many different parts, each with different geometrical properties such as slope or curvature; they cannot be completely described by one equation. Thus techniques that involve a single equation for a whole surface are limited in their use, and alternative methods for describing surfaces are necessary. However, for computer graphics applications it is essential that we have mathematical descriptions for every part of a surface so that we can determine positions on it, and calculate surface normals. The usual procedure, for a completely general surface, is to divide the whole surface into small pieces called **patches** and to obtain a mathematical formula for each patch. Any surface can be represented piecewise by a set of surface patches: we can think of these like patches in a quilt, stitched together to form the whole surface.

The simplest surface division is into triangular **plane facets**. If we have a set of points in a surface then we can always join them up by straight lines so that plane triangles result, as shown in Figure 21.1(a). This set of plane facets gives us an approximation to the original surface; the facets touch, so we have no gaps, but each joins the next at a ridge, so the approximated surface is not smooth. However, dividing the surface up into many plane facets can give an acceptable approximation to the original surface.

When we join up a set of points in a surface by straight lines that form quadrilaterals, as in Figure 21.1(b), then these patches are unlikely to be planar. The use of **quadrilateral patches** which are non-planar, and which can have their four sides straight or curved, gives us a better approximation to any surface. We start with a simple example on a sphere, and then we shall focus on patches where the opposite sides are straight lines (**bilinear patches**) and where they are curves

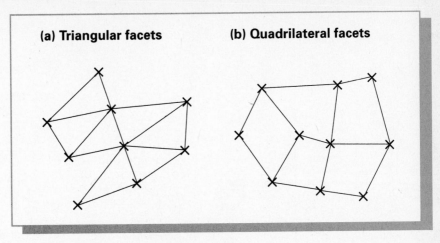

(a) Triangular facets

(b) Quadrilateral facets

Figure 21.1 (a) Triangular and (b) quadrilateral facets.

(**linear Coons patches**). In both these latter cases we can arrange for patches to join each other with no gaps, so that the approximated surface is continuous (this idea may be compared with continuity of a curve, as discussed in Section 17.2), and we have the means of defining the entire surface within the patch. However, it is likely that there will still be ridges, even if small ones, where patches join.

Parameters remain an essential tool when we use patches to approximate a surface. There are several reasons why parameters are so valuable: they are independent of the axis system used, and ambiguity is avoided even when a surface folds back on itself. In addition they are easily compatible with homogeneous vectors, and thus with all the three-dimensional transformations that might be applied.

21.2 A quadrilateral patch on a sphere

We start our consideration of patches with an easy illustration, a patch on a sphere. Approximating a spherical surface using patches is not novel since, before high-quality rubber mouldings were available, the balls for many sports were traditionally made by actually sewing together patches of leather or rubber around a bladder or other filling. A spherical soccer ball was made by sewing together twelve pentagons (or sometimes eighteen rectangles), and a tennis ball was formed from two patches; these shapes are shown in Figure 21.2. We have already investigated spherical surfaces in Section 19.10 and Example 20.3, so in this case the formula for the complete surface is already known; we shall consider a curved quadrilateral patch on a unit sphere where all four curved edges are specified.

Using the result of Section 19.10 we have the following vector equation for a spherical surface of unit radius:

$$\mathbf{S}(\theta, \phi) = \cos\theta \, \sin\phi \, \mathbf{i} + \sin\theta \, \sin\phi \, \mathbf{j} + \cos\phi \, \mathbf{k}$$

where the angles measured by the parameters θ and ϕ, for a general point P, are shown in Figure 21.3(a). We consider the patch ABCD shown on the sphere in Figure 21.3(b). It is obviously a curved patch, with curved boundaries, which can be defined relative to the above equation by limiting the parameter values: for ABCD

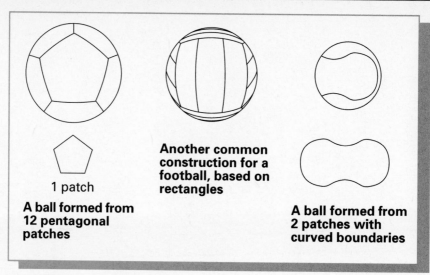

Another common
construction for a
football, based on
rectangles

1 patch

**A ball formed from
12 pentagonal
patches**

**A ball formed from
2 patches with
curved boundaries**

Figure 21.2 Balls formed using patches.

$$\begin{cases} \pi/4 \le \theta \le \pi/2 \\ \pi/4 \le \phi \le \pi/2 \end{cases}$$

From the parameter values at the four corners we determine the coordinates at the corners. At A we have $[\theta = \pi/4, \phi = \pi/2]$, so A has coordinates

$$(\cos \tfrac{\pi}{4} \sin \tfrac{\pi}{2}, \sin \tfrac{\pi}{4} \sin \tfrac{\pi}{2}, \cos \tfrac{\pi}{2})$$

that is, approximately,

$$(0.71 \times 1, 0.71 \times 1, 0)$$

$$= (0.71, 0.71, 0)$$

Exactly similarly, since at B $[\theta = \pi/4, \phi = \pi/4]$ the coordinates of B are $(0.5, 0.5, 0.71)$; at C $[\theta = \pi/2, \phi = \pi/4]$ so the coordinates of C are $(0, 0.71, 0.71)$; and at D $[\theta = \pi/2, \phi = \pi/2]$ so the coordinates of D are $(0, 1, 0)$.

By the methods of Section 20.5 we can find surface tangents at these corners, using partial differentiation. From the surface equation we obtain:

$$\begin{cases} \mathbf{t}_\theta = \dfrac{\partial \mathbf{S}}{\partial \theta} = -\sin \theta \, \sin \phi \, \mathbf{i} + \cos \theta \, \sin \phi \, \mathbf{j} + 0 \mathbf{k} \\ \mathbf{t}_\phi = \dfrac{\partial \mathbf{S}}{\partial \phi} = \cos \theta \, \cos \phi \, \mathbf{i} + \sin \theta \, \cos \phi \, \mathbf{j} - \sin \phi \, \mathbf{k} \end{cases}$$

Thus at the point A we have two surface tangents:

$$\mathbf{t}_\theta = -\sin \tfrac{\pi}{4} \sin \tfrac{\pi}{2} \mathbf{i} + \cos \tfrac{\pi}{4} \sin \tfrac{\pi}{2} \mathbf{j}$$

$$\approx -0.71 \mathbf{i} + 0.71 \mathbf{j}$$

and

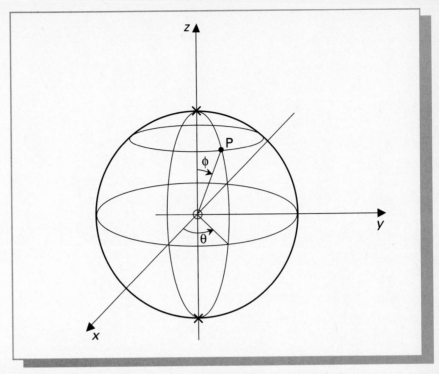

Figure 21.3 (a) The parameters used for the surface of a unit sphere.

$$\mathbf{t}_\phi = \cos\frac{\pi}{4}\cos\frac{\pi}{2}\,\mathbf{i} + \sin\frac{\pi}{4}\cos\frac{\pi}{2}\,\mathbf{j} - \sin\frac{\pi}{2}\,\mathbf{k}$$

$$= -\mathbf{k}$$

Using the method of Section 20.5 again, we calculate $\mathbf{n}$, a surface normal at A:

$$\begin{vmatrix} \mathbf{i} & \mathbf{j} & \mathbf{k} \\ 0 & 0 & -1 \\ -0.71 & 0.71 & 0 \end{vmatrix}$$

so

$$\mathbf{n} \simeq 0.71\mathbf{i} - 0.71\mathbf{j}$$

The directions of these three vectors are shown in Figure 21.3(b). Similar calculations can be performed to obtain the surface tangents and normals at the other corners of the patch.

In this special case we already have the equation of the whole surface we are considering, and so all the points in the interior of the patch can be determined. However, in general, if we are given only the four boundaries of a quadrilateral patch then we do not necessarily know anything about the surface in between them. In fact the four boundaries alone do not determine the shape of the interior; it might be tight and smooth, or it might bulge inwards or outwards.

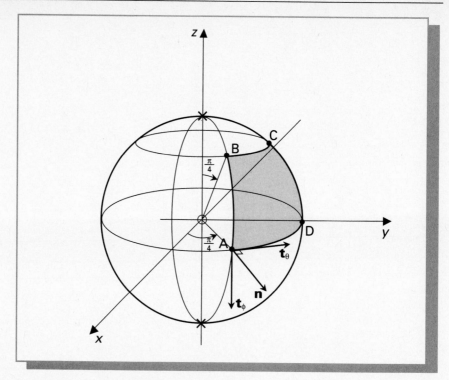

Figure 21.3 (b) A quadrilateral patch on a sphere.

21.3 Bilinear patches

There is a simpler situation than the one described above, which has the added advantage of allowing us to find out about the interior of the surface. We can be given just a network of points in the surface, with no specific edges joining them and no formula given for the surface as a whole, but by forming **bilinear patches** we can construct equations for portions of a curved surface which allow us to interpolate all the interior surface points. With computerization, bilinear patches are now among the most favoured methods for dealing with surfaces in industrial design projects.

To construct a bilinear patch we take four points A, B, C and D in the surface under consideration. These points have position vectors **a**, **b**, **c** and **d**, and they are arranged as shown in Figure 21.4(a). The points will not usually lie in a plane. First we obtain the opposite straight sides of the patch: from the position vectors of the points we use interpolation formulae to construct the vector equations $\mathbf{Q}_1$ of the line from A to B, and $\mathbf{Q}_2$ of the line from C to D. We note that these lines go in the same direction, from left to right in the Figure 21.4(a). We apply the method of Section 18.2, using the same parameter u which takes values between 0 and 1 for both lines. The position vectors of general points along these lines are

$$\begin{cases} \mathbf{Q}_1(u) = (1 - u)\mathbf{a} + u\mathbf{b} \\ \mathbf{Q}_2(u) = (1 - u)\mathbf{c} + u\mathbf{d} \end{cases}$$

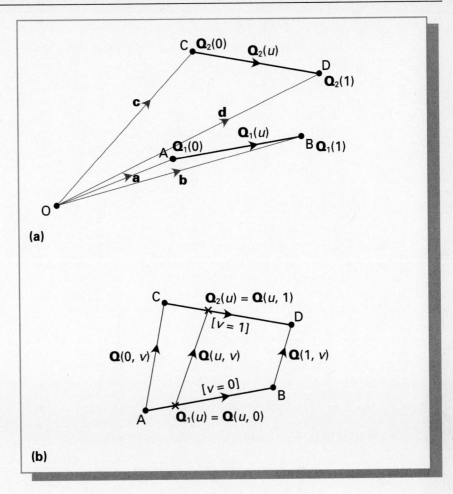

Figure 21.4 (a) Four points joined by the first linear interpolation.
(b) The second linear interpolation.

We next take the points on these lines that have the same value of the parameter u and join them with the vector $\mathbf{Q}$. To construct a vector equation for $\mathbf{Q}$ we use a second parameter v (which again goes from 0 to 1) and then the equation for the straight line in the direction of $\mathbf{Q}$ is

$$\mathbf{Q}(v) = (1 - v)\mathbf{Q}_1(u) + v\mathbf{Q}_2(u)$$

We use the formulae for $\mathbf{Q}_1(u)$ and $\mathbf{Q}_2(u)$ from above, and since $\mathbf{Q}$ depends on two parameters we get

$$\mathbf{Q}(u, v) = (1 - v)\big((1 - u)\mathbf{a} + u\mathbf{b}\big) + v\big((1 - u)\mathbf{c} + u\mathbf{d}\big)$$

which when simplified becomes

$$\mathbf{Q}(u, v) = (1 - v)(1 - u)\mathbf{a} + (1 - v)u\mathbf{b} + v(1 - u)\mathbf{c} + vu\mathbf{d}$$

We have used interpolation to combine the equations of the two boundary lines we formed to start with, and now we have an equation in two parameters which represents a surface. This is the bilinear patch which approximates to the surface required; its four edges are all straight (see Figure 21.4(b)) but the surface itself may well be curved or twisted. From the formula for $\mathbf{Q}$ we can obtain the coordinates, surface tangents and normals for all the points in the interior of the patch, which is fully determined.

As in Section 19.6 we can represent the patch in the parameter plane. In Figure 21.5 we show the patch ABCD as a square on a graph which has the parameters as coordinates.

The word 'bilinear' means 'involving two lines' and it is used here because linear interpolation is used twice over: first in constructing lines between A and B and between C and D, and then in constructing lines between these two. The patch we have constructed has both pairs of opposite boundaries linear. We obtain the individual boundary lines from the surface equation by setting each parameter equal to 0 and 1 in turn. Thus when $[v = 0]$ we have

$$\mathbf{Q}(u, 0) = (1 - u)\mathbf{a} + u\mathbf{b}$$

which is $\mathbf{Q}_1(u)$, along the line from A to B. Similarly when $[v = 1]$ we have

$$\mathbf{Q}(u, 1) = (1 - u)\mathbf{c} + u\mathbf{d}$$

which is $\mathbf{Q}_2(u)$, along the line from C to D. In exactly the same way we can show that $[u = 0]$ gives $\mathbf{Q}(0, v)$, along the line from A to C, and $[u = 1]$ gives $\mathbf{Q}(1, v)$, along the line from B to D; all these are labelled on Figure 21.4(b).

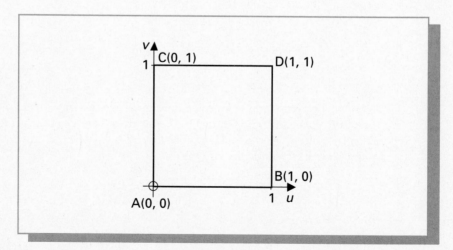

Figure 21.5 The patch shown in the parameter plane.

Example 21.1 A bilinear patch based on four given points

We here construct the bilinear patch based on the points A(0, 0, 0), B(1, 0, 0), C(0, 1, 0) and D(1, 1, 1), and then we find the equation of the curve that joins A to D in the surface so formed. In envisaging this patch we note that the points A, B and C are coplanar, in the plane $z = 0$, but D is a point above that plane: it is as if we have a square piece of stretchy fabric with three corners pinned to the corners of a square board, and the fourth corner is lifted up vertically.

We first write down the position vectors of the points: the position vector of A is

$$\mathbf{a} = 0\mathbf{i} + 0\mathbf{j} + 0\mathbf{k} = \mathbf{0}$$

the position vector of B is

$$\mathbf{b} = 1\mathbf{i} + 0\mathbf{j} + 0\mathbf{k} = \mathbf{i}$$

the position vector of C is

$$\mathbf{c} = 0\mathbf{i} + 1\mathbf{j} + 1\mathbf{k} = \mathbf{j}$$

and the position vector of D is

$$\mathbf{d} = 1\mathbf{i} + 1\mathbf{j} + 1\mathbf{k} = \mathbf{i} + \mathbf{j} + \mathbf{k}$$

The line from A to B is $\mathbf{Q}_1$, and the line from C to D is $\mathbf{Q}_2$, so using the same parameter u in the vector equation of each line we have

$$\mathbf{Q}_1(u) = (1 - u)\mathbf{0} + u\mathbf{i}$$

and

$$\mathbf{Q}_2(u) = (1 - u)\mathbf{j} + u(\mathbf{i} + \mathbf{j} + \mathbf{k})$$

Combining these as above we get the equation of the surface patch:

$$\mathbf{Q}(u, v) = (1 - v)(1 - u)\mathbf{0} + (1 - v)u\mathbf{i} + v(1 - u)\mathbf{j} + uv(\mathbf{i} + \mathbf{j} + \mathbf{k})$$

which we simplify and get

$$\mathbf{Q}(u, v) = u\mathbf{i} - vu\mathbf{i} + v\mathbf{j} - vu\mathbf{j} + uv\mathbf{i} + uv\mathbf{j} + uv\mathbf{k}$$

$$= (u - vu + uv)\mathbf{i} + (v - vu + uv)\mathbf{j} + uv\mathbf{k}$$

$$= u\mathbf{i} + v\mathbf{j} + uv\mathbf{k}$$

To sketch this patch we examine its boundaries. When $[v = 0]$ then $\mathbf{Q}(u, 0) = u\mathbf{i}$, which is the line along the x-axis as u takes values from 0 to 1; it is the line from A to B. When $[u = 0]$ then $\mathbf{Q}(0, v) = v\mathbf{j}$; this is the line along the y-axis, as v takes values from 0 to 1; it is the line from A to C. When $[u = 1]$ then $\mathbf{Q}(1, v) = \mathbf{i} + v\mathbf{j} + v\mathbf{k}$; as v takes values from 0 to 1 this line has gradient 1 in the plane $x = 1$; it is the line from B to D. When $[v = 1]$ then $\mathbf{Q}(u, 1) = u\mathbf{i} + \mathbf{j} + u\mathbf{k}$; as u takes values from 0 to 1 this line has gradient 1 in the plane $y = 1$; it is the line from C to D. These boundaries are shown in Figure 21.6.

The patch ABCD is shown in the parameter plane in Figure 21.7(a). From this diagram we see that on the line from A to D the parameters are equal: $v = u$. Thus to find the equation of the curved line joining A to D we put $[v = u]$ into the equation of the surface patch:

$$\mathbf{Q}(u, u) = u\mathbf{i} + u\mathbf{j} + u^2\mathbf{k}$$

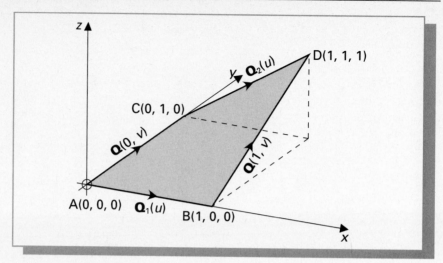

Figure 21.6 The bilinear patch A, B, C and D.

The components of this are

$$\begin{cases} x = u \\ y = u \\ z = u^2 \end{cases}$$

that is

$$\begin{cases} x = y \\ z = u^2. \end{cases}$$

Thus we see that the result lies in the plane given by $x = y$ and takes the form $z = u^2$ as u increases from 0 to 1. This is a parabola in the plane $x = y$, as indicated in Figure 21.7(b). A computer-generated version is shown in in Figure 21.7 c).

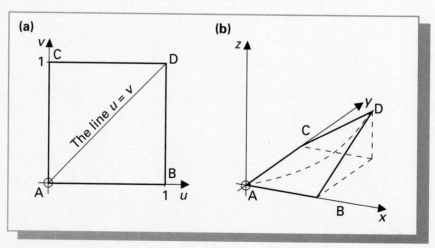

Figure 21.7 (a) The bilinear patch shown in the parameter plane.
(b) The curve in the surface patch.

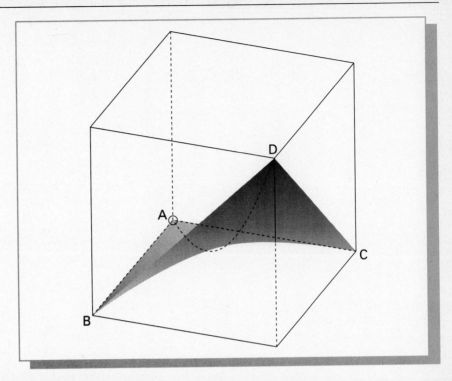

Figure 21.7 (c) The bilinear patch (*source: John Dormand, University of Teesside*).

21.4 Linear Coons patches

Linear Coons patches provide a development of bilinear patches: they are more strongly prescribed than bilinear patches and can provide more intricately varied surfaces. The surface patch is defined by its four boundary curves (they are not usually straight lines) and the interior of the patch is obtained by interpolating between the curves.

We start with the four boundary curves $\mathbf{P}_1$, $\mathbf{P}_2$, $\mathbf{P}_3$ and $\mathbf{P}_4$, and the four points A, B, C and D where pairs of curves intersect; these points are the corners of the patch. We assume that the boundary curves are already expressed by vector equations using parameters. Each is a space curve, and so employs a single parameter: as with bilinear patches we arrange that opposite boundaries use the same parameter, taking values between 0 and 1. Thus we have $\mathbf{P}_1(u)$ and $\mathbf{P}_2(u)$, $\mathbf{P}_3(v)$ and $\mathbf{P}_4(v)$, with each pair having the same sense of direction. Each curve starts and finishes at a corner of the patch, so we have alternative representations for the position vectors of the points at the corners. As shown in Figure 21.8, at A $\mathbf{P}_1(0) = \mathbf{P}_3(0)$, at B $\mathbf{P}_1(1) = \mathbf{P}_4(0)$, at C $\mathbf{P}_2(0) = \mathbf{P}_3(1)$ and at D $\mathbf{P}_2(1) = \mathbf{P}_4(1)$.

We use interpolation between these curves to construct the equation of the surface patch they enclose. Simplistically, since the surface depends equally on all the four boundaries, we could model the formula on that obtained in Section 21.3 and get

$$\mathbf{P}(u, v) = (1 - v)\mathbf{P}_1(u) + v\mathbf{P}_2(u) + (1 - u)\mathbf{P}_3(v) + u\mathbf{P}_4(v)$$

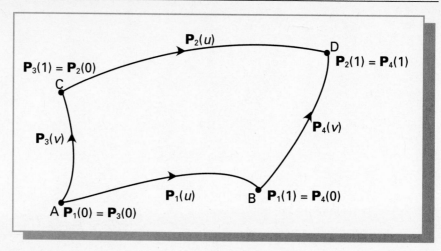

Figure 21.8 The corners and boundaries for a linear Coons patch.

Unfortunately this formula is incomplete. We illustrate one instance where it is inadequate by considering the corner A. At A $[u = 0, v = 0]$, so using the formula gives the position vector of A to be

$$\mathbf{P}(0, 0) = \mathbf{P}_1(0) + \mathbf{P}_3(0)$$

But we have seen above that $\mathbf{P}_1(0) = \mathbf{P}_3(0)$ is the position vector at A, so '$\mathbf{P}(0, 0) = \mathbf{P}_1(0) + \mathbf{P}_3(0)$' is false. At the corners and on the boundaries our simplistic formula counts data twice, thus the correct formula for the surface patch is obtained by subtracting appropriate terms. The correct equation for the surface patch is

$$\begin{aligned}
\mathbf{P}(u, v) = &(1 - v)\,\mathbf{P}_1(u) + v\mathbf{P}_2(u) + (1 - u)\mathbf{P}_3(v) + u\mathbf{P}_4(v) \\
&- (1 - v)\,(1 - u)\mathbf{P}_1(0) - (1 - u)v\,\mathbf{P}_2(0) \\
&- u(1 - v)\,\mathbf{P}_1(1) - uv\mathbf{P}_2(1)
\end{aligned}$$

Since the points A, B, C and D and the boundary curves all lie in the surface patch, they can each be described alternatively in terms of both parameters u and v as indicated in Figure 21.9(a); the equivalent information is shown in the parameter plane of Figure 21.9(b). When two parameters are used throughout, the equation of the surface patch becomes

$$\begin{aligned}
\mathbf{P}(u, v) = &(1 - v)\mathbf{P}(u, 0) + v\mathbf{P}(u, 1) + (1 - u)\mathbf{P}(0, v) \\
&+ u\mathbf{P}(1, v) - (1 - v)(1 - u)\,\mathbf{P}(0, 0) \\
&- (1 - u)v\mathbf{P}(0, 1) - u(1 - v)\mathbf{P}(1, 0) - uv\mathbf{P}(1, 1)
\end{aligned}$$

Example 21.2 A linear Coons patch based on intersecting parabolic arcs

We here construct the linear Coons patch based on the curves given by

$$\begin{cases}
\mathbf{P}_1(u) = u^2\mathbf{i} + u\mathbf{k} \\
\mathbf{P}_2(u) = u(2 - u)\mathbf{i} + \mathbf{j} + (1 - u)\mathbf{k} \\
\mathbf{P}_3(v) = v^2\mathbf{j} + v\mathbf{k} \\
\mathbf{P}_4(v) = \mathbf{i} + v(2 - v)\mathbf{j} + (1 - v)\mathbf{k}
\end{cases}$$

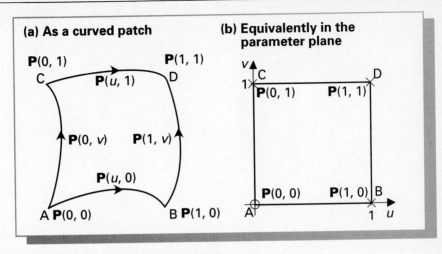

(a) As a curved patch

P(0, 1)   P(1, 1)

C   P(*u*, 1)   D

P(0, *v*)   P(1, *v*)

P(*u*, 0)

A P(0, 0)   B P(1, 0)

(b) Equivalently in the parameter plane

v

C
P(0, 1)   P(1, 1)   D

1

P(0, 0)   P(1, 0) B

A   1   *u*

Figure 21.9 The surface patch fully labelled.

which intersect, in pairs, at the points A(0, 0, 0), B(1, 0, 1), C(0, 1, 1) and D(1, 1, 0). We then find the equation of the curve joining B to C in the surface so formed.

These curves are all arcs of parabolas, based on those already met in Section 7.3, and they define the patch shown in Figure 21.10. We start with the equation for a linear Coons patch

$$\mathbf{P}(u, v) = (1 - v)\mathbf{P}_1(u) + v\mathbf{P}_2(u) + (1 - u)\mathbf{P}_3(v) + u\mathbf{P}_4(v)$$
$$- (1 - u)(1 - v)\mathbf{P}_1(0) - (1 - u)v\mathbf{P}_2(0)$$
$$- u(1 - v)\mathbf{P}_1(1) - uv\mathbf{P}_2(1)$$

and into this we substitute the components of the boundary curves and the position vectors of the corners:

$$\mathbf{P}(u, v) = (1 - v)(u^2\mathbf{i} + u\mathbf{k}) + v(u(2 - u)\mathbf{i} + \mathbf{j} + (1 - u)\mathbf{k})$$
$$+ (1 - u)(v^2\mathbf{j} + v\mathbf{k}) + u(\mathbf{i} + v(2 - v)\mathbf{j} + (1 - v)\mathbf{k})$$
$$- (1 - u)(1 - v)(\mathbf{0}) - (1 - u)v(\mathbf{j} + \mathbf{k}) - u(1 - v)(\mathbf{i} + \mathbf{k}) - uv(\mathbf{i} + \mathbf{j})$$

Once this has been simplified by multiplying out the brackets and collecting together the components of **i**, **j** and **k** we get the following formula for this surface patch

$$\mathbf{P}(u, v) = (u^2(1 - 2v) + 2uv)\mathbf{i} + (v^2(1 - 2u) + 2uv)\mathbf{j}$$
$$+ (u + v - 2uv)\mathbf{k}$$

From Figure 21.11(a) we see that on the curve joining B to C [$v = (1 - u)$]. We use this expression instead of v in the surface equation, and we get

$$\mathbf{P}(u, (1 - u)) = (2u^3 - 3u^2 + 2u)\mathbf{i} + (-2u^3 + 3u^2 - 2u + 1)\mathbf{j}$$
$$+ (2u^2 - 2u + 1)\mathbf{k}$$

This is the equation of the curve joining B to C in the surface. To identify it we examine the parametric equations:

$$\begin{cases} x = 2u^3 - 3u^2 + 2u \\ y = -2u^3 + 3u^2 - 2u + 1 \\ z = 2u^2 - 2u + 1 \end{cases}$$

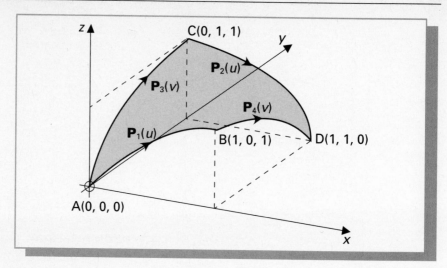

Figure 21.10 The linear Coons patch between four parabolic arcs.

By adding the first two we get

$$x + y = 1$$

thus the curve lies in the plane $x + y = 1$. From the third component we see that the curve is an arc of a parabola, as indicated in Figure 21.11(b). A computer-generated version of the surface is shown in Figure 21.11 (c).

21.5 Conclusion

This completes the chapter on surface patches. Although the ideas embodied in this topic are very important, with many practical applications, there is a heavy demand on algebraic skills needed in manipulations. We are now at the limit of what we set out to achieve; it would be unrealistic, at this stage, to accomplish immediately many more of these types of calculations. Thus there is just one exercise included below: if you have followed and understood all the material in the preceeding sections, then that should be reward in itself!

Exercise

21.1 Construct the vector equation for the bilinear patch based on the line segments joining A(0, 0, 0) with B(1, 0, 0), and C(0, 1, 1) with D(1, 1, 0). Sketch the resulting patch, and find the equation of the curve joining A to D in the surface.

Answer

21.1 $\mathbf{Q}(u, v) = u\mathbf{i} + v\mathbf{j} + (v - uv)\mathbf{k}$; the parabola $z = u - u^2$ in the plane $x = y$.

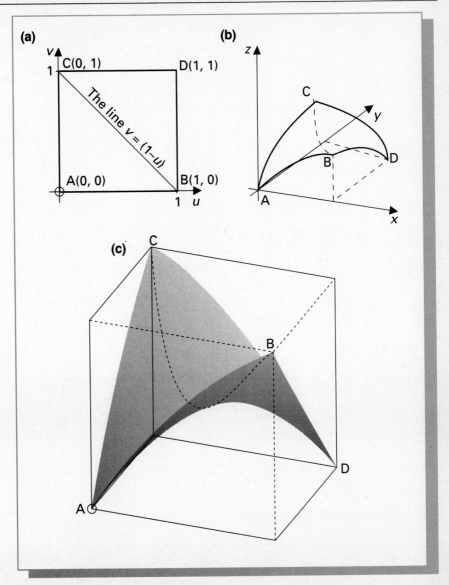

(a)

v

C(0, 1)   D(1, 1)
1

The line v = (1–u)

A(0, 0)   B(1, 0)

1   u

(b)

z

C

y

B

D

A

x

(c)

C

B

D

A

Figure 21.11 (a) The linear Coons patch shown in the parameter plane.
               (b) The curve in the surface patch.
               (c) The linear Coons patch (*source: John Dormand, University of Teesside*).

22

Computer graphics:
Next steps

Having reached the end of this book, you are now in a position to understand the basic mathematics needed for computer graphics. Where do you go from here? There is a variety of possible directions to take: from operating existing graphical packages with enhanced knowledge, to applying your new knowledge in graphical applications to developing the packages, or even to progressing to further mathematical techniques using more advanced books, which will lead you to be able to create still more realistic objects in the computer.

Let us look ahead at the steps required for creating and manipulating realistic computer displays so that we can recognize the landmarks (the key words and ideas) with which we can orient ourselves in the future. (In what follows we write the landmark words and phrases in *italics*.) First of all, where are we now? We have the mathematical capability to produce lines, simple curves and surfaces, and wire frame images. We are also able to manipulate and display these through transformations, including perspective and projection. We already have all of the basic techniques required for the creation and manipulation of simple objects and images, but with regard to display we have not dealt with any methods relating to the pixel nature of the screen display, nor importantly, with colour. However, it is in the production of realistic looking objects that we have furthest to go.

A common way of creating an object or image is to represent its surface by flat polygons or *facets* (which were introduced in Chapter 19) joining up given points on the object. This produces *polygon mesh*. The surface may also be created from the *patches* of Chapter 21 in a surface fitting process. Both of these methods are *boundary representations* or *B reps*. The points themselves can be introduced by hand, by *digitizing* an actual object with a *laser ranger* or can be obtained from a mathematical formula for the object (perhaps a shape such as an ellipsoid, or a swept surface, see Chapter 19). More complicated curves and surfaces can be produced from *Bézier curves* and *Bézier surfaces*, *B splines* and *NURBS* (*non-uniform rational B splines*). These last are very important in creative graphical design.

In contrast to the above methods, in which an object is represented by its surface, there are methods by which an object can be created using its volume; that is, it is represented by *constructive solid geometry* or *CSG*. Here standard solid shapes, such as cubes, cylinders or spheres, known as *primitives*, are combined to make more complicated objects. Thus, for example, a set of long cylinders can be added to make a multicored wire, or a cube with a hole in it can be formed by subtracting a cylinder from a cube.

Once a three-dimensional object or scene has been created in the computer, it must be visualized on the computer screen in a process generally called *rendering*, which involves a variety of operations including the fixing of a *viewpoint, perspective projection, hidden surface removal, shading* and *rasterization. Anti-aliasing* may also be needed to counter the staircase effect which is sometimes encountered with pixel representations. The *shading* of an object (by, for example, *Gouraud shading* or *Phong shading*) needs to be carried out, taking into account the interaction of light with each surface. For this a *reflection model* is needed, which, at a basic level, depends on the angle between the normal to the surface and the direction of the light from a point source. Even at its simplest, the reflection model can include *diffuse, specular* and *ambient* light. An *illumination model* may include more sophisticated sources of light than just that emanating from a single point, as well as *radiosity*, which involves the multiple diffuse reflections of light between surfaces. Usually *colour shading* is used from a three component *colour space*, or if colour output is not available then *grey shading* is implemented. Graphics images produced using these techniques are very realistic in some ways; however, they sometimes have an unearthly floating-in-the-air aspect to them which is best dispelled by the appropriate use of radiosity and the introduction of *shadows*.

A more advanced technique for improving the realism of scenes is *ray tracing* which takes account of the actual paths of rays of light. Ray tracing takes things forward by allowing, for example, an improved interaction of light between objects, and the possibility of light passing through partially transparent objects. However, this technique is extremely time consuming, and it is often prohibitive to compute ray-traced scenes even though the level of realism can be significantly improved.

By the means described above, an object with a very realistic shape may be created and placed in a scene, fully lit and viewed in colour; however, all the surfaces are plain and untextured. There is nothing in the picture to indicate the materials from which objects are made, which might be supposed to be wood or marble, for example. This deficiency can be supplied by *texture mapping*, in which realistic patterns are placed on a surface. Examples of images created using this technique are shown in Figures 1.2 and 22.1.

What then are computer graphics practitioners doing with all these advanced possibilities? It is certain that the field is so active and creative that any current list soon becomes dated. However, at the present time entertainment and advertising are major interests, particularly with *virtual reality* and *animation*. There is also *medical imaging* with techniques being developed to help with non-invasive, 'keyhole' surgery; *scientific visualization* showing, for example, the complex fluid flows around an aircraft; and the *virtual reality environments* used in many aspects of engineering and architectural design and also in *simulators* for skills training.

Computers have already revolutionized our capabilities for calculating, storing information and communicating with words and numbers, and now the potential of graphical images in all types of computing activities is being explored and extended. Most people use mental 'visualization' as part of their thought processes, and it is natural to wish for an increasing use of computer-generated images, incorporating high-level visualization techniques in constructing, manipulating and displaying images. Very many impressive examples already exist of three-dimensional computer graphics at work and at play, and sophisticated graphics packages support both high-quality production and also further development. This work is all ongoing, and still much remains to be achieved; for example, virtual environments are now used for stage set design and lighting, but the *virtual actor*, realistic in form and movement, is still, as we write, in the future. Research in all areas of computer graphics will continue well into the next century, and present achievements are showing the way to a society that is at ease with, and understands the value of, three-dimensional graphical imagery.

Figure 22.1 A graphical image produced with texture mapping (*source: Matthew Holton, University of Teesside*).

Appendix A
Pythagoras' Theorem
(Reference Example 1.1)

Suppose we have any triangle containing a right angle, as shown in Figure A.1, with the lengths of the sides denoted by a, b and c as indicated. We note that c is the length of the side opposite the right angle: the name of this side is the **hypotenuse** of the triangle.

Pythagoras' Theorem states that the squares of the lengths of the three sides of the triangle are related by this formula:

$$a^2 + b^2 = c^2$$

We can illustrate this geometrically by drawing a square based on each side; the areas of these squares, shown in Figure A.2, are a^2, b^2 and c^2. We see that the area of the square based on the side of length c is the largest, and thus from a geometric point of view Pythagoras' Theorem states that this area is equal to the sum of the areas of the other two squares.

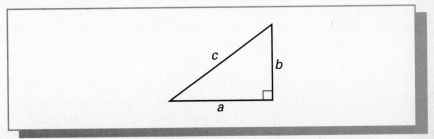

Figure A.1 The sides of a right-angled triangle.

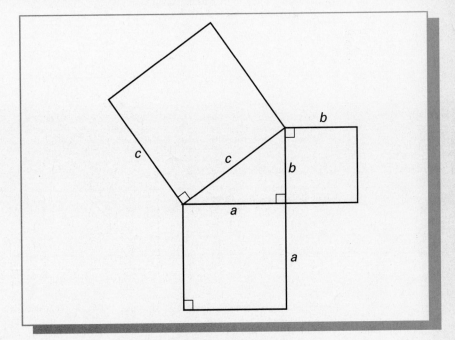

Figure A.2 The squares on the sides of a right-angled triangle.

Appendix B
The form of a rotation matrix
(Reference Section 9.4)

The effect of a planar rotation about a fixed point may be examined by considering a rectangle ABCD, fixed at one corner A, and rotated through an angle θ, as shown in Figure B.1. The transformed positions of the corners are denoted by A*, B*, C* and D*.

We draw the perpendicular C*F from C* onto the x-axis, and the perpendicular B*E from B* onto the x-axis. The perpendicular from B* to the line C*F meets it at G, and thus the line GB* is parallel to the x-axis.

These construction lines are now used to generate the formulae for rotation which will relate the new corner position C*, with coordinates (x^*, y^*), to the original corner position C which had coordinates (x, y). The angle AB*G is opposite to the angle EAB*, and hence has the value θ. Because angle AB*C* is 90°, the angle GB*C* is (90° − θ); and the angle B*C*G is θ because it is in a right-angled triangle with angle GB*C*. We now have all the geometric quantities in place to produce the rotation formulae, and hence the rotation matrix.

The coordinate x^* of point C* is given by the length AF, and thus

$$x^* = AF$$

$$= AE - B^*G$$

$$= AB^* \cos \theta - B^*C^* \sin \theta$$

from triangles AB*E and GB*C*. However, the shape of the rectangle remains unaltered by the rotation and thus the length AB* is the same as the original length AB, which is x. Similarly, B*C* is the same length as BC, that is y. Thus

$$x^* = x \cos\theta - y \sin\theta$$

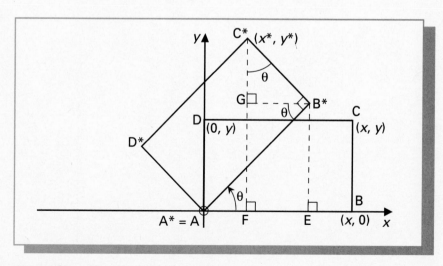

Figure B.1 Rotating a rectangle.

In the same way the coordinate y^* of C^* is given by the length C^*F, with

$$y^* = C^*F$$

$$= GF + GC^*$$

$$= AB^* \sin\theta + B^*C^* \cos\theta$$

$$= x \sin\theta + y \cos\theta$$

These two formulae can be gathered together:

$$\begin{cases} x^* = x \cos\theta - y \sin\theta \\ y^* = x \sin\theta + y \cos\theta \end{cases}$$

and then written in matrix form, as follows:

$$(x^* \quad y^*) = (x \cos\theta - y \sin\theta \quad x \sin\theta + y \cos\theta)$$

$$= (x \quad y) \begin{bmatrix} \cos\theta & \sin\theta \\ -\sin\theta & \cos\theta \end{bmatrix}$$

Thus the matrix which multiplies the original position vector $(x \quad y)$ to give the new position vector $(x^* \quad y^*)$ is

$$\begin{bmatrix} \cos\theta & \sin\theta \\ -\sin\theta & \cos\theta \end{bmatrix}$$

so this is the required rotation matrix.

Appendix C
Sines and cosines for sums of angles and double angles
(Reference Examples 10.1 and 10.4)

When two angles θ and ϕ are added as in Figure C.1, the sine of the sum, $(\theta + \phi)$, is related to the sines and cosines of the separate angles by the formula

$$\sin (\theta + \phi) = \sin \theta \cos \phi + \cos \theta \sin \phi$$

There is a similar formula for the cosine of the sum of two angles:

$$\cos (\theta + \phi) = \cos \theta \cos \phi - \sin \theta \sin \phi$$

By putting $\theta = \phi$ we can obtain the following formulae for double angles:

$$\sin (\theta + \theta) = \sin \theta \cos \theta + \cos \theta \sin \theta$$

that is

$$\sin 2\theta = 2 \sin \theta \cos \theta$$

and also

$$\cos (\theta + \theta) = \cos \theta \cos \theta - \sin \theta \sin \theta$$

so that

$$\cos 2\theta = \cos^2\theta - \sin^2\theta$$

These formulae may be quoted and used in simplifying trigonometric expressions.

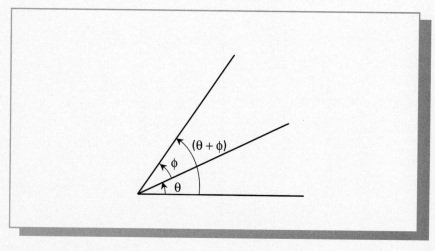

Figure C.1 The sum of two angles.

Appendix D
The geometric relationship between coordinates transformed by perspective-projection
(Reference Section 14.5)

As shown in Figure D.1, we have a point $P(X, Y, Z)$ which is viewed from the viewing point at $E(0, 0, z_c)$ on the positive z-axis; as in Section 14.5 we are here assuming that the z-coordinate of P is actually a negative number. Under perspective-projection this point is transformed to $P^*(X^*, Y^*)$ on the viewing plane $z = 0$.

Investigating this diagram geometrically we see that triangles EP^*F and EPG are similar, so that corresponding sides are in proportion:

$$\frac{EF}{EG} = \frac{P^*F}{PG}$$

In addition, triangles EOF and EHG are similar, so that

$$\frac{EF}{EG} = \frac{OF}{HG} = \frac{EO}{EH}$$

Obviously all these ratios are equal, and in particular

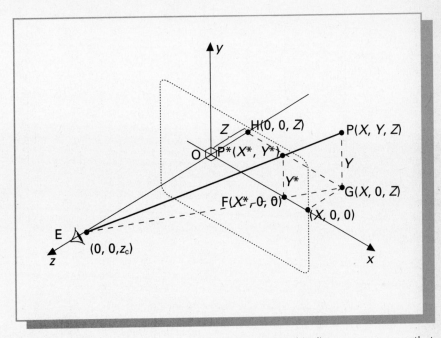

Figure D.1 Perspective-projection onto the plane $z = 0$. (By convention, in this diagram we assume that Z is a negative number.)

$$\frac{OF}{HG} = \frac{P*F}{PG} = \frac{EO}{EH}$$

If we use the given coordinate measurements in these ratios (remembering that here Z is a negative number) we get

$$\frac{X*}{X} = \frac{Y*}{Y} = \frac{z_c}{z_c - Z} \qquad\qquad \textbf{(D1)}$$

If we focus on the last ratio here, we can change it as follows

$$\frac{z_c}{z_c - Z} = \frac{1}{1 - Z/z_c}$$

Next we can replace z_c by $-1/r$ (as stated in Section 14.5), so that

$$\frac{1}{z_c} = -r$$

and so we get

$$\frac{z_c}{z_c - Z} = \frac{1}{1 - Z/z_c} = \frac{1}{1 + rZ} = \frac{1}{rZ + 1}$$

Using this in equation D1 above gives

$$\frac{X*}{X} = \frac{1}{rZ + 1}$$

so that

$$X* = \frac{X}{rZ + 1}$$

and similarly

$$Y* = \frac{Y}{rZ + 1}$$

These two results, obtained geometrically, correspond exactly to those we arrived at by multiplying the position vector of P by the matrix for perspective-projection. They remain equally valid even when the diagram is drawn in such a way that Z is a positive number.

Appendix E
Differentiation from first principles
(Reference Section 16.3)

In order to differentiate the function $y = x^2$ 'from first principles' we need the limit of $\delta y/\delta x$ as δx gets smaller and smaller, and thus we first consider δy which is given by

$$\overline{P_1\, Q_1} = \delta y = y_1 - y$$

[handwritten: $\frac{dy}{dx}$]

as shown in Figure E.1.

Each of the values y and y_1 corresponds to a point on the curve, and thus can be obtained from its formula $y = x^2$. Thus $y_1 = x_1^2$ and $y = x^2$ so that

$$\delta y = x_1^2 - x^2$$

To bring in δx, we remember that

$$P\, Q_1 = \delta x = x_1 - x$$

so that

$$x_1 = x + \delta x$$

and this illustrates another way of thinking of the difference δx: that is the amount to be added to the first value of x to obtain the second. Using the fact that $x_1 = x + \delta x$ we get

[handwritten: or $dx = x_1 - x$]

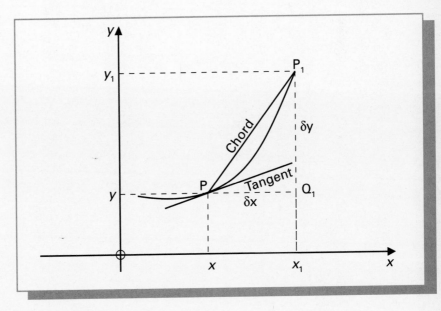

Figure E.1 A tangent and chord at P.

$$\delta y = (x + \delta x)^2 - x^2$$

which we then simplify to

$$\delta y = x^2 + 2x\,\delta x + (\delta x)^2 - x^2$$

$$= 2x\,\delta x + (\delta x)^2$$

Dividing this all through by δx gives *Here's the "trick", treating $\frac{dy}{dx}$ as a*

$$\frac{\delta y}{\delta x} = \frac{2x\,\delta x + (\delta x)^2}{\delta x}$$

quotient. A method much reviled by mathematical purists & fundamentalists.

that is

$$\frac{\delta y}{\delta x} = 2x + \delta x$$

Thus for the derivative dy/dx we have

$$\frac{dy}{dx} = \frac{\text{limit}}{\delta x \to 0} \left(\frac{\delta y}{\delta x} \right)$$

$$= \frac{\text{limit}}{\delta x \to 0} (2x + \delta x)$$

$$= 2x$$

since the term δx, being infinitesimally small, will *in the limit* disappear.

Thus when we differentiate the function $y = x^2$ we obtain the derivative

$$\frac{dy}{dx} = 2x \quad \text{\textit{I'm convinced.}}$$

which gives us the slope of the line at x, whatever x is. This is true if the function defining y is $y = x^2$, that is, a parabola. The line is tangent to the curve of the parabola at x. We could generate the curve with an envelope of such tangent lines.

Postscript
Row vectors vs column vectors

In this postscript we offer an explanation for the decision, made at the outset of the book, that in all the descriptions, explanations and examples using vectors we use **row notation** throughout, and not columns. Thus to express **OP**, the position vector from the origin O to the point P with coordinates (3, 7), we write (3   7), a row vector; the corresponding homogeneous vector is (3   7   1). An alternative convention is to express **OP** as

$\begin{bmatrix} 3 \\ 7 \end{bmatrix}$, a **column vector**, with homogeneous column vector $\begin{bmatrix} 3 \\ 7 \\ 1 \end{bmatrix}$. The adoption of either notation

is perfectly valid, and allows the development of a completely consistent system. Consequent upon the choice of notation for the vectors, the transforming matrices may need to be transposed, and the order of consecutive operations is reflected differently in the ordering of the matrices; the systems cannot be mixed, but either one can be used with perfect consistency.

It is certainly true that the mathematical approach would be to use column vectors throughout. Many computer graphics textbooks follow the row vector convention, while others use column vectors. Programmers' Hierarchical Interactive Graphics Standard (PHIGS) has adopted the use of column vectors. So why have we decided to use row vectors in this book?

To appreciate the literature fully, it is necessary to be able to understand and to use both systems of notation. However, we believe that there are real educational advantages in introducing vectors using the row notation. We discuss now several of the considerations that swayed us.

As an initial teaching tool, we feel that row vectors are to be preferred since their meaning and format follow so closely the standard notation for coordinates, and also the component form for vectors. For example, the above row vector which expresses **OP** is (3   7), which is closely related in format to (3, 7), the coordinates of the end point P, and also to 3**i** + 7**j**, the component form of the vector. *Component form where i designates x direction and j designates the y direction.*

We feel that when applying a transformation to a set of vertices (as in Section 9.5) it is more natural to adopt an 'object oriented' approach; so we first set down the details of the row vectors to be transformed, and then the matrix by which the transformation is performed. For example, we suppose we have the two end points (3, 7) and (5, 8) of a line segment that is being translated 6 units in the *x*-direction. Using row vectors, the 'object' comes first, as in Section 9.5:

object then transformation

$$\begin{bmatrix} 3 & 7 & 1 \\ 5 & 8 & 1 \end{bmatrix} \begin{bmatrix} 1 & 0 & 0 \\ 0 & 1 & 0 \\ 6 & 0 & 1 \end{bmatrix} = \begin{bmatrix} 9 & 7 & 1 \\ 11 & 8 & 1 \end{bmatrix}$$

3 + 6 = 9
5 + 6 = 11

However, if column vectors are being used, then they are written down after the transforming matrix, so that the object under consideration has less apparent significance; the above matrix is transposed (see Section 8.2) and the object comes second:

Transform ↓ ↓ this object ↓ ↓

$$\begin{bmatrix} 1 & 0 & 6 \\ 0 & 1 & 0 \\ 0 & 0 & 1 \end{bmatrix} \begin{bmatrix} 3 & 5 \\ 7 & 8 \\ 1 & 1 \end{bmatrix} = \begin{bmatrix} 9 & 11 \\ 7 & 8 \\ 1 & 1 \end{bmatrix}$$

action object

When dealing with a sequence of transformations on vertices represented by row vectors, then the transforming matrices follow the row vectors in the same order as the operations are being applied. For example, taking the above line segment, first translating it and then reflecting it in the y-axis, we have (as discussed also in Sections 10.2 and 11.3)

$$\begin{matrix} \rightarrow \\ \rightarrow \end{matrix} \begin{bmatrix} 3 & 7 & 1 \\ 5 & 8 & 1 \end{bmatrix} \begin{bmatrix} 1 & 0 & 0 \\ 0 & 1 & 0 \\ 6 & 0 & 1 \end{bmatrix} \begin{bmatrix} -1 & 0 & 0 \\ 0 & 1 & 0 \\ 0 & 0 & 1 \end{bmatrix} = \begin{bmatrix} -9 & 7 & 1 \\ -11 & 8 & 1 \end{bmatrix} \begin{matrix} \leftarrow \\ \leftarrow \end{matrix}$$

1) translation 2) reflection

and the order of the matrices is the same as the order of the operations as stated. On the other hand, when column vectors are used, the transposed matrices precede the vectors and as a consequence the order in which they are written down is the reverse of the order in which the corresponding transformations are applied.

$$\begin{bmatrix} -1 & 0 & 0 \\ 0 & 1 & 0 \\ 0 & 0 & 0 \end{bmatrix} \begin{bmatrix} 1 & 0 & 6 \\ 0 & 1 & 0 \\ 0 & 0 & 1 \end{bmatrix} \begin{bmatrix} 3 & 5 \\ 7 & 8 \\ 1 & 1 \end{bmatrix} = \begin{bmatrix} -9 & -11 \\ 7 & 8 \\ 1 & 1 \end{bmatrix}$$

2) reflection 1) translation

We feel strongly that the advantage of being able to follow the natural order used in speech makes the use of row vectors very much preferred, at this introductory level.

We use row vectors to introduce essential concepts in the mathematical underpinning of computer graphics. We firmly believe that once someone is experienced in these techniques, and confident in their applications, then they will have no trouble in converting to an alternative convention as and when required. Row vectors are not an end in themselves, they are a tool used to facilitate the learning of graphical techniques. They supply us with a compact notation that can be augmented and/or superseded by other forms as we progress in our knowledge.

Glossary
Valuable concepts and their definitions

Angle: the amount of rotation from one line to another measured in degrees or radians.

Axes: mutually perpendicular lines which form the basis of graphs, for example the x-axis, the y-axis, and the z-axis.

Biparametric forms: formulae containing two parameters, which correspond to surfaces.

Cartesian equation of a line or curve: an equation involving the relationships between the x-, y- (and z-) coordinates of points on the line or curve.

Chord: a straight line joining two points on a curve.

Component form: a vector written in terms of the unit vectors $\mathbf{i}, \mathbf{j}, \mathbf{k}$, for example $\mathbf{r} = 2\mathbf{i} - \mathbf{j} + 3\mathbf{k}$.

Continuous: (of lines, curves or surfaces) without gaps or holes.

Coordinate planes: planes at right angles to each other formed from pairs of axes, for example the x–y plane.

Coordinates: distances from perpendicular axes that fix the position of a point in two or three dimensions, for example (x, y) or (x, y, z).

Cosine: a number associated with an angle. In a right angled triangle it is obtained by dividing the length of the side adjacent to the angle by the length of the hypotenuse.

Cross product: (also known as a vector product) the result of multiplying two vectors together so that the result is another vector at right angles to both the originals.

Curve fairing: finding a curve that passes close to a given set of points.

Curve fitting: finding a curve that passes through each one of the given set of points.

Degree: a measure for angles; there are 360 degrees in a complete rotation.

Derivative: the gradient function for a curve.

Determinant: an arrangement of numbers set out in a square pattern from which a single numerical value can be obtained.

Differentiation: the process of finding the derivative of a function.

Direction cosines: cosines of the angles that a vector makes with the positive coordinate axes.

Dot product: (also known as scalar product) the result of multiplying two vectors together in a way that produces a scalar quantity.

Eye point: the point from which a scene is viewed (see also Viewing point).

Factor:	a multiplying quantity.
Free vector:	a vector that is not constrained to pass through any particular point.
Function:	a rule (usually a formula) by which a single value can be calculated from one or more other values.
Gradient:	the slope of a line, found by dividing the amount by which the line goes up or down by the amount it goes along.
Homogeneous vector:	notation for position vectors which includes an *extra* component; the three-dimensional vector (x y z) has homogeneous form (x y z 1), or (cx cy cz c) for any non-zero scalar c.
Horizon:	a line at eye level that joins the vanishing points.
Hypotenuse:	the side opposite to the right angle in a right-angled triangle.
Interpolant:	a line or a curve drawn to fill in between points.
Linear interpolation:	the process of filling in between points using straight lines.
Local scaling:	scaling in the direction of one axis only.
Locus:	the path produced by a point moving in a plane or in three-dimensional space.
Magnitude:	the size or length of a vector; a positive quantity (see also Modulus).
Matrix:	a rectangular array of numbers, used to describe transformations.
Modulus:	the length of a vector.
Normal:	a line at right angles to a line, plane, or surface.
Normalization:	the process of proportioning the coordinates (x, y) of objects in a viewing screen so that they lie between 0 and 1.
Origin:	the point where the axes meet.
Orthogonal:	a description of lines that are at an angle of 90° to each other.
Orthographic projection:	a projection onto the coordinate planes using parallel projectors.
Overall scaling:	scaling in the directions of all axes simultaneously.
Parameter:	a quantity whose variation in a formula produces a line, curve or surface.
Parametric lines:	the lines on a surface given by constant parameter values.
Parametric plane:	formed by taking the parameters that occur in a formula for a surface in three dimensions as the coordinates of a plane.
Parametric vector equation:	the equation of a line, curve or surface given as the moving end point of a position vector depending on one or two parameters.
Partial differentiation:	differentiation with respect to one variable, while keeping other variables fixed.

Perpendicular:	see Orthogonal.
Perspective:	a transformation in which parallel lines meet at point; resulting in a 'perspective view'.
Perspective–projection:	a projection of a perspective transformation.
Pixels:	the small divisions into which the computer screen is divided.
Plane facet:	a plane bounded by straight lines, which approximates to part of a surface.
Plane of projection:	a plane onto which an object or scene is projected.
Point at infinity:	the 'point' on a line which is as far along it as can be imagined.
Polygon:	a plane shape bounded by straight lines.
Polygonal modelling:	making up a shape from polygons.
Polynomial:	a formula consisting only of powers of a variable and numbers.
Position vector:	a vector that starts from the origin.
Primitives:	simple shapes such as spheres and cubes which may be put together to make more complicated shapes.
Principal vanishing points:	the points at which lines parallel to the coordinate axes meet after a perspective transformation.
Projection:	a two-dimensional representation of a three-dimensional object or scene.
Projector:	the line joining a point on an object to the corresponding point of its projection.
Quadrants:	the quarters of a plane produced by dividing it by the x- and y-axes.
Quadratic curve:	a curve corresponding to a formula containing at most squares of the variable.
Quadratic interpolation:	the process of joining up points with quadratic curves.
Radian:	a measure for angles; there are 2π radians in a complete rotation.
Ray:	a straight line in a scene coming from the eye or from a light source.
Rectangular coordinate system:	a system of perpendicular axes by which the position of any point in space can be determined.
Reflection:	a way of transforming a shape in the way that a flat mirror does.
Right angle:	the angle which is one quarter of a complete revolution, measuring $90°$ or $\pi/2$ radians.
Right-angled triangle:	a triangle in which one of the angles is a right angle.
Right-hand screw:	the direction of movement in driving forward a right-hand threaded (normal) screw.

Right-handed set:	a set of three axes obeying the right-hand screw rule, so that for example twisting from the x-axis to the y-axis corresponds to movement along the z-axis.
Rotation:	a way of transforming a shape so that every point moves through the same angle about a fixed point.
Scalar:	a quantity that only has size (either positive or negative) like a real number.
Shift:	a way of transforming a shape so that every point moves by the same distance and in the same direction; also known as a translation.
Sine:	a number associated with an angle. In a right-angled triangle it is obtained by dividing the length of the side opposite to the angle by the length of the hypotenuse.
Single point perspective:	a form of perspective in which there is one vanishing point.
Slope:	see Gradient.
Space curve:	a curve that passes through space and is not confined to a plane.
Splines:	specific curves that produce curve fairing to a given set of points.
Surface normal:	a line that is normal to the tangent plane of a surface.
Surface of revolution:	surface formed by rotating a curve round a line.
Surface tangent:	the tangent line to a curve that is lying in a surface.
Swept surface:	surface formed by sweeping a curve through space.
Tangent (1):	a number associated with an angle. In a right-angled triangle it is obtained by dividing the length of the side opposite to the angle by the length of the side adjacent to the angle.
Tangent (2):	the line just touching a curve at any point; the slope of the tangent gives the slope of the curve at that point.
Tilt:	a transformation caused by successive rotations about two axes.
Trace point:	the point at which parallel lines that are not in a plane parallel to one of the coordinate planes meet after a perspective transformation.
Transformation:	a specified change to an object or image; it can include translation, rotation, reflection and perspective and projection.
Translation:	see Shift.
Unit vector:	a vector whose magnitude is 'one'.
u-parametric curve:	a curve in a surface obtained by keeping the value of the u parameter fixed.
Vanishing point:	the point at which parallel lines in the direction of one of the coodinate axes meet after a perspective transformation.

Variable: a quantity that can take a variety of values. The independent variable can be chosen independently; the dependent variable is the resulting quantity calculated from a formula.

Vector: a quantity that has both magnitude and direction.

Vector equation of a line or curve: the equation of a line or curve given as the moving end point of a variable position vector; it always involves a parameter.

Vector product: see Cross product.

Vertex: a corner on a figure, usually where two or more straight lines join; for a parabola, its extreme point with maximum curvature.

Viewing plane: the plane, such as a computer screen, onto which an image or scene is projected.

Viewing point: see Eye point.

Viewport: the bounded part of a computer screen displaying an image.

v-parametric curve: a curve in a surface obtained by keeping the value of the v parameter fixed.

Window: the bounded part of an image or scene being viewed.

Wire frame: a form of a surface, defined by lines lying in the surface; or a way of visualizing objects using lines in their surfaces.

Further reading

J. D. Foley, A. Van Dam, S. Feiner and J Hughes,
Computer Graphics – Principles and Practice, 2nd edn, Addison Wesley, 1990.

D. Hearn and M. P. Baker,
Computer Graphics, Prentice Hall International, 1986.

R. A. Plastock,
Schaum's Outline of Theory and Problems of Computer Graphics, McGraw-Hill, 1986.

D. F. Rogers and J. A. Adams,
Mathematical Elements for Computer Graphics, 2nd edn, McGraw-Hill, 1990.

J. Vince,
Virtual Reality Systems, Addison-Wesley, 1995.

A. Watt,
3D Computer Graphics, 2nd edn. Addison-Wesley, 1993.

Index

Princeton Univ. Store, NJ
22 Mar 2000 (Special Order)
$42 with 30% discount
 2.52 tax
$44.52 $60 list